LOVE AT FIRST HIKE

LOVE AT FIRST HIKE:

A Memoir about Love & Triumph on the Appalachian Trail

Michelle "Brownie" Pugh

STACKPOLE
BOOKS

Published by
STACKPOLE BOOKS
5067 Ritter Road
Mechanicsburg, PA 17055
www.stackpolebooks.com

Printed in the United States of America

10 9 8 7 6 5 4 3 2 1

FIRST EDITION

Cover design by Tessa Sweigert
Cover photo courtesy of www.shutterstock.com

Cataloging-in-Publication data is on file with the Library of Congress

ISBN 978-0-8117-1366-5

Table of Contents

PART THREE

Acknowledgments

Many people contributed to the completion of my Appalachian Trail journey in incredible ways. I feel very blessed to have had so many people who supported me, cheered me on, and helped me achieve my dream. Not only because of my own determination and hard work, but also because of the support of so many others, I am now a two-thousand miler. I'd like to thank all those who helped me along the journey.

Thank you to all of the trail angels who helped in innumerable ways, including (but certainly not limited to) providing food, places to sleep, car rides, transportation to the hospital, and encouragement. Every single bit of help was a nudge toward my completion of the trail. I could never list you all by name, but I appreciate the efforts, however big or small, of each trail angel.

Thank you to the many businesses that provided discounts in order to help long-distance hikers like me finance the trip. I will continue to patronize small businesses and trail towns as much as possible.

Thank you to the trail maintainers, ridge runners, volunteers, and Appalachian Trail Conservatory employees who put in sweat, tears, and time to maintain the trail so that hikers are able to enjoy the path. Without you, I wouldn't have had a trail to hike. I appreciate the painting of each blaze, clearing of each fallen tree, and building of each shelter.

Thank you to everyone who sent letters and packages to the many post offices along the way: Lark, Nicole, Giggles, Brenda (in memory), Nanny, Grandma, Aunt Barbie, Uncle Dwight, Aunt Betsy, Uncle Steve, the Littles, and the Grazianos. Each of your support meant so much. The encouragement and care powered me through difficult days. Every athlete needs cheerleaders, and I found mine in you.

Thank you to everyone who drove extra miles to get me to and from the trail, those who took me into their homes and fed me, and those who brought me supplies: Climber, the Phelps, the Novaks, the Grazianos, the Soules, and the Boyds. These gestures of hospitality allowed me to visit family, rest, and complete town errands.

Thank you to my trail friends, without whom I never would have finished the Appalachian Trail. I will always be grateful for the short time we shared together. And a specific thank you to Souleman, who encouraged and supported me for over two thousand miles. May each of my hiking friends have feet that always seek new trails to conquer and hearts that always find new goals to achieve.

Thank you to my amazing support team: Carrie Armstrong, Nicole Bernard, Allison Byers, Randy Motz, Anna Ottosen, Lark Wells, and Sarah Worth. Randy, Lark, Sarah, and Anna each edited the first edition of my book and offered priceless suggestions. Allison and Nicole reviewed the proof copy and helped make sure the final product was polished. This book never would have been published without the generous efforts of each of you.

Most importantly, thank you to my biggest role models and strongest supporters, both on the trail and throughout life: my parents, Donna and Burv Pugh. Thank you for teaching me to believe in myself and to reach for my dreams while staying firmly seated in reality. I appreciate your guidance and encouragement more than you know. Mom, thanks for serving as trail-mom extraordinaire. Your mail drops, photo management, supply runs, and trailside chauffeuring were nothing short of amazing. Dad, you picked us up, cooked us hearty meals, suggested ways to increase our energy reserves, and even planned to hike a portion of the trail with us. (I'm sorry my injury ruined that.) I am so lucky to have you two as parents. I hope that you both continue to reach for your dreams as you settle comfortably into retirement.

The generosity of others—friends, family, and strangers alike—was the greatest gift I received on the Appalachian Trail. Now it's my turn to give back.

Prologue

My favorite place is so remote that you cannot get there by car or even by horse. From one direction you have to canoe across Big Pond, past an island, and around the bend. From the other you must walk through miles of wetlands and mud so high it reaches your waist. Either way, it is a long journey, and when you arrive your surroundings completely change. Pine and birch trees as tall as giants encircle this place with their great leafy arms stretched wide to shelter and protect. You are in a forest, but this is not just any forest—it is the Enchanted Forest.

Here, there are more shades of green than on a painter's palette. Colors are heightened by spots of sunshine that pierce through the canopy of trees like a million tiny arrows. Large, elephant-sized boulders scattered throughout the forest create a natural playground. Each time I visit, I am so captivated by the magic of the forest that I almost expect to see a gnome peek out from behind one of the many rocks. Refreshing pine needles, wet and gritty mud, sun-baked leaves, budding wildflowers, and pollution-free air all mix together to perfume the entire area with a smell that people in cities could never understand.

The Enchanted Forest was part of the primitive Girl Scout camp I attended as a girl. Tucked away in the Berkshire Mountains of Massachusetts, Camp Bonnie Brae provided a haven where I could immerse myself in nature. The Enchanted Forest is significant to me not just because of its splendor, but because of the hobby—the passion—it sparked in me. Journeying to the Enchanted Forest was my first exposure to hiking. I relished being surrounded by nature and having the opportunity to learn new skills in this initially unfamiliar setting. Over the years, I developed skills in outdoor cooking and leave-no-trace ethics while making friendships that would last a lifetime. I progressed from short day hikes to mini backpacking trips off camp property. I learned to purify water, pitch a tent, and properly pack a backpack.

From the first summer I was introduced to backpacking, I was in love. As much as I enjoyed the Enchanted Forest, I yearned for longer backpacking trips in new locations. One summer session, my small group ventured away from camp for my longest backpacking trip yet. Our poorly fitted backpacks, bulging with gear, had extra supplies tied to the outside with rope. We stuffed giant Coleman sleeping bags (definitely not intended for backpacking) into black trash bags that we carried in our arms. I staggered under the ridiculous weight and impatiently anticipated reaching the campsite and unburdening my weary body.

As we trudged laboriously up the trail, a man hiking in the same direction caught up to our group. He was about thirty, wore a small, faded backpack, and carried what looked like a metal ski pole in each hand. The man introduced himself as

Gadget. I eyed him questioningly. He chatted with us as our exhausted group stepped to the side to let him pass.

"Hey, ladies. Where are you headed?" he asked in a friendly tone.

"We're on a Girl Scout overnight," one of our counselors informed him.

"If you're headed to Hill Campground, it's not too much further," Gadget offered.

"Are you camping there too?" one girl asked.

He shrugged casually. "Probably."

"Do you know how much further?" another girl questioned, dropping her sleeping bag and sitting down on it wearily.

Gadget took his pack off in one smooth motion and pulled out a tattered Ziploc bag. After thumbing for the right page in a well-worn book, he told us, "About half a mile."

"Did you hike all the way from the road too?" another girl wanted to know as she struggled to re-tie her shoe without removing her pack.

Gadget chuckled. "Well, I started about fifteen miles before that," he explained as he ripped open a king-sized Snickers bar.

"FIFTEEN MILES?" we all chorused, exchanging stunned looks.

"How far is your hike going to be?" I asked.

"This weekend I'm only doing about forty-five miles. I don't have much time to hike this year." He shoved his book back into the Ziploc and slid it into his pack.

"You've done more than *forty-five* miles before?" I asked incredulously.

Gadget nodded. "I did the Appalachian Trail."

I shrugged and shook my head blankly.

"It goes from Georgia to Maine."

"What part did you do?"

"All of it." He smiled sheepishly.

I was speechless. I remembered driving from Massachusetts to Florida with my family over the course of two very long days. *No one can walk that far.*

He interrupted my thoughts. "It's about twenty-two hundred miles."

I gaped at him speechlessly. Anyone who has spent any time with me knows that speechlessness and I are rarely compatible.

That night around the campfire, Gadget told us that the trail had taken him six months. He had hiked through fourteen states. He had slept outside and cooked on a miniature stove. He talked about mountains and rivers, animals and plants, rain and snow. By the end of the conversation, I was captivated. Gadget retired for the night into a tiny, one-person tent. I stayed awake for hours staring at the hole in the roof of my borrowed tent and imagining a 2,200-mile hike. *How many nights under a nylon roof would that be?*

When I awoke, Gadget was gone. Only a small patch of flattened grass indicated that he had ever been there. His story, however, stuck with me. That one glimpse of the possibility of spending half a year in the woods was all it took. I was hooked. At the age of twelve, I went home and told my parents I was going to hike the Appalachian Trail from start to finish. They smiled, probably thinking, "This, too, will pass." The idea remained subdued for years to come, brewing quietly under the surface until my junior year of college.

Part One

1

Planning a Dream

"Be careful," Mom almost whispered. She pressed her cheek against mine. Her forced smile and too-big eyes were reminiscent of her face as she dropped me off at college freshman year. I wondered if, like then, she would cry as soon as I was out of sight. Dad kissed my forehead. His voice was just a little more gravelly than normal as he said, "Good luck."

I slipped a letter I'd written into their hands. This is it. I hugged them both, though my enormous pack made it awkward. Now or never. I blinked hard, making sure there weren't any tears trying to escape before I looked at them one last time. They stood close—their shoulders pressed together as though supporting each other gave them the strength to support me.

I fell in line behind my fellow hikers, taking my first step toward Maine. We looked like a motley re-creation of the Seven Dwarves trudging off for a day of work. Our farewell group—well-wishing family and friends—yelled "Bye!" and "Good luck!" until we rounded the bend and they could no longer see our string of multi-hued backpacks bobbing up the trail. Filled with enthusiasm, we screamed "KATAHDIN!"—the name of the final mountain in Maine—in unison every couple of seconds, our eager voices blending together, until we suspected our audience could no longer hear.

That first step toward the Appalachian Trail was preceded by years of preparation. During my first three years at Furman University, I escaped the stress of my studies to hike as often as possible in the mountains of North and South Carolina. I explored Pisgah National Forest, Table Rock State Park, Caesars Head State Park, and Jones Gap State Park extensively. My fondness for the outdoors grew, and I scheduled backpacking trips whenever possible, often dragging my roommate or boyfriend along. I rediscovered how happy I was in the woods and started making vague plans for a thru-hike on the Appalachian Trail. Researching mileage, potential starting dates, safety information, and trail statistics became a regular hobby and was a welcome break from my challenging course load.

Through my research I became more and more excited about the prospect of immersing myself in the woods for half a year. The thought of being surrounded by trees, mountains, and fresh air was vastly appealing. I learned about www.trail place.com, a website run by seven-time Appalachian Trail thru-hiker and trail enthusiast Dan "Wingfoot" Bruce. Reading the information posted by past and future thru-hikers on his website, I started to feel confident that hiking the Appalachian Trail was something I could do.

The next step was telling my parents. While I knew I was legally an adult, my parents had always been quick to remind me that age means very little when your parents are still footing the majority of your bills. I still felt like a high school student approaching my parents for permission to attend an event. Even though I knew they couldn't actually say no this time, my gut churned with the same familiar nervousness.

To strengthen my resolve, I started rehearsing the conversation with my confidante, roommate, and best friend, Lark. We had spent hours cross-legged on her bed with chips and salsa between us as she gamely suggested ways to tell my parents, brainstormed responses, helped with wording, and role-played the conversation.

"What if they think it's a bad idea?" I asked Lark.

"What if they think it's awesome?" she responded, licking the salt from the chips off her fingertips. "You're not going to know their reaction until you tell them."

"I know." I pushed the salsa around the bowl with a chip. "Let's practice one more time."

"Michelle!" she exclaimed, exasperated. "What are you so worried about? You're an adult. They can't really tell you no. Just call and tell them."

"I know."

"Promise me you'll call them tonight. I can't handle having this conversation again."

"Ok, I will." *Maybe.*

I returned to my room, and after many more practice rounds in which I paced the length of the hallway and carried on both sides of the conversation, I called home.

My mom answered the phone after the first ring. We chatted about my classes, the Girl Scout troop I led, her tennis group, and any topic I could come up with to avoid divulging the actual reason for my call. Finally, having run out of distractions, I asked her to get my dad on the phone too. My parents have always had this rule that you have to talk to them together about anything important.

Dad picked up on the extension, and after a quick greeting, he got down to the point. "So, what's up?"

"Well, I, uh, wanted to tell you guys that I think I want to, um, go to summer school this year?" I blushed at my childish mumbling. *Slow down. Just relax.*

"You aren't coming home?" Mom asked.

"Well, I'd like to." I consciously slowed my speaking. "Of course I want to see you guys. It's just that I want to get a couple of classes out of the way this summer."

"Well, that's certainly an option," Dad responded. "But why?" Naturally, my parents had wanted to know *why* I would inflict extra courses upon myself at a university where the word "overwhelming" was an understatement when used to describe a normal course load.

"Well, because if I take two classes this summer and I overload this spring, I can graduate early," I told him.

"Okaaay . . . ?" Mom's voice was skeptical.

I took a deep breath. *Now or never.* "Do you remember when I told you guys a long time ago about that trail that goes from Georgia to Maine? The Appalachian Trail?"

"Yes," Mom replied warily. "You learned about it at camp."

"I remember," Dad added.

"Exactly. Well," I sucked in one more deep breath before I took the plunge. "I want to hike it. All of it. You have to start in March, so I'll need to graduate early." *There, I've said it.* "That's why I want to go to summer school." I exhaled with relief.

After an interminable pause, during which I wondered if my parents were still breathing, Mom said, "Okaaay, tell us more."

"The trail is a little over two thousand miles. Everyone just calls it two thousand for simplicity, though. It goes from Georgia to Maine—oh, but I already told you that." I was tripping over my own words in my excitement to get it all out. *Slow down.* "It goes through fourteen states. I've done a ton of research over the last year and I already know some of the gear I'll need. I have the guide book right here. I think it'll take me about six months to hike, and—"

Mom interrupted. "Alone? You want to hike two thousand miles, up mountains—for half a year—*by yourself?*"

"Yes."

They had a lot of questions. Dad's questions were technical: How would I finance this trip? How would I get to the trailhead? How would I prepare my body physically? Mom was more concerned about safety and my emotional health: Would this endeavor be safe for a young woman? How would I get help if I were hurt in the middle of the woods? Would I be scared?

"I'll answer all your questions," I promised.

Before we hung up the phone, Mom said, "Just keep us informed, please."

"I will."

"And Michelle?" Dad added. "Good luck!"

Once my plan was tentatively approved by the "powers-that-be," I took my planning to a different level. I spent hours of would-be study time exploring www.trailplace.com and any other Appalachian Trail website I could find. I researched gear obsessively, determined to spend my hard-earned money in the most efficient way possible. During this time, any unsuspecting person who came within plausible conversation-holding distance of me was subjected to copious amounts of trail information, gear statistics, and hiker gossip. By the time I had finished my research, I could have written a thorough dissertation on the Appalachian Trail, its history, and the gear required to take it on. Somehow, I was also doing enough research and coursework in my philosophy classes to maintain respectable grades and learning enough Chinese to have coherent conversations with fellow students. I was exhausted but invigorated.

You might assume that a girl who decided at a young age to hike the Appalachian Trail had spent her childhood hiking. On the contrary, I had hiked almost exclusively at camp. During the summers at resident camp, I had taken hikes of varying lengths with my counselors and camp friends, and I had attended a few winter camping programs. But during the school year I had not been exposed to hiking, other than an errant school field trip or family camping trip. I had become proficient in fire building, cooking over a campfire, and outdoor survival, yet I had no idea what type of gear was required for a long-distance hike. Preparing for a trip of this magnitude necessitated extensive online research, hours of grilling experts in local gear stores, and many practice hikes in order to teach myself the necessary information and skills.

Over Easter weekend of 2004, my boyfriend at the time and I went on my longest backpacking trip yet—around twenty-four miles over three days. I got lost once, had my gear soaked in a surprise downpour, and suffered numerous blisters. It wasn't a glamorous hike, but still I was proud. At that point, I considered each backpacking trip to be training for my upcoming adventure. I told other hikers I ran into that I was preparing for an Appalachian Trail thru-hike. The more people I told, the more committed I became.

I finished my junior year at Furman and needed to complete only seven more courses to graduate early, as planned. I was confident that this would not be a problem. That summer, I took two classes and worked three jobs to save money for the trail. Although my body was busy doing homework, babysitting, being a resident assistant in the dorms, and working in a church nursery, my mind was almost always on the trail.

While my parents continued to be supportive of my upcoming hike, their predominant worry was the fact that I would be hiking alone. My efforts at explaining the floating trail community and the unlikelihood that I would ever find myself *truly* alone did little to abate my parents' concerns. My complete lack of experience with being entirely alone in the woods legitimately fueled their fear. I promised I would keep researching and get back to them with a solution.

Although I was prepared gear-wise, I did still have some nagging doubts surrounding my physical ability to hike 2,200 miles. I planned to use the initial weeks as a sort of self-inflicted boot camp. Those first painful days would relentlessly prepare my body for the rest of the journey. The trail would take care of *my* concerns, but I needed to address my parents' biggest concern: namely, that their young adult daughter would be hiking *alone* in unfamiliar woods. Knowing that I wasn't going to cancel my hike, and unsure of whether I could find a hiking partner, I decided to practice hiking solo.

One Friday I skipped class. It was a spur-of-the-moment decision, and because I am not the kind of person who would typically blow off class, it was exhilarating. I packed my daypack, grabbed my trekking poles, pulled on my hiking boots, and drove to the mountains. The road was winding and narrow, which forced me to focus on my driving instead of what I was about to do. I left the windows down and enjoyed the liberation of the wind whipping my hair into wild disarray.

Thirty minutes later I was sitting in the Jones Gap parking lot staring at the trailhead, my heart racing. *Did I tell enough people where I am?* I stuffed my cell phone and map into my pack and locked the car. *What am I forgetting?* I tightened my bootlaces with shaking fingers. *Are they laced tightly enough?* I had gone about ten steps before I realized I'd forgotten my trekking poles. *Slow down!* I dug out my keys and went back. *Breathe.* I adjusted the poles, rechecked my boots, and left again. This time I realized I didn't have my ID or money for the hiking fee. *You can do this.* Forcing myself to swallow, I turned around again.

I reminded myself that this was not a completely new experience. I'd hiked in several states, in unreliable weather, and on trails of varying difficulties. I'd hiked through snow, in mud up to my waist, and with a dislocated shoulder. But this hike was different. This hike was of monumental importance. It was the first concrete step toward making my dream, my plan for after graduation, a reality. It was my first solo hike.

That day would stand out as the most important day in my hiking history until the following March, when I would begin the 2,174-mile journey from Georgia to Maine on the Appalachian Trail. It was by no means my first training hike. I had been doing shake-down hikes—hikes to test the weight of my pack and determine what gear was extraneous and could be eliminated—for months. I registered at the trailhead and, for the first time ever, wrote only my own name on the sheet. I stepped onto the trail with my thoughts racing. *How far will I go? Will I see other people? What if I get hurt? If I can't do this alone, I surely can't walk to Maine.*

Soon, nature stepped in and slowed my thoughts. Recent hurricanes had done severe damage to the trail. I had to focus all my concentration on maneuvering around the natural obstacle course that resulted. I traversed rivers, scaled small cliffs, shimmied under fallen trees, and used my poles to bushwhack through tangled tree branches. A couple of times, I came up against what at first appeared to be impossible challenges. With the help of a partner, the branches could have been held aside easily enough. Alone, I had to remove my pack and drag it behind me or push it ahead of me. I had to think so hard about where to place my foot next that I couldn't worry about anything else.

The first time I looked at my watch was an hour after my initial step onto the trail. Ecstatically, I realized that I hadn't been scared at all. I hiked on without stopping for another hour. Since I didn't have anyone to talk to, I sang, counted the number of bridges I crossed and how many snakes I saw, practiced my Chinese, and daydreamed about meeting a cute hiker boy on the Appalachian Trail. After what I guessed was four miles, I stopped for a snack and to let the blood drain from my feet for a little while. I tried out my new MIOX water purifier in the stream and was happily satisfied with its simplicity.

Choosing gear had been a stressful process. Every hiker prefers different equipment, and every gear review offers varying opinions. Deciding which water purifier to purchase seemed especially important since staying hydrated is a necessity and drinking unpurified water can lead to all types of illnesses. While I had researched this purifier extensively, this was my first time using it on an untreated water source. I was very impressed with the natural taste of the water.

Rejuvenated by my break and by the realization that at least one important gear decision had been successful, I turned around and manipulated my way through the jungle gym of foliage for a second time. As I headed back toward the parking lot, I recalled conversations with my parents concerning my upcoming hike. In spite of how scared they must have felt, they had been incredibly supportive. Now that I had answered all of Mom's safety questions and directed her to books and websites on the subject of women who hike alone, she was much more comfortable. *My hike is only four months away!*

I got lost in thought speculating about that first day on the Appalachian Trail. When I crossed what I knew would be the last bridge, I was shocked. Even though I was undoubtedly more tired on the return hike, I had surprised myself by completing it in less time. I stopped to chat with a park ranger in the parking lot. He told me I had just hiked ten miles.

I tossed my pack into the trunk of my SUV. *Ten miles?* I shortened my trekking poles and attached them to my pack. *Ten miles in five hours . . . I might make it to Maine after all.* I knocked my boots together, watching the clumps of dirt scatter below me before unlacing the boots and sliding them off. When I was packed to go, I sat in my trunk with my bare feet dangling above the ground and procrastinated leaving until the last possible moment. I dreaded exchanging the simplicity of nature for the overstimulation of busy streets and honking horns. My mind started to shift uncomfortably to all the responsibilities I needed to take care of—homework, cleaning my apartment, volunteer work, ordering backpacking gear. *In a few months, hiking will be my only responsibility.* That thought was enough to push me through the rest of the semester. I headed back to campus with the windows down and the radio off.

When the smell of asphalt and exhaust replaced the smell of leaves and pine needles, I rolled up the windows and called my mom to tell her about my hike.

"With whom did you hike?" she asked. Mom is a grammar fanatic and has always had a particular fondness for the rule of not ending a sentence with a preposition.

"Myself." I could practically see her close her eyes and swallow the lecture on safety she wanted to throw my way.

"Were you good company?"

A grin spread across my face as I realized I had been.

"Yep."

"Good enough to hang out with for two thousand miles?" she challenged.

"You bet!"

Armed with the knowledge that I *could* in fact handle hiking by myself, I attempted to push the Appalachian Trail from my mind for long enough to finish college. Surely I could multiply this ten-mile feat a few hundred times and make it from Georgia to Maine. I approached my schoolwork with the same thoroughness with which I was preparing for my hiking trip. Although I had trouble prioritizing between the two, I always managed to squeeze in both homework and trail preparations. I would type an introduction to a paper about "the gendered approach to art in a phallocentric society," and then I'd spend an equal amount of time debating the merits of a down sleeping bag versus a synthetic one with other soon-to-be hikers in an online forum. Painstakingly, but successfully, I completed two overloaded semesters. All I had to do was finish three classes in the last semester—only one in my major—and I would be a college graduate.

During my last semester, I began corresponding with other hikers who were planning to start the Appalachian Trail on the same day in March. Initially, it was exciting just to talk to other people with a similar goal. But as we got to know one another, plans gradually developed for the six of us to meet in Atlanta and begin the journey together. We had no commitments past the first day, but for at least those first twenty-four hours, it guaranteed us a support system. We were a diverse group. We represented both genders, six states, and a seven-year age span. We were a recent high school graduate, an REI employee, a factory worker, a ski bum, a town recreation department worker, a soon-to-be college graduate, and a manual laborer. We had little in common, it seemed, except a shared goal of hiking the 2,200 miles between Springer Mountain in Georgia and Mount Katahdin in Maine. But, as far as we were concerned, that common goal was all that mattered.

While most of my fellow college seniors were applying for their first full-time jobs and looking at ads for apartments, I was researching tents and guide books. For weeks, it seemed like the UPS man was knocking on my door daily to deliver some carefully selected and highly anticipated piece of gear. In between laboring over term papers, cramming Chinese characters into my brain, and studying for exams, I opened boxes containing a sleeping bag, tent, zip-off pants, and countless other dizzyingly exciting, mercilessly overpriced items.

After unpacking each item, I rushed to the computer to regale my future trail partners with the details of my newly acquired equipment. Only fellow hiking enthusiasts could understand my exuberance over opening a four-hundred-dollar sleeping bag. I wore my new zip-off pants to class, slept in my sleeping bag in my living room, walked around campus in my hiking boots, and pitched my tent on my balcony. I was absurdly proud of my new gear. As my final pieces of equipment arrived in the mail, I handed in my term papers and graduated from Furman University three months early with a bachelor's degree in philosophy.

2

Before the Beginning

The following week was a flurry of activity as I said goodbye to college friends and professors, moved out of my apartment, and drove home to Massachusetts to see my family. Amidst all the other activity, I finished preparations for my hike. Planning for this journey had occupied the majority of my waking moments for the better part of the previous year. Even so, the week before the hike I obsessively packed and repacked my backpack. I was intent on somehow lessening my pack weight without sacrificing a single item that I *knew* I needed.

I erected my tent several times in the living room, my bedroom, and the back yard. I seam-sealed my tent, stuffed and un-stuffed my sleeping bag, and learned to tie my bear-bag rope into a daisy chain. My mom walked into the kitchen one night and was horrified to find me practicing cooking with an open flame on an alcohol stove on her kitchen counter. I was immediately banished to the garage along with all of my gear.

Although Mom was not amused by my cooking antics, she patiently sat beside me on the kitchen floor as I counted, sorted, resorted, evaluated, weighed, and repacked my mail-drop items—packages that would be sent to me at various points along the trail. With pink-painted nails she attached the mailing labels and sticky-noted each box with a mailing date so that she would know when to send each box of precious cargo. Slyly, she suggested leaving the boxes unsealed, "just in case" I needed her to add anything. This would become her means of slipping surprises into each package.

Eventually, I determined that I was as ready as I was going to get. Passing the minutes, hours, and days until my departure was difficult. I tried to enjoy relaxing and doing mundane activities like watching TV, but I was incurably restless. My legs were ready to walk. I spent endless amounts of time on the computer communicating with my soon-to-be hiking companions. A plan solidified that we would all arrive in Atlanta by March 13 to get acquainted in person before beginning our journey two days later. Relieved that my plans for starting the hike were in place, I made sure to enjoy some time with my family. I had been hundreds of miles away at college for almost four years, and now, rather than really coming home, I was disappearing into the middle of the woods.

My sister, Allison, helped me mail packages containing maps of the Appalachian Trail to family and friends so that they could track my journey. In each package was a letter that read:

March 2005

Hey People Who Are Important in My Life, GUESS WHAT I'M DOING IN LESS THAN A WEEK?!?!? I'm flying to Atlanta to start my Appalachian Trail thru-hike. Now that we've established that, let's back up. I hope you are all doing awesome. As most of you know, I graduated from Furman in February with a BA in philosophy. I'm now enjoying a couple of weeks at home before moving on to the next chapter in my life (gulp!).

On March 15, against Shakespeare's advice ("beware the Ides of March"), I will start hiking the Appalachian Trail. Over the next six months, I will hike about 2,200 miles from Georgia to Maine. Hiking the AT has been a goal of mine since I first heard about it when I was twelve. Hiking, camping, and nature have been a big part of my life since I started Girl Scouts as a little girl. I'm excited to continue that exploration on the AT. Some people might say I'm crazy (I mean, seriously, who decides to take a 2,200-mile hike in the woods for fun?), but I love a challenge and this will certainly be one. I have worked hard to plan and prepare for my thru-hike for two years, so I am very excited to finally be starting this adventure.

For those of you who haven't been within earshot of me for the last six months, here are some facts about the Appalachian Trail. The AT is a continuous footpath that goes through fourteen states, starting at Springer Mountain in Georgia and ending on Mount Katahdin in Maine. Three to four million visitors hike parts of the AT annually. The first person to hike the entire trail was Earl Shaffer in 1948. Since then, thru-hiking has become more common—about three thousand people attempt a thru-hike annually. Last year, 24 percent of attempted thru-hikers completed their hikes. To forewarn you about the obsession I will develop with food, the average thru-hiker burns six thousand calories a day! This is understandable since the elevation gained throughout the hike is equivalent to climbing Mount Everest sixteen and a half times. Although the physical aspect of this hike is daunting, most hikers say the mental component is the hardest.

I know that you are all asking yourselves how you can be supportive and encouraging during my hike. The best ways to do this are by sending pack mules, high-calorie, sugar-based goodies, and GPS devices. Seriously, though, please send emails and letters and remember me in your prayers.

In between sleeping in your nice, warm bed, flushing the toilet, using electricity, and sitting on your soft squishy couch, check your email often while I'm gone so that you can read about my inevitable encounters with bears, moose, and crazy, starving hikers. . . . If you have questions about how to reach me while I'm wandering around in the woods, contact my mom. Take care!

Love,
Michelle

Finally, I had mailed my letters, packed my gear, said my goodbyes, and after months of anticipation, it was March 13—two days before the official beginning of my Appalachian Trail journey. After a largely sleepless night, my mom and I drove from Massachusetts to Connecticut so we could fly from Connecticut to Georgia so I could walk from Georgia to Maine. Ironically, I had to fly south in order to walk north. I would be meeting most of my starting group for the first time that very evening.

My mom and I were not seated together on the plane. Since I had no one to talk to, I distracted myself by flipping through my *Thru-Hiker's Handbook* for the hundredth time and then left it lying, rather conspicuously, on my little plastic fold-down tray. This book, alternately referred to as "The Handbook" and "Wingfoot," was written by Dan "Wingfoot" Bruce, the webmaster of www.trailplace.com, and is the reference book of choice for most thru-hikers.

Finally, after drinks had been served, the middle-aged man sitting next to me waved his chubby hand in the direction of my book, pointing at the title on the cover. He raised his eyebrows, asking, "The Appalachian Trail?"

I nodded. "In two days I'm going to start hiking it."

"Oh, yeah?" He tilted his head a little.

"Yes." I nodded proudly, straightening a little in my seat.

"Where's that?"

It had never even occurred to me that he might not know what the Appalachian Trail was. "It starts in Georgia . . ." I began.

He nodded, not appearing nearly impressed enough.

". . . and ends in Maine," I continued.

"MAINE?!" he sputtered, nearly choking on his coffee. "How far are you hiking, exactly?" He shifted in his seat, looking at me out of the corners of his eyes while I took a deep breath.

"About twenty-two hundred miles!" I had learned in my research that since the exact trail mileage changes every year due to re-routes, hikers generally refer to the trail as being 2,200 miles for simplicity.

I was confident that he would understand the enormity of this feat I was attempting. Some part of me expected him to be awed or perhaps impressed.

Instead, he wrinkled his eyebrows, cracked his neck, and then shaking his head bewilderedly, asked, "Why?"

"Well . . ." I faltered. "Because . . ." I trailed off, realizing that simply wanting to hike that distance was not a reason that made sense to most people. In a society where success is measured in terms of money, possessions, and position, hiking the Appalachian Trail would seem like an utterly pointless undertaking to many people.

Saddened by this reminder that I was in the minority in wanting to spend an extended period of time surrounded by nature, I finally managed to mumble something about wanting to see everything between Georgia and Maine and walk in the woods for a season. In that moment, before I even stepped onto the trail, I realized that I would never be able to completely articulate the desire to walk 2,200 miles in the woods to any non-hiker. I spent the rest of the flight in contemplative silence.

Mom and I checked into our hotel and realized we had two hours remaining before the cookout where we would meet the rest of my hiking group. We retired to our separate rooms and half-heartedly attempted naps, but neither of us could sleep. I stared up at the speckled ceiling thinking about the daunting statistics regarding completion of the Appalachian Trail: 2,174 miles, fourteen states, approximately five million steps, and about 165,000 signature white blazes. In 2004, twenty-six percent of attempted thru-hikers succeeded, and less than one-third of those were women. Any one of these statistics alone would be enough to spark apprehension, but combined, the information was beyond intimidating.

Meanwhile, in the next room, my mom was undoubtedly imagining bear attacks, broken legs, and stalkers in the woods. She poked her head into my room and together we sprawled across the hotel's itchy, germ-infested comforter discussing my rapidly approaching trip. Our anxiety levels seemed about equal.

"I started reading a book about the Appalachian Trail," she told me, picking at a pill on the comforter. "I borrowed it from your bookshelf."

"Oh, yeah?" I mentally inventoried my growing AT book collection and wondered which of the dozen dog-eared books she had selected. "Which one?"

"*A Walk in the Woods* by Bill somebody."

Oh no! Not that one. Of all my Appalachian Trail books, not that one. I searched her face for signs of terror. Surely Bill Bryson's somewhat wild rendition of trail life hadn't helped ease her worries. She looked unruffled. Maybe she realized how much dramatic humor and creative license Bryson had used? I swallowed hard and made sure to keep my voice neutral. "What do you think of it?"

"It's funny. He makes the trail sound fun."

Fun? Fun is good. How far has she read? I told her that Bryson wasn't the best role model since he didn't really hike the whole trail. We talked about some of the more memorable scenes in the book, and I told her it was supposed to be made into a movie.

Eventually, I stood up and stretched and declared it time to get ready for the cookout. Mom retreated to her room, and soon I found myself standing at the bathroom mirror curling my eyelashes. I realized that this moment was a perfect representation of the two starkly different sides of myself. I often joke that I'm delicate *and* tough—equal parts girly girl and tomboy. Standing in front of a mirror with a curling iron and mascara, dressed in my favorite pink shirt, I was preparing to attend a kick-off for my six month hike—six months during which I would wear the same clothes every day, forego deodorant, and rarely shower.

As I picked up my curling iron, I looked at the reflection of my pack in the mirror. The pack was stuffed to the gills, and my Handbook, already slightly worn, rested on top. Mentally cataloging my gear for the thousandth time, I put the finishing touches on my hair. I really *could* be feminine *and* a hiker, delicate *and* tough.

With a final glance at my pack, Mom and I headed to the car. I thought that I concealed my nervousness rather smoothly. Rather than retreat into fear-induced silence, I found topic after topic with which to entertain my mom. She saw right through my loquaciousness, though, and asked if I wanted to drive by Katie's house and check things out before turning into the driveway. I applauded her devious recommendation and peered curiously through the tinted window of our rental car as we passed the house. There were people milling around everywhere. Lots and lots of people.

Mom pulled onto a nearby street to turn around and glanced over at me. My face must have conveyed the oh-man-what-am-I-doing-am-I-making-a-big-mistake feeling that was bubbling up in my stomach and threatening to burst out at any moment. Mom, ever prepared, suggested a plan involving a story that loomed somewhere between truth and fiction.

"Michelle, no one knows our plans with Elissa are cancelled, right?"

"Right."

I was born in Atlanta, so my family has old friends in the area. Originally, we had hoped to find time to visit with these friends while we were in town, but right after we landed in Atlanta, we found out they were unavailable. I had mentioned the possibility of these plans to Katie a few days in advance so it wouldn't seem rude if we had to leave the cookout early.

"Ok, so every now and then at the party I'll ask you if Elissa has called. If you say 'no,' I'll know you want to stay at the party. If you say 'yes,' I'll know you're ready to go."

Relieved at the prospect of having an exit strategy if necessary, and grateful that my mom had known I'd be nervous, I managed a wobbly smile as we pulled into the driveway. As we parked, I could feel the eyes of everyone at the cookout boring through the windows of our rental car.

People surrounded us like vultures as we stepped out of the car. My eyes roamed from person to person as I learned names one by one. First was Katie, the only other girl in our starting group. Here I was in my pink shirt and makeup, and Katie was barefoot in an old t-shirt with ripped capris and a haphazard ponytail. While I was feeling very self-conscious, she looked completely comfortable in her own skin. She had a beer in one hand and the other wrapped possessively around a guy's waist.

Katie hugged me like an old friend and introduced Kevin, her hip attachment, who nodded his head slightly in acknowledgment. Next was John, a man in his mid-twenties, who was bouncing around giddily like a puppy. He hugged me—and my mom—as Mom and I both discreetly took a step back, protecting our personal space. Blake, whom I had met once before on a day hike, approached and immediately overtook the conversation.

"Hey! How the heck are you? How was your flight? Was it, like, totally crowded? I hate that. Did your pack make it through inspection ok? I guess it must have, right? Was your drive bad? Atlanta traffic can be really awful, you know?" He didn't seem to require answers.

As Blake continued his virtual monologue, I counted in my head. *Katie (one), Kevin (two), John (three), Blake (four), me (five) . . . two hikers are missing.* I scanned the crowd, searching for the remaining two, and my eyes landed on one guy who was hanging back from the group. He had the beginnings of a beard and was wearing a worn Red Sox cap and zip-off pants. Sitting in a lawn chair slightly off to the side, he was casually watching everything unfold. After everyone else had scattered, he approached me.

"Hey. Michelle, right?"

I nodded. *(Six.)*

"I'm Jeremy. Sorry I didn't come over when you first got here. It was a little crazy, you know?" He fingered the brim of his faded Red Sox hat.

We shook hands and then I tucked my hands in my back pockets. "There are so many people here."

His eyes scanned the large crowd and then landed back on me. "I guess soon we'll be out in the woods away from all this."

"I guess." I peered around. "We're missing one person, right? Your friend. Where is he?"

"Yeah, Eddie. He's stuck in an airport. He had a flight mix-up, but he should be here in a few hours."

"Well, good. Then we'll all be here."

I wasn't sure where I fit in with this diverse group. Everyone was nice, but no one seemed at all similar to me. Then again, I wasn't so sure they were similar to each other. This was reassuring. We may not have been best friends, but we were pursuing a common goal, and that was enough to link us together for now. While Katie's unending stream of aunts, uncles, cousins, and brothers rendezvoused outside, the hikers congregated in the living room to exchange statistics: pack weight, food content, tent size, sleeping bag degree, and any other possible gear fact or figure. Once we started covering a common topic, we all relaxed.

Mom floated in and out of conversations, making herself available but unobtrusive. She asked me twice if I had heard from our friends, and both times I emphatically shook my head no. I was nervous, but I was determined to get to know my hiking companions. Finally, we all made plans for the next day, the final day before starting our hike, and then said farewell. I waved goodbye as I climbed into the car, feeling socially exhausted but much more confident than when I had arrived.

"Sooo," Mom crooned the second the car was in reverse. "What did you think?"

We dissected the evening and determined that it had been a success. She had been able to meet Katie's mom, which fulfilled her need to know another hiker's parent. They had exchanged email addresses so that they could communicate parental fears as we hiked. I could now put faces to names with five of my soon-to-be hiking companions.

"Who was the guy in the Red Sox hat?" Mom asked.

"That's Jeremy. He's from Vermont."

"He's cute, don't you think?"

"Mom."

"Well, he is."

I blushed in the darkness of the car. "Yeah, he is."

"You never know." I could feel her grinning beside me in the dark car.

Right then we passed a Kripsy Kreme store with a "HOT NOW" sign in the window. The car practically drove itself into the parking lot, and once we were inside, I unabashedly devoured three doughnuts.

"I need to store up calories," I explained to my mom between mouthfuls of warm, sugary, gooey goodness.

Mom licked the sugar off her fingers and picked up her second doughnut. "Maybe I should hike too," she joked.

Back at the hotel, we changed into pajama pants and settled in to wait for my dad to arrive in Atlanta from his business trip. I packed and repacked my gear a few more times, each time trying on the pack to check out the weight distribution. Mom watched from the couch with an amused smirk.

When I removed my bulging first aid kit for about the eighth time in an effort to find a better place, my mom picked it up. Then she scooted onto the floor beside me and unzipped the pouch. She spread the contents out in front of her, inventorying my most recent set of selections. She had recommendations for additions—Chapstick, body lotion, Vaseline, anti-itch ointment—but I just shook my head. Dry hands and itchy mosquito bites were not big concerns of mine. Besides, I wasn't planning to add an ounce; I wanted to reduce the weight, not increase it. As I fiddled with my gear, I wondered what the other hikers, who were all sleeping at Katie's, were doing. *Am I missing anything by not staying with them?*

The next day Eddie (*seven*) arrived, and the entire group was able to make our final preparations. We gathered at Katie's house that morning with the intention of helping to lighten each other's pack weights. Upon arrival, however, only Jeremy and I seemed invested in the task. The others were engrossed in *South Park* episodes. While they lay around watching TV, we sifted through each other's gear, asking questions.

"How many shirts did you pack?" he wanted to know.

"Two long-sleeved wicking shirts," I said, laying out a light blue and a lavender shirt between us. "One long underwear shirt and one full-zip fleece," I continued as I set the white nylon and mesh shirt and the black and raspberry-colored fleece on top. "Oh, and my raincoat," I added, pulling a chocolate brown jacket out of my pack and plopping it on top of the pile. I looked up at him. "And I need to buy a short-sleeved shirt tomorrow."

He nodded his approval. "Mine's about the same, except I only have one long-sleeved shirt." He pushed his clothing aside. "What do you have for cooking gear?"

We compared stoves and cooking pots. Although we had made some different purchases, it was clear that we had read many of the same gear reviews.

"There were so many choices to make for gear. I'm really afraid I'll get out there and I will have chosen the wrong sleeping bag or the wrong stove," I confided.

"Me too. And it was all so expensive."

I nodded. My bank account was still a little shocked at the expense of all the new gear and clothes. I pushed my clothing and cooking gear aside and dug in my bottomless pack. "So, what's in your first aid kit?" I asked Jeremy as I pulled mine out.

"First aid kit?" He raised an eyebrow.

"You don't have one? Mine's monstrous."

"Let's go through it. I'll bet you can toss some weight from that," he offered, reaching for the green stuff sack.

We weeded out Band-Aids, Neosporin, all but two Benadryl tablets, a number of hair elastics, and other assorted extra items. My satisfaction grew in proportion to the size of my discard pile. This preliminary shake-down had probably shaved two unnecessary pounds from my pack. To a non-backpacker, this amount may seem inconsequential, but knowing I would be hauling this load up mountains for months, I had a great sense of accomplishment and gratitude.

Our whole entourage visited the local REI outfitter, where I searched fruitlessly for a pink hiking shirt. Pink was without question my favorite color, and it was sadly under-represented in hiking gear that year. I settled for red. While I wandered through the aisles, my dad held up a dehydrated food pouch that read "Ice Cream Sandwich" from across the store and pointed at my shopping basket, raising his eyebrows comically.

Satisfied that our gear lists were complete, the seven of us paraded to the grocery store next door and bought our first food supply. My parents patiently shuttled us around as I watched their facial expressions volley back and forth between amusement and blatant parental fear. I began piling granola bars, crackers, cheese, Lipton noodles, and peanuts into my cart.

When at last the purchases were complete, my parents offered to treat us all to our last "civilized" meal. The group hemmed and hawed at making a selection. Knowing that we would be eating mostly prepackaged food for the next several months, it seemed impossible to settle on a restaurant. My dad stuffed his hands into his jean pockets and scuffed his loafers on the ground, barely disguising his impatience at our inability to make such a simple decision.

In a moment of silence, Jeremy suggested, "How about Pizza Hut?"

Murmurs of agreement came from around the circle. Dad slapped Jeremy on the back and thanked him for being decisive, then ushered us into the car.

Lunch was full of laughter and conversation. With our bellies full, we went our separate ways for the afternoon. At my parents' suggestion, I invited two hikers back to the hotel for the night. We had extra beds, and Katie's house was more than crowded. We all needed a good night's sleep. Jeremy and Eddie jumped at the opportunity, so the three of us spent the last restless pre-trail hours together.

We made a late-night trip to Dairy Queen, during which we talked about everything but the trail. Our nervousness was starting to intensify. In a completely uncharacteristic event, I pushed my ice cream around with my spoon, unable to force the treat past my bubbling anxiety. The Appalachian Trail was no longer a hypothetical trip sometime in the future. *This is happening. Tomorrow.*

I have had a lifelong struggle with insomnia, so it came as no surprise that, with both excitement and nerves competing to be recognized in my body, falling asleep that night proved impossible. Hearing me get up for about my sixth drink of water, my mom insisted that I take a sleeping pill so that I would start the first day on the trail well-rested. Within thirty minutes of swallowing the little white miracle pill, I drifted into dreamless sleep.

3

The Ides of March

On the morning of March 15, 2005, I found myself standing in the parking lot at Amicalola Falls State Park. In spite of the innumerable hours I'd spent preparing, I suddenly felt completely inadequate to embark on this adventure. I mean, who walks 2,200 miles? I discreetly studied the hikers around me, convinced that each one was somehow more suited to this task. My preparations seemed inconsequential. Forcibly pushing those thoughts away, I hefted my pack and poles from the car and joined my fellow hikers.

The air had been charged with anxiety from the moment we awoke that morning. My dad had brought us breakfast before the drive. I'd choked it down, knowing I would need the fuel, but Jeremy and Eddie could barely force down a few bites.

While the three of us in the backseat had exchanged halting, nervous remarks about random topics, my dad had remained silent, his frequent glances in the rearview mirror the only indication of his unease.

"We'll be there in fifteen minutes . . . ten . . . five . . . look, there's the park sign." Mom kept updating us on the distance to Amicalola Falls State Park.

As we dawdled in the parking lot, nervousness emanated from our group. Each person expressed it differently: John couldn't stop touching and hugging people, Eddie kept laughing, Jeremy had sweat rings the size of manholes around the underarms of his shirt, Katie and Kevin were once again glued together, Blake was talking nonstop to anyone and everyone, and I, quite uncharacteristically, remained silent.

Leaving our precious packs outside, we went into the Amicalola Falls Visitor Center, and all seven of us crowded around the trail register, waiting for a turn to sign in and officially become an attempted thru-hiker. In turn we recorded our names, addresses, and emergency contact information. We lined up as a group, each of us darting sidelong looks at the door through which we would soon pass, and took our official group picture for the record book. The picture was labeled "Beware the Ides of March," as though we were an entity to fear.

We paraded outside to participate in the important tradition of weighing our packs. This hiker ritual is mentioned in nearly every Appalachian Trail book and website. The famous metal scale hung intimidatingly from the side of the building.

One by one, we hefted our packs up onto the hook and announced our pack weights. Jeremy's was the largest at fifty pounds, which seemed impossibly heavy. *He must have too much stuff.* Blake's was the lightest at thirty pounds. *I bet he forgot something.*

"Ok, your turn, Michelle," Jeremy told me.

Much to my embarrassment, I had to have help lifting my pack high enough to reach the hook. My dad quickly stepped in to help. "Forty pounds," he read out, and I thought I detected a note of pride in his voice. *That sounds just right!*

We had to go back through the Amicalola Falls Welcome Center to begin our journey. Hefting our packs, we quickly passed by the touristy exhibits and walked through the wooden door marked "Approach Trail." Once outside, we migrated toward the stone arch as though some unseen magnetic force was silently compelling us. We lined up as a group to take our last pre-hike photo in front of the Appalachian Trail's approach trail sign. It brazenly declared the distance to the official trailhead to be 8.7 miles. *In 8.7 miles I'll be on the Appalachian Trail.*

After the final photo, I stood beside my parents on the stone terrace. Around us tourists snapped photos, day hikers looked at trail maps, and other thru-hikers made final pack adjustments and said goodbye to family. I blocked out the commotion and focused only on my parents.

"Be careful," Mom almost whispered as she pressed her cheek against mine. Her forced smile and too-big eyes were reminiscent of her face as she dropped me off at college freshman year. I wondered if, like then, she would cry as soon as I was out of sight. Dad kissed my forehead. His voice was just a little more gravelly than normal as he said, "Good luck."

I slipped a letter I'd written into their hands. *This is it.* I hugged them both, though my enormous pack made it awkward. *Now or never.* I blinked hard, making sure there weren't any tears trying to escape before I looked at them one last time. They stood close—their shoulders pressed together as though supporting each other gave them the strength to support me.

I fell in line behind my fellow hikers, taking my first step toward Maine. We looked like a motley re-creation of the Seven Dwarves trudging off for a day of work. Our farewell group—well-wishing family and friends—yelled "Bye!" and "Good luck!" until we rounded the bend and they could no longer see our string of multi-hued backpacks bobbing up the trail. Filled with enthusiasm, we screamed "KATAHDIN!"—the name of the final mountain in Maine—in unison every couple of seconds, our eager voices blending together, until we suspected our audience could no longer hear.

Beginning our hike at Amicalola Falls State Park and hiking the 8.7-mile approach trail to the official beginning of the Appalachian Trail represented the first of many controversial decisions we would each make on our journey. The official start of the Appalachian Trail is on top of Springer Mountain. The terminus is accessible only from other trails since no road reaches the trailhead. We had all chosen to park at Amicalola Falls State Park and hike the trail up to Springer Mountain. Other hikers opt to drive a different route and hike a much shorter approach. Much debate exists in the hiker world as to the "right" or "best" decision in any given situation, and whether or not to hike the approach trail is no exception. When debates regarding trail decisions come up, the commonly repeated advice is, "Hike your own hike." While the approach trail was rumored to be very difficult, each of us had chosen this route.

True to rumor, this trail was grueling. At first the adrenaline and excitement propelled my legs at a seemingly unstoppable pace. Even so, I realized almost immediately that my pack was loaded incorrectly. It was top-heavy, causing me to feel like I might flip over backward. *I feel like a weeble-wobble.* I kept fiddling with my straps as I hiked, but my adjustments weren't helping.

"Is something wrong with your pack?" Jeremy asked. He had stopped ahead of me on the trail to wait for the rest of our group to catch up, and saw me messing with my straps as I joined him.

"It seems like it's top-heavy. I feel like I'm going to flip over. Plus it's hurting my shoulders."

"Maybe you should rearrange stuff?"

"Probably." At the next level spot, I stopped, took off my pack, and removed all my gear, tossing it on the ground in a colorful pile.

"Want some help?"

Katie, an REI employee who was much more knowledgeable about appropriate weight distribution, stopped beside me.

"Please. I have no idea how all this stuff should be arranged."

"Yeah. It's tough to figure out. Men and women have to pack their stuff differently, too."

"Really?"

"Yep. Here, try putting your food bag down lower. That has a lot of weight. And put your clothes up higher because they don't weigh much." Katie shoved my gear into my pack in new locations as she talked. "This should be better."

"Thank you so much."

She smiled. "There are some benefits to working at an outfitter."

I clipped my pack shut and awkwardly swung the forty pounds onto my back.

Katie shook her head. "Next time try lifting your pack like this." She lifted her pack onto her knee, slipped one arm through a shoulder strap, and slid the pack around her waist onto her back. "This is easier on your whole body."

"Thanks." *I haven't even reached the beginning of the trail, and I've already learned that I don't know how to pack my pack or put it on. Maine, here I come.*

Katie's suggestions were effective, and I was able to continue my excitement-driven ascent. We were one long train of hikers pounding away the steps to Maine. At the top of Amicalola Falls, our first picturesque stop on the trail, I pulled out my camera. The beauty of the waterfall was lost on me amid the delight of the first day of hiking. After snapping a picture of the cascade, I pushed on toward the official start of the Appalachian Trail.

As the steps grew into miles, my pace slowed, almost imperceptibly at first. As I gave in to my groaning and protesting muscles, I gradually fell farther behind each of the six hikers I'd started with. First, two were out of my sight, then three, and eventually all six. I relegated myself to a position at the end of the "train to Maine" and hiked steadily at my natural pace. *Surely all five feet and two inches of me shouldn't be expected to keep up with men who are over a foot taller.* Of course I was aware of their lightning speed and my comparably snail-like pace, but I would not let this dissuade me. *It's only the first day. I knew the first few days would be painful and challenging. Why should the approach trail be any different?*

The trail climbed steadily upward, and my legs discovered the strain of hauling a forty-pound pack in addition to my body weight. I tried to use my shiny new Leki hiking poles to lessen the strain on my knees, but I had rarely hiked with poles before and felt as though I had suddenly grown two gangly, awkward appendages. I tripped over the poles, got them stuck in the ground, and couldn't seem to figure out what length was most comfortable. Just as I was getting comfortable hiking alone and starting to get into a rhythm—pole, step, step, pole, step, step, pole—I heard voices.

I rounded a corner and saw a half-dozen hikers seated on fallen logs eating lunch. The contents of their backpacks had spilled onto the ground. Grateful for the break and the company, I plopped down on a log and pulled out my own blasphemously heavy food bag. I devoured an outrageously heavy orange and the rest of my lunch while introductions were made. Some of the hikers had been part of my starting group, but I was introduced to new hikers as well.

There were two sisters who were already going by the name the Gypsy Sisters. The older sister had designated herself Gypsy, and the younger didn't have a trail name yet. She would later become Touk.

Trail names are a well-known tradition in which hikers take on an alias for the duration of their hike. This aspect of trail life often completely baffles outsiders. The silly monikers ensure safety because no one knows each other's real names, and they also create a low-key atmosphere. It's hard to be too serious while being called Rudolph or Dreamer.

Life on the trail is so different from what's commonly referred to as "real life" that I think having a different name to suit the different lifestyle makes sense to most hikers. After a few days, it becomes customary to meet people with names like Pixie and Princess. Even in towns hikers go by their trail names, which adds to the mystique surrounding long-distance hikers. I wondered what my trail name would be. I had considered using my camp name, Hershey, but decided I wanted my trail experience to stand on its own. Gypsy was the first hiker I had met with a trail name.

In addition to the Gypsy Sisters, there were two women from Albuquerque, one with dreadlocks and the other with a severely short haircut, who would soon become the first hikers I had met to leave the trail. I was surprised at the number of women I saw, but my companions assured me that this was quite unusual and would change as I progressed up the trail.

Although the break had been enjoyable, we still had about four-and-a-half more miles to hike before dark. As I started back up the trail, my body was well aware of all forty of the unforgiving pounds I had strapped onto my back. It seemed incomprehensible that after the number of times I had packed and repacked in anticipation of this trip, there were still non-essential items in my pack. Yet suddenly, with my pack on, headed yet one more mile up Springer Mountain, I began to mentally sort through my gear and select the items that could be ditched without regret at the first town stop. *Do I really need an extra flashlight? That first aid kit is still too heavy. I don't need two long-sleeved shirts, do I? And that orange for lunch, that'll never happen again—water weight AND a peel that has to be packed out. I don't need matches and a lighter—the matches can go.*

Hauling the burdensome pack, I pushed on. The mid-March winter landscape was barren and drab, even in Georgia. The woods were a muted dual-tone of brown and grey. Luckily, the seasons change more quickly in the south, so we hikers would begin to see more color in the woods before long.

After what seemed like an impossible amount of time, I made it to the top of Springer Mountain—the official start of the Appalachian Trail. Sitting on a rock at the summit was Jeremy. I returned the smile on his cute, bearded face and plopped down next to him.

Jeremy patted the plaque on the ground next to him with a ready smile. "You made it!"

I looked down at the tarnished plaque: "Southern terminus of the Appalachian Trail." Breathlessly, I unbuckled my pack. "I can't believe we hiked all that way and we're just now at the beginning. Today's miles don't even count. Who starts a trail on top of a mountain?"

"I don't know," he murmured, shaking his head.

We sat in companionable silence for a few minutes. Then, he took my picture beside the plaque and showed me the metal slot with the first official trail register. Trail registers are notebooks left along the trail where hikers record thoughts, share information, and leave notes for other hikers. Since this would be my first-ever trail entry, I sat for an interval trying to think of something profound to write. Giving up on creativity, I scrawled a brief note and signed my name. Then I rewarded myself with a snack for making it up Springer Mountain. I chose GORP ("good old raisins and peanuts") because it was the heaviest snack in my pack.

"The shelter is right up the trail," Jeremy told me after a while.

We stood and shouldered our packs. I looked up and grinned when I saw the first official white blaze on the trail ahead. Exhausted, sweaty, and already 8.7 miles into my day, I touched the white paint with my hand before taking my first real step onto the Appalachian Trail.

4

I'm Going to Get Arrested

With one last glance back at the Springer Mountain plaque, I stumbled past that first trail blaze. A few short steps later, stuck in the hard cold ground, was a wooden post about four feet high. It was splintered and weathered and irreparably crooked. There was one word carved into that post: "Shelter." Even on that first day, I recognized the magnificent symbolism of those carved wooden posts. Each shelter sign represented triumph—a goal achieved, a milestone met. I had arrived at Springer Mountain Shelter.

Shelters along the Appalachian Trail are generally three-sided, wooden structures. This was the first shelter I had seen, and I was impressed. It was clean and large. Since this was an oft-visited shelter, it had a loft to provide extra sleeping space. The roof extended far enough in front of the shelter to cover two picnic tables. As I would learn over the next few months, the shelters vary in size and capacity as well as quality. Each shelter is built by the club that maintains that section of the trail, which accounts for the many variations. Most shelters have picnic tables, fire circles, privies, water sources, and flat spots for tents, though even these details vary. Some shelters, like the Springer Mountain Shelter, are built right along the trail, while others are a few tenths of a mile down a blue-blazed side trail.

I survived my first night on the trail without any major mishaps. Surprisingly, my gear all functioned and it appeared that I hadn't forgotten to pack anything. There were fifteen of us at Springer Mountain Shelter that first night, and the group was even more diverse than our "Beware the Ides of March" clan. The age span in the shelter was easily forty years. Our hometowns ranged from Albuquerque, New Mexico, to Burlington, Vermont, to Atlanta, Georgia. As for previous camping experience, our group consisted of everything from a previous Appalachian Trail thru-hiker to one person who had never even slept outside before. After animated introductions, each of us began the process of figuring out a comfortable and efficient nighttime routine.

There were many "firsts" in the shelter that night. Some hikers needed help working their water purifiers, while others didn't know how to light their stoves. Jeremy released too much fuel while priming his WhisperLite MSR stove and shot a flame three feet into the air, to the vast amusement of the group. I, however, had the opposite problem. I didn't pour enough denatured alcohol into my Brasslite Stove, and the flame went out halfway through cooking my noodles, causing me to doubt my decision to buy an alcohol stove. It was completely dark by the time I finished cooking dinner.

At some point during my preparations, a new person walked up to the shelter. He came from the north, which immediately caught everyone's attention. He explained that he was a trail runner. Trail runners are state employees who are in charge of hiking a certain section of the trail and teaching leave-no-trace camping ethics, as well as helping hikers. He imparted some of his trail wisdom to us, including the fact that using poles while hiking burns an extra thousand calories a day. He answered questions about the trail and also reminded us to use the bear bag cables for our food and other scented items.

Bear bags are containers, often nylon stuff-sacks, used for storing food. The bags are strung up with rope on a high tree branch to protect both hikers and their food from hungry, thieving animals. In Georgia and some other locations on the trail with heavy bear populations, cables with pulley systems are provided for hikers to use in lieu of trees. This method of bear bagging suffices for eluding the black bears found on the East Coast, but in other areas of the country and on other trails, more extreme bear-proofing is required.

Just before the trail runner left, he cautioned us, "Don't forget to bear-bag your cameras; bears are attracted to something in film."

"Do I need to bear-bag my digital camera?" I asked.

"No, bears haven't learned to smell pixels yet," he joked, soliciting a chuckle from nearby hikers.

I ate dinner and finished cleaning up and preparing for bed by the light of my headlamp. On previous hiking trips, I had always used a Maglite flashlight, so wearing a headlamp was new to me. I kept tilting my head at awkward angles in an attempt to shine my light in the desired direction. My fingers were clumsy inside my fleece gloves, and everything took longer than it had when I had practiced inside my living room. It took me a few days to learn how to angle my headlamp so that I didn't get a crick in my neck from doing chores in the dark.

Finally, after everyone had purified water, eaten, and set up sleeping gear, someone lit a fire. Despite what many non-southerners may think, it *is* cold in Georgia in March. I layered on all my clothes, stomping my feet and wiggling my toes in an attempt to stay warm beside the fire. Souleman (pronounced "soul-man"), as Jeremy was now called, looked at the thermometer attached to the outside of his pack.

"It's thirty degrees," he announced.

Now, thirty degrees doesn't seem bad when, in a matter of seconds, you can dash out of your warm house and into your waiting, heated car. However, when you're outside all night long without a four-sided building to shield you, thirty degrees is bitterly cold.

Almost all fifteen of us were huddled around the crackling fire exchanging stories and jokes as we created new friendships. KTR (Kick the Rocks) and Cupcake were the resident experts that night. They had both attempted thru-hikes before and had a lot of trail knowledge between them. Domino, Snowbunny, Hairball, and Big John were there, too. Many friendships that would last the duration of the trail were sparked that night. Although meeting new hiking companions was fascinating, the cold chased us all into our sleeping bags at an early hour.

I wiggled the lower half of my body into my twenty-degree Western Mountaineering mummy sleeping bag. The down bag had been entirely too hot inside my apartment in South Carolina, but it was comfortable outside. With anticipation, I pulled out my journal. During my trail preparation, I had put considerable effort into setting up my trail journal. The first few pages had quotes, songs, and other items that I had glued inside for inspiration. The next five pages were motivational letters from my mom, dad, sister, and two best friends. I had asked them each to prepare one for me before my departure. My plan was to read one letter of encouragement each day for the first five days. My mom had glued the letters into my journal for me so that I wouldn't have an opportunity to sneak a peek at them ahead of time.

With much anticipation, I flipped to the first letter.

THE OLYMPIC GAMES – 1968 –
MEXICO CITY

Almost seventy-five minutes after the last runner had crossed the finish line in the marathon, fans had filled the stadium for the next event when a noise was heard outside. A runner was approaching the stadium and was being cheered on by fans who lined the road leading into the stadium. Over the twenty-six miles, John Stephen Aguarre had dislocated a knee and sprained an ankle. His shins and elbows were bloody and bruised from the falls he had taken. But still he was running!

He made his way into the stadium and as he began the final lap, the crowd began to rise as he passed them. When he finally collapsed across the finish line, the entire crowd was standing in an ovation that lasted for several minutes. To this day it is described by many people as the most poignant moment in Olympic history.

In the newspaper the following morning, a reporter said: "Yesterday we saw a young African runner who symbolized the finest and best in the human spirit. His was a performance that lifts athletics out of the category of grown people playing games. This was a performance that gives meaning to the word courage. All honor to John Stephen Aguarre."

Twelve years later the journalist Bud Greenspan went to Aguarre's homeland in Ethiopia to ask just one question: "Why? With the winner having crossed the finish line so long ago, were you still running?" Aguarre replied: "I didn't travel across the world to win a medal, I went there to finish a race."

As you make your way across the Appalachian Trail, it strikes me that you have a lot in common with Aguarre. Like him, you are in a long distance event. You are going to have your share of bumps and bruises along the way. And, just like Aguarre, what you are doing is not about a trophy, it's about the race.

In preparing for the hike, you have already shown a level of commitment and sacrifice that most people are unwilling or unable to make. I am proud of what you have done to get ready for the experience and will be leading the cheers when you get to Maine. But I know that the ultimate satisfaction will not come from the congratulations that you get from others, it will come from the feelings about yourself that you will carry around for the rest of your life for having followed—and realized—a dream.

Your biggest fan – Dad

My heart sped up a few beats knowing that my dad was so proud of me before I had even spent a full day striving for this dream. I knew that his words would push my feet forward when stopping seemed a preferable option.

I pulled my winter hat off and zipped myself the rest of the way into my sleeping bag, cinching the cord until only my eyes and nose were visible. My headlamp was placed right next to my head in case of an emergency. I had never slept in a shelter before, and I was most worried about the mice. The many www.trail place.com posts that I had read on the subject had me envisioning organized mouse races across our bodies during the night. I lay listening to the nighttime noises and tossed and turned as much as possible in the confines of a short mummy sleeping bag on top of a narrow Therm-a-Rest sleeping pad.

Most hikers carry some type of sleeping pad to provide insulation and cushion between themselves and the ground. My Therm-a-Rest was an inflatable version of a sleeping pad. Other, more lightweight options exist, but I had decided that the increased comfort of an inflatable mattress was worth a little additional weight. On this first night on the trail, as my body repeatedly slipped off the thin, narrow mattress, I wondered if I had made the right decision.

I was on the end of the top level of the shelter, and a crisp, cold wind was blowing directly into my ear through a crack in the wall. The thin pad did not seem to be protecting me from the cold floor. Finally, I pulled my hat back onto my head and retightened the mummy bag hood around my face. I spent most of the night awake, curled into a ball trying to avoid the wind and attempting to ignore the screams of my full bladder. My ears desperately strained to hear tell-tale mouse sounds through the two layers of hat and thick sleeping bag that surrounded them.

I woke up from a short sleep with fabric pressed over my eyes and mouth. *Oh my God, someone is trying to suffocate me!* I was trapped and terrified. My arms tried to fly up and pull the fabric away from my face, but they were pinned to my sides. *I'm trapped!* I awoke fully as I suppressed the urge to scream in panic. My hand brushed a zipper, and I remembered that I was in a sleeping bag. I had twisted around while asleep, and my face was no longer sticking out of the little face hole. Instead, when I opened my eyes, I could see only the pitch black of the interior of my sleeping bag. It is nearly impossible to twist around inside a mummy sleeping bag because your hands are completely immobilized. I spent a few panicky seconds trying to get my face lined back up with the breathing hole. Much to my surprise, it was still dark outside when I emerged from my nylon prison. I located my headlamp and stole a glance at my watch. It was only two in the morning.

With the mummy bag hood carefully away from my face, I lay back down. It would be weeks before I would be brave enough to try tightening the drawstring around my head again. Miserably, I dozed in and out of slumber, exhausted from the effort of trying to fall asleep, and finally awoke to muted chatter and the distinctive sound of raindrops on the shelter roof. When I opened my eyes, I was disheartened to realize that it was still mostly dark. Based on the levels of noise and activity, it seemed that everyone else had slept soundly. Groggily, I packed my gear and, decked in my rain coat, followed Jeremy and Eddie to the bear bag ropes. The bags were still hanging like upside-down balloons from the line, confirming that the bears and other large animals had been dissuaded from devouring our food.

Upon lowering my bag, my previously unwarranted hatred of mice was substantiated. There was a hole—with telltale chew marks—in the bottom of my stuff sack. I dumped the contents onto the picnic table to take inventory. The culprit had somehow known *exactly* which item in the food bag was most treasured and had chosen to target only that particular Ziploc bag. The entirety of my mom's special-made GORP had been tainted with mouse germs. Now, not only could I not eat the heavy treat, I would have to carry the ridiculous weight until I passed the first trash can.

I wasn't in the habit of eating breakfast, so I stuffed granola bars in my cargo pockets. This meant I could wait until I was hungrier to eat and that my body heat would thaw them to a consistency that wouldn't break my teeth. I wrestled my pack into its new rain cover and left the shelter at the same time as Jeremy and John.

The rain was icy, and even inside my rain clothes and many layers, I was cold. The chill crept down my spine, causing me to tighten my back and further strain my tired muscles. Unaccustomed to carrying around forty extra pounds, my body was adamantly indicating its indignation over the weight. Luckily, my excitement about being on the trail overrode my stiffness and the disappointment that it was raining. Two and a half miles into the day, Blake and Eddie caught up to us, and the five of us continued up the trail together.

For a few minutes, the guys had gotten ahead of me. I was walking down the trail, lost in thought and enjoying the misty morning air. I rounded a corner to see four men in camouflage kneeling on a rise above me with guns pointed in my direction. I became a statue with concrete feet. *I'm going to die on the second day of my hike.*

"Wow, uh—you, uh—really, uh—blend in. I—uh, didn't even—uh, see you," I finally stammered.

"That's kind of the point," one told me quietly without moving his eyes from the trail. I started to ask him what they were doing, but before I could get the question out, he darted his eyes around and then whispered, "We're doing training. We're not allowed to talk to you." He handed me a discarded bullet shell and then stepped backward, fading into the woods.

A little rattled, I pocketed the shell and continued up the trail, all the while scanning the woods in search of more camouflaged soldiers waiting to ambush me. A few officers were standing at random intervals along the trail, but they didn't acknowledge me as I passed. Over a small hill just past the last officer, Eddie, John, Blake, and Jeremy were waiting for me. After passing all the soldiers, they had thought I might be scared and had decided to wait for me.

Even including the brief stop following the camouflaged mafia invasion, which we later found out was part of a training expedition for a local ROTC group, we had hiked the first five miles in two and a half hours. This meant we had hiked thirty-minute miles. Granted, the trek had been mostly downhill, but nonetheless I was proud.

I slowed down for the last few miles and reached Hawk Mountain Shelter after the guys. Still, I arrived at the shelter by two o'clock. Immediately, I reserved my spot for the night by inflating my Therm-a-Rest and placing it between two others. Then, already settling in to my evening routine, I went to the stream to get water.

The second day on the Appalachian Trail, it was still very exciting to use my MIOX water purifier. Since many hikers choose water pumps instead, I was often asked for a demonstration. This early on, almost all hikers were still learning about gear and were excited for any bit of confident knowledge, so I willingly acquiesced. As the miles progressed, many hikers turned into self-proclaimed experts on every possible topic related to hiking. At that point, I stopped discussing gear because I didn't care for the endless debates and disagreements about the virtues of one choice over another. As long as my gear worked for my purposes, I was satisfied.

By three thirty in the afternoon, I had eaten dinner and was settled in for the night. I sat on a picnic table and did a crossword puzzle with other hikers while the new arrivals cooked and ate. As I sat there, I watched a hiker attempt, rather unsuccessfully, to string up a clothes line. The hiker tied a rope between two trees, placed a shirt on it, and proceeded to watch the shirt sag to the ground. After seeing this happen repeatedly, I walked over and offered assistance. With practiced ease, I used a clothesline hitch to secure the rope to each tree. I then hung the shirt to demonstrate the line's weight-holding ability.

"Where'd you learn that?" he asked.

Searching the recesses of my brain in an attempt to recall where, exactly, I had learned that particular knot, I finally replied, "I've been a Girl Scout for a long time."

Later that night, another question arose about tying a knot, and someone suggested, "Ask the Brownie Scout."

"Who?"

"The Brownie." He pointed in my direction as I sheepishly waved a hand to get the hiker's attention.

"You're the Brownie?"

I smiled and started to explain that Brownies are young Girl Scouts in first through third grades, but seeing his blank face, I realized it was futile. I helped him tie the knot, and as he walked away, he called over his shoulder with a smile, "Thanks, Brownie."

And just like that, I had my trail name. It is said that trail names are given in the most unusual ways. At first I protested and scorned the name Brownie, thinking it unnervingly effeminate for a hiker. I wanted my name to sound tough so that I would be respected. But Brownie stuck, and the more I thought about it, the more appropriate it seemed since Girl Scouting was where I had first heard about the Appalachian Trail. I've since grown to adore the name.

As I crammed my food into its stuff sack, I realized that I was dealing with my first gear malfunction. The mouse attacker from the previous night had chewed straight through the stuff sack in his frenzy to get to my GORP, ripping it completely, and I had no way to hang my food for the night. Jeremy, who had a food bag the size of Texas, offered to let me bear-bag with him until we arrived at the first town with an outfitter to replace my bag.

That night, I secured myself a spot in the middle of the shelter and snuggled into my sleeping bag, keeping my hat on this time. I pulled out my journal and, with great anticipation, flipped to the second inspirational letter. This one was from my high school best friend, Meagan.

Mich – You are an amazing person. I have faith in you and I know you can definitely do this, definitely.

What lies behind us . . . and what lies before us . . . are tiny matters compared to what lies within us.—Emerson

And what lies within you is nothing less than pure QUALITY. I love you.

Meag

I smiled at the obviously intentional uses of the words "quality" and "definitely," which had been jokes between us for over six years. It was nice to know that even my friends who considered backpacking a form of cruel punishment were supportive. Meagan would sooner agree to clean a men's locker room every day for a year than to hike 2,200 miles and sleep outside.

Yawning, I looked at my watch—it wasn't even six o'clock yet. My whole body was tired, and my muscles quivered like they could slide right off my limbs. Apparently, my body was already getting used to a hiker's schedule. Since it gets dark so early and is so cold outside in the spring, hikers often go to bed by six or seven in the evening. In the hiking community, this is jokingly referred to as "hiker midnight."

I spent the night sandwiched between Jax (Eddie's trail name) and Souleman and stayed nice and toasty. Much to my surprise, I slept. I opened my eyes in the morning and was shocked to see snow. The woods around the shelter were dense with fog. I pulled on layers of clothes and packed my gear as quickly as possible. Already I had developed a systematic routine, and each piece of gear had a designated place in my pack. I could go from sleeping to hiking in a matter of minutes.

I crammed granola bars in my pockets, donned my gloves, and readjusted my fleece hat, which had not come off my head in over twenty-four hours. Especially noteworthy in this case is the fact that I hate to wear hats: my head becomes claustrophobic and I can't hear as well. Keeping a hat on my head for twenty-four straight hours was a testament to the unrelenting cold.

Momentarily, my shivering body envied the steaming mugs of coffee and bowls of oatmeal being enjoyed by other hikers. Since I'm not a morning person, I had decided to eat cold breakfasts and reduce the number of morning chores. Besides, knowing that I hiked slowly, I hadn't wanted to waste any more moments than necessary before getting back on the trail each day.

For the first time I tried to use my hiking poles while wearing gloves. I hated it. The thick fleece gloves pushed my fingers uncomfortably far apart, and trying to grip the poles was awkward. I pulled the gloves and hat off and on all day. It seemed I was not capable of adequately regulating my body temperature. While hiking, I got overheated in the layers of clothing and began to sweat. I would peel off a few layers to cool down, which would work nicely until the air cooled my sweat. Any time I stopped, I would become so cold that I had to re-dress immediately. It was nearly impossible to get comfortable, and I spent the entire day dressing and undressing. I hated removing the rain pants the most. They blocked the wind and prevented the snow from dampening my pants, but they also trapped my body heat and made me sweat. How to maintain a consistent body temperature while hiking in cold weather was a puzzle I never completely solved.

It remained foggy and continued to snow all day. The snow painted the trees with delicate crystals, and I enjoyed the beauty of the storm even as I was frustrated with my body temperature, uncooperative gloves, and ever-heavy pack.

"Hi. Who are you?" a high-pitched little voice called out as I rounded the turn after the sign for Gooch Gap Shelter on the third night.

I leaned on my Leki poles, mercifully taking some of the weight off my throbbing feet, and thanked myself for at least the hundredth time since Springer Mountain for deciding to purchase them, in spite of the extra calories they caused me to burn.

"I'm Brownie." *How many times will I have to say that before it sounds natural?*

I squinted my eyes, trying to find the source of the voice among the surrounding bushes and trees. Branches rustled in front of me, and out popped a little boy. He was wearing a plaid kilt and had a Mohawk. I guessed he was about nine years old.

"I'm Oblivious," he informed me with a grin.

I couldn't help but laugh. *Oblivious? What a perfect name.*

He tossed a ball in the air as I followed him up the trail to the shelter and introduced myself to his parents, Troll and Anchor. Little did I know at the time that this family, who would become known as "The Troll Family," would continue to pop up when least expected for the duration of my hike. We would exchange trail information, share rides to and from town, convene in towns, and leapfrog back and forth up the trail in a bizarrely aligned dance.

Our "Beware the Ides of March" group started separating on the third day. Once we had all lived safely through the first days and nights, we each became confident in our ability to survive without the security of a designated group. First, Krazy Katie and Radio (Katie and Kevin) passed the rest of us. Their meager funds and trail-ready legs propelled them forward. Jax (Eddie), Souleman (Jeremy), and I became a threesome. They hiked much faster than I did, but we set a destination each morning and rendezvoused for lunch, and again each evening, with stories about our respective journeys. Mercifully, they often saved just enough space between their Therm-a-Rests in the shelter to squeeze me in. This served a dual purpose for me: I had space in the shelter and a warm body on each side, so I could guiltlessly steal their body heat during those relentlessly cold March nights.

Other hikers around us were settling into their trail aliases as well: Draggin', Chestnut, Just Gary. I socialized around the picnic tables with my new, funnily named friends until my fingers and toes grew cold, and then I settled into my increasingly familiar sleeping bag. By the third day, not only was I actively looking forward to my nightly letter of encouragement, but other hikers had come to know the tradition of the letters as well. The previous two nights, I had shared quotes from the letters out loud. Now, these letters had become a bit of a tradition, and other hikers asked about the reading material for the night. That day's letter was from my sister, Allison. It was written on brightly colored, hand-decorated paper and was scattered with stories and quotes in collage-type fashion.

In emergency situations, you can survive in the wilderness by shooting small game with a slingshot made from the elastic waistband of your underwear.

Check the washing instructions before purchasing any apparel to be worn hiking. Buy only those that read, "Beat on a rock in a stream."

Sherlock Holmes and Doctor Watson were on a camping and hiking trip. They had gone to bed and were lying there looking up at the sky.

Holmes said, "Watson, look up. What do you see?"

"Well, I see thousands of stars."

"And what does that mean to you?"

"Well, I guess it means that we will have another nice day tomorrow. What does that mean to you, Holmes?"

"It means someone has stolen our tent!"

"When you come to a fork in the road, take it."—Yogi Berra

"Do not go where the path may lead, go instead where there is no path and leave a trail."—Ralph Waldo Emerson

Be safe and have fun. I love you.
Allison

I shared the quotes with my fellow hikers and tried to envision my non-outdoorsy sister hauling a backpack and sleeping on the ground. This scenario was about as likely as my attending a video game convention.

Jax, Souleman, and I shared many wonderful trail moments. During the day I rarely attempted to keep pace with them, knowing that hiking at their speed would have probably killed me. Occasionally, one or both would slow to my crawling pace for part of the day. On one such afternoon, they entertained me with their rendition of Tom Cruise's "You've Lost That Loving Feeling" from the movie *Top Gun*. On other days we told jokes and climbed fire towers searching for the best views. In the evenings we played shelter baseball, watched sunsets from mountaintops, did crossword puzzles, and enjoyed the company of fellow hikers. I found myself looking forward to reuniting with them at lunch and at the end of the day. Souleman's easy smile and peaceful attitude were contagious, and Jax provided comic relief.

The first few days, we kept the mileage completely manageable. We were all still getting our trail legs and adjusting to hiker life. Typically, we were on the trail before eight in the morning and finished hiking for the day by two or three o'clock in the afternoon. Stopping on time was important because it grew completely dark before five o'clock. Reaching the shelter, completing chores, and settling into bed before hiker midnight meant finishing early in the day.

While I enjoyed spending time with Jax and Souleman at night, I was grateful for the time spent alone during the day. The first few days of hiking were painful and difficult. I was slow moving and paused frequently during the uphill climbs to rest my legs and rejuvenate. I never doubted my ability to complete the hike, but I knew that I was slow and out of shape and would have been embarrassed if someone else had seen just how much I struggled in a given day. To take my mind off the difficulty, I sang camp songs from my limitless arsenal and spoke to myself in broken Chinese and Spanish. Although I hiked many miles alone, I was never isolated. Most hikers I encountered were friendly and up for conversation. I came across a lot of other hikers—day hikers, thru-hikers, section hikers, weekend hikers—and enjoyed meeting new people and learning their stories.

On some days I hiked a section of the day with other thru-hikers. Gypsy Lulu, of the Gypsy Sisters, was about my age. Touk, her sister, hiked incredibly fast and was often keeping pace with Bassline (Blake from the original Ides of March group), while Gypsy preferred to dawdle behind at an unhurried pace. She took breaks to practice playing the penny-whistle or to take in a pretty view. Gypsy and I hiked together a few times, and I learned that Gypsy and Touk had six other siblings and that all eight of them had been homeschooled. Gypsy described in detail their parents' very interesting educational plan, antics with their siblings, and other life adventures she had pursued. We also talked about issues surrounding female hikers and theoretical concepts like destiny and fate. Spending time with other women on the trail was rare, and for that I valued Gypsy's intermittent and always happy presence.

That night, everyone from our starting group was present in the shelter except for Bassline. Before retiring for the night, Jax and Souleman invited me to watch the sunset with them. We bushwhacked through trees and bushes looking for the perfect viewing location. Eventually we settled on some fallen logs, and from that vantage point I saw my first Appalachian Trail sunset. As the sun changed from yellow to orange to purple, the conversations grew deeper. When I looked over, Jax was holding a Ziploc bag and a piece of paper. Curious, I watched. With some amount of shock, I realized that he was rolling a joint. I had never seen marijuana before, nor had I been in the presence of anyone smoking it. *I'm going to get arrested.* I tried to pretend I didn't notice as a lighter appeared and he lit the joint.

I was seated in the middle of a log between the two guys. From one side, Jax held the joint out toward me. My heart thumped wildly in my chest, and I didn't trust my voice to respond. I shook my head no.

"You sure?"

I nodded and leaned back slightly. They passed the joint across me and the conversation continued. As the joint made its way back around, they offered it to me again, but again I shook my head no.

"You don't smoke?" Jax asked.

"Noooo . . . " I drew the word out, shaking my head and looking around nervously. I had spent all of my high school and college years making sure I didn't get in trouble. I had been afraid to make any grade below a B+ in school, much less do anything illegal. Though rationally I knew we were in the middle of the woods, as far away from law enforcement as possible, I was terrified that somehow I could get in trouble.

"Have you ever tried it?" The question was curious but didn't sound judgmental or pressured.

"No," I answered too quickly. "I've never even *seen* it." Then, embarrassed, I stood up and paced a little. *Shut up, Michelle, just shut up.* I was torn between my desire to head back to the shelter and my desire to do something totally outside of the norm and stay.

Souleman pulled out the Ziploc and came over to me. He opened it so I could look inside. "This is from Vermont," he told me. "It's the good stuff." He smiled a slow, relaxed smile.

I looked inside and saw dry, green leafy material. It looked like dried seasonings. I leaned in to smell and wrinkled my nose.

The guys laughed. "You sure you don't want to try?"

"I don't want to get in trouble."

Jax looked around us at the trees and encroaching darkness as if to say, "With whom?" No one spoke. After a few seconds of silence, Jax handed the joint to me, nodding his head toward Souleman, and indicating for me to pass it. The conversations continued, and the sun dipped further behind the neighboring mountain. The guys rolled another joint, and this time when it got to me, I hesitated.

"If you're going to try that, don't inhale too much," Jax advised.

"Yeah. You'll cough like crazy."

I nodded. I held it in my hand a few seconds, balancing it between my thumb and middle finger, and held a raging internal debate. The curious part of me won, and I tentatively put the joint to my lips after casting a last uneasy glance over my shoulder.

I inhaled timidly. Nothing happened, so I inhaled a little more and there was immediately a powerful burning in the back of my throat. My nose tickled, my insides burned, and I couldn't stop myself from coughing. The guys both laughed good naturedly. Shaking my head and wiping my watering eyes, I passed it on. *What am I doing?* I tried it a few more times as the joint made its way around. Each time I coughed and the back of my throat burned in protest. When the joint was gone and we stood up to go back, Jax asked if I felt anything. I shook my head no.

I didn't feel any different. *Is this what being high is like?* All I felt was guilt. Guilt over doing something illegal. Guilt over giving in and trying something I'd spent my life avoiding. I was afraid that everyone back at the shelter would somehow know that I was now tainted. And yet a small part of me was also proud. Proud that I had tried something new. Proud that I wasn't always the goody two-shoes. Proud that I had a streak of rebel in me.

I cooked dinner quietly, thinking about the previous few days. Already I had been on the trail for what felt like an eternity. What other unexpected situations and decisions would I encounter over the next six months? Jax, Souleman, Krazy Katie, Rawhide, Radio, and I crammed into a very tiny shelter and spent a pleasant evening talking and laughing in our sleeping bags. Katie and Radio passed around a container of Bailey's Irish Cream, and we had a late St. Patrick's Day celebration. By flashlight we filled in a few Mad-Lib puzzles, and then in a moment of childish humor, we did the wave back and forth by kicking our sleeping-bag cocooned legs into the air. Cutting up was really nice after a few days of rigorous exercise, and it also eased my inner tension at the earlier events of the evening.

By this day, the fourth on the trail, I had only two treasured inspiration letters remaining. One was from my mom, and the other was from Lark. When the antics quieted and people started going to sleep, I pulled out my journal and was treated to a really remarkable letter from my mom.

Dear Michelle,

I AM YOUR MOTHER . . . therefore, I, of course, have lots of advice to offer, warnings to issue, and blessings to bestow. How very sneaky of you to limit me to such a little page!

You are about to take the first step of an adventure that you have dreamed of for years. I am so proud of you for having the perseverance, courage, enthusiasm, and stubbornness to get to this point—so you can only imagine how I will feel as you take steps two, three, four . . . ! Keep focused on each day, each hour, each step and enjoy ALL of it. Happiness is a journey, not a destination.

There WILL be times of frustration, exhaustion, and doubt. That's part of the journey. There will be rain, hunger pains, and sore feet. But it will all be worth it.—To reach any significant goal, you must leave your comfort zone.

Always keep your goal in mind, but take time to enjoy the unexpected pleasures along the way . . . the sound of a stream, the smell of the mountain air, the sight of a tiny butterfly.—Nature is the art of God.

Remember that things may not always go as planned . . . and sometimes that's not a bad thing. Be resourceful, spontaneous, and creative.

Improvise.—Blessed are the flexible, for they shall not be bent out of shape.

You have prepared well for this trip. After all, you're a Gold Award Lifetime Girl Scout! Use what you have learned and be open to learning even more. Absorb each experience and let it become part of who you are and who you will become.

Remember your manners. Be kind, helpful, and polite . . . and those same things will come back to you. Smiles will be returned, laughter will be shared, acts of kindness will be bestowed upon you. —The test of good manners is to be able to put up pleasantly with bad ones.

Be careful! You have reliable outdoor skills and good common sense. Just make sure you always use them!—Lint from your belly button makes a handy fire starter. Warning: Remove lint from navel before applying match!

Remember that you have many people rooting for you, praying for you, and walking with you every step of the way. Keep going. —Consider the postage stamp: Its usefulness consists of the ability to stick to one thing until it gets there.

Maintain your curious nature and use this time to ponder the world's great mysteries. Perhaps this would be a good time to revisit some of your very first questions (and I quote):

"If I touched the clouds, would my hands get messy?"

"You know at night time when the sun goes to bed? Does it have covers on its bed like me?"

"If Bingo (my cat) had been born at the hospital like me, would he have been a people like me?"

Please let us know the answers upon your return.

Be safe, be well, be happy. Stay true to who you are. Have the adventure of a lifetime, then come home to your family and share it all with us.

You will be on my mind and in my heart every day. I love you.
Mom

Warm with happy thoughts from my mom, I tried in vain to sleep. For the most part, my bad sleeping habits hadn't changed so far on the trail. I spent much of the night awake, listening to the nighttime noises of six people crammed together. Sleeping in shelters was a bizarre experience if I really analyzed it. A bunch of strangers going by weird names squished themselves as close together as possible and went to sleep. Often someone else's sweaty socks or muddy boots were inches from my head, and usually at least one tired hiker was snoring.

Even without much sleep, I woke up motivated to approach the next day. That day we would hike into Walasi-Yi, a hiker store/hostel in Blairsville, Georgia. This, for me, was the first real milestone along the trail. Walasi-Yi was located about forty miles from Springer Mountain, which would be the longest distance I had ever hiked in one backpacking trip.

But before I could make it to Walasi-Yi, I would have to climb Blood Mountain. Jax and I started the mountain together, but about halfway up he pushed ahead, and I finished the climb alone. I expected the mountain to be a real challenge because of the hype it had generated among hikers over the last few days. Much to my surprise, I didn't find the climb to be very difficult.

When I reached the summit, huge boulders protruded from the ground, with the occasional brave tree bursting through rock at a precarious angle. A stone shelter was perched near the highest point of the mountain. I pushed the door open and squinted into the darkness. Wind whipped through the leaky walls, and the floor was covered in debris and mouse droppings. I was really glad we hadn't decided to push ahead and sleep here the previous night.

I walked back outside and climbed the nearest boulder to get a better view. There was ice on some of the rocks on the mountain, so I watched my footing carefully. The view over the vast expanse of valleys and mountains stretched so far in either direction that I felt increasingly small as I spun around to take it all in. It was humbling to stand on top of a boulder and realize, yet again, how insignificant I was in the grand scheme of the world. Grateful for those few minutes alone on top of the mountain, I soaked the surroundings in while I ate a second breakfast.

When I was ready to resume hiking toward Walasi-Yi, I followed the trail for another tenth of a mile or so before the blazes disappeared. I stopped walking and turned in a circle, scanning the ground, nearby trees and rocks, and any other visible surface for the familiar white blazes. Nothing. I tilted my head various ways, hoping to hear the sounds of other hikers nearby.

I walked a little way in each direction in search of a reassuring white blaze. I couldn't find one. I tugged at one pigtail as I consulted my Wingfoot book and determined that the trail *should* be nearby. My heartbeat sped up as more time passed without sight of a blaze. The thrill of enjoying the view by myself was long gone. Without a comforting white blaze to guide me, being alone didn't seem as appealing anymore.

I was by myself on top of a mountain in the middle of the woods, and I couldn't find the trail. My heartbeat quickened and I had to remind myself that all the hikers who had gone up this mountain before me had to have gone somewhere. *I am ok.* I turned in a circle again. Nothing. I looked for a worn path on the ground, but the ground was almost entirely slab rock. *Ok, Michelle . . . Brownie, THINK*

Never lose the place where you realized you were lost, I remembered from my survival training. I placed my pack on the rock to mark the point. Then I decided to pick a direction and walk a few steps. The first few tries were not successful. I returned to my pack and scanned the area again. This time my eyes noticed some rocks that seemed out of place. I walked closer. It was a tiny little cairn that someone had built out of pebbles and marshmallow-sized stones. Cairns are piles of rocks that are sometimes used to designate the trail when there is nowhere to place a blaze.

I walked to the cairn, feeling more assured, but stopped short when again I could see nowhere to go. *The trail has to go somewhere.* This was getting old. I had spent about half an hour walking around the top of this mountain, looking at the ground trying to locate a blaze. I sat down on the ground next to the cairn and ate a snack.

Eventually, I noticed a blaze and was able to follow a series of miniature cairns to a spot where I could see another blaze. I stopped beside the last cairn and took a picture of it so that I would remember the unease that being lost and alone had produced. While I had the camera out, I also snapped a picture of my hiking boots. It occurred to me that I had now spent the better part of four days looking at my feet. I had been so worried about tripping on a root or sliding on ice that I had hardly looked around at the scenery while I walked. I couldn't have told you much about the landscape, but I could have picked out my hiking boots from any shoe rack. I made a silent vow to learn to look up as I hiked.

Soon after I started the descent of Blood Mountain, I could hear the sound of cars. I knew the road must be close. A few switchbacks later, I saw a large stone building and realized that I had reached the Walasi-Yi. My fellow hikers were already beginning the process of cleaning themselves and their gear, but they stopped what they were doing to congratulate me and show me around.

I went straight to the pay phone, planning to immediately amuse my family with stories of my adventures, but no one answered. So instead I headed back to the hostel where Souleman, Jax, and I shared a load of laundry. After only four days in the woods, we already stunk. The shower facilities reflected the general hiker filthiness: strange hair clung to the shower walls, and unidentified debris clogged the drain. My Crocs, which protected my feet from the grunge and diseases I was sure lurked on those floors, temporarily became my favorite piece of equipment.

Once we had showered, the three of us sat down with unappetizing microwaved cheeseburgers and our Handbooks and planned our next few days of mileage. It was already established that the three of us were a team. All around us, hikers were gathered in groups discussing mileage and resupply locations. Each stop had to be planned, along with the next place to resupply, so that we would know how many days' worth of food to purchase. Once our next segment was planned, I headed straight for the pay phone with my calling card in hand.

This time my parents answered, and in a rush of excited words I detailed my hike. They were surprised to hear from me so soon and were relieved that I was all right and having fun. I promised to call again from the next town.

In the small store, I bought enough food to last until our next town stop in Hiawassee. Each food item was carefully selected based on weight and calorie composition. *Apples?—No way, too heavy. Beef Jerky?—Expensive, but full of protein. Cheese?—Calories and fat. Good. Protein Bars?—Expensive, heavy, and taste like chalk. No. Little Debbie snacks?—Oh! Lots of calories and they weigh nothing.* This was so different from my usual grocery shopping where I tried to watch calories and balance food groups. After purchasing the odd collection of food, I remembered that I no longer had a stuff-sack in which to keep it. I headed back into the store to replace my mouse-eaten sack.

The store was crowded with hikers. Souleman was in the shop buying a new headlamp, and Rawhide was getting treatment for painful blisters. I picked out my food sack and then watched the store employees do a shake-down of one hiker's gear. After observing a shake-down and watching the employee weigh the excess gear at five pounds, I decided I needed to give it a try.

Just as I was shoving my gear into my pack, Souleman came in with our clean laundry. I told him of my plans to go back to the gear store for a shake-down, and he immediately starting packing his gear to come along. He stood beside me as the employee dumped all my gear on the ground and methodically sorted through each Ziploc bag and stuff-sack. When the expert finished, there was a small pile of rejected gear, including the cell phone my parents had insisted was non-negotiable, excess duct tape, assorted first aid supplies, pajama pants, and an extra long-sleeved t-shirt. Without another thought, I scooped all of the rejections into a box.

While the expert sorted through Souleman's pack, I scribbled my parents' address on top of the box and penned a note. Souleman packed his rejected gear, and exchanging high-fives we happily mailed our boxes home without further reservation. The shake-down had shed less than two pounds from my pack, about which I was disappointed. On the other hand, I was proud that the experts thought I had packed well.

I stood outside with Souleman and Jax to plot our next move. We were huddled over a Handbook with our packs in a pile beside us. While we talked, I noticed visitors walking up from the parking lot pointing and whispering. This was our first encounter with thru-hiker stardom. The general public, or at least those who are aware of the concept of thru-hiking, are fascinated with the idea. Most people have a lot of questions. One gentleman approached us with questions and congratulations for making it this far. On the way back to his car, he even brought us each a soda and told us to keep up the good work.

Many hikers decided to stay the night at the Walasi-Yi Hostel to recharge, but the three of us decided to save the money for later on up the trail and instead pushed on three more miles to camp. I laced my boots and hefted my now thirty-eight-pound pack. About three steps into the first mile, I broke a sweat. *So much for that shower.* During the last mile of the climb, I noticed a pain in the arch of my left foot and made a mental note to check on it later. We stopped for the night in a small clearing and, for the first time, set up camp away from a shelter. We pitched our tents in a tight triangle and then built a fire and cooked dinner, discussing the next day's short seven-mile day with anticipation.

While we enjoyed the fire, I removed my left sock and examined my tender foot. I found a lump on the side of my arch. It was not raw like a blister; it was just painful and extremely swollen. The lump was the length of two quarters side by side and was at least as thick as my thumb. I had no idea why this injury had happened, but I knew I had to keep an eye on it.

While the boys hung the bear bags, I climbed into my tent by myself and immediately noticed how much colder it was tenting alone than sleeping in a shelter with other warm bodies by my side. I was tempted to go straight to sleep but made myself pull out my journal. I knew that the memories of this trip would fade over time, and I wanted a detailed journal to help me remember them. Before writing, I read my fifth and final letter of encouragement. This letter was from Lark, and in true Lark fashion, it was both long and funny.

Dear Michelle,

This inspiration letter is a lot harder than I thought. I have to write something that you can read over and over again and always feel like you can walk a thousand more miles just because of it. That's a lot of pressure! So I'm getting organized.

Purpose: To Inspire My Best-Favoritest Roommate Ever

Thesis: You are the Little Engine That Could. You can do it!

Reasons:

- First of all, I (probably) don't need to remind you that you are on the most amazing journey of your life! Not only are you hiking from Georgia to Maine, you are doing it all at once. You'll see the most beautiful vistas, encounter the most interesting people, and find yourself in the most remarkable (and probably strange) situations. What an adventure! I'm so excited for you!
- It has never occurred to me that you won't get to the end of the trail. Always when people ask, "Do you think she'll finish?" I've said, "Yes, she's very strong. I don't think she'll let herself quit." I know you can do it, and I can't wait to see you reach the end!
- If any stupid hikers or rangers or people in general discourage you, I know you won't be (too) upset. You are very good at dealing with weird and intense situations, so I know you can handle anything that needs handling on the AT. You rock!

Techniques (to get you through the tough parts):

- Imagine: you're about to see the most beautiful view of the entire trip, just over the next mountain. You can't give up now!
- Think about bubbles. Floating all around you. You're in a bubble wonderland, and nothing exists but you and the bubbles, and you are actually inside a bubble, and it's floating you away over the next hill. Happy bubbles.
- Focus on the way the trees are whispering to you overhead . . . they are whispering secret tree-words of encouragement, pulling you along, waiting for you to arrive at the next one so they can pass it on. The trees love you (almost as much as I do) and want you to succeed.
- Repeat: I am stronger than steel, faster than pain, and more intense than hunger. Trail, you are my bitch.

Conclusion: You are the most strong-willed (often known as "stubborn," but we're being positive here) person I know, and you will make it.

May the [trail] rise to meet you, may the wind be at your back. May the sunshine be warm upon your face, the rains fall soft upon your fields. And until we meet again, may God hold you in the palm of His hand.

I'll miss you a whole lot while I wait on the edge of my seat for updates! Have fun! I love you!

Lark

The letters had served their purpose already. I was more motivated and excited than I had expected to be five days into the trail. Although I was as exhausted as the other hikers, I had no doubts about my ability to succeed.

5

One Tough Cookie

The weather was sunny and uncharacteristically warm for March. I hiked along happily in a long-sleeved t-shirt, enjoying the clear day. This was our second week on the trail, and I was feeling strong. The bruises on my shoulders underneath my pack straps were fading, the blisters on my hips were healing, my legs were less like Jell-O, and I could finally use my hiking poles smoothly. While crossing a road, I met a day hiker who gave me the first "trail magic" of my journey: peanut butter crackers. It amazed me that people thought the feat of hiking from Georgia to Maine was interesting or noble enough to go out of their way to help.

Shortly after receiving the trail magic, I passed another day hiker who was headed south. We had a conversation, and I inquired about Souleman and Jax. He recalled having passed two guys together about an hour earlier. Considering their usual speed, I was impressed that I was even that close to them. About a mile later, I met Souleman and Jax at our pre-determined destination in time for lunch. The guys were sprawled across the picnic tables, nibbling on snacks and dozing in the sun. I plopped down on a table and pulled out my shiny new food sack. I devoured a lunch of raisins, peanut butter straight from the container, cheese, crackers, and cookies.

As I was raising a dirt-smeared, peanut-butter-coated finger to my mouth, a large object came hurtling toward me. I heard the sound of barking, and given my lifelong aversion to dogs, I immediately scrambled over the picnic table to a spot behind Souleman and Jax. A male hiker dressed in a kilt was close on the dog's heels. He kept calling the dog, and when it wouldn't come he tackled it in a pile of leaves. As the man wrapped his legs around the dog, his kilt bunched up around his waist in a most indiscreet fashion. Let's just say the kilt was his only layer and I got quite the eyeful. Blushing, I turned my gaze to my lunch as the man lumbered over and introduced himself as Bramble.

Bramble told us that he had adopted the dog after she had been rescued from a hurricane and they were still getting used to each other. Bramble was hiking for five straight years to raise money for cancer patients, in memory of his aunt who had recently died from cancer. He had a large tattoo on his back with the names of survivors and those lost to the disease. According to Bramble, people paid to have their names added to his tattoo. As he told us his story, he propped his leg up on the picnic table to tie his shoe. When I looked up at him to say something, I was eye-level with his crotch. I blushed severely and averted my gaze as Souleman and Jax tried to control their laughter. Eventually, the dog heard other hikers coming and galloped away. Bramble took off after the dog, yelling a hasty farewell over his shoulder.

Still slightly traumatized, I turned back to my food. The boys had already eaten, and I noticed that they had not started unpacking their gear as usual. I anticipated what happened next.

"Hey, Brownie?" Jax looked my way.

"Mmhmm?" I had a mouthful of crackers and cheese. *Here it comes.*

"We were thinking that with it still being so early and all, maybe we would hike on to the next shelter."

I didn't have to look at my Handbook to know that the next shelter was 7.5 miles up the trail.

"It's just that it's so early and we've already reached our original destination. It seems like a waste of daylight," Souleman added as he sat down on the picnic table next to me.

Not wanting to appear weak, I nodded in agreement, although inside I was terrified. *Can I make it that much further?* That would be almost *double* any distance we had yet hiked.

"So that's ok?" Jax clarified.

Not trusting my voice to hide how terrified I was, I stuffed more food in my mouth and nodded my head. *You're not going to make it to Maine going only eight miles a day.*

"We'll hike with you for a while," Souleman told me, elbowing me gently.

We rested for a bit longer, and then the three of us started hiking together. As we began the climb out of the small valley where the shelter was nestled, we came upon a large, blue tent. Laughter emanated from inside. Jax called out and two guys came over to meet us. Their names were Veni Vidi Vici (V3) and Toolman. They were high school friends who were out hiking in an effort to get closer to God. They shared a tent so that they could hold daily Bible studies together. Part of their hiking philosophy included a belief that they should not hike on Sundays. Today was Sunday, which was why they had their tent set up at midday.

The trail attracts people of all varieties. I continued to be surprised at the reasons people decided to hike—to honor God, in memory of a loved one, to raise money for a cause, to recover from divorce, to celebrate retirement; the reasons were endless. The trail is a moving community constantly in flux. Few of the inhabitants share any great similarity, other than the aspiration to hike from Georgia to Maine, and even that one similarity has variations.

First, there are thru-hikers (those who hike the whole trail in one hike) and section hikers (those who hike the whole trail in sections). Then there are purists (those who hike only on white-blazed trails), blue-blazers (those who sometimes take blue-blazed side trails), and yellow-blazers (those who sometimes hitch-hike partway on roads). Some hikers believe in slack-packing (hiking without their full load of gear), while others insist on carrying all of their gear the whole way. Some hikers hike only in one direction (north or south), while others mix it up based on terrain or town events. There are all different types of hikers with different philosophies on the best way to make it to Maine.

Since the trail offers a lot of time for talking, hikers sometimes have debates about what being a "real" thru-hiker entails. Some hikers believe that those who fall into the blue-blazing or yellow-blazing group cannot be "true" thru-hikers since they have not walked past every white blaze. Usually this conversation ends with someone stating the inevitable mantra, "Hike your own hike." While I respected each hiker's decision, my personal plan had always been to thru-hike as a purist, always carrying my full gear, and always walking north. So far I had been meticulous.

We wished Toolman and V3 a good day and said we hoped to see them up the trail. Both Jax and Souleman stuck with me for the first three miles. Their constant chatter kept my mind off my aching feet. The terrain was flat and I tailed behind them without too much struggle.

I was concentrating on the conversation more than my foot placement when I had my first fall. The weight of my pack had propelled me toward the ground faster than I could recover. With my hands tied up in my poles, I couldn't catch myself and scarcely avoided striking my knee directly on a pointy rock. Because of my sore legs and heavy pack, I had trouble returning to an upright position. Jax offered me a hand and inspected my knee. The scraped knee was of minimal concern, but my embarrassment at not being able to remain upright was considerable.

Shortly after my fall, the boys sped up and I dropped behind. On this flat terrain, their legs were probably itching for a faster speed. At first I could see them in the distance and could occasionally hear their voices carried by the wind. Finally, I saw and heard nothing and returned to hiking in solitude.

The terrain became more challenging, and my legs were screaming in complaint of this first truly long day of hiking. The "foot egg" on my left foot was really bothering me, and I had developed a noticeable limp. I leaned heavily on my trekking poles and shifted my pack weight often to relieve my once-again bruised shoulders.

As I was limping down the trail, I saw a colorful blob lying on the ground. I determined that it was immobile and therefore non-animal and non-threatening. I approached curiously and recognized a familiar item—an orange, brown, and green cargo hat. Domino, a fellow thru-hiker, had been wearing a hat just like this one. A mental replay of the day's leap-frogging confirmed that Domino was ahead of me. Certain that he would miss wearing this hideous fashion statement, I dusted the hat off and plunked the monstrosity on my head, deciding to carry it on.

I was becoming disheartened at my impossibly sluggish pace—step, drag, step draaag, step draaaaag. I was mumbling to myself and worrying about the sun slipping away behind the mountains. *You had better learn how to hike these distances if you're going to make it to Maine.* The woods were becoming increasingly dark. As the shadows lengthened, I pulled out my Handbook to determine my location. Distressingly, the book helped little. I didn't know if I had crossed four streams, or five, or maybe even six. The endless miles blurred together. I had no option but to keep hiking into the increasing darkness. I would hear voices and get excited, only to round the bend and realize I had heard only the gurgling of yet another stream. Just as I was contemplating pulling out my headlamp, I heard voices again. This time I saw moving shapes and the outline of a shelter, too. *I made it.*

Limping up to the shelter, I must have looked rough because a number of people approached me.

"Brownie, are you ok?" questioned Big John.

"What happened to you?" asked Jax, eyeing me from head to toe.

"What's the matter?" asked someone else.

"We were starting to worry about you," added Domino, joining the group.

While I was flattered by the concern, I was in no mood for an interrogation. I unhooked my hip belt to take the weight off my hips and leaned heavily on my poles. I plunked the unsightly hat onto Domino's head and he leapt into the air.

"Brownie! You're my hero. I thought my hat was lost forever."

I smiled weakly and collapsed onto the bench.

"I'm going to pay you back, you'll see," he promised repeatedly.

People continued to approach me in an attempt to help me settle in at this late hour. Finally, still catching my breath, I held up my hand and declared, "I—will—not—be—sociable—for the next—ten minutes." Then, giving myself an internal pep talk, I set about doing all the evening camp chores before my body ceased to function. *Just a few more minutes and I can sit down. Just one more chore. Almost done.* Souleman offered to cook for me, but I shook my head no. I needed to prove that I could do this on my own. I allowed the adrenaline still coursing through my veins to propel me through my remaining chores.

I was offered a space in the crowded shelter, but in my exhaustion I couldn't stand the thought of another snore-filled night. Upon my refusal of the offer of a shelter spot, Jax shook his head and said, "That Brownie is one tough cookie." Begrudgingly, I cracked a smile, and everyone within earshot giggled a little at the pun.

I pitched my tent, boiled water for a meal, and finally settled on a log by the fire to eat. I did accept Souleman's offer to use his extra water rather than stumble down to the water source in the dark. My headlamp cast a faint glow onto my pot, and I began to eat greedily. Before I'd had half a dozen bites of my mashed potatoes, I noticed a dark splotch land on the surface of my food.

A dab of my bandana and a flick of my headlamp confirmed that I had a nose bleed. *Really? Now?* I ducked my head and pinched the bridge of my nose. My potatoes grew cold and my frustration increased. For an hour my nose continued to leak blood as I repeatedly moved positions around the fire, trying to avoid the smoke. Souleman sat with me, poking at the fire.

"You should try and eat," he suggested.

Stubbornly, I shook my head and willed myself not to cry as my potatoes became increasingly pink.

"Want me to make you something else?" he offered.

"No, thanks," I managed.

Two of my bandanas were saturated with blood before my nose finally stopped leaking. I spooned my tie-dyed mashed potatoes into the fire and then sat on a log and took off my shoe to examine my next failing body part: my aching left foot. There were no blisters, for which I was grateful. I had been watching my fellow hikers treat painful blisters since Springer. There was, however, still an egg-shaped bump protruding from my arch. It had turned varying shades of blue, green, and purple and was horribly tender. *How is this going to heal? What's causing it?* I poked the lump and scowled into the dark. *As if hiking so many miles and having a bloody nose weren't enough bodily punishment for one day. . . .*

The day's hike had humbled me. I wasn't quite the tough hiker I had thought myself to be. Fifteen miles had completely done me in. Parts of my body hurt that I had never even realized were affected by hiking. In the privacy of my tent, I donned my headlamp and lowered my hiking pants to expose my hip bones. I had raw red spots on each hip where my pack had rubbed all day. I poked at my shoulder blades where I had matching raw spots. *What doesn't kill you makes you stronger,* I told myself sarcastically. There was nothing I could do. I barely had the energy to zip myself into my sleeping bag before falling asleep. For once I slept soundly.

The sun rose through the trees the next morning with a myriad of colors, spreading a rainbow of reds, yellows, purples, pinks, oranges and other indescribable shades before me. Surprisingly, I was awake and able to enjoy this stunning display through my open tent door. My legs were gelatinous before I even put any weight on them, and they screamed with fury at each movement. It took me three tries to stand up from my tent. Determined not to let this dissuade me, I resigned myself to an unhurried day. I was extremely grateful for the short 7.7 miles we had planned.

Gypsy and I hiked much of the day together, talking about our varied beliefs and her upbringing. Her parents had followed a very unique style of homeschooling that included classical book read-alouds, family music sessions, and individual-interest-inspired lesson plans. One of her brothers had built a canoe by hand as part of his education. Learning about lifestyles different from my own was becoming one of my favorite aspects of meeting new people.

Although it had been a short day, I was so tired that night that I settled into the crowded shelter in a tiny spot between Jax and Souleman, rather than pitching my tent. The shelter was packed and many tents were already pitched nearby. Stories floated through the air as a fire crackled in the fire ring. I met two hikers in their seventies who were thru-hiking and was both impressed at their endurance and embarrassed by my own exhaustion.

The next day was our first town stop in Hiawassee, Georgia. Hiawassee was the opposite of a perfect trail town. The town itself was located a good number of miles off the trail, and the services were spread out and hard to reach on foot. There were a couple of hostels, but they filled quickly that early in the season and forced many hikers to settle for the expensive chain hotels in town.

Our group of worn-out hikers moved rapidly with the promise of town food and showers. Jax was battling a sore Achilles tendon, so he hiked with me at my slower pace until the pull of town caused him to move faster. Even I made it the 10.5 miles to the road before one o'clock.

We hitched a ride into town with the father of a hiker named Bottoms Up. He drove a tiny little Honda Element that we crammed full of hikers like a clown car at the circus. Packs, poles, bandanas, and sweaty hiker appendages poked out the windows at odd angles. Upon finding out that the Blueberry Patch Hostel, famous for its pancake breakfast, was full, we drove on into town. Six of us split a hotel room. I was the only woman, but this was becoming increasingly more common on the trail. For the first time we enjoyed the cleanliness of a town shower after days of hiking. For the first time we checked our email. For the first time we attempted to satisfy our already blossoming trail appetites with town food.

When it came my turn to shower, I joyously closed myself in the bathroom. I had been picturing a steaming shower, a dry towel, and a refreshed body. I blinked at the bathtub in horror—it was ringed in brownish-greenish grime. A dusting of dirt covered the tile floor, the countertop, and the back of the toilet. Dirt-tinged footprints were scattered on the tile, and wet, grayish towels were piled in the corner under the sink. I looked down at my bare feet and wished feverishly that I was wearing my Crocs. I peeled off my salty, sticky, damp shirt and looked around trying to decide where to put it. Realizing that my clothes couldn't get any dirtier, I simply tossed them on the filthy floor.

The soap was gritty, the rough washcloth burned my weather-beaten skin, and there was no conditioner for my straw-like hair. But the water was hot, and I had never been so grateful for a shower. As I watched the dirt swirl down the drain, I studied my hairy legs. I didn't have a razor. *Should I get one from the front desk tomorrow?* I looked past my legs to the filthy tub. The idea of smooth legs seemed absurd in this setting. Then and there I decided I would not shave my legs for the rest of the trail. My increasingly hairy legs would become a source of pride as I progressed north.

I dried off and eyed my pile of filthy clothes. I did not want to re-dress in the same sweat-drenched outfit. Weighing my options, I cracked the door and called out, "Hey, Souleman?"

"Yeah?" His still dirt-smudged face appeared outside the door.

"Would you look in my pack and grab my rain pants and rain coat, please?"

"Sure. Where are they?"

I told him where they were stashed in my pack and he returned momentarily. Thanking him and closing the door, I put on my rain clothes with nothing underneath. My shower-damp skin stuck uncomfortably to the nylon. I vigorously brushed my teeth and then stood for a minute in front of the mirror, realizing that this was the end of my personal hygiene routine on the trail. I had no face lotion, no deodorant, and not even a hairbrush or a much-desired Q-tip. My rumbling stomach reminded me of my priorities. I ran my fingers through my hair and hurried to join my new friends.

Although I had daydreamed extensively about the hiking and camping aspects of the trail, it had never occurred to me to imagine town stops. Visiting countless small towns was a rewarding, if unexpected, part of hiking the Appalachian Trail. I met curious and supportive locals, patronized local businesses, and was able to get a taste of mountain communities up and down the East Coast.

While I loved exploring new towns, completing a long list of semi-urgent tasks on foot never ceased to be time-consuming and exhausting. As our first order of town business, we filled our empty bellies at Hardee's. With thick, creamy milk-shakes in hand, we headed to the local grocery store. Walking around town with a group of hikers never failed to elicit stares in public places. This grocery outing was no exception. Our brightly colored Crocs and mismatched, dirty outfits alone would have been enough to make others do a double-take. Factoring in our offensive smell and the already wild beards on the men, it was no wonder we gained unsolicited attention. As I pushed my cart up and down the aisles, methodically choosing my items, I watched people point, stare, and whisper.

Since this was our first town resupply, we had yet to learn the important trick of bringing an empty backpack to stuff the groceries in after checking out at the register. Instead, we were stuck carrying awkward plastic bags back to the hotel. The route to the grocery store from the hotel had been circuitous and lengthy. Laden with bags, we decided to take a shortcut. There was a steep dirt incline that connected the grocery store parking lot with the hotel parking lot. This route was notably steeper than the sidewalk but was also considerably shorter. While we all loved to hike, we were decidedly against doing any extra walking in town. We were completely unprepared for such a climb since most of us were wearing Crocs and weighted down with grocery bags. The hill was covered in mud and extremely slick.

As we eyed the incline and debated the merits of this shortcut, Souleman offered to take my shopping bags for me. Determined to be tough, I shook my head no. Souleman went first, charging ahead in an effort to go against gravity. He slid back down partway and broke his flip-flop in the process. Jax went next in his boots and made it with only one hand muddied. I was third up the embankment and made it clear that I didn't want to be "helped" (for fear of being thrown off balance). I wrapped my hands carefully around my grocery bags and tested my footing. When I was two-thirds of the way up and almost touching Souleman's outstretched hand, another hand touched my back. Rawhide had grabbed my shirt, and this change of weight flung me forward into the muck. I was completely covered in thick, red mud and thoroughly annoyed. I nodded thanks to Souleman, collected my muddy grocery bags, and headed inside without looking back.

I tracked mud through the tiled lobby and into the carpeted elevator, where I continued to fume. When you have only minimal clothing in your possession, you are protective of your one clean set of layers. Now I would have to pass the evening in muddy rain clothes while my hiking clothes washed. I hated the thought of my temporarily clean body being trapped in muddy, sticky clothes.

Struggling with my dirty grocery bags, I clumsily unlocked the hotel room door and swung it open. The stench of six hikers' gear assaulted my nose and nearly sent me stumbling backward. My nose had yet to become immune to the hiker stench.

After I caught my breath, I hurried into the bathroom to clean some of the mud off of myself. I heard a knock on the door as I was scrubbing my rain pants with a wet hand towel. When I cracked the door, Souleman was standing there. He leaned toward me and confidentially told me, "You are one of my best friends. Really. You already are."

As if to prove this statement, he held out a clean, long-sleeved shirt for me to wear while mine washed. Appreciatively, I dressed in his shirt and my semi-clean rain pants and rejoined my friends, making sure to stop and give Souleman a big, gracious hug.

While I was in the bathroom changing, a conversation had started in the hotel room about where everyone was going to sleep. There were two double beds and a pull-out couch, which meant that no one would have to sleep on the floor.

I was the only girl, and Jax spoke up, "I call the bed with Brownie!"

I shook my head in amusement while the rest of the guys grumbled their disdain and split themselves up.

V3, Toolman, Weatherman, and many other hikers whom we had met on the trail were at the hotel as well. We invited them into our room to play cards and have a few beers in celebration of completing the first section of the trail. We had hiked sixty-seven miles. While this was nothing compared to the approximately 2,200 miles we were attempting, we all had a sense of accomplishment. None of us had hiked sixty-seven miles in one stretch before.

Typically, I hate beer. I am one of those girls who orders the expensive, fruity drinks. Martinis with girly names like Appletini are my drink of choice. But in Hiawassee, Georgia, I finished my first whole beer of my life—a tribute to the trail. My dad had joked that beer would be good for me in trail towns because it would help replace important electrolytes lost during strenuous physical activity.

Later that night, we each found a make-shift swimming outfit and ventured down to the empty hotel hot tub. We casually ignored the sign warning against alcoholic beverages and enjoyed drinks concealed in Nalgene bottles while soaking some of the abuse out of our extremities. The men smoked cigars while I simply enjoyed being off my aching feet. Sinking down into the water so that only my face stayed above the surface, I tried to count the number of places on my body that hurt. *My shoulders hurt, my hips hurt, my back hurts, my ankles hurt, my foot egg hurts, my thighs hurt, my arms hurt . . .*

Soon my eyelids grew heavy. It was all I could do to stumble back to the hotel room and re-dress in Souleman's shirt. It had been so cold on the trail with rain, snow, and wintry mixes that I was grateful to be indoors, free of wind or weather and dressed in a dry shirt. While card games continued at the coffee table behind me, I fell into a dreamless sleep on the coily mattress.

My body was still hurting the next morning and begged for more rest. Everyone else agreed. We all lay in bed, talking lazily and delaying the process of getting up. Someone turned on the TV, and we lay there in relaxed quiet, staring at the screen. When Jax got up to use the bathroom, Souleman turned to me and, throwing a sidelong glance at his bedmate, Rawhide, whispered, "Next time I call the bed with you." The darkness hid my amused smile.

Everyone agreed that a full day of hiking would not be in our best interest. Instead of spending the money on a hotel room for a second night, we lounged around until checkout at eleven and then went back to the trail. In trail terms we had taken a "nero" because we hiked nearly zero miles.

Despite the relaxing images one might dredge up involving the word "zero," the name is deceptive. A "zero" day is a day when a hiker completes no trail miles. These days are almost always work days: They are used for laundry, shopping, showering, post-office runs, gorging on "town food," and running other errands. These days are exhausting, at best, and perhaps even painful at worst. Imagine yourself in an unfamiliar town trying to accomplish a long list of pressing tasks—on foot.

After our "nero," we hiked a short 4.3 miles to Plum Orchard Gap Shelter. It was seventy degrees and sunny—a perfect day for hiking. The forecast predicted thunderstorms and excessive rain over the next few days. I would later learn that hearing weather forecasts is sometimes a positive part of town visits and sometimes a negative one. When you wake up in the woods, you hike no matter what the weather is because you have no choice. When you wake up in town and the forecast is bad, it is easier to hunker down in the hotel and wait out the weather. Luckily, we were still so new to the trail that no weather prediction would have stopped us.

The next morning Jax, Souleman, and I were anticipating our third big Appalachian Trail milestone. First we had made it to Walasi-Yi. Then we had made it to Hiawassee. Next we were about to cross our first state line. I hiked in giddy anticipation of the state line sign all morning. I had my camera in my hip pouch, ready to snap candid photos of the momentous occasion.

We saw Gypsy and Touk taking a break underneath a very large tree and stopped to say hello and check our Handbook. Somehow we had all passed the state line sign. I lamented missing this photo opportunity and wondered how we had all walked right by the same sign without noticing. Was the sign missing? We had a few sips of wine that someone had carried for the state line celebration and joked that our theme song had changed from "Georgia on My Mind" to "Carolina on My Mind."

The hiking that day was difficult, with some very large and long uphill climbs. I kept up with the men for ten miles and was very proud of myself. We spent part of the day in conversation and probably an equal part in companionable silence. Occasionally, I sang quietly from my spot at the back of the line. On one challenging uphill, I stopped singing mid-song to catch my breath.

Souleman turned around and said, "Don't stop. I like it when you sing. It makes for nice background noise."

I laughed because my family had always teased me relentlessly about my inability to carry a tune.

"What are you singing, anyway?" he asked.

"Mostly. Camp. Songs." I explained between labored breaths. "I went to camp. For years. As a kid." I continued to hyperventilate as I walked. "Then worked. As a counselor. For years. I know lots. Of silly. Songs."

"I like hearing you sing. It's sweet." He offered a warming smile over his shoulder and kept hiking.

I smiled at his back, embarrassed. *How is he able to hold a normal conversation while walking uphill?*

As we finished hiking the last couple miles of the day, I allowed my sore legs to relax the pace and dropped behind to enjoy an hour of solitude before entering the noisiness and busyness of the evening shelter. I saw lots of birds and reflected on how strong I was becoming. This twelve-mile day, with considerable elevation gain, had seemed easier than some of the seven- and eight-mile days at the very beginning. I was already starting to get my trail legs. I walked along thinking about how exciting it was to be in North Carolina, the second of fourteen states, and hummed to myself.

The swelling had lessened in my left foot, and it hurt less. Loosening my shoelaces had made a world of difference. I had made another important clothing adjustment recently: I was now hiking without underwear. I had heard other women hikers talking about their choice to hike commando and decided to give it a try. The elastic from underwear is somewhat constricting and can cause chafing on tender skin. Plus, when sweating a lot and not showering often, the increased airflow helps prevent raw skin and infections. This was only my second day hiking without underwear, but so far I was planning to make this my general mode of operation.

That night at the shelter, I sat on a fallen tree and wrote in my journal. I looked around at my surroundings and, for the millionth time, thought about how lucky I was to be out here on this trip. I was surrounded by trees, breathing in fresh cool air, and meeting interesting new people. Most of my friends were struggling through their last courses in college, writing papers, and studying for the GMAT or LSAT. The months I had spent overloading on courses and preparing for this journey had been exhausting, but the payoff was proving much greater than the sacrifice.

My sense of peace and excitement carried over into the next day, and I resolved to enjoy every moment. As we hiked 7.6 miles, I thought about Lark and wondered what class she was sitting in as I summited Standing Indian Mountain. I wished that she could have been beside me on the mountaintop. After climbing Standing Indian Mountain, the terrain was pleasant. The afternoon was essentially a rolling walk. As my boots ticked off the mileage, I started to formulate a plan to get Lark to come hike with me for a while. I would have to call her in the next town and make plans.

That afternoon Souleman, Jax, and I convened in a sunny patch by the shelter's water source and talked. We sat there until the sun shifted across the sky and the patches of ground became cold. The three of us were becoming very close. With so much time spent together, we had learned a lot about one another. When we returned to the shelter, we saw KTR, our friend from the beginning of the trail. We had thought he was a day behind us, but we were excited to see him and immediately struck up a conversation.

KTR cocked his head at an unnatural angle and politely waited for a pause in our banter before saying, "I don't think we've met."

Souleman looked at Jax. Jax looked at me. My gaze swiveled from the two of them to KTR.

"I'm Solace."

The three of us just stared at him.

After a few uncomfortable moments of silence, he said with a grin, "I think you might know my brother, KTR?"

"*Twin* brother?" I asked incredulously.

It turned out that KTR and Solace were identical twin brothers. They also had sisters who were identical twins. Solace and KTR had decided to hike the Appalachian Trail together a few years back. They had made a number of attempts together, but different obstacles had kept preventing them from finishing. The farthest they had ever made it was to Fontana Dam, North Carolina. This year KTR was hiking by himself, but Solace had hiked in to surprise him for a couple of days. These twins were not only identical in appearance, but in sarcastic sense of humor, bouncy body movements, and bigger-than-life personality. I loved Solace immediately.

During the evening we spent together, Solace told us a popular hiker joke: "How do you tell the difference between a day hiker, a section hiker, and a thru-hiker? If a day hiker sees an M&M on the trail, he will pass it by; if a section hiker sees an M&M on the trail, he will pick it up; if a thru-hiker sees an M&M on the trail, he will eat it and then get on the ground and look for more."

6

Angels in Many Forms

The hiker rumor mill loves to intimidate hikers with information about what lies ahead on the trail. Mileage, elevation gain, distances between water sources, and poor correlations with reference guides are all popular topics. Gossip had been heavy the last few days. Albert Mountain was on the agenda for that day, and it was supposed to be the steepest climb we had yet encountered.

In the morning Souleman and I left the shelter at the same time. While we had been planning to stop at the same location each night for a while, we did not always hike together along the way since our natural strides made us hike at different paces. Today, since the first miles were relatively easy, I managed to match pace. The conversation flowed naturally as we hiked, and we realized we had a lot in common. Though the two of us and Jax had spent a lot of time together, we were usually in our group of three. We hadn't actually talked one-on-one very much.

The terrain became more intense, and I was forced to slow my pace. I offered to let Souleman pass as usual, but he said he was enjoying the conversation and was in no hurry.

"We're headed to the same destination," he joked.

We hiked along, enjoying the sunshine while sharing stories about our lives and really learning about one another. Souleman wasn't always talkative in a group, but in this setting he talked without restraint. I learned that he had grown up in Vermont and started college in Vermont but then had decided to leave school and work at a resort out West, where he had met Jax. He had two sisters, loved to snowboard, and was a fan of the Boston Red Sox. He talked about his dreams for a family of his own, his desire to coach children's baseball, and his fears surrounding his mom's health. The further we walked, the more I was drawn to his comfort in his own skin.

The mild terrain had helped us to have long conversations without gasping for breath. Albert Mountain loomed not far up ahead. Other hikers had been studying this mountain on profile maps in anxious anticipation for days. Neither Souleman nor I had ever carried maps on the AT, and at this point on the trail we weren't even paying too much attention to elevation details in our Handbook.

My theory was that I would have to hike the terrain that lay in front of me no matter what, so worrying about it ahead of time would be useless. I simply tackled whatever the trail put in front of me at the moment. Still, the anticipation of other hikers had rubbed off, and both Souleman and I were a little nervous about the ascent of Albert Mountain.

According to my internal odometer, which was becoming more and more reliable, we were about half a mile from Albert Mountain when I saw a strange sight. In front of me on the trail was a red bandana attached to a post. The post had painted lettering that I couldn't make out from a distance.

"What do you think it is?" I asked, leaning to the side to let Souleman see. "A warning?"

"I dunno."

I took a few steps closer and squinted my eyes. The words came into focus and a huge smile spread across my face as I read out loud to Souleman, "Trail Magic!"

We grinned at each other. Without discussion we picked up our pace. Thirty yards down the trail, we encountered a large awning with a fire circle and lawn chairs. We were invited to take off our packs and fix ourselves a plate. These "angels" had vegetarian burritos with a whole host of fixings, soda, and other goodies. We joined Cuppa Joe, Scholar, Break-a-Leg, and Weatherman around the fire. Shortly thereafter, Jax arrived. I stuffed myself with three burritos brimming with beans, onions, corn, peppers, and cheese while listening to Cuppa Joe and Break-a-Leg discuss books.

Cuppa Joe, Weatherman, Break-a-Leg, and Scholar were a mismatched foursome. The girls, Break-a-Leg and Scholar, were both around my age, while the men, Cuppa Joe and Weatherman, were in their early forties. Scholar and Cuppa Joe were on second thru-hike attempts. Weatherman and Break-a-Leg had constant, painful injuries that slowed their progress and made hiking more difficult.

Somehow the four had formed a group and were rarely found apart in the early days of the trail. Cuppa, Break, and Scholar were famous for carrying multiple books at a time because they read so fast and were rendered immobile at the thought of being without something to read. I let their literary conversation float through my ears while I layered hot chocolate on top of the burritos in my swimmingly full stomach. Mexican food is my favorite, and I feared I had let my enthusism allow me to eat too much.

Eventually, Souleman and I determined that we had been gluttonous for long enough. I profusely thanked the trail angels and hefted my burdensome pack onto my aching shoulders. With smiles and uncomfortably full bellies, we began the ascent of Albert Mountain.

I was prepared for the worst. The need to use handholds and other such tedious endeavors had been described to me repeatedly. The incline definitely became steeper and I had to pull myself up using tree trunks a handful of times, but the trail was decidedly easier than it had been portrayed. This was one of my first lessons in believing very little when other hikers described the upcoming trail sections. I summited Albert Mountain still smiling at my stomach full of warm food.

Souleman and Jax were waiting at the top, and together we climbed the fire tower to get a panoramic view of the area. With awe we propped our sweaty elbows on the ledge and gazed at the mountains stringing along to the north. The peaks bobbed along in a continual pattern—up and down, up and down. We would summit many of the mountains that lay before us as we followed the white blazes northward.

Just past Albert Mountain, we encountered a southbound hiker. She was wearing a brightly flowered skirt with leggings and a daypack. A folded bandana held back her long hair.

"Hola! I'm Swiss Miss the Chocolate Bandito."

We introduced ourselves and stopped to chat. Swiss Miss told us she had attempted a thru-hike the previous year. She hadn't finished the trail but had had a wonderful experience and wanted to come out and treat other hikers.

"Here, take some candies," she offered as she passed out Easter candy. Swiss Miss extended her generosity by inviting us to come back to her house for Easter dinner the next day. My eyes widened at the invitation. *A complete stranger is inviting me to Easter dinner?* While it was very tempting, we had a schedule to keep, so we politely declined.

Minutes later we ran into a man and his young son out for a day hike. They stopped and the father asked us questions about thru-hiking.

"How many miles do you hike a day?"

"Usually somewhere between ten and fifteen," Souleman answered as he pulled out his water bottle.

"How do you know where to stop each night?"

I pulled out my *Thru-Hiker's Handbook* and held it out. "This is the reference we use. It helps us know where to get water, what roads we're crossing, where we can sleep at night, and other stuff like that." I pointed at various symbols in the book, making sure to angle it so the young boy could see too.

He leaned in to look at the book but still didn't speak.

"How do you get food on the trail?" the father wanted to know.

"We go into town about every four to seven days and buy food at a store. There are a few places further north where we will have food mailed to us by family members because the stores are scarce," I explained.

"Our next stop will be in Franklin, North Carolina, tomorrow, actually," Souleman added.

"How do you get to town?"

Souleman and I glanced at the little boy and then exchanged glances, knowing people often disliked this answer.

"We hitchhike," I confessed quietly.

"What time do you think you'll be at the road tomorrow? I'll pick you up. It's Easter and I'd love to do something nice."

We objected, knowing this would be an inconvenience and would interrupt his family's holiday. But the man insisted, so we did some quick math and arrived at a tentative time when we would reach the road. Gratefully, we made arrangements to meet the man the next day. Before we continued up the trail, I leaned down to the boy's level.

"I bet you could hike the whole trail someday if you wanted to."

His eyes got big and he puffed out his little chest.
"Really?"
This was the first word he'd spoken in our presence.
"Sure."
"Definitely," Souleman chimed in.

All of the unexpected events had caused the day to fly by. Almost before it seemed possible, we had arrived at the next shelter. As we were unpacking our gear, a woman with a dog approached the shelter from the south side. She introduced herself as a trail angel and asked who wanted hot dogs. A bag filled with hot dogs, buns, ketchup, and chocolate candies materialized on the picnic table. The brick-like mass of burritos was still sitting in my stomach, but in true thru-hiker fashion, I didn't say no.

It had been an eventful day on the trail. Although I had greatly enjoyed the unexpected trail magic and the triumph of Albert Mountain, I was even more pleased with the pleasant conversations and newfound friendship with Souleman. Over the next few days, it became increasingly common for Souleman to hang back and hike with me.

"I see more when I hike with you. With Jax I just hike so fast that we don't see anything along the way. Besides, your butt is much nicer to walk behind," Souleman told me.

I smiled at him and wondered what exactly he was up to. *Is he flirting or just being nice? Do I want him to be flirting?* Souleman might have been slowing down, but Jax seemed to have a powerful magnet pulling him quickly north. The three of us continued to rendezvous in the evenings, but during the day we rarely stayed together as a threesome.

We woke on Easter morning to a miserably cold and wet day. The only thing more unlikely than three dirty hikers getting a hitch on Easter would have been three *wet*, dirty hikers getting a hitch on Easter. Luckily, we avoided the whole debacle because of the generous man from the previous day.

We devoured our breakfasts and practically ran to the meeting point, slipping and sliding on the mud. Our trail angel arrived at precisely the pre-determined time and beckoned us into the warmth of his minivan. Inside, there were three adorable, food-laden Easter baskets his wife had prepared. We devoured the contents during the short ride to town as a sort of second breakfast.

In town we wandered the grocery store in search of resupply. This town chore was one we were still adjusting to. Our already grumbling stomachs greatly complicated the goal of selecting just enough food to last until the next town without adding unnecessary weight. After we had selected many items, analyzed them for calorie-to-weight ratio, and then re-shelved them, we eventually made it to the checkout line.

Just as we made it to the front of the line, but before we relinquished our carefully selected items to the clerk, we remembered that it was Easter and we needed something with which to celebrate. Jax suggested Easter dinner a la campfire, and we split up to collect the ingredients. Properly outfitted with a bottle of Foxhorn wine, canned green beans, corn, and a can of mystery meat, we checked out and wandered outside to reload our packs.

I sat cross-legged on the covered sidewalk outside the grocery store among a massive pile of Ziploc bags, discarding excess packaging and repackaging my food. I was faced with the task of fitting five days of food into a damp, not-yet-easily-pliable pack, and I wrestled the groaning bag into obedience while sampling bites of my selections. After entirely too much time, we shouldered our packs and were prepared to hitch back to the trail. It was then that we saw a flicker of light through the rain: a neon sign that read "All You Can Eat."

Within minutes we were seated at Shoney's with our packs safely tucked under the adjacent table. Surrounding us were families dressed in their Easter best. We could smell their noxiously sweet perfume and soap, which I'm sure meant they could detect our not-so-sweet, not-so-clean hiker funk. By this point on the trail, our smell was ripe but not yet to the point of heinous repulsion.

We ate copious amounts of fat- and calorie-infused goodness—bacon, sausage, pancakes, toast, and hashbrowns—and even managed to squeeze in some healthful options like fruit, salad, eggs, and milk. This was our first experience at an AYCE (the hiker term for all-you-can-eat restaurants). We suddenly understood the appeal to hungry hikers and the risk to restaurant owners who were trying to make some money. Happily stuffed, we stumbled back onto the road two hours later with swollen stomachs and big smiles.

Our original plan had been to head straight to the trail from the restaurant. Technically, our *original* plan had been to leave straight from the grocery store, and our *subsequent* plan had been to go back to the trail after leaving the restaurant. But then we heard about an outfitter in town. And since hikers can't resist the temptation of perusing gear, we marched down the road toward the store. I walked with my waist belt unhooked to accommodate my bulgingly full stomach.

The outfitter was complete with a plentiful selection of gear, Appalachian Trail books, and a hiker register and photo log, which we dutifully signed and posed for. Many of our hiker friends were there, including Mother Nature and Red Hat, who had been staying at a nearby hotel. As it happened, their ride soon arrived and offered us transportation back to the trail. The driver turned out to be the hot dog trail angel from the previous night.

The weather, which had previously been eerily dark and drizzly, changed to an outright downpour of icy cold rain as we headed back up the trail. I tried to hike quickly to create body heat, but my pack was full of resupply and my stomach uncomfortably stuffed. My body simply wouldn't move any faster. Jax and Souleman took off up the trail. I, on the other hand, resigned myself to a cold, wet day and petulantly trudged alone up the river the trail had become. My teeth were chattering, and my fingers had gone numb inside my fleece gloves to the point that only the straps were holding my hiking poles to my hands. I couldn't think of much besides a warm meal (yes, I was thinking about food again) and being horizontal in my sleeping bag. My burning legs exclaimed that I had hiked at *least* the four miles of expected distance to the shelter, yet the shelter sign was simply not appearing. It began to hail and lightning simultaneously. This combination of weather phenomena had been unknown to me until that day.

My exhaustion began to turn into fear when I had continued at least a half mile farther without seeing a sign. *Did I read the mileage wrong?* I shrugged out of my soaked pack and located my Wingfoot book with awkward, numb fingers. Turning my back on the storm, I tried to stand so that my hood and body shielded my precious book from the unforgiving rain. My wet glove traced the appropriate line in the book, and I saw I had read the mileage correctly. *Where the heck is the shelter? Did I miss the sign somehow?*

As I was shrugging back into my pack, I heard a shout. Someone was jogging toward me from the opposite direction. I tensed and narrowed my eyes. Then I realized it was Souleman. His hair was plastered to his head under his hood, and raindrops were running like little waterfalls off his beard.

"I was worried about you out here alone in this weather."

Lightning crashed near us as if to justify his statement.

"Here, let me take your pack."

He reached his arm out. Squinting up at him through the rain misting into my eyes, I shook my head no. Carefully reseating my heavy, wet pack on my bruised shoulders, I told him, "Thanks, but I want to carry my pack the whole way. I decided before I started that I was going to be a purist."

He didn't fight me a bit.

"I get that. You walk in front. I'll stay right behind you." As we started up the trail, he yelled over the storm, "The good news is, the shelter is right up ahead."

Detecting a trick, I asked, "And the bad news?"

"The shelter is full of Boy Scouts. Tons of them. They took up the whole shelter, so we have to tent. Jax and I are set up in the field already."

Looking up at the dark clouds surrounding us, I growled under my breath. True to Souleman's word, Siler Bald Shelter was just ahead. The only place to tent was in a small field behind the shelter. Souleman selflessly stayed with me in the wet field, offering help and encouragement as I erected my tent as best I could in the rain, hail, lightning, and cold. After talking to Jax, we decided to forego the celebratory Easter dinner. Cooking multiple things in the rain or inside the crowded shelter did not sound like fun. Instead, I huddled inside my rain coat in a corner of the shelter for just long enough to cook my fastest-cooking hot meal, Ramen noodles. Once again full, I crawled dejectedly into my semi-dry tent. Jax and Souleman were in their respective tents, which made a triangle with mine. We yelled back and forth over the relentless weather.

"I am *not* carrying that wine again tomorrow," Souleman declared over the pelting rain. "We either have to drink it or dump it. And I didn't carry it all that way just to pour it out."

"We could pass it from tent to tent?" Jax offered.

"We'd let all the rain in," I yelled back, barely lifting my heavy head from my damp sleeping pad.

"We could all get in one tent," Jax hollered.

I was skeptical. "No way would we fit. We all have one-man tents."

"It could work," Souleman yelled. "Brownie, you have the biggest tent."

Next thing I knew, I heard two zippers being undone. Souleman showed up at my vestibule first, toting his sleeping bag. He shoved that in ahead of him and crawled over me and into my tent. Before we had even settled comfortably, Jax appeared, wiggling his way in. Unavoidably, some water came in too. We stuffed my sleeping bag and Souleman's around the three of us.

Astonishingly, we did fit, though we stretched the confines of the walls considerably. The guys were laying head to toe lengthwise in the tent. I was sitting at their waists with my legs bent. The wine was passed around and consumed. We laughed and talked in the dark while the rain steadily beat the top of the tent and the Boy Scouts up at the shelter yelled and laughed over the storm.

During our conversation, I felt someone playing with my hair and realized it was Souleman. I got very still, hoping he wouldn't stop. Finally, my legs cramped and I had to stretch them out. I lay down, intentionally placing my head near Souleman's shoulder. Jax dug in his pocket and lit a joint to pass around. I hated the thought of my tent smelling like smoke and worried that my sleeping bag would be forever ruined. *Please let the Boy Scouts be asleep. I don't want to be a bad example.* Preoccupied and enjoying Souleman's fingers gently running through my hair, I became quiet. Shortly, tired of being cramped, Jax retired to the comfort of his own tent.

Souleman stayed in order to "make sure everything was dry." After a brief examination, he determined that my sleeping bag was wet and therefore useless. I collapsed onto my stomach on my Therm-a-Rest, my head in my hands, and cursed my much-debated decision to purchase a down bag. *How am I going to avoid hypothermia when the temperature drops tonight? What was I thinking cramming all these people into my tent? How will I ever make it to Maine?*

"We'll dry it out tomorrow, Brownie. It'll be ok," Souleman reassured me as he lay on his side next to me and covered us both with his oversized, synthetic sleeping bag. He rhythmically rubbed my back, and soon the exhaustion of the extremely long day, combined with the wine, began to overtake me and I succumbed to sleep—but not before we shared our first kiss.

7

Our Trio's Down to Two

I woke up the next morning damp and cramped, but without hypothermia or frostbite. Jax's tent was already gone when I poked my head out to survey the clearing. With admittedly large grins, Souleman and I climbed out of my tent to pack our gear. I had to pause every few seconds to warm my hands in my armpits as I took down my tent and stuffed my gear into my pack. Souleman's hand was warm on my lower back as he sympathetically watched me wrestle my sleeping bag. The traitorous bag was cold as ice when I crammed the heavy, wet mass into its stuff sack. Finally packed and still smiling foolishly, Souleman and I started up the trail together. The weather remained bitterly cold, and it began to snow before our second breakfast.

The snow was dampening our attitudes, so to lift our spirits we dreamed out loud about warm drinks and food. Souleman talked about cheeseburgers and steaks, while I tended toward cookies and sweets. We settled on our joint craving: Krispy Kreme doughnuts. My mouth watered at the thought of doughnuts, and I dejectedly thought of the less-appealing contents of my food bag, wondering what I'd eat for lunch.

Souleman was walking in front of me, and he interrupted my thoughts, exclaiming, "It's so rude when people do this. Don't they care at all? I do not want to pack out someone else's trash, but how can we just leave this here to make the trail all gross?"

I leaned around him to see the grocery bag he was poking with his hiking pole.

He pulled the handles apart to reveal a Krispy Kreme doughnut box.

"You don't think . . . " he wondered out loud as he leaned down to open the box.

Sure enough, inside were half a dozen glazed donuts and a sticky note that simply said, "Enjoy, Hikers!" A finger-poke assured us that the donuts were fresh. What were the odds of the exact food we were craving showing up trailside? We devoured two doughnuts each and rejoiced at our luck as we enthusiastically pushed on through the snow.

Not two miles further, we reached a stone fire tower and stopped to get out of the wind and thaw our aching fingers. Inside, we found a family who offered us food and showered us with encouragement. We stood indoors avoiding the blustery wind and talked with them while we ate snacks. They declared us "the most positive hiking couple they had ever met."

We exchanged sheepish glances at the word couple.

"You'll end up married someday," they predicted.

Married? Could that be possible? I looked from their eager grins to Souleman's smile and chided myself. *Don't get ahead of yourself.*

Grinning and still tossing the marriage comment around in my head, I gulped my hot chocolate so fast that I burned my tongue and the roof of my mouth. My toes tingled, so I stamped my feet on the frozen ground to keep my blood flowing. The pounding on my foot pressed on the swollen, egg-shaped lump and reminded me of that nagging injury.

Souleman reached for my empty cup, and my heart skipped a beat when his hand brushed across mine. We pulled on our gloves, and I awkwardly squeezed his hand before we ducked back outside. As the snow began to fall harder and the wind picked up, my concern about drying my drenched sleeping bag heightened. It was too cold to stop hiking for long enough to eat a real meal. I couldn't take my gloves off for long enough to find food in my pack. There was no way I could stop for long enough to dry my sleeping bag, and even if I could, the temperature was too cold and the weather too awful for drying to be feasible.

I sent up a prayer for the family that had provided us with food earlier in the day. We traveled uphill for five straight miles. The bitter cold prevented me from indulging in my normal habit of stopping every couple hundred yards or so to re-energize. Eventually, the day's rhythmic pattern of right—left—right—left and repetitious replaying of the previous day's unexpected kiss took my mind off of the sleeping bag dilemma. In spite of carrying a good four pounds of extra water trapped in my sleeping bag and clothes, and being ravenously hungry, my mood remained upbeat.

That night the shelter was again full—this time with thru-hikers and not Boy Scouts. Souleman and I stood under the ledge of the shelter roof and tried to shield our stoves from the wind and snow enough to cook a hot meal. Jealously, I listened to the sounds of my cocooned co-hikers. They laughed and sang along to the strumming of someone's guitar. Our hiking companion, Jax, was wedged in there with the rest of them.

As I was preparing my dinner, I sliced right through my thumb with a knife. My fingers were so numb that I didn't notice until blood was dripping everywhere. I performed haphazard first aid while Souleman generously finished my food preparation. Shivering, I leaned against the shelter wall and sucked down my Lipton noodles with record-breaking speed. I stuffed the empty pot into my bear bag. Cleaning up was not even a consideration. After that night I never again cleaned my cooking pot.

My thumb was still throbbing and bleeding at bedtime. I had wrapped it in a bandana that was turning increasingly crimson in color. Since my sleeping bag was now partially frozen, Souleman again shared his sleeping bag and body warmth. This arrangement was now mutually beneficial because he had discovered that he was somehow missing a pole for his tent. I shared my tent, and he shared his sleeping bag. Between the two of us, we had one complete sleeping arrangement. He curled his body around mine, and this time I inched even closer.

We had pitched my tent under a group of trees, hoping that they would provide some protection from the snow and wind. Nearby, V3 and Toolman were in their tent. The four of us yelled back and forth in friendly conversation until exhaustion and cold lulled us to sleep. If I somehow expected a reprieve from the snow and rain that night, I was sorely wrong. Throughout the night, snow thumped down on the tent as the branches overhead became laden with weight and released their burden. Worried about freezing or bleeding to death, I slept little.

I lived through the night and woke up warm with Souleman's arm around me and his sleeping bag tucked tightly around us both. I dreaded getting out of the tent into the cold. An inspection of my thumb revealed a blood-soaked bandage but no current bleeding. My wiggling around woke Souleman, and begrudgingly we crawled out into the white wonderland.

Surprisingly, the weather warmed up quickly and the day was pleasant. Souleman and I stopped for a lengthy lunch on top of the Wesser Fire Tower. We spread out our socks and my wet clothes in sunny spots on the wooden planks in an effort to dry them while we devoured beef jerky, cheese, crackers, cookies, and anything else we could spare. Our appetites had become voracious, and no meal seemed adequate.

The miles passed quickly as the day progressed. For the first time on the trail, I was actually warm all day. The sun was out, and my body warmed considerably with the heightened pace. We passed a rapidly flowing stream, and with mischievous grins, Souleman and I both dunked our heads in the water. The water was frigid and made my skin tingle, but it felt wonderfully refreshing trickling down my neck and back, washing away some of the salt and dirt.

As we were nearing the end of our planned mileage, we passed a day hiker headed in the opposite direction. As most hikers do, he stopped to chat with us. When he realized we were thru-hikers, he had a number of questions. He was an avid hiker himself and had encountered numerous thru-hikers over the years. He enjoyed hearing about what motivated people to hike, what they ate in the woods, and what gear they carried.

As we parted ways, he shook our hands. He held my hand in both of his, and while looking into my eyes he said, "You're going to make it to Maine. You just have that look in your eye."

That was precisely the motivation I needed to push on to the shelter. I was so thrilled by the day hiker's prediction that I couldn't even recall my feet touching the ground for the rest of the day. I floated down the trail, elated that a stranger had so much confidence in me.

When we reached our destination for the evening, Krazy Katie, Radio, Jax, and many others we knew were already set up for the night. We decided to stay in the shelter and avoid having to take down a tent in the morning. As nice as tenting could be, it always seemed to take longer to get going in the morning. I was already so familiar with my pack that packing and unpacking could be accomplished in a matter of minutes.

Now that the rain and snow seemed to have finally abated, I decided to attempt drying my sleeping bag, which was still soaked from the Siler Bald disaster days before. It smelled grossly like a wet bird as I draped it over the clothesline. As I was spreading the fabric out, I heard a loud "c-r-r-rack!" My head snapped up just in time to watch a fully grown tree fall to the ground. Ever the philosophy major, I immediately rekindled the debate about whether or not there would have been a sound if none of us had been there to hear it. My friends seemed more worried about whether or not there would be cheeseburgers in town if we didn't go in to eat them.

The guys, who apparently still had some energy left, engaged themselves in a game of trail baseball using a stick and a wadded-up ball of duct tape. Once they had exhausted themselves, we joined all the other hikers at the campfire and shared our belated Easter meal. While we passed corn, green beans, and canned mystery meat around the campfire, we talked about cheeseburgers, fries, milkshakes, and other greasy, heavy foods.

Chatter abounded around the campfire. Everyone was excited because we would be heading into the Nantahala Outdoor Center (NOC) first thing in the morning. Haiku, another thru-hiker, and his uncle, who were camping at the shelter, had given in to their cravings and hiked the mile in for hamburgers that night. They sauntered back into the campsite gloating about their full stomachs and how wonderful the town food had been. It seems everyone was starting to get the infamous trail appetite because there were many questions.

"Just *how* big was the burger?"

"Did they have onion rings?"

"What about veggie burgers?"

"Were there free refills on drinks?"

The answers were really just to appease our salivating taste buds. We knew we would all be eating at the restaurant tomorrow regardless of price, size, or selection. Eventually, I couldn't hear about food anymore. It was time for bed.

My sleeping bag was finally dry enough for me to consider using it. Since it was still wet enough to be chilly, Souleman and I decided to put it on top of our Therm-a-Rests and throw his sleeping bag over the top of us. Our body heat would dry my bag further while his bag trapped in warmth. And, let's be honest, it was another reason to sleep closely again.

Just as we had switched off our headlamps and settled our heads onto our makeshift pillows, we heard voices approaching in the dark. Headlamps swept over us and I looked up to see two familiar faces staring down at me. Toolman and V3 had night-hiked in to the shelter. At first they tried to whisper and set up quietly, but then they got louder and louder. They went behind the shelter to hang a bear bag and we could hear them arguing.

I squeezed Souleman's hand in the dark and wiggled closer. Hiking with a partner can certainly be a challenge, especially when you share food and other important gear. Although we had yet to experience hiking-partner drama, we had witnessed plenty. Everyone pretended not to notice they were fighting and just waited for them to settle into their sleeping bags. Normally, being kept awake so late would have been extremely frustrating, but we were in excellent spirits because we had only nine-tenths of a mile to hike the following day and a restaurant on the agenda.

As the bickering continued outside the shelter, Souleman's hand traced circles on my stomach. I tuned out the arguing as his hand moved under the hem of my shirt, drawing larger and larger circles. Finally, all became quiet, and he kissed the back of my head before I drifted off to sleep, dreaming about human-sized cheeseburgers and mountains of ketchup-covered french fries.

In the morning I hurried to the NOC. It is mainly a kayaking center, but the employees are notorious for treating the hiking community well. We rented a bunkroom and then raced to the restaurant, still dirty and sweaty. Eating was our first priority. My package of Pop-Tarts had been digested long ago, and cheeseburgers, my favorite, were on the menu. Souleman, Jax, and I shared a table with Gypsy, Touk, Bassline, and numerous other hairy, stinky hikers. We ordered appetizers, salads, burgers, desserts, sides, milkshakes, and drinks. Not a bite of food was left on the table. Our stomachs satiated for the moment, we headed to the showers.

Once the three of us were fully scrubbed and wearing the cleanest clothes we had, we tackled the job of finding food for our next stint in the woods. We walked the winding road to a nearby gas station and loaded up on frozen pizza, Pop-Tarts, and other calorie-rich resupply items. One of the benefits to spending the night at the NOC was that we could cook in the kitchen. Therefore, a whole new array of microwaveable foods provided options for our evening meal.

We unanimously determined that we were not excited about walking back to the NOC from the gas station. We may have been *hikers*, but that didn't mean we liked to *walk*. Walking is a whole different beast, particularly on a hardtop road with blind curves. Thus began the process of soliciting a ride. Jax approached a young woman, but she hastily locked her doors and shook her head no. Souleman tried an older gentleman, who just blatantly refused

Finally, the three of us started a conversation with a rather questionable-looking guy. He was probably in his early thirties and was wearing surfer shorts and a tank top. His hair was long and greasy, and he had a number of prominent tattoos. In addition to his musky odor reminiscent of foliage, his eyes were curiously red.

He offered us a ride, but I couldn't figure out where he intended for us to sit. When we approached his car, there were already two children inside, one in a dirty old car seat, and one who *should've* been in a car seat. In the end, I sat in the front with the car-seat-less child in my lap, and the guys squeezed in back with the car seat, a vacuum, a set of weights, and other assorted items. Sublime was playing on the CD player as we made our curious return to the NOC.

I spent the afternoon lying on a picnic table by the river, eating, walking around the gear store, and updating my journal. I called my parents to let them know I had now made it 142 miles. Dad answered and yelled for my mom and sister to pick up extensions. After greetings, they got down to business.

"How does your body feel? Do you have sore muscles? What about blisters?" Dad asked.

I took an inventory of my body. "No blisters. Yes, my muscles hurt some, but overall I'm fine. I expected to hurt some." I poked at my foot-egg while I spoke but decided it wasn't worth mentioning. Surely it would be gone before the next town.

"Have you been stretching?" he wanted to know.

"No, not really. But I've never been good about that." I rolled my stiff neck as we talked.

"It might keep you from getting hurt."

"Ok." I knew I'd never stretch, but maybe saying I'd try would ease his worries.

"Make sure you fill up on food in town," he advised.

Mom cut in, "Are you meeting people?"

I looked at all the hikers stretched out on tables and rocks around me. "Yes. Lots of people. Learning how everyone gets their trail names has been interesting. There's Bottoms Up, Cuppa Joe, Scholar, Panoramic, Toolman . . . all kinds of funny names, and everyone has a story. Oh, did I tell you I got mine?"

"What is it?" my sister wanted to know.

"Brownie."

Mom laughed. "How appropriate."

"So, when is the last time you showered?" my sister asked.

"This morning, actually."

"And before that?"

"Umm . . . in the last town. Maybe four or five days?" I inspected my leg hair and was proud to see a fine layer of stubble accumulating. *If only Allison could see this!*

"Gross."

I hung up with my family and rejoined my new friends. That night a generous rafter, who was also staying at the NOC, invited all the thru-hikers to join his group on the deck for beer and snacks. The deck was enormous—a huge wrap-around structure with staircases connecting to other levels of decks and walkways. The rafter was giving out what appeared to be a limitless supply of beer that he was determined to deplete before his return home in the morning. Not wanting to let him down, we sat around in lawn chairs and helped put back a few drinks. The men all smoked cigars, and we traded stories about paddling and hiking. The rafters were impressed with the distance we had walked and how far we had yet to go.

Before we crashed, Souleman asked me to go for a walk. *Sure, a walk . . . since we aren't getting nearly enough exercise these days.* We followed the railroad tracks to the Nantahala River, where we sat on a picnic table and talked. After some time we lay on the table side by side, looking up at the stars with our hands clasped on top of our stomachs, and traded stories about the first time each of us had gone backpacking.

"I'm really glad we're hiking together now," he told me, squeezing my hand.

"Me too. I love hiking with you. But I'm afraid you'll get tired of my slow pace."

"I'm not worried about it." His thumb traced circles on mine. He pulled me toward him and we kissed, our bodies melding together on top of the picnic table. We heard voices approaching but didn't have time to sneak away. We sat up just as we were joined by Jax and a few others.

After a little conversation, the guys passed around a joint, this time in a pipe. At first I declined. I had no intention of making a habit out of smoking, and outside of Jax and Souleman, I was also embarrassed for anyone to know I had ever tried it. Still, since I hadn't felt any effect the first time I had smoked, I wanted to know what being high was like. After glancing over my shoulder many times to determine whether anyone was watching, I joined in.

After more laughter and musings about what lay ahead of us on the trail, Souleman and I snuck away from the group and walked hand in hand to the bridge over the Nantahala. We curled up in a nook of the bridge to hide from the relentless wind and continued talking. The many days of hiking caught up with us, and we became overwhelmingly tired. We lay lazily curled around each other in the alcove. I distinctly remember being mesmerized by the flapping of an American flag over our heads. When we followed the levels of decks back toward the bunk, we re-encountered the rafter and his group still enjoying beer. Stopping to talk for a few more minutes was inevitable. Although I didn't feel any different after smoking, I had a sense of paranoia, like everyone could tell I had smoked.

Nervously I eyed everyone in the circle, certain they knew my secret. The rafter told me nonchalantly that he worked for the Drug Enforcement Administration, and I became convinced that my guilt was palpable. Although Souleman assured me the man was just messing with me, I lay awake all night fearing that he actually worked for the DEA and I would be arrested. I imagined the phone call I would have to make to my parents. *"Hi, Dad, I'm in jail. I got caught smoking marijuana. Will you bail me out?"* He would kill me. Souleman and I curled up on one twin-size bunk and I finally fell asleep, but I dreamed about jail and the police all night. I awoke further convinced that I could never live a life involving anything illegal.

The first thing I heard in the morning was the loud pitter-patter of raindrops on the roof. When I sat up and peered out the window, the rain was pouring down. Souleman and I made a stop at the gear store before heading into the downpour. He bought a new headlamp and I purchased gaiters to protect my lower legs, along with what would soon become one of our most valued possessions—a hitchhiking bandana. It was white and on one side said "Hiker to Town" in large green letters, with "Hiker to Trail" on the other side. This simple creation helped us procure numerous rides over the next thousand miles. When we left the outfitter, Jax had already headed up the trail. We expected to meet him at the pre-determined shelter.

The climb out of the NOC was brutal. It was purported to be the steepest climb until the Great Smoky Mountains National Park. I trudged along steadily, but my steps were small because my pack was heavy with resupply. The mud and rain made the trail slippery as I continued my unchanging pattern of right, left, right, left. Sharing nonstop conversation with Souleman over the noise of the rain made the time pass more quickly. I felt tough and was proud of my determination to remain positive in spite of the weather and terrain. We arrived at Sassafras Gap Shelter and hurried in to see Jax. I peered inside as Souleman stated the obvious.

"He's not here."

"Nope."

Souleman grabbed the register and flipped to the most recent entries. I watched him scan the pages.

"He didn't write an entry." He set the register back on the shelter floor.

I waited a few seconds before observing, "I think that, in the words of Timon from *The Lion King*, 'Our trio's down to two.'"

"Well, I guess you'll have that," he said as he shook his head.

I would soon learn that "You'll have that" was a phrase from Vermont that Souleman often used. The best I could determine, it meant something to the effect of "Well, that happens."

"Do you think we'll see him again?" he asked.

"Probably." I shrugged. "The trail is strange. The way people disappear and then reappear, he could show up later today, or next week, or a month from now even. Every time I think I've seen the last of a particular hiker, poof, there he is again."

"I guess so."

We sat on the edge of the shelter and stared out at the rain. I thought about the ebb and flow of hikers on the trail. Sometimes we were drowning in a sea of fellow hikers. Other times we were nearly alone in the woods. Some people you saw almost daily; others you met once and never saw again.

There was a lot of space in this two-story shelter, so after a while we spread out our sleeping gear under the skylights on the second level and settled in. It would be nice not to get our tent wet. We would still be sharing my one-man tent until Souleman could get a replacement pole shipped to him at a town up the trail. While lying close was nice, our aching bodies appreciated a little space to spread out while we slept. My small tent made for rather cramped sleeping quarters, so cramped that we used only his Therm-a-Rest and we both squeezed on top. After a meal in the dry shelter, we fell asleep with our fingers intertwined, listening to the hypnotic sound of rain on the roof.

I heard rain still drumming on the metal roof before I even opened my eyes the next morning. After being wet the entire previous day, I was well past the point of trying to stay dry. In fact, I splashed right through a puddle as I left the shelter to get the inevitable over with.

We trudged up and down muddy hills all day. When it rained this hard, I found it hard to stop for breaks. I got chilled as soon as I stopped moving, and everything in my pack got wet if I tried to take anything out. I tried to avoid stopping to go to the bathroom in the rain at all costs because that would involve putting my pack on the waterlogged ground. It would also mean exposing to the rain the one part of my pack that was usually protected by my back and might possibly still be dry. And of course, I would have to pull down my rain pants and squat in the mud, which meant risking falling over on the slippery, uneven ground.

That day was so wet and muddy that Souleman and I looked like mud wrestlers. Our rain pants and gaiters were covered in layers of mud, and our jackets had as much moisture inside as out. Still, we trudged on with smiles. Souleman's relentlessly positive attitude helped me remain upbeat. He viewed life with such positive enthusiasm that it was hard to be negative in his presence. Our conversations that day covered challenging topics like abortion, patriotism, universalism, family, and relationships. Although our opinions often differed, we were able to share our ideas without diminishing each other's point of view.

That night we had the privilege of sharing the shelter with a very experienced trail couple, Jake Brake and Low Gear. These two were much more seasoned than we, both at hiking and at life. Jake Brake and Low Gear were in their mid-sixties and were thru-hiking for the second time in their married life. The four of us braved the rain together inside the uneven and slightly leaky little shelter. We played a few games of Spades and traded many stories and laughs. These two were truly an inspiration and would become a constant presence in both our trail and post-trail lives.

The sun glistened off of every visible surface in the morning. The rain had changed over to snow in the coolness of the night, and everything I could see was white and sparkling with snow. I was grateful for my gaiters, gloves, hat, and other winter gear as we trekked up the mountain toward Fontana Dam. In some spots the snow drifts touched my knees. The snow was coming down so swiftly that the footprints of hikers who had preceded us only a short time before were no longer visible. I tucked my chin down against my chest, trying to block some of the snow from hitting my bare cheeks. Souleman's breath froze on his beard and mustache, creating giant icicles.

We started out in our usual line-up, with me leading our two-man train. Quickly we realized that we were not making much progress. Breaking through snow while traveling uphill with a heavy pack is hard work.

"Let me lead for a while," Souleman offered when we stopped to put on more clothes. I nodded gratefully. I had my hands balled into fists inside my gloves, and my fingers were still getting colder and losing mobility. *This is miserable.* I tucked my chin against my chest and focused on stepping in Souleman's footprints. I glanced up to see another hiker coming toward us. It was Scholar, and she was wearing sandals and no hat. Her ears were already questionably red and her feet must have been ice blocks. The road was still a few miles away.

Scholar mentioned that some other hikers had been turned back from entering the Smoky Mountains because the snow drifts were dangerously high and the park rangers were concerned about safety. We discussed the situation as we trekked on. Should we keep going? Did we really need to stop in town again? Could it be that bad? Ultimately, while neither of us wanted to delay our trip, we decided we shouldn't hike into a winter storm against park ranger advice.

We arrived at the road and called a shuttle from a roadside phone. On the way to the phone, Souleman stepped on a spot of slick mud and took his first trail fall. His legs shot out in front of him and he landed on his rear end in the puddle of mud. I busted out laughing. I laughed and laughed until I realized he wasn't getting back up. He also wasn't laughing. When I knelt down beside him, he was holding his wrist and gingerly rotating it. I helped him to his feet and we examined his sore wrist. It seemed his pride had taken the brunt of the damage.

"I can't believe my first fall was in a parking lot," he lamented.

"I can't believe you made it a hundred and seventy miles without falling."

Fontana Dam was a tiny little trail community with just enough amenities to accommodate hikers. We spent two days lazing around town, waiting for the weather to clear in the mountains ahead. As soon as the rangers deemed it safe, we would enter the Great Smoky Mountains National Park with all of the other stranded hikers—Serenity, Freedom, Free, Thatch, Jake Brake, Low Gear, Domino, Fireball, Tex, Bassline, Gypsy, Touk, V3, Toolman, and, in the funny and unexpected way of the trail, our friend Jax. A whole horde of us had taken over the little town. We played miniature golf and ping pong, swung on the playground swings, ate pint after pint of Ben and Jerry's ice cream, and piled into hotel rooms to watch TV.

While stranded in town, Souleman and I ventured to the miniature post office to check for a package from my mom. I had not one, not two, but seven packages. My mom, aunt, grandmothers, best friend, a trail friend, and the kids I babysat had all sent me packages. *So many people are rooting for me.* I sifted through the contents of the packages and shared the goodies with my friends.

The most memorable item was a giant chocolate bar with the words "161 down, 2,012 to go" written in icing on top. This treat was from Giggles, a friend I knew from working at summer camp years before. She had thru-hiked the previous year and had provided invaluable advice and encouragement in preparation for my hike. I was so proud of that candy bar that I *almost* didn't want to eat it.

Only another long-distance hiker could appreciate how big a deal it was to have made it to Fontana Dam. It was one of the most common quitting locations on the trail. Knowing the statistics made being waylaid in this particular spot even more worrisome. Luckily, between the thoughtful care packages, encouraging letters in my journal, excitement surrounding my budding relationship, and of course my own drive and stubbornness, I still had more than enough motivation to continue. The longer we stayed in town, the more restless and antsy I became to get back on the trail headed north.

Town food became expensive after a day or two, so the hikers got creative: We dug out our camp pots and made chili dogs and Reese's Pieces fondue in the fireplace in the lodge, much to the amusement of other guests. While sitting around the fire during the fondue-making session, Souleman unconsciously reached for my hand, and just like that all of our hiker friends became aware of our changing relationship.

8

I'm Tough!

Finally, after three days in town, the rangers cleared us for departure, and a whole troop of thru-hikers stampeded north. Various sections of the trail are highly anticipated by different hikers. I had grown up hearing stories about my mother's childhood vacations in the Smoky Mountains and was looking forward to visiting them myself. Everyone said that this park had one of the most beautiful sections of trail. I was excited to be surrounded by so many friends, but worried about how crowded the shelters would be.

After leaving Fontana Dam, we had to register for passage through the park. Locating the form and figuring out how to fill in the dates was complicated and more stressful than it should have been. When we finished, no one ever even looked at the paperwork we had so diligently prepared. I resolved to worry less about such paperwork further up the trail.

Finally, we stashed the form in a Ziploc in my pack and stepped into Great Smoky Mountains National Park. Jax had departed town before us and had left us, quite literally, in his dust. We kept track of him for the rest of our hike, reading his entries in shelter journals and emailing occasionally from towns.

The morning was a challenging one. I was ready for a break when we stopped at a fire tower in time for lunch. I wanted to eat on top of the tower, but the wind and chilly temperature made that impossible. I settled for a rock in a patch of sunshine underneath the tower. Souleman and I lay side by side on the rock and talked and giggled our way through lunch. We were surprised to realize how much time had passed before we started up the trail again.

Day One in the Smokies had been rumored to be the most difficult. I hoped that the rumors were true because the hike was taking everything out of me. By the end of the day, it took all the energy I could muster to simply place one foot in front of the other. I had also expected to see a plethora of animals in the park, but that didn't happen on the first day. In fact, I had come across surprisingly few animals on the entire trail. A fox outside the hotel in Fontana Dam was the only wildlife I had seen so far.

My first night in the Smokies largely contributed to my disillusionment with the park for the rest of the trip. I had reached the shelter exhausted and ready to eat a warm dinner and get into my sleeping bag. A glance into the shelter revealed an explosion of gear and an overflow of people. Rain coats, tent pieces, socks, and food bags dangled from every visible hook or nail.

Knowing that more hikers with reservations would likely show up and need the few remaining bunk slots, Souleman and I pulled out our tent and began searching for a flat spot of ground. As we were spreading the tent's footprint, a uniformed ranger approached and informed us that we could not pitch our tent because the park was trying to cut down on damage to the forest. We would have to wait to make sure it wasn't possible to stay in the shelter first. I pointed out the number of people already inside, but the ranger was insistent that we wait. We could not tent, but we also could not put our belongings inside the shelter because the spots were reserved.

Annoyed, we prepared dinner, got water, and hung our bear bags. By that point it was completely dark and, as we had predicted, the shelter was full. Now we would have to pitch our tent and set up our sleeping gear in the dark. Since we had to choose a spot in the dark, we ended up sleeping on an angled piece of ground sprinkled with protruding roots. I spent the night tossing from side to side, attempting to evenly distribute the discomfort of my sore body on the pointy rocks. It was an uncomfortable and frustrating night.

The second day in the Smokies proved to be equally as challenging as the first, according to my internal difficulty-o-meter. The terrain went endlessly up-up-up. Everything was muddy and slippery, and it seemed that for every two steps forward, I slid backward one. I became frustrated quickly and wanted to blame everyone and anyone. *Stupid rangers with their rules, stupid trail maintainers who can't manage rain runoff, stupid horses that create ruts in the trail.* I had to remind myself that no one had forced me to do this hike. *You chose this. You wanted to be here. Suck it up and find the silver lining.* Although I was struggling to keep an upbeat attitude, Souleman's demeanor was as serene as always.

While Souleman and I shared a passion for hiking, our personalities were polar opposites in many ways. This was probably a good thing because the world certainly doesn't need two of me. I am high-strung, high-maintenance, and obsessively organized. I am the epitome of a perfectionist and a stickler for the rules. I can't sit still. I get worked up easily and can't stand it when things aren't "fair." I don't like loud or repetitive noises, and I value my personal space.

Souleman, on the other hand, is about as calm as a blue-skied summer day. He is never stressed, never worked up, and can find the positive in any situation. He likes to bend the rules, loves to relax, and maintains the attitude that things will always work out one way or another, so there is no sense in worrying.

For Souleman, hiking was an extension of his normal life. Before the trail he had worked outside at a local park in the extreme cold of Vermont. He had hitchhiked cross country and had often picked up other hitchhikers in his own car. He had lived independently without consulting anyone about his decisions since finishing high school. Souleman thought nothing of spontaneous plans and didn't own a calendar. Knowing the date mattered little to him unless there was a Red Sox game. He wore the same fleece and Red Sox hat practically every day. None of his friends or family batted an eye when he told them (last minute) that he was going off to hike the Appalachian Trail.

For me, the trail was a break from the "real world," where I measured a day's success by how many things I checked off my never-ending to-do list. *Study for psych test. Read philosophy text. Exercise. Pick up prescription. Schedule appointment with Dr. Worth. Check mailbox. Do laundry. Pay phone bill.* I typically lived by a meticulously over-scheduled calendar, worried about wearing the appropriate outfit for every situation, and planned at breakfast what I would eat for dinner. While I strived to be independent, I still consulted my parents about big life decisions.

On the trail I tried not have a list. Instead of constantly accomplishing things, I made an effort to find contentment in being a part of my surroundings. I breathed in the fresh air perfumed with leaves, mud, sweat, and fire smoke. I enjoyed lazy lunches on rocks warmed by the sun. I listened to raindrops on my tent fly, owls in the trees, and logs crackling on the fire. I worked at embracing the spontaneity that the trail relentlessly forced me to accept.

On this second day in the Smokies, I ignored the mud and steep ascents and focused on the joy of being in nature and enjoying the company I had so luckily found. I envisioned Clingmans Dome, the mountain we would be summiting the following day. Clingmans is the highest mountain on the Appalachian Trail. I imagined the views to be spectacular and well worth the struggle through the rest of the Smokies to get there.

My Handbook claimed that we had hiked a mere 11.7 miles that day, but my body believed otherwise. Although Wingfoot's Handbook was an invaluable guide to the trail, there was no way for the information to be one hundred percent accurate. Many hikers enjoyed poking fun at Wingfoot and attributing their painful days to his miscalculations. I tried to assume that these discrepancies were not intentional and were due to trail relocations or other such occurrences. On unending days like this, though, it was sure easier to just blame the book—or its author.

When we arrived at the shelter, I shook my head at the sight. Many shelters in the Smokies are encased in wire fencing and look rather foreboding. The fencing is allegedly there to protect the hikers from bears. So many hikers have been irresponsible with their food storage in the past that bears have been known to frequent shelter sites in search of food. Now the sites have large metal poles where hikers are supposed to hang their food bags. Although these poles are bear-safe, they are not human-friendly. Actually getting the food bag onto one of these poles requires extreme patience and often an inordinate amount of time.

The interiors of shelters in the Smokies were frequently as disappointing as their exteriors. Oftentimes, the bunks were scattered with trash and discarded gear, the walls were stained with graffiti, and the fireplaces were littered with cigarette butts and empty tin cans. Thru-hikers are obviously not immune to making a mess, but few would have the audacity to leave a shelter in such ill repair. For one thing, long-distance hikers rarely carry enough extra items to leave anything behind. Many thru-hikers, including myself, attempted to pack out some of the debris in an effort to keep shelters the pristine, welcoming environment one should find in the middle of nature. Thru-hikers bestow a lot of respect on their nightly resting spots, which is why shelters used almost exclusively by long-distance hikers rarely ever have these issues.

Rumor around the picnic tables that night suggested that the weather would be bad the next morning. We cooked dinner, and as we prepared for bed, Souleman picked up our food bags to hang. I surprised him by taking the bear bags from his hand.

"I'll hang the bear bags tonight," I told him.

"I don't mind. I always do it. You go get our sleep stuff out." He went to kiss my forehead, but I ducked and tugged on the food bags.

"Let's trade tonight, ok? I can do this."

"These bear poles are tricky," Souleman warned.

"I'm tough."

He placed the food bags in my hands and walked toward the tent, shaking his head in amused defeat. I needed to prove I was able to perform all of the camp chores myself. Even though we were hiking as a pair and had certain tasks we tended to divvy up, I wanted to reassure myself that I was self-sufficient.

I carried the heavy bags to the bear pole and set them on the ground. This particular bear pole was tall like a tetherball pole. Sticking out from the top of the pole were a number of long hooks. The goal was to loop the handle of the food bag over one of the hooks so that it would be suspended in the air. A thin pole with a small hook on the end, much like the poles used to get merchandise down in a department store, was provided for hikers to lift the bags up to the larger hooks on the bear pole. *No problem.*

I hooked our bags' drawstrings onto this small pole and started to lift it up in the air. The weight of the two food bags together surprised me, and I dropped them when they were only a few feet off the ground. Undaunted, I re-hooked the drawstrings and, with significant effort, lifted the pole until the bags were over my head. The bags began to swing wildly, causing me to lose my balance, and slammed into the top of my head before crashing to the ground directly on top of my Croc-clad foot. I hopped around in circles, mumbling to myself. *This is ridiculous. I can hang a bear bag. There are other bags up there. This has to be possible.* I looked up to see Souleman leaning against a tree watching me. Wordlessly, I held the bags out toward him.

"Oh, no." He shook his head smiling. "You can do this." He crossed one ankle over the other and leaned back on the tree.

Glaring at him, I decided to change my strategy. I hooked only one food bag on the pole this time. Shakily, I lifted the bag up almost to the hook on the bear pole. With my arms fully extended, I was just inches shy of my target. *Dammit.* I stood on tiptoe and touched the hook. *Almost.* Then, at the last minute, I lost my balance and stumbled forward, dropping the bag on the ground. *Stupid bag.*

Angry now, I hooked the drawstring once more and launched myself at the bear pole. Miraculously, I reached the hook and transferred the bag. I was about to yell in triumph when the pole snagged on something. The hook had caught someone else's bright red food bag and yanked it off the bear pole. It landed inches from my toes. Now one of our bags and this red bag both lay at my feet. I picked up one bag to start over again.

Then, instead, I laid it back on the ground. *I don't always have to be tough. Right?* I scrunched up my eyes, poked out my lower lip, and looked at Souleman. Chuckling, he picked up the bags, and while I sulked nearby, he made much quicker work of getting them on the bear pole.

Our chores finally finished for the night, he slung his arm around my waist and asked with a grin, "What was that about being tough?" as he escorted me to our tent. I felt slightly defeated but was simultaneously reminded how incredibly lucky I was to have a hiking partner who balanced my weaknesses.

Our tent spot was flatter that night. Settling into the tent was becoming an increasingly treasured part of the trail routine—both for the opportunity to stretch out my aching body and for the chance to be physically close to Souleman. I ran my hands through his hair, which was growing shaggy already, as I waited impatiently for sleep.

Despite the hectic evening, we slept well and woke up early in a cloud of dense fog. Our tiny tent was wet with condensation. Although it was tempting to slink further into our sleeping bags and stay in bed, we had a deadline to meet. My aunt and uncle were meeting us at the top of Clingmans Dome at one o'clock, which meant we had to hike more than ten miles to the top of the tallest mountain on the Appalachian Trail within the next six hours.

The hike was foggy and misty and completely without views. Clingmans Dome was my first real experience with missing an incredible view on the trail. One of the disadvantages of thru-hiking is having to hike whatever comes next on the trail regardless of the conditions. Sometimes this means missing beautiful views due to hitting a particular point during bad weather. A day hiker, on the other hand, can simply pick a more appropriate day.

Because we feared being late, I pushed through the fog and moisture as quickly as I could, with Souleman on my heels. We didn't take any breaks and didn't slow down much on the steep sections. Much to our surprise, we reached the top of Clingmans Dome shortly after noon. We had arrived early. We plopped our packs on the ground, eager to remove them for the first time that day. Sitting on a stone wall at the base of the observation tower, we dug through our packs looking for long-sleeved shirts and rain jackets. Tourists milled around us, hoping for a break in the fog to see the view. Souleman and I watched the tourists as they rather indiscreetly stared at us. In a group of clean, nicely dressed vacationers, we stood out like proverbial sore thumbs.

A family of four stood off to one side talking in hushed tones. They looked up at us occasionally, and finally the father sauntered over and asked, "Are you hiking the Appalachian Trail?"

We nodded yes and he motioned to his family, who surrounded us like a flock of seagulls. As they asked us question after question, other people stepped slightly closer to eavesdrop. We answered inquiries about mileage, weather, gear, and other aspects of trail life. The father told us that his daughter and her husband were thru-hiking and wanted to know if we had met them.

"What are their names?" I asked.

"Karis and Brian."

Souleman and I exchanged looks.

"We wouldn't know them by those names. Hikers usually have a trail name in the woods. Do you know their trail names?" I questioned.

A look of confusion crossed his face.

I explained the concept of trail names and then added, "For example, I'm Brownie, and this is Souleman."

The dad just shook his head.

His wife jumped in then. "Karis is about five feet tall, brown hair, glasses. Brian is tall, curly hair. He has a mandolin with him."

Souleman and I both shrugged. We knew a number of couples, but none that fit that description.

"He's a musician and she's a nurse in the Navy," the mother continued.

"We don't really know what our trail friends do for a living," Souleman tried to explain.

The parents exchanged surprised glances, as did many of the eavesdroppers.

Souleman shrugged. "What you do in the 'real world' doesn't matter much in the woods."

People quit trying to disguise their curiosity at that point. We answered questions from numerous others and let the kids try to lift our packs. This was our first extended experience with thru-hiker intrigue, and it was flattering but also somewhat awkward.

The parents were disappointed that we didn't know their family members and very surprised by some of the nuances of trail life. Before they left, they gave us a handwritten note for Karis and Brian, which we assured them we would leave in the next trail register with a note explaining its origin.

Eventually, my Aunt Betsy and Uncle Steve arrived at the observation tower, and we strolled to the top hoping for a view. There was no view, but at least we could say we had climbed to the highest point on the Appalachian Trail.

Aunt Betsy and Uncle Steve drove Gypsy, Touk, Souleman, and me into Gatlinburg, Tennessee. After having spent the better part of a month in the woods and in small trail towns, the commercialism and tacky charm of Gatlinburg were shocking. Souleman and I promised that this was just a temporary stop for lunch and resupply, and that we were heading back into the woods that afternoon. But as we entered McDonald's for lunch, the rain started and never stopped.

A huge number of hikers joined us for lunch, including Gypsy, Touk, and Bassline. This was the first time our appetites had been positively insatiable. Souleman ate two double cheeseburgers, two McChickens, a large fry, a Big Mac, and a large milkshake. He even went back for an ice cream sundae. My aunt and uncle watched us eat in disbelief.

Gatlinburg became an inescapable vortex, luring all the hikers to hide out in the dry stores, hotels, and restaurants. Betsy and Steve shuttled us to a hotel, where they gave us a package from my mom. Inside, along with assorted treats, was my other, larger tent. Souleman had been unable to locate a replacement tent pole, and we had become rather attached to sleeping side by side. Now we could share a two-person tent and actually have enough space to put two Therm-a-Rests one beside the other.

At the grocery store, my Uncle Steve tried to help us resupply by suggesting nutritious options. As we piled squeeze cheese, fruit roll-ups, bagels, and king-sized Snickers bars into our grocery cart, Steve kept appearing with cashews, dried cranberries, and low-carb snacks. While we appreciated his efforts, we had pretty much settled into a food routine at that point and didn't want to mess with it. In retrospect, our food selections could have used some improvement. My body was probably forgetting that vegetables and fruits existed. Nonetheless, we bought our standard items, dashed through the downpour back to the car, and headed to the hotel.

After the day's busy events, we were more than ready for a nap. We said our goodbyes to my aunt and uncle and, without even showering, curled up on the hotel bed and slept for the rest of the afternoon. We woke up ravenously hungry and ordered pizza. Domino's "5-5-5" deal, where three pizzas cost just five dollars each, was a hiker's dream. After taking much-needed showers, we sat on the floor in a hotel room with other hikers and devoured two pizzas along with beer.

We met Jake, Trip, and Chuck that night—a crazy trio of guys, two of whom had escaped getting trail names. It was fascinating to be two hundred miles into this journey and still meeting new people all the time. The strategies of different hikers shocked me. Trip carried only the clothes on his back—literally. He didn't have a warmer shirt, extra socks, or rain gear. If he got wet, he walked himself dry. Meeting people with such vastly different approaches really proved to me that anyone who has the desire can hike the trail. It also reinforced the popular motto, "Hike your own hike," which in this case refers to bringing the necessary items for success. It doesn't matter whether one hiker's choices align with another's.

In the morning Souleman and I hitchhiked back to the trail using the hitchhiking bandana we had acquired at the Nantahala Outdoor Center. Since it was raining and we had to go all the way back up to the top of Clingmans Dome, we thought that finding a ride would be nearly impossible. A man stopped and said he could take us partway. His wife was attending a business conference in Gatlinburg, and he had tagged along for a vacation. We were all enjoying talking, and he ended up taking us all the way back to the trail. We offered him money as reimbursement for gas, but he firmly refused.

It was absolutely pouring and we got soaked just taking our packs out of the trunk. We waved hearty goodbyes and then ran for the cover of the trees. Luckily, we hadn't planned much mileage that day, so we would be able to dry out shortly. The relentless rain had turned the trail into a miniature river. Narrow gullies of water rushed down the trail, making it impossible to place our boots anywhere else. Under the water, hidden, jagged rocks that littered the ground tried ferociously to trip me with each laborious step.

As we trudged through the rain, Souleman asked, "When I talk to my mom in town, can I tell her that you're my girlfriend?"

"Am I?" A grin spread across my face.

"Will you be?"

"Definitely."

"The way I figure, we've been dating since Easter," he informed me before turning around in the downpour to kiss me. Our poles dug into each other's backs and rain dripped into our eyes as we stood in a muddy puddle in the middle of the trail, lip-locked. We let seconds turn into minutes before we pulled apart and continued up the trail.

Getting to know another person romantically while in the midst of such an intense physical and psychological endeavor was both thrilling and exhausting. As we ticked off the mileage each day, we had the opportunity to learn more and more about one another. We learned and explored, questioned and debated.

This was a very unnatural dating environment. Souleman and I were together twenty-four hours a day, seven days a week. If dating were a sport, this would qualify as extreme dating. We came to know each other very well, very quickly, and those who met us during our hike were often surprised to learn we had only just met on the trail.

Later that day we met two memorable hikers. The first was a weekend hiker named Tater. He was a previous thru-hiker who had met his wife on the trail. It seemed like we were meeting more and more hikers with similar stories. *Could we be so lucky?* The second notable hiker was a southbounder named Dude.

Dude had a giant, whitish beard, filthy clothes, and a threadbare pack. He was the first thru-hiking southbounder we had met. For many reasons, including snow, heat, the growing seasons for poisonous plants, and the hibernation seasons of snakes, most people choose to hike from south to north. Dude was very encouraging and told us that if we had made it this far and had hiked a fifteen-mile day, then *physically* we had what it would take to make it to Katahdin. After that, he said, it was just *mental*. He also told us that being a couple would be very beneficial emotionally.

That night, we settled into the shelter well past "hiker midnight," spooned against each other as much as two slippery nylon bags would allow, and were nearly asleep when we heard approaching voices. A man and his two young sons stomped into the shelter. They were loud and made us extremely jealous with their elaborate dinner of steak, potatoes, and other fancy treats. The youngest boy regaled us with ghost stories as the temperature dropped and the shelter became more and more frigid. I fell asleep with a smile, listening to yet another narrated ghost story by the enthusiastic young boy.

While the Smokies as a whole were a letdown, they did give us one enjoyable day. We hiked our longest mileage yet, but only if we counted the blue-blazed mileage to and from the shelters. Mileage on the trail is a funny thing. The

Handbook only describes the mileage on the official Appalachian Trail. These official, white-blazed trail miles are what hikers usually refer to when recounting daily
mileage. But in actuality, a hiker also hikes to and from shelters, to and from water,
and to and from privies every day. Many more miles are additionally accumulated in
towns. I often wondered what the total mileage for my Appalachian Trail trip would
be if I had included all of those added miles.

For the first time since entering the Smokies, I understood why they were called
the Smoky Mountains. Even on this clear day, the mountains had wisps of clouds
and fog swirling around their tops, like smoke from a chimney. When I told Souleman my observation, he just laughed at my statement of the obvious.

In addition to the smoke-topped mountains, we saw a two-headed bird that we
managed to capture on camera. The trail through the Smokies was not well maintained, so we spent much of our time climbing over fallen trees and negotiating our
way around trail debris. While navigating obstacles was fun, it slowed our pace considerably. We used the time to explore topics including homosexuality, faith, fate,
and predestination. The list of controversial subjects we had explored together was
growing daily. In between conversations and climbing mountains, we spent a lot of
time leaning against trees and rocks kissing.

Just as we approached the shelter that day, there was a torrential downpour. It
couldn't have lasted more than five minutes, but it was enough to completely soak
all of our belongings. Normally, I wasn't bothered by my snail-like pace, but when
sections of the trail were crowded, speed could mean the difference between securing shelter space and having to tent. With the amount of rain that had fallen recently,
we really weren't looking forward to tenting, even with our new, larger tent. Luckily, we were able to snag two of the last spots in the shelter, between Bassline and
Red Hat.

We tried to hang our gear and clothes to dry. With all the hiker gear hanging on
ropes, nails, mouse hangers, hiking poles, and every available knob, the shelter
looked like it had been decorated for Christmas by some overactive, eccentric elves.
It was a miracle that hikers rarely grabbed the wrong gear when repacking in the
half-light of the early morning hours.

The following day contained two important milestones: first, it was our last full
day in the Smokies, and more importantly, it was also the ten-percent mark. We had
completed ten percent of the Appalachian Trail—ten percent of the mileage between
Georgia and Maine. We cheered the accomplishment, though the joy was somewhat
tainted when I mentioned that this meant we had ninety percent left to go. Yikes! We
wondered aloud what it would be like to say we had ten percent left instead of ten
percent finished.

Surprisingly, our final day in the Smokies was a beautiful time of ridge walking. At one point I rounded a corner and was shocked to see a large, black animal
trotting down the trail toward me. Without yet having registered what I was seeing,
I flew backward into Souleman. Our poles tangled and we narrowly avoided collapsing in a pile. As the animal stopped abruptly, I looked up into the face of a

horse. The rider apologized, and we stepped aside to let four horses and their riders pass. Horses are not allowed on many sections of the Appalachian Trail, but this section in the Smokies was an exception.

When the horses passed and I had returned to breathing normally, I asked Souleman, "You wanna lead for a while?"

9

Tollbooth

Davenport Gap was just outside the northern boundary of Great Smoky Mountains National Park. We reached it eight miles into our next day. From there a road wound 1.3 miles down to Mountain Moma's (pronounced "Mama's") Kuntry Store and Bunkhouse. Entries from southbounders in the trail registers had raved about the enormous cheeseburgers at Mountain Moma's for days. Although we had not originally planned to stop there, our stomachs begged otherwise. Plus, after having endured the tortures of the park, I deserved a reward.

Not wanting to walk the extra mileage, we parked ourselves on the roadside waiting for a car. In the first half hour we didn't see a single vehicle. Just as we were considering giving up, a rusted pick-up rattled down the road toward us. We sprang to life and stuck out our thumbs. The driver ground to a noisy halt and motioned us into the truck bed. As if on cue, three other hikers came tumbling out of the woods just in time to clamber into the truck bed with us.

At Mountain Moma's, I slumped down in the booth waiting for my cheeseburger. Looking down, I realized how filthy my hands were. I very briefly considered going to the bathroom to wash my hands before eating. Then I rationalized that I had been eating with those same dirty hands every day on the trail and I was still alive. I remained in the booth relaxing until my mountainous cheeseburger was delivered to the table. The cheeseburgers were worthy of the lavish praise. They were smothered with lettuce, onions, and ketchup and served with a large pile of greasy fries.

After filling our bellies, we lazed on the front steps in the sun with our fellow hikers. We took turns on the pay phone and played with the resident cat. I got in touch with my parents, and during our conversation I told them of my developing relationship with Souleman. Ever the detectives, they weren't surprised. My mom reminded me that she had told me he was cute when she had first met him. My dad had observed that we had been getting closer and closer in the trail pictures I had been mailing home. It was a relief to tell my parents about the budding romance. I had started the Appalachian Trail hoping to discover myself. I hadn't even dreamed of finding someone to share myself with. But as the saying goes, sometimes you have to stop looking for something in order to find it.

In addition to my parents, I got through to Lark.

"Larkness!"

"Hey! Oh my gosh, how are you? *Where* are you? I can't believe we actually connected live."

"I know, right?" I caught her up on our location. Then I gushed about the trail. "It's just so great. The people are so nice, and every single day I see new things. The trees and mountains and even the little towns are all just amazing. You should come hike with me for a while."

"It does sound amazing. I'd love to come out for a while. I just don't think I have the gear. Plus, I wouldn't be able to get enough time off work."

"Well, could you maybe meet us in a town somewhere?"

Before hanging up, we made a tentative plan for a weekend visit in Hot Springs, North Carolina.

Many hikers succumbed to the temptation and spent the night at Mountain Moma's. We had given in to temptation in Gatlinburg and didn't want to set the precedent of staying in town every time we had the opportunity. If we continued in that manner, we would never make it to Maine. We got a ride back to the trail and continued a mile and a half further before setting up camp. Plenty of daylight remained, but our full stomachs rioted at the idea of further mileage.

Wolfhound shared a campsite with us at the fork of a river. He claimed one bank and we the other. To make up for the missed shower opportunity at Mountain Moma's, I rinsed my hair in the stream and hung our wet clothes on a tree like Christmas ornaments.

Around a campfire, Wolfhound told stories of his previous Appalachian Trail thru-hike, his Pacific Crest Trail thru-hike, and other escapades on the Lewis and Clark Trail. While he talked, Souleman brushed my hair with his fingers.

"You want me to braid it?" he asked.

"You can braid?" I raised my eyebrows curiously.

"Of course. I used to have long hair." He touched halfway down my back. "My hair was at least this long."

"Wow. Well, sure."

He wove my hair into a tight braid, and then I settled back against his chest and watched the sun set over a flowering tree, wondering if there was any other place in the world I'd rather be.

Wolfhound retired early, and Souleman and I lay on a Therm-a-Rest by the fire. He ran his fingers across my face and neck as we stared into the flames and talked about the past and the future. He leaned in close and said he had something to tell me. I looked up expectantly in the flickering firelight, but he didn't speak. He slid his hand under the edge of my shirt, and with his fingertip, traced letters on my stomach while I held my breath.

"Do you know what I wrote?" he asked.

I nodded silently. Three words. Three short words. Three powerful words.

This time he spoke the words aloud. "I love you."

I was surprised. *Does he really love me? Already? Do I love him?* Too scared to respond, my hand found his, and I tilted my head up and kissed him. I couldn't imagine finding someone I would be happier with. Although we were complete opposites in so many ways, our differences worked well together. My constant need for organization and planning, together with his laid-back approach, meant that our hike was well organized without being obsessively planned. His drive to hike fast and my desire to go slow meant that we hiked at a pleasant, moderate pace that allowed us to make progress while still seeing as much as possible along the way. I imagined that our differing perspectives would balance us out in the "real world" just as they did on the trail.

Souleman often told me how much he cared about me, and I didn't think I'd ever cared as much about anyone else. But I didn't want to reciprocate with those all-important words until I was sure—completely sure.

I awoke early, still thinking about the previous night. The happy and nerve-wracking thoughts carried me quickly through the day. The terrain was mild, and although my body felt tired, my mind was hyperactive. The day was not as carefree for Souleman. His tooth had been bothering him for a few days, and the ache had now become unbearable. Though he had been taking Ibuprofen regularly, it was no longer alleviating the pain. He was going to have to find a way to get to a dentist in Hot Springs.

We took a brief break in the middle of the day at Standing Bear Hostel. We didn't stay long, but we ran into Bassline and the Gypsy sisters, along with Sunshine, another female hiker, who was now hiking with them. They were all staying a second night at the hostel. The girls entertained everyone there with their angelic voices and any instruments they could get their hands on. They were singing "The Boxer" as we left, and I had Simon and Garfunkel floating through my head for days afterward.

Souleman's toothache came and went throughout the day. He complained very little, but he barely spoke. I knew he was in serious pain when he wouldn't eat dinner. He sat on a rock with his head between his knees, silent tears rolling down his cheeks. He wanted to be alone, so although I checked on him often, I spent the evening around a campfire with V3, Toolman, and No Worries. Since I'm normally a night owl, it was nice to be around hikers who stay up a little past dark. While we were talking, a mutant, baseball-sized bug leapt toward us. The guys jumped up and beat it into oblivion with sticks and a hiking pole. I laughed at the spectacle but felt sorry for the poor bug, who probably only wanted to dry his wings by the fire.

Luckily, Souleman's discomfort disappeared overnight and we were able to get in another day of cold, rainy hiking. Even though the weather was less than agreeable, the terrain was flat and I felt motivated. We made it to Walnut Mountain Shelter and squeezed in with all the other hikers. When it's raining or snowing, an unspoken rule among hikers dictates that room should always be made in a shelter. Everyone adhered to the custom that night, and we packed an unseemly number of people into a too-small shelter.

Sometimes quarters were so tight that everyone had to sleep on one side in order to fit. Turning over in these packed shelters could be a challenge. Although I was squished, I snuggled under Souleman's arm and quickly fell asleep. I woke often, needing to turn over and having to carefully maneuver so that I wouldn't wake those on either side of me. Even though I didn't sleep well, I remained excited because the next day we were going into Hot Springs, North Carolina, and I would get to see my Lark.

In the morning I literally ran part of the way to Hot Springs. I had to call Lark by a certain time to tell her where to meet me, and we were cutting it close. Souleman and I jogged the last 3.2 miles in an hour to make it to a pay phone on time. I was able to contact her by phone as scheduled, and only hours later she arrived in Hot Springs.

We stayed in a treehouse-style cabin by the river with V3, Toolman1, and Souleman. We all ate dinner at a local pub where we regaled her with stories about trail life. She enjoyed meeting Souleman, whom she had heard about during our phone calls, and being introduced to other trail friends. I relished hearing her updates on life at Furman and the adventures of our mutual friends, though I felt so removed from typical college experiences like lectures, final exams, and job applications.

I was sad to see Lark leave the next morning, but she had to get back to school to finish her final semester. She was excited to have gotten a glimpse into thru-hiker life and expressed a desire to join me further up the trail if possible.

After waving final goodbyes, Souleman and I moved our belongings to the Duckett Inn up the street and took a long and much-needed nap. Our room featured a king-sized bed, and we were able to sprawl across the bed to stretch our aching muscles. The soft, cotton sheets were a welcome change from my nylon sleeping bag.

After resting, we took care of our town chores, including collecting our mail-drop package. My mom, the divine goddess of packages, had sent a card with money for us to enjoy the famous hot springs in town. This was a special treat because we might not have sprung for this luxury on our own. We made an appointment and hurried through the rest of our chores. During the obligatory trip to the outfitter, I bought a wrap skirt to wear while doing laundry in towns, and we checked email for the first time in weeks. Finally, hand in hand, we walked down the road to the hot springs.

When I thought of a hot spring, I had visualized a giant rock with an upside-down, cave-type hole filled with nearly boiling water. Wrong, wrong, and wrong. Instead, regular hot tubs sat positioned on wooden platforms that bordered the river. Each platform rested on a mound of dirt and was surrounded by a privacy fence. The hot water was piped in from the spring.

Even though this was not the natural water-filled hole I had pictured, the hot water relaxed our abused muscles, and every impurity released from my body. I hated to imagine the quantity of sweat and dirt that escaped from my pores into that water and was thankful that the employees changed the water and cleaned out the tub after each set of customers. I had expected to smell more normal after getting out. Shockingly, I could still get a whiff of my hiker funk, though it had been slightly lessened by two showers and one soak in the hot spring.

For dinner we returned to the pub, the only restaurant in town, which was completely packed with hikers. More than thirty thru-hikers were seated at a long table down the middle of the restaurant. We squeezed in near KTR and Domino. Looking around the table, I was surprised at the number of unfamiliar faces. Hikers are a welcoming bunch, though, and we immediately connected like old friends as we traded trail stories.

Souleman decided to hang out at the Cody House Hostel that night while I went back to the inn to catch up on my journal writing. He asked if I would be ok walking back by myself. Since I had not yet been scared in the woods on this trip, I figured I would be fine walking the short distance through town. Hot Springs is a very small town with few amenities, and the entire town is compacted onto one quaint street. This is convenient for hikers, though I would imagine it to be claustrophobic for residents. I had to walk to the end of town to reach the Duckett Inn, but I figured this was nothing compared to the hours I'd spent on the trail alone.

As I was walking down a hedge-lined sidewalk in the middle of town, anticipating sliding between clean sheets shortly, I heard rustling in the bushes and my heartbeat quickened. I stopped walking and strained my ears. Again, I heard the rustling nearby. Instinctively, I reached up to switch on my headlamp. My hand brushed over my bare forehead a couple of times before I realized that I wasn't wearing it. A dog barked nearby, and I took off running. I ran the rest of the way to the inn and was out of breath when I let myself inside. I leaned against the closed door to catch my breath before making my way up the stairs. I was ashamed of my cowardice. *I just ran from a dog. Am I not the same girl who sleeps in the woods? The same girl who started the Appalachian Trail alone? Wimp.*

I sprawled across the king-sized bed with my journal. Just as I finished penning the last sentence, Souleman returned. We lazily discussed the next day's plan. I knew that before I left I needed to take advantage of the inn's amazing shower. Even though I was already clean from the hot spring, I headed down to the communal bathroom, tugging Souleman behind me.

The inn had a large bathroom with stained glass windows and a porcelain sink. It also housed a claw-foot tub and a separate shower with two massive showerheads. One showerhead was high-powered and streamed down from overhead like rain.

"Shower? Or bath?" I asked, holding my hand out like Vanna White to illustrate our options.

"Shower," he said, turning on both showerheads.

Souleman had only ever seen my bare skin in the darkness of a tent. Shyly, I turned my back and pulled off my clothes with record-breaking speed. I didn't look back to see if he was watching before I dashed under the water.

Stepping under the dual shower heads was like entering a carwash for humans. The harsh stream of water felt so incredible on my sore muscles that I almost forgot I wasn't alone. Souleman's arms snaked around my waist as he joined me in the shower, and we stood together letting the water pound the remaining soreness from our shoulders and backs.

Cleansed and recovered, we fell asleep almost instantly in the fantastically large and luxurious bed.

Breakfast the next morning was award worthy. The owner, who doubled as the chef, had created a breakfast masterpiece for his guests. Domino had also spent the night, and we joined him at the breakfast table.

Halfway through the meal, out of the blue, he asked, "Have you planned your honeymoon yet?"

I blushed and hid my face by intently studying my plate as I cut my pancakes. My mind flashed back to our shared shower the night before, and as I wondered if he knew, my cheeks turned even redder.

Domino elbowed me. "Brownie, I'm just kidding. You two just look so happy." Domino got a lot of mileage out of teasing me all the way up the trail.

The large breakfast, the zero day, and the cleansing of the hot spring had filled Souleman and me with energy. We returned to the trail with enthusiasm. As we neared the top of a peak that morning, we heard another hiker scream one long, drawn-out word.

"Siiiiiilence!"

Souleman and I exchanged perplexed looks and pushed harder to the summit in case someone needed help.

"Siiiiiilence!" it echoed again.

When we arrived at the top, KTR was standing on a tall rock looking out over the surrounding peaks.

I gave him a hug and asked, "KTR, are you ok? We heard yelling."

He laughed. "I yell my brother's name off of every peak."

"Ohhhhh. You were yelling 'Solace?'"

"Yep."

"Why?" Souleman asked the obvious question.

"So that he's here with me to share the joy on every mountain top even when we aren't hiking together. We started this trail together, and even though we can't always be out here together, I want to share the hike with him."

"That's really cool. Hey, did he connect with you a few weeks ago?" I asked. "We met Solace when he was hiking in to surprise you. We were so confused. We knew you had a brother, but not a *twin* brother. He was great—just like you."

"He did find me." replied KTR. "We hiked together for three days. He really liked both of you and said he had a great time."

The three of us spent the afternoon hiking together, and on every peak Souleman and I joined KTR in screaming "Solace!" into the wind. Later in our hike, and even on occasion after finishing the Appalachian Trail, Souleman and I would remember KTR by screaming his name off random mountaintops.

KTR had many stories of his previous hikes and big dreams for making it further up the Appalachian Trail this time. On one ridgeline, KTR positioned himself sideways across the trail. Looking up with a grin, he declared, "I have one butt cheek in North Carolina and one butt cheek in Tennessee."

The frequent laughter and companionship helped ease the distance. Eleven miles later, we found ourselves in a shelter with other friends. As we were preparing dinner, KTR pulled a six-pack of beer out of his pack. Souleman's eyes nearly exploded out of his head with awe. KTR just winked and said, "It's our one-month trail anniversary. How else did you think we were going to celebrate?" *It's only been a month? It seems like I've been out here a year. A lifetime.* KTR chilled the beer in the nearby stream and later shared with each hiker there who was celebrating a trail anniversary.

As KTR handed me my beer, I gave him a hug and thanked him for being so thoughtful. When he pulled away, I asked, "KTR, how do you always smell so good?"

"It's my deodorant."

"You wear deodorant on the trail? I thought everyone stopped wearing deodorant a few days in when the hiker funk took over."

"Of course I wear deodorant." He looked indignant. "You never know when you might run into Claire Danes."

We enjoyed our beers and celebrated one month and almost three hundred miles of hiking. According to Wingfoot's writings in the Handbook, this meant we were nearing top thru-hiking shape. Page ninety-nine states, "Studies of Olympic track and field teams have shown that it takes about six to eight weeks for a male athlete doing strenuous, all-day exercise to reach peak performance, and usually a week longer for females." *I'm well on my way to becoming a thru-hiker.* While I wasn't quite ready to join an Olympic team, I was infinitely more resilient than I had been at the beginning of the journey. My pace, though still unhurried, had increased, and my stamina was more substantial.

Every day I inched a few miles closer to Katahdin. People were dropping off the trail all around me, but my spirits and body were still strong. Two days after our one-month trail anniversary, Souleman and I hiked our longest day yet at 17.2 miles. This feat seemed fantastically easier than our first fifteen-mile day that had nearly killed me back in Georgia.

Throughout this long-mileage day, we leap-frogged back and forth with Montreal and Kutza. We would pass them sitting on the trailside, enjoying a snack. Then, a few hours later, they would pass us taking a break. At one point I rounded a curve in the trail to find Montreal sitting in the shade on a fallen tree. He had one foot propped up on his other knee and was humming quietly. I stopped in front of Montreal, and Souleman came to a stop beside me.

"What's up, Montreal?" Souleman questioned.

"I'm waiting on the woman of my life," he said in his crisp accent, with a nod back down the trail.

We stood and chatted with Montreal and learned more about his relationship with Kutza. He was a movie producer from Canada, and Kutza was from Israel. They had met on the Appalachian Trail a few years ago and were out again that year to do a complete thru-hike together. They had dreams of producing a movie about the Appalachian Trail in the future. After learning about their history, Montreal asked about ours and was shocked to learn we had just met on the trail a month ago. He winked and told us that we could end up like them.

Montreal wasn't the only person who had mentioned marriage lately. It seemed we were running into more and more married couples who had met on the trail: Jake Brake and Low Gear, Spike and Hopper, Montreal and Kutza. These encounters spurred numerous conversations between Souleman and me about marriage itself as well as our individual beliefs about marriage.

Both Souleman and I had parents who were still married. We considered them to be exemplary models of faithfulness and commitment and hoped to have our lives turn out the same way. We both believed in sharing everything in a marriage, from the fun things like dreams and goals to the tough stuff like bank accounts and bills. We found that we both had strong opinions about the lifelong commitment of marriage. I couldn't believe we were having conversations about marriage after having known one another for only a month, but then again, nothing about this trip seemed normal.

The next day, for the first time, I had a complete lack of motivation to hike. We stayed in our tent until nine in the morning, which was unprecedented. Then, even once we had started hiking, we stopped often at my request and spent much of the day lazing by the side of the trail. When we did hike, we kept stopping to create "tollbooths" along the way. Tollbooths were my excuse for getting random kisses throughout the day. I would stop unexpectedly in the middle of the trail and spread my arms out wide to block the path.

"Tollbooth."

Invariably, Souleman would tell me, "I have no money."

"You can pay in kisses."

He would lean in and kiss me. "Is that enough?"

Usually it wasn't, and very seriously I'd tell him, "You have to pay more. You can't pass until you pay the full amount."

Tollbooths were initially my idea, but both of us were soon exploiting the concept. After a late start, a number of tollbooths along the trail, and countless uncalled-for breaks, attempting to go into town for hamburgers became a way to further procrastinate hiking and fill our aching bellies. We sat on the curb laughing, talking, and sneaking kisses as we listened attentively for engine noises—our cue to jump up and stick out our thumbs. That idea was squelched when after an hour no cars had passed in the right direction. We shouldered our packs and pushed on up a small hill. Though we had just taken a break, I immediately started looking for an inviting spot to stop for lunch.

Half a mile up the trail, we stopped underneath a huge tree. Souleman reclined with his pack propped against the massive trunk. He pulled me back against him, and we lay in the sunshine eating lunch. We fed each other crackers and cheese with dirt-covered hands and kissed between bites. The conversation turned to how unusual a dating experience this was, and we wondered about the implications of spending so much time together so quickly.

We took out a piece of paper and did some estimates. We guessed that the average dating couple spends roughly ten hours a week together. Multiplying that by fifty-two weeks in a year results in approximately 520 hours per year of time spent together. On the other hand, multiplying the fifteen waking hours per day we had been spending together on the trail by seven days in a week gives 105 hours together each week. We had been hiking for five weeks, which meant that we had spent 525 waking hours together so far. This meant that we had spent the equivalent amount of time together of one year of "normal" dating in only slightly more than a month on the trail. If we finished the trail in six months, our time spent together would be comparable to almost six years of civilized dating.

Souleman ran his hand across the pink bandana tied atop my head as we wondered what it would be like to summit Katahdin. Would it be sunny or cloudy? Cold or hot? Would we cheer or cry? What would happen to our relationship then? As we pondered the future, both of the trail and of our relationship, he told me he would propose right then if he could. My friend Nicole once told me that when you meet the person you're supposed to marry, something inside you just clicks and you know. She said you're absolutely certain that it's right. *How do you know? When do you know? Right away? When he actually proposes? If I don't know right now, is that my answer?*

The talk of the future, and more specifically of Katahdin, finally got us motivated to hike. We certainly weren't going to make it to Maine by sitting around. Although it was already mid-afternoon, we pushed on eight more miles to Bald Mountain Shelter. The productivity of the late afternoon made up for the extreme laziness of the morning.

Just before the shelter, we saw a spectacular golden sunset on Big Bald. A bald is a mountaintop without trees, and the views extend forever since they aren't obstructed. We would have erected the Blue Mansion, our affectionate nickname for my giant blue tent, right on top of Big Bald if we had had enough water to make it through the night. Unfortunately, our nearly depleted water supply required us to push on. Although I hated to leave the attractive camping spot, I was more than happy to reduce the next day's mileage. I made a mental note to return to that spot in the future with enough water to sleep right on the bald.

Bassline, from our original Beware the Ides of March group, was at the shelter that night. The three of us reconnected while Souleman and I cooked and settled in to the shelter. Some southbound section hikers were staying in the shelter and had numerous questions about locations we had passed earlier in the trail. We talked about mileage, difficulty, and gear until late that night. It was after ten thirty when I turned off my headlamp for good. By hiker standards, it was probably equivalent to going to bed at three in the morning. I knew the following morning would be rough.

I do not function well without sleep. Being tired is challenging enough in real life, but on the trail it is insufferable. I lose the ability to estimate mileage, so a day seems interminable. *Have I hiked three miles or thirteen?* My pack feels like it's packed with enough bricks to pave a driveway. A task as simple as purifying water can become a monumental effort that brings on tears. Even activities that I normally enjoy, like writing in my journal, become excruciating without sleep. Figuring out upcoming mileage or resupply needs can seem like abstract mathematics.

Not only does a lack of sleep make day-to-day activities more challenging, it also means that as the day progresses I have less and less ability to control my mood. True to form, I became increasingly grumpy as the next day progressed. My feet had developed red spots underneath each toe that were painful and swollen. There was foul-smelling slime on top of the sore spots and a gooey layer under my toes. Plus my head was feeling woozy. I think all the junk food may have finally been getting to me. Apparently, my body really *does* require protein and vegetables.

After a few hours of feeling sorry for myself, I realized that I needed an attitude adjustment. I took a deep breath of fresh mountain air and soaked in my surroundings—the big round knot on the nearby cedar tree, the grass just poking through the dirt, the mountains looming in the distance. Having the opportunity to hike the Appalachian Trail was a gift, and I vowed to recognize my blessings and be more positive.

Bassline walked with us and talked about his inability to make a decision about his future. At nineteen, he had ample time for new experiences but lacked direction. He was waiting for God's indication of his path, which hadn't yet been made clear. He knew he wasn't ready to find one person to spend his life with and expressed awe at the fact that a close friend of his was getting married. Souleman said that at twenty-four, he was completely ready for a serious relationship and marriage. He tried to express the satisfaction in having had a number of adventures and now being ready to get married and start a family. I hoped that the conversation had been beneficial to Bassline. I knew that it had *certainly* been informative for me.

Every fiber of my being had always known I wanted marriage and children. Back in kindergarten, the what-do-you-want-to-be-when-you-grow-up board in my classroom said "Mom" underneath my name. While I had worked hard in school and in every activity I had pursued, I knew that deep down my deepest desire was to be a wife and mom. Although I really liked Souleman, I was hesitant to trust myself in making a love-life decision with life-long implications—particularly so soon.

In college I had been engaged to a great man. We dated for over two years—years filled with trips to the beach, fraternity activities, study sessions, tennis matches, shared classes, and time spent with our families—and then he had proposed on a cold winter day on the lawn overlooking the Biltmore house in North Carolina. While I did love him, I began to realize that we fought too much and that it was not what I wanted for the rest of my life. In some ways we were just too much alike.

Months after he had given me a ring, I finally admitted to myself that I simply couldn't marry him. In a teary, late-afternoon conversation in my apartment, I explained my feelings and returned his ring. It had taken almost three years for me to realize that we weren't compatible long-term.

After my dream of marrying straight out of college had disappeared, I had focused on hiking the Appalachian Trail. I had imagined all kinds of experiences on the trail, but a romantic relationship wasn't one of them. Now that I found myself falling in love, I was worried about the implications. *What if I make another mistake? I want marriage, but I want the* right *marriage. How will I know?*

The unexpected relationship was not the only way the trail had surprised me. So far it had been a balanced mixture of exactly what I thought it would be and the complete opposite. I had been hoping for meaningful relationships, deep conversations, and a better understanding of my body, my thoughts, and my place in the world. And all of that had happened. But I had also thought I would see a lot of animals and that my body would get used to hiking. On the contrary, my body still hurt, and the only animal sighting of late had been a snail.

To take my focus off of the challenging inclines, Souleman started up a game of Twenty Questions. We also made up songs about the trail, played the alphabet game, and vocalized our most powerful food cravings in exquisite detail. One of our favorite games became pretending to spar with our Leki hiking poles during breaks.

I was really enjoying hiking with a partner and found that sharing the experiences of the trail made them seem more concrete and powerful. I had trouble explaining to friends and family the significance of events on the trail, but Souleman always implicitly understood because he had been right there for every single step. Our trail experiences were so intertwined that we couldn't separate them. We knew how many times each of us sneezed. We knew when the other person used the bathroom. We suffered the same insatiable appetite, the same intolerable heat, and the same mind-numbing cold. We shared equipment failures, clothing mishaps, and interactions with other hikers. Every single mountain summit, sunrise, sunset, animal sighting, and delicious cheeseburger was enjoyed side by side. No matter how carefully I described these events, only Souleman would ever be able to completely understand our hike.

In addition to our tollbooths, we had started a silly tradition of tapping our Leki poles against one another. This had begun one day when we were hiking with other people. Souleman had tapped my pole to get my attention, and when I had turned around he had mouthed, "I love you." Tapping our Lekis became our secret communication of affection when we were around others.

10

I . . . Can't . . . Do . . . This

For days, all I could think about was gorging on greasy McDonald's food. My stomach was loudly demanding a higher caloric intake, and my mind was chronically occupied by thoughts of food. I dreamed about McGriddles at night and marched to the cadence of "cheese-burger, cheese-burger, cheese-burger" each day.

One night, overtaken by the longing to eat breakfast food, I brazenly suggested heading into Erwin, Tennessee, the next morning in time to eat at McDonald's during breakfast hours. Souleman immediately agreed and we broached the idea with our fellow shelter-mates. Jake was immediately on board and so was KTR. Jax was in the shelter with us that night, too, and he was definitely up for the McDonald's challenge. Within a few minutes, the entire shelter was in agreement on waking before the sun in hopes of arriving in Erwin in time for a gluttonous, satisfying breakfast.

We emerged from the warm confines of our sleeping bags at four in the morning and stumbled onto the trail by four thirty. We had already hiked two miles when a pale pink light spread across the lowest edge of the horizon, creating a daring contrast with the thick blackness of night. I paused beside Souleman for a few minutes to watch. As I leaned on my poles with my shoulder pressed against his, the pink color was followed by salmon and then raspberry. Soon a muted sherbet orange, a crisp burnt sienna, and a vibrant red eased their way onto the palette. I was watching the colors so intently that I was surprised to realize that the black night sky had completely disappeared and the sky above me was now a pale blue.

"I don't even think there are names for all of those colors," I whispered, breaking the trance.

He nodded solemnly.

"It's amazing." I leaned my head on his shoulder.

He kissed the top of my head. After a few seconds of silence staring at the fading colors he said, "We better get moving."

"True." I started back up the trail. "Because you know what else is going to be amazing?" I asked over my shoulder.

"What's that?"

"McDonald's."

I practically flew up and down the hills, clicking off the miles. Soon, from the clearings in foliage, we could see a town through the trees to our left. That was the last push I needed. I took off at lightning speed, careening down the mountain with the force of gravity. My Pop-Tarts were long gone, and I was intent on making it to McDonald's in time for a second breakfast.

Briefly I feared we might not make it in time because we struggled to get a hitch. But we persisted, and our hitchhiking bandana saved the day yet again. We were in town before nine o'clock. I stood in line at McDonald's feeling like Pavlov's dog, salivating at the mere suggestion of food. I ordered a ridiculous quantity of breakfast items and joined my fellow hikers in the booths.

I ate that first McGriddle without even chewing. I just swallowed bite after satisfying bite. Grease ran down my chin and coated my dirty fingers. I grinned at the indulgent joy of this meal even as I sensed my arteries screaming in revulsion. My stomach begged for more and I readily complied, picking up the second McGriddle and eating with vigor. It disappeared almost as quickly as the first. I wiped my greasy fingers on my hiking pants and grabbed my third sandwich.

Two bites into the third sandwich, something inconceivable happened. I simply could not swallow another bite. The hikers around me were still gorging themselves. *What kind of thru-hiker am I? I can only eat two sandwiches?* Souleman was already on his fourth menu item. I stared at my sandwich feeling disappointed in myself. *Normally I would never even consider eating this amount of fast food. Why in the world do I feel embarrassed?* Someone else observed my dilemma and offered to "dispose of" the sandwich. I hesitantly, but gratefully, passed it on.

We passed around a newspaper with the idea of updating ourselves on the events of the world. We realized that the depressing content of the paper—house fires, the war in Iraq, and stock market updates—was too much for isolated hikers. Souleman scanned the sports page in search of Red Sox news before discarding the paper in disgust.

Leaving McDonald's, Souleman, Jax, and I stopped in a gas station to stock up on snacks for the rest of the day. In spite of my disillusionment at not being able to finish a third breakfast sandwich, I hoarded snacks for the afternoon as though food was going out of supply. While I waited my turn in line, a flash of color caught my eye from among the touristy roadside displays. A pair of Pepto-Bismol-pink sunglasses was beckoning me. I decided that I *had* to have them. I handed over the money and proudly wore them as I walked along the paved road toward Miss Janet's Hostel, our home for the evening. These unforgettable sunglasses became a mainstay of my hiking attire.

During our stay at Miss Janet's, we explored Erwin, Tennessee, and had the opportunity to meet one of its unique residents. While returning from the bank, we ran into an elderly gentleman who was perched precariously on a bicycle. We watched his wobbly approach and were debating bailing from the sidewalk when he abruptly stopped pedaling. He leaned near us conspiratorially and asked, "You'uns hikers?"

We nodded. *Aren't our packs the first clue?*

"Joker, that's what they—the hikers—call me," he told us, pointing his finger in the direction of Miss Janet's. He proudly regaled us with an explanation of his senior citizen's bike-of-the-future. It was complete with a rear-view mirror, horn, flag pole, and front and rear supply baskets. Joker pointed out each attribute and rambled on semi-coherently about free apples at the food shelf, Miss Janet's good breakfasts, his son, and other equally random topics. He lacked any ability to segue between topics and showed no signs of halting his verbal attack. We made polite excuses and continued on, never expecting to meet Joker again.

Many hikers enjoy hostels, but I found them to be suffocating. Staying in shelters on the trail was as much group sleeping as I could handle. In town, I wanted the ability to control my environment—temperature, lighting, noise level. However, hostels are considerably less expensive than hotels in most cases, and sometimes they're the only option. In this instance, we had decided to stay in the hostel to capitalize on bonding time with our fellow hikers. As expected, the noise level in the hostel was high late into the night, and I went to sleep many hours after I had hoped.

Following the restless night, we left Erwin and enjoyed the flat mileage to Curley Maple Gap Shelter. There we encountered Joker, the elderly trail enthusiast we had met in town. Joker had brought a bunch of apples in a satchel and immediately offered us one.

"Take a' apple. Come on, take one."

"No, thanks. I'm full," I smiled at him.

"From the senior center. Have a' apple," he insisted, waving the open bag at me.

I took an apple and gestured for Souleman to take one too. "Joker, what are you doing out here?" I asked, concerned about his safety alone in the woods.

"Jus' walkin'. I brings these apples fer th' hikers." He shuffled his feet in the dirt.

"Are you out here all alone?"

He ran his hand across his stubble-covered face, then stuffed it in his pocket. "Yep."

"How far are you going to hike?" I was worried he would get lost.

"'Til I get tired, I reck'n."

I exchanged a glance with Souleman. "Do you know where you are?"

"I'm right here!" Joker grinned lopsidedly at me.

Can he make it back to town? I wondered. "Joker, how will you get back to Miss Janet's?"

He proudly pulled a rumpled piece of construction paper from his pocket. Crayon handwriting said "TRAIL PLEASE" in blue on one side and "TOWN PLEASE" in red on the other.

"Miz Janet?" He looked at me for recognition. "She gived me this. I jus' show it ta the person drivin', 'n I get back. The red side?" He pointed. "Red gets ta town. The blue side?" He pointed at his paper again. "Blue gets me here so's I can brought my apples from th' senior center."

The paper was well-worn, so we assumed he was accustomed to this method of travel. Uncertain of Joker's fate, Souleman and I waved goodbye and watched him walk awkwardly down the trail, tripping once or twice before he was out of sight. He was clutching his satchel of apples and mumbling under his breath.

We hiked along chatting, wondering about Joker's safety. Within a mile, I stopped abruptly. In front of me was a black rat snake sunning on the trail. We watched him for a minute and then threw a rock to startle him off the trail. He slithered up a nearby tree and wound around the branches. I made an arrow out of rocks so that Marshmallow and Colorado, two hikers we had met in Erwin who were just behind us, would see. Then we safely passed our first slithery creature. Prior to my hike everyone had asked me how I would handle snakes and bears, yet this harmless creature was the first snake I had encountered.

In the shelter that night we cooked macaroni and cheese, our favorite trail meal, and sat around the picnic table with Marshmallow and Colorado. After a dinner of sticky, overcooked pasta, I looked into the bottom of the pot and saw a charred, black mess. Some of the noodles had burned onto the titanium pot. I decided to do something unusual and wash the pot in the stream. I had long since given up washing my cook pot in any fashion. First, I had given up soap and used only leaves or sand to scrub out excess food. Then, I decided that even *that* was unnecessary because the boiling water would kill any bacteria the following night. This time, I made an exception because I didn't want to taste burned noodles all week. I headed for the water source with my pot in hand.

I took my time at the stream. First, I cleaned the burned mess out of the pot, and then I filled our water containers with crisp, cool water. I still couldn't get over how much better mountain water tasted than tap water. Before I went back up to the shelter, I spent a couple of minutes playing in the refreshing water. I splashed my face and arms to rinse off the layers of salt, and noticed how dark my arms had become. *Is that dirt or a tan?* I unwound my pigtails and ran my wet fingers through my tangled hair before neatly rebraiding them. Even that minor attempt at hygiene was rejuvenating.

When I returned to the picnic table, Souleman was dealing cards for a Spades game with Colorado and Marshmallow. The sound of raindrops on the tin roof halted the Spades game after a few rounds and we dashed for our tents. Although there was space in the shelter that night, we wanted to sleep in our "new" blue tent.

The blue walls of the two-person tent seemed positively cavernous in comparison to the confines of the one-man tent we had co-inhabited for so long. Our Therm-a-Rests fit comfortably side by side. We performed the ritual of getting them as close as possible. I pulled out my journal and found out that Souleman had written a guest entry while I had been down at the water source. His sweet words were a welcome addition to my accounts of our trip thus far.

Guest Entry # 1

It's been a wonderful trip up to this point. I really like this girl, and I think she likes me. She is the most wonderful girl in the world, but she knows it. I'm watching her clean her pot, but she doesn't know it, and she is very cute. I can't wait to show her how much I love her someday! Erwin (TN) was great, but Hot Springs (NC) was better! Can't wait to have another day of hiking with her tomorrow. Rain or shine, it will be nice to be making miles again back on the AT. 'Til next time, love ya!

You-Know-Who

I kissed him to thank him for the message, and then we lay side by side with our fingers interlaced and listened to the rain bouncing off the blue nylon walls. Taking the pressure off my aching legs was such a relief. The temperatures dropped, and we scooted our sleeping bags closer so that we could share body heat. We whispered about the future and kissed as the lightning crashed down all around us, adding eerie ambient lighting to our tent. Overhead, thunder boomed.

When I woke up and stretched my painfully complaining muscles, Souleman was already sitting up beside me. The mere ability to sit was a novelty after having endured the cramped quarters in the one-man tent we had shared. This alone made the extra weight of the new tent worth it. As I blinked myself awake and rubbed his lower back lazily, I realized that it was raining heavily. Very little daylight filtered through our nylon roof, and the darkness gave no hope that the weather would change soon. Wordlessly, we knelt and packed as much of our gear as possible without leaving the dry inside of the tent. Finally, we had even rolled our Therm-a-Rests from underneath us, and we had no choice but to get out.

It was a race against the clock to dismantle the tent and stuff it into the groaning stuff sack before our packs got soaked. Wet tents and tent footprints are impossibly heavy and difficult to maneuver. Within seconds, our hands were covered in mud and our rain clothes were already drenched. Souleman shoved the heavy mass into his pack and awkwardly wrapped his pack cover around the whole giant, soggy mess. He had a hate-hate relationship with his pack cover on even the mildest of rainy days.

It rained and rained, and when we thought it couldn't possibly get any wetter, it started pouring. I had never been so thoroughly waterlogged. My rain clothes kept the rain off of me, but the fabric became saturated and confining. Inside the non-breathable, restrictive barriers, my body heat was trapped, causing me to sweat profusely. Even under the protection of the trees, the cold rain blew into our faces as we trudged up mountain after slippery mountain. With rain assaulting the nylon bubbles of our rain hoods, we couldn't hear each other talking, so we hiked in unusual silence.

We reached the top of a bald mountain just as the storm intensified even further. Wind was whipping water at us so forcefully that my cheeks stung with the attack of each droplet. Lightning crashed down all around us, so close at times that I cringed involuntarily. The bald in front of us offered no protection, but we certainly couldn't stand still and wait out the storm.

"We'll have to run for it!" Souleman yelled at me over the rain and wind.

I eyed the long expanse of the bald in front of us, looked up at the sky, and finally looked at him like he was crazy.

"On three!" Souleman screamed. "One–"

"We're holding metal poles," I interrupted, yelling frantically over the noise of the storm.

"We're wearing metal framed packs, too," he called back. But we both knew that in order to get out of the storm, we would have to make it to the next shelter, which meant going over the bald. We hid under the marginal shelter of tree limbs for a few minutes before mustering up enough courage. Souleman clicked his hiking pole against mine and caught my eye.

"One . . ." he started again as he took my hand.

I nodded.

"Two . . ."

A lightning bolt hit the ground in front of us on the bald.

"Three!"

Holding hands tightly, we ran across that fog-shrouded bald like we were being chased. Bright lightning crashed down on the ground all around, illuminating the path. I looked heavenward. *It's not my time to die.* A bolt struck too close for comfort, and I dropped Souleman's hand and started to cry in fear. *Don't let me die. Please don't let me die.* My tears blurred my vision even further and slowed my pace.

"Hurry! Come on! You can do this!" Souleman waited for me to catch up, and beckoned me across the bald.

We made it to the trees on the other side, and I sunk into a brooding silence. I was cold and wet and mentally exhausted. Even my spirit was waterlogged, and I might have let it ruin the entire day if it weren't for Souleman's unending encouragement. The rain let up just enough that we could hear each other over the slurping of our boots in the mud and the drumming of the rain all around us. In an effort to preserve the day, we started a happy conversation about holidays.

"What's your favorite holiday?" I asked him.

"Thanksgiving."

"Why?"

"Because of all the food. We have this huge get-together with all of my aunts and uncles and cousins. There are at least thirty people, and we have tables covered in food. Everyone brings different dishes and all."

"Christmas is my favorite. My family has all kinds of traditions."

We talked about future dreams for big Christmases and Thanksgivings full of family and laughter. We discussed elaborate Christmas decorations, possible traditions to start, and spreads of holiday food. *I'm seeing a future together more and more clearly.* Though I was still wet and tired, my disposition had improved significantly.

Slugging through the mud and muck all day had been thoroughly draining. Each step took twice the effort as the mud sucked our boots deep into the sticky earth. I began to shiver inside my damp clothes and was so relieved when we finally saw the shelter sign that tears prickled the back of my eyes. I was so relieved that the day's hike was over. Considering my level of exhaustion, I found it hard to believe that we had hiked a mere twelve miles. Since the rest of our day had been less than ideal, it came as no surprise that the shelter was already completely full.

Mustering a reserve of energy, we went about setting up the Blue Mansion. Although tent set-up was usually my job, we typically teamed up for all of the chores on bad weather days without shelter space. The ground surrounding the shelter was completely saturated. Just finding level ground that didn't have standing water was a challenge. Stashing our packs in the shelter, we erected the already wet tent in record time. We threw our sorry-looking, dripping packs under the tent's vestibule and slithered into the tent, attempting in vain to leave as many water droplets outside as possible.

Zipping ourselves into our damp cave, we began sorting wet from dry gear. We attempted to string wet gear up above our heads in hopes that it would dry at least a little. I was wet and shivering, and my skin had the wrinkled texture of someone who had stayed in the bathtub for too long.

"Can you hand me my clothes stuff-sack?" I asked.

Souleman passed it to me and watched me take out clothes. "What are you doing?"

"I have to get out of these wet clothes. I'm miserable."

He tried to pull the bag away from me. "I don't think that's a good idea. You've got to wear them dry. Otherwise, you'll have no dry clothes tomorrow."

"I know. But I can't do it. I'm so uncomfortable. I'm just going to wear my dry shirt and pants to cook and all." I pulled the bag back.

"I'm wet and cold, too. It'll be ok. Let's just cook fast and then get in our bags to dry our clothes out. You have to have dry clothes tomorrow."

"I can't. I have to get dry now." I removed my wet clothes and changed into my only dry clothing—a pair of long underwear pants and a long-sleeved shirt. The dry material felt sensuous on my cold, wrinkled skin. I hung my wet clothes over a pole at the top of the tent.

"Those won't dry up there with the weather this cold," Souleman stated.

"I know. I'll put them in my sleeping bag tonight. I just had to put them somewhere for now."

He shook his head quietly.

We rolled our Therm-a-Rests out on top of the damp tent floor and stretched out our aching bodies. Without discussion, we mutually agreed to rest for a minute before venturing back into the rain to cook at the shelter. Souleman pulled me close and I laid my head on his damp chest. The rhythm of his breathing, combined with the staccato of raindrops on the tent, must have lulled me to sleep because the next thing I knew, my grumbling stomach woke me. There was a puddle of drool on Souleman's shirt where my mouth had been. *Why is it dark outside?* I shook Souleman awake, and we realized, after rummaging through our vestibule in the dark to locate a headlamp and a watch, that it was almost midnight.

Rain was still steadily pouring down, and neither of us was enthused at the prospect of trying to cook. We briefly considered eating dry food but decided that our stomachs could wait until morning. One problem remained—the food bag. We *always* put our food up in a bear bag. We debated the pros and cons of sleeping with the food in our tent just once. In the end, our wish to remain as dry as possible outweighed our concern over the possibility of an animal invading our tent. We shoved the food to the bottom of our tent (what animal would dare go near hiker feet?) and immediately went back to sleep.

When I awoke the next morning, everything seemed darker than usual. I thought perhaps I had woken earlier than normal due to our accidental early bedtime. Peeking out of the tent, I saw white—lots and lots of white. The color had vanished from the woods overnight. The ground was white, the trees were white, and our tent, normally a vibrant blue color, had turned into a white igloo. Snow was coming down steadily at an angle.

On the clothesline above my head, I touched my forgotten clothes from the day before and was dismayed to realize they were frozen. I picked up my shirt, hoping to knock off the ice, and found that the fabric was as stiff as cardboard. That would have to wait. The matter we needed to tend to immediately was nourishment. My moving around had awakened Souleman, and our stomachs were threatening mutiny. They were so empty they hurt. I grabbed our food bag from its safe haven under our feet, Souleman located the stove and fuel, and we shuffled, shivering, through the snow to the shelter.

In the shelter we found Burning Man, Train, Raindrop, Marshmallow, and Colorado. They were all propped against the back wall, cocooned into their sleeping bags. A brief conversation revealed that they had all decided to take a zero day in the shelter rather than brave the still-falling snow and the cold. I loved the idea immediately and raised my eyebrows excitedly at Souleman.

A quiet conversation about our schedule followed at the picnic table. Although we had been lucky to avoid big arguments over mileage and scheduling, we certainly did not always agree. In this instance, he hated to change our schedule and thought we should push on that day. I was cold and sore and couldn't stand the idea of trudging through snow while still more continued to fall. After watching me shiver through breakfast and listening to me beg shamelessly, Souleman begrudgingly agreed to stay.

We moved our gear to the shelter and left our igloo-tent outside. The snow continued to come down sideways. We made a group effort to snow-proof our three-sided shelter, tying tarps together to cover the open fourth side and stuffing rocks and debris in holes. Snow still found its way in. As secure as we possibly could have been, the whole group huddled close.

Both of the other couples, Train and Raindrop and Marshmallow and Colorado, were warm inside their mated sleeping bags. Souleman and I huddled closely, an awkward endeavor when wrapped in slippery fabric with our arms pinned to our sides, and bemoaned our inability to zip our bags together. Someone asked if we had tried, and we realized that we had just assumed that since we had different brands of sleeping bags, they were incompatible. We braved the cold for long enough to unzip our bags and try to rematch the zippers. Much to our surprise, our sleeping bags were semi-mate-able. Most mate-able bags zip together on both sides. Due to differences in zipper thickness—mine being tiny and feminine, his being enormous and manly—ours zipped together only on one side, the bottom. This was, nonetheless, an improvement.

We zipped the mate-able side and flipped our bags upside down so that we could tuck the unattached ends underneath us. Beneath our giant, semi-mated bag, we could share body heat from our knees up. We spent most of the day horizontal in our sleeping bag, trying to stay warm and entertained.

As we lay facing each other in our cocoon, I pushed my hat-covered forehead against his and whispered, "Thank you."

"For what?"

"Giving in."

He shook his head. "You're welcome. We're hiking tomorrow no matter what."

I nodded and put my frozen clothes in the sleeping bag with us to defrost them.

It was bitterly cold and snowing in the morning. Although I still couldn't stand the idea of being cold and wet, I knew we had to hike. We would run out of food if we kept stalling. Besides, snow or not, Maine was still calling. This would certainly not be the last snow we encountered on our journey, and now that my clothes were thawed, I was determined to face the weather with bravado.

Souleman made a deal with me: He would go get our frozen tent, which we had abandoned in the elements during our escape to the shelter, if I would pack our sleeping gear. Readily, I agreed. My numb fingers gratefully stuffed snow-dusted sleeping bags and rolled up stiff Therm-a-Rests. After only a few minutes, Souleman returned to the shelter, stamping his feet in the cold.

"Can you toss me our lighter?" he asked.

"Our lighter?"

"Yeah. The tent poles are frozen. I'm going to try to melt the ice with the lighter so that I can take them apart."

I tossed the lighter down to him, and he disappeared into the snow again. After what seemed like ages, he was able to pry apart the frozen poles and manipulate the frozen tent into an equally frozen stuff sack. In the shelter, I had loaded both of our bags and was zipping his headlamp into place when he returned. He stuffed the icy tent sack into his waiting backpack. I just had to put on my boots, and we would be completely ready to start hiking. That morning's preparations had taken much longer than usual.

I scooted to the edge of the shelter and attempted to shove my right foot into my boot. I pushed and shoved and wiggled, but my foot would not go in. The leather was frozen solid. Souleman put my boot on the ground and literally jumped up and down on the rigid shoe in order to loosen the leather. After a few minutes of working on my boots, I could finally open them enough to slide my feet in.

I stood up to stomp my right foot into place. My foot slid into the boot and landed on top of an insert that was completely frozen. I blanched at the pain. The rigid cold against my tender, trail-abused skin was unbelievable. *Oh my gosh, that hurts.* My foot was scorching hot and extremely cold at the same time. I curled my toes and attempted to reduce the surface contact with the bottom of the boot. *You can do this.* Tears threatened as I hastily laced the boot. Glancing around me, I realized that I was in a shelter almost entirely full of men. *I cannot start crying.* I bit my lip and grasped the left boot. I got my left foot settled into its frozen casing and a hot tear singed my cheek as I sat down and fumbled with the laces.

Souleman put two fingers under my chin and attempted to lift my face to meet his gaze. Stubbornly, I tucked my chin to my chest and refused to look up. Finally laced into both pain-inducing boots, I stood awkwardly, curling my toes and arching my feet so that neither foot fully touched its frozen insert. *How am I going to hike like this?* I avoided looking at Souleman, knowing I wouldn't be able to hold back the threatening tears. Already, my toes were throbbing from the intense cold. Souleman sunk down to my height and looked me in the eyes.

"Brownie. Look at me. What's the matter?" he asked, his voice full of concern. His cold fingertip caught a searing tear from my eyelash before it had time to splash on my cheek.

"It . . . hurts," I choked out.

"What hurts? Your boots?"

I nodded as my lower lip started quivering. Hot tears ran in rivers down my cold-reddened cheeks. Noisy hiccupping sobs escaped the confines of my throat. Embarrassed, I awkwardly fled the shelter, trying to move without touching the bottoms of my shoes. I stumbled twice and almost fell before I made it around the corner. Alone behind the shelter, I hopped from foot to foot as I sobbed and sobbed. I cried all the tears of frustration and pain and struggle that I had kept in for all these miles. My tears turned to ice on my cheeks and eyelashes, and my fingers, uncoordinated from the cold, poked my eyes as I tried to brush the tears away.

Souleman appeared beside me and pulled my face to his chest, wrapping his arms around me. "Talk to me. Tell me what's going on."

I shook my head against his chest. I was breathing much too fast. *I can't talk. I'm going to die.*

"Brownie, come on. I need to know what's going on." He tried to pull back so that he could look at me, but I locked my arms behind his back and wouldn't let go.

I continued to cry. My sobs were loud and shook my whole body.

One of his hands cradled the back of my head and the other firmly held me against him. "Brownie?"

I shook my head no again, clinging tightly to him.

"Michelle. You have to talk."

I startled at the sound of my real name. *He never calls me Michelle.* I sucked in a shaky breath and forced myself to answer him. "I . . . can't . . . do . . . this," I sobbed.

"Yes, you can. You've hiked almost three hundred and fifty miles." He squeezed my shoulders.

"No!" I squeaked. "You . . . don't . . . understand."

"Tell me, then."

"I'm too . . . cold."

He kept rubbing my shoulders. "It's going to be ok—I promise. You have to trust me."

I cried and cried, struggling to get enough air in through my sobs. *I can't feel my feet anymore. I'm not sure if I have ears. I'll never be warm again. I'm going to die in this cold shelter in the snow.*

"Michelle! Calm down. It's going to be ok. We just need to warm you up."

"Nooo. It's . . . not . . . ok," I wailed. "My feet . . . could get . . . frostbite. I . . . will . . . never . . . get warm."

Souleman looked more and more concerned as he tried new phrases of reassurance. "You're all right. You can do this. I don't think you have frostbite. Ok? I love you. I'm not going to let anything happen to you."

I kept crying, and he wrapped his arms around me.

"Brownie, it's going to be ok."

"I'm . . . going . . . to . . . die." *I'm too cold. I can't warm up. My toes will fall off. I'm going to die out here. I can't walk anymore. Why did I ever think I could do this? Why am I out here? This is crazy!*

"No, you're not." His voice was stern now. "Let's go back in the shelter, all right?" He tried to guide me toward the front of the shelter.

"No." I used what little energy I had left to jerk away from him. I was still shaking and crying loud, hiccupping sobs. I was also under the delusion that my meltdown had been private behind the thin-walled shelter. Eventually, I lost the energy to protest and let him steer me, stumbling, back inside.

Butterfly Moon, a friend of ours who was an ER nurse, had arrived at the shelter at some point during my meltdown. As I sat at the edge of the shelter, I heard her talking to Souleman as though through a thick layer of fog. I simply didn't care. I had long ago stopped shivering, but still all I could think about was being cold. I couldn't hold on to any other thought. Fleeting phrases trickled through to my brain—"blue lips," "not shivering," "irrational." I found out later that Butterfly Moon had expressed extreme concern over my condition. She was worried I might have been hypothermic and thought I needed to go straight into town.

As I sat, spaced-out, on the shelter ledge, still unable to stop crying, people around me sprang into action. Butterfly Moon used her cell phone to arrange a ride for us from the next road. Souleman wrapped my shoulders in his sleeping bag and wiggled my uncooperative hands into my gloves. He removed my frozen boots and put his own extra pair of dry socks on my feet and rubbed them until I once again had circulation. As my feet thawed, they burned and tingled, and I cried and mumbled under my breath. *I'm too cold. So cold. Not ok. I'll never warm up. Want to lie down.* Although on some level I knew I was going to be all right, I couldn't seem to get control of myself. I continued to cry quietly, and he wiped the tears off the end of my nose with his sleeve and reassured me in a comforting voice.

"We're going to go to town, ok? We'll get you warmed up and get some food in you. You'll feel much better."

Town? I nodded, though I only heard half of what he said. The people seemed to be swirling around me. *What are they all talking about?*

In a final attempt to raise my core temperature, Souleman fired up our stove and made noodles. I was too cold to use my spork, so he shoveled the steaming noodles into my mouth. I became vaguely aware of all the people in the shelter watching this and turned my back in embarrassment. Once I was lucid enough to listen, he explained what we were going to do. I had to get my boots back on and hike approximately four miles to a road where Phoenix, a friend of Butterfly Moon's and a hiker whom we'd met numerous times, would meet us in a van to take us back to Erwin, Tennessee.

I nodded at the plan but teared up again when we had to put the sleeping bag away. With awkward fingers, I managed to lace myself back into the traitorous boots. An extra pair of socks served as a futile barrier against the unrelenting cold. Putting on my pack seemed like cruel punishment since the weight pushed my feet deeper into the frozen shoes. *Just keep moving.* Souleman offered to carry some of my pack weight, but I emphatically declined, determined to be tough even in my misery.

"It doesn't . . . count . . . if I . . . don't carry . . . my whole . . . pack."

"Brownie, this is different."

"No." I took a shaky breath. "I'd have . . . to . . . come back. Redo . . . the . . . miles."

Souleman shook his head in annoyance but helped me settle the pack on my shoulders. I cried for the first few minutes. As we hiked, I gradually regained sensation in my feet. The pain was so intense that I realized I preferred numbness. Souleman walked in front of me, breaking through the thick layer of snow so that I could walk with less effort in his footsteps. After about a mile, I started shivering. The violent shaking reverberated down my back. I ached all over. *Shivering is a good sign.* Even in this condition, I hiked the four miles at an almost normal pace, though I continued to sniffle for much of the way. My breath came in those loud, erratic gasps that are common after hard crying.

We arrived at the road sooner than I expected and waited by the roadside with Marshmallow and Colorado, shivering in the wind and snow. At this point I was still cold but had regained control of myself. I probably would have been in good enough shape to continue hiking, but a ride had already been arranged, and there was no sense in taking a risk. I had also worn myself out with all the emotion. A van slowed across the street, and we instinctively reached for our packs. We were shocked when a woman stuck her camera out of the passenger side window and snapped our picture as though we were an unexpected wild animal sighting. Our disappointment was extreme.

Phoenix arrived shortly after the paparazzi had departed. He jumped out and took my pack from me after a big hug, then ushered me into the front seat where the heaters were blowing full-force. The hot air thawed my extremities, which, it turns out, were still colder than I had realized. My tears returned in full force as I thawed.

In extreme embarrassment, I cried all the way to town. Souleman politely declined the offer to return to Miss Janet's hostel and instead opted for the isolation and quiet of a nearby hotel in spite of the price.

Souleman checked us in while I sat in the car with Phoenix. He came back with keys and lifted my pack from the trunk. For once, I didn't argue. I thanked Phoenix and heard them whisper a conversation involving my name. As we entered the room, Souleman threw both of our packs on the carpet. My muscles were incredibly tight and sore. I immediately headed for the warmth of the bed. I was almost under the covers when Souleman stopped me by sliding his arms around my waist.

"I think you should take a hot shower. Warm up your core."

"I can't." I flopped on the edge of the bed. "I'm too tired."

"I'll help. Come on." He pulled my filthy shirt over my head and tugged on my hands.

Begrudgingly, I let him lead me into the bathroom, where he already had the shower going. I stood staring in the mirror in a daze while he adjusted the water, got a towel, and opened the soap. Gently, Souleman peeled my clothes off and piled them on the floor. He pulled me toward the shower and held my arm while I stepped under the steaming water. I moaned out loud as the water washed over my tired, aching body.

Eventually, I stood motionless under the hot water. As I warmed completely, I realized how close a call I'd had. I started crying again and let my hot tears mix with the even hotter water. After a few minutes, Souleman stepped into the shower behind me. While I stood still hogging all the water, he scrubbed shampoo into my filthy hair. I watched numbly as swirls of dirt ran across the white tub and down the drain.

Finally clean, dry, and warm, I snuggled into the double bed with a surplus of blankets for a long nap. I roused hours later, still tired but more or less back to my usual self, in time to join other hikers at an all-you-can-eat restaurant.

In the morning I was still so tired that lifting my arms and legs required a huge effort. I elected to spend one more night in the hotel. Souleman and I spent the day and night alone, rarely leaving the bed, much less the room. I napped, watched TV, and soaked in the hot tub. I was frustrated at the amount of time we had spent in towns lately and was hoping to rejuvenate my body so that we could really tackle some mileage once we returned to the trail.

As we lay in bed that night, we massaged each other's sore muscles. Souleman's head was in my lap as I traced the lines of his face and watched his eyelids flutter and his expression relax.

"Thank you."

He peered up through sleepy eyelids. "For what?"

"Taking care of me. I was so stupid. You tried to warn me, but I didn't listen. That whole thing could've been avoided. I could have died out there."

"But you didn't." He held my hand.

"So many people had to help me."

"Brownie, that's what the trail is all about. You'd have helped someone else, right?"

I nodded in agreement. "Still, I just want you to know how much I appreciate your taking care of me."

He squeezed my hand. "It's all part of it. I'd do anything for you."

All I could think was how happy I was and how lucky we were to be sharing this journey. All of our time together on the trail and in various towns was building up an arsenal of experiences we would never forget.

"Pssst." I nudged Souleman.

"Hmmm?"

"Let's go eat."

He groaned. "That involves moving."

"Then we can come back to bed."

He nodded and staggered to a standing position. As I ran my fingers through my hair in front of the mirror, he wrapped his arms around my waist from behind. I studied our reflections side by side in the mirror. *Wow, we look alike. Same eyes, same hair, same skin tone.*

He interrupted my thoughts. "You know, we'd make some beautiful babies."

11

I Hear Banjos

After two nights of warm, food-laden days in the hotel, I was anxious to return to the woods. We had spent more than enough time and money in Erwin, Tennessee. I hoped that the lapse of time would have allowed some of the snow to melt, but no such blessing occurred. Phoenix drove us back to the trail, and after many hugs and rounds of thanks, we started walking north once again. The temperature was a comfortable fifty degrees, but a brutal wind kept our shoulders hunched and our hoods wrapped protectively around our ears. The trail was covered in snow, but fortunately for us, enough hikers had preceded us that there was a well-worn, snow-edged path.

I knew immediately that the stay in town had been a good decision. The cold wind was trying even after such a relaxing break. That day, I was so excited to be back on the trail that I didn't complain about the snow or the cold or the wind. Every day on the trail was a blessing, and my brush with hypothermia had reinforced that.

Souleman must have been equally appreciative because he turned around and asked, "Do you know what I'm thinking about?"

I shrugged my shoulders.

"I'm thinking about everything we've been through on this hike and how we're not even a quarter of the way done and we have so many more exciting things to experience together."

"Yeah, but if you weren't hiking with me you'd have a lot fewer problems."

"If I weren't hiking with you, I wouldn't be experiencing things the same way. I'll take the good and the bad of a hiking partner."

I smiled and said the only thing I could think of. "Tollbooth."

We spent the night in Clyde Smith Shelter and faced climbing Roan Mountain the following morning. The wind was blowing violently and threatened to fling us right off the mountain. The ascent was snowy and windy. I observed the trees glittering with snow, tramped over the frozen ground, and wondered what worms do in the winter.

As I pondered the coping mechanisms of worms, it started to hail. I tucked my chin into my chest and crunched through the snow up the mountain. By the time we made it to the stone shelter on top of Roan Mountain, my pigtails were frozen solid and Souleman's growing beard was covered in icicles. We unbolted the shelter door and slid inside in hopes of eating lunch protected from the elements. Unfortunately, the wind blew right through the holes in the rock walls, so the shelter provided no protection. We ate some dry snacks, and then I had to take a bathroom break before hiking on.

Finding a place to use the bathroom in the winter can be a real challenge for women on the trail. The trees and bushes without leaves provide little concealment. I walked off into the trees and finally found a place that seemed remote enough. Dropping my pants and baring my most delicate parts to the wind and snow was a special kind of torture. I wondered if my pee would freeze before it hit the snow on the ground. Balancing in a squatting position over the snow while simultaneously making sure to avoid soaking my clothes was a monumental task. I wished briefly that I had been born male.

I watched the snow underneath me turn yellow and then had the horrifying realization that the yellow snow was getting precariously close to my foot. Just then, warmth spread across the top of my foot. *Seriously!?* I had peed on my own shoe. Rolling my eyes in frustration, I wiggled my pants back on. The thin layers of my hiking pants and rain pants were comfortably protective. I kicked my shoe in the snow and reminded myself, *Urine is sterile.*

We pushed on toward Overmountain Shelter, eager for warmth. On the way, we passed a tombstone. The epitaph read, "He lived alone, he suffered alone, he died alone." Souleman and I questioned what type of life a person must have lived for those to be the final words selected to represent it.

"You about ready?" Souleman asked me.

I shook my head no. As cold as I was, I had to take a few moments to stand beside the gravestone. *Why is he buried here? What's his story? Does anyone who loved him visit his grave?* I dug in the snow with my pole as I reflected on my recent brush with hypothermia.

I looked up at Souleman. "This could have been me."

"But it wasn't."

"But it could have been. What if I had been alone?"

"You weren't." He snaked his arms around my waist and gave me a squeeze.

I shook my head sadly. "Who would have found me? How long would it have taken?"

"Brownie, you're ok. And we aren't going to let it happen again. It was just a fluke."

I nodded and tipped my head up for him to kiss me. He went through the routine of kissing my forehead, my nose, each eye, and finally my mouth. Before we walked away I placed my hands on top of the gravestone. "You aren't alone now," I told him. "Every hiker who passes this place shares a moment with you."

The backside of Roan Mountain was ice-coated and decidedly slippery. As we fought to remain upright, it began snowing. I was leaning heavily on my Leki poles and had visions of one of them snapping under my weight. I feared that a fall would send me sliding down the rest of the mountain pack-first. Souleman and I struggled across a series of balds as the snow continued to fall.

My body was tired and begged for a break, but it was too cold to stop. My ankles and knees were sore, and my feet were throbbing. I felt guilty for slowing Souleman's progress. I really wanted to increase my daily mileage, yet it seemed that my body wasn't cooperating with my mind. I trudged on. I was ready to stop long before the shelter sign appeared.

Overmountain Shelter had originally been a barn. It had three levels, including a loft overlooking a vast field. We sat on a ledge off the back side with other hikers, including Gypsy, Fireball, and Tex, and watched the sky turn shades of yellow, gold, and bronze as we cooked a warm dinner.

Although the converted barn was rustic and charming, it was also a wind tunnel. Souleman and I spent a chilly night on the third floor. Some people pitched their tents inside to combat the cold. The wind whipped relentlessly through the open hayloft door and seeped up through the cracks between the floorboards. Souleman and I mated our sleeping bags and curled our bodies together. I remembered the tip about getting naked in a sleeping bag to share body heat. I wasn't willing to revisit hypothermia, but I also wasn't going to get naked in a shelter full of hikers. As a compromise, I lifted both of our shirts so that his bare stomach was pressed against my bare back. Even huddled together, we shivered the whole night and rose at the first sign of daylight.

Unfortunately, the following day was slow going once again. My hips had joined the rest of my body in revolting against movement. I hated the dichotomy between my mind's desire to hike quickly and my body's inability. Every single step hurt like I was walking barefoot on sharp rocks. Though my pain slowed our progress, we hiked steadily, pausing only for a morning snack.

After covering just over nine miles, we were looking for a place to eat a late lunch when we came upon a piece of paper pinned in the middle of the trail by a rock. An arrow on the paper pointed to the bushes beside the trail, where we found a case of beer.

"I'll bet it's empty," Souleman predicted.

Surprisingly, it was a full case with the words "Enjoy, hikers" written on the box.

"I don't have to be asked twice," Souleman said, sticking one in his pack for later.

"Take mine, too, since I don't drink beer."

"Nah, I'll leave them for other hikers. We'll have to work on that whole 'you not drinking beer' thing, though."

I laughed and then turned abruptly to look up the trail. "Do you hear cars?"

We headed toward the sound of vehicles and soon reached a sparsely traveled road. According to Wingfoot, a diner called Buck's was located a few miles down this road.

It was becoming increasingly hard to say no to food, so we hitched to Buck's for cheeseburgers. Buck's was a tiny, family-run restaurant and store, and if it had a busy season, this wasn't it. As we stared at the "menu," a handwritten piece of paper streaked with coffee stains and crusted food, someone behind the counter called out, "You'uns wants somethin'?"

We ordered cheeseburgers, onion rings, and milkshakes and settled in to the vintage, mint-green diner furniture to wait. Since there were no other customers and I was too tired to say much, we could clearly hear the loud conversations of the employees, all of whom were from Buck's family. We deciphered enough of the conversations to learn that Buck was away on vacation, his daughter was pregnant (again), the mobile home needed repairs, the grandmother was sick of watching the kids, the nephew was moving out, and no one shot anything on the hunting trip.

I got up and hobbled around the store while we waited. I couldn't figure out the random selection of items for sale on the shelves. Among the odd assortment were aging canned goods, maxi pads, unidentifiable first aid supplies from 1950, Tic Tacs in unusual flavors, fluorescent orange hunting hats, a couple of touristy t-shirts, a box of tissues, a broom, and some plastic flowers. My stomach growled angrily as I finally settled back onto the bench beside Souleman and rested my head on his shoulder.

When our food arrived, it was passable, although the cook himself was questionable. I took one glance at the large man with long, unrestrained, greasy hair, a stained apron, and saggy pants and redirected my eyes to my cheeseburger that he slid to my place. I raised it to my mouth with my eyes closed and savored the crisp lettuce and crunchy onion. I lowered my head as my tongue fully experienced the grace of the melted cheese and thick burger patty. *Hallelujah.* I looked up at Souleman as ketchup oozed from the edges of my mouth and dripped down my chin. We ate in reverent silence. I chewed and swallowed bite after satisfying bite. Once I had wiped up the last smudge of ketchup with my final french fry, I collapsed back in the mint-green booth and wiped my mouth with the back of my hand.

When I went to pay our bill, a woman with one toddler on her hip and another perched on the counter was pushing buttons on the register. She informed me that the fine establishment of Buck's took only cash. We had none. One of Buck's many relatives—the grandfather, I think—offered to drive us to an ATM. In hushed tones, Souleman and I whispered about whether only one of us should go to the ATM. In the end, we opted for safety in numbers and piled into the truck's cab with our packs. For once I did not worry about my smell in the confines of someone's personal vehicle. *He's probably had a dead animal in here recently.*

"We's been thinkin' ta turn the 'partment ov'r the rest'rant into a hostel fer th' hikers. What you'uns thinks?" he asked on the way.

We encouraged the idea and told him that if a town has food and a place to sleep, many hikers would be attracted.

After getting money from the ATM and grabbing some snacks from the shelves at Buck's, we counted out cash to pay our bill. Then we grabbed our packs and sat out front, packing the new snacks into our bags and waiting for motivation to return to the trail. As seemed to be a constant lately, my body was aching and tired.

One of the relatives came out, and with a toothpick hanging out of his mouth, asked, "You'un's wanna stay the night?"

"Oh, thank you very much, but we're going to head back to the trail," Souleman explained.

"Well, if'n you'uns change yer mind, you'uns come on in an' lemme know, awlright?"

"Will do."

The man headed toward the door of the restaurant but then changed his mind and turned back to us. "Why dontcha come an 'av a look at 'er. You'uns can tell me what the hikers ar' gonna think."

"Um, sure, we can take a look," I answered. I stepped over bicycle parts, discarded folding chairs, miscellaneous cardboard pieces, and an old musty quilt on my way up a narrow outdoor staircase.

"My grandson 'n sum kids was livin' here," he told us as we approached the door. He shoved the door open and led us inside.

There were two small bedrooms, a nice-sized living area, and a tiny, very dirty kitchen. Random belongings were strewn throughout the apartment as if it had been abandoned unexpectedly and without much time to pack, or perhaps as if it had been ransacked and the intruders had been disturbed mid-heist. The walls had tacks where pictures used to hang, and some left-behind posters were still taped in place. A folded pile of faded sheets sat on a couch, and he pointed at those and said, "Those'r fer the hikers."

"Oh, you're already preparing, that's great," I offered with a forced smile.

"We had sum hiker guys dat stayed here las' night. Two of 'em." He looked around and added, "Th' place still needs sum work."

"I'm sure it will be great once you fix it up a little. The hikers will appreciate it," Souleman encouraged.

"If'n you'uns wanna stay 'ere, you's can stay. Guys last night paid ten dollurs each."

"Thank you again for the offer," Souleman started, "but we really weren't planning to spend the night anywhere. Staying in town tonight wasn't in our budget."

The Buck relative said he would leave us to talk about it and disappeared. We found a clock in the kitchen and realized that it was much later than we had thought. The long wait for food and the drive to town had whittled away much of the afternoon. With it nearing five o'clock, we would either have to stay there or camp a few miles up the trail.

"We could just stay here, have a few drinks, relax, and then leave early in the morning," Souleman suggested.

I looked around and imagined all sorts of nasty germs crawling around. *This place can't be dirtier than we are, can it?* We went and sat on the porch with our packs and weighed our options. The Buck relative reappeared next to us.

"Ya know, you'uns can stay here if'n you want. Fer nothin'. Jus' talk good 'bout us on the trail so's hikers might come here. Somebody tol' me dat hikers talkin' good would git more of 'em ta come."

Souleman and I exchanged looks. I glanced at my watch, then nodded my head slightly. Already formulating a journal entry for that evening, I hauled my pack up the cluttered stairs. I glanced over my shoulder to make sure Souleman was right behind me.

Buck's family also owned a liquor store on the same property. We ventured over there and found a number of older men clustered around a wood stove, drinking whisky and telling stories about their recent hunting trips. I'd never seen so many men in denim overalls. I tried not to crack a smile or stare as we made our selections and left with haste.

"I think I hear banjos," Souleman whispered in the parking lot, tossing a glance over his shoulder.

"What?"

"This is definitely *Deliverance* territory."

I shrugged my shoulders. "What's *Deliverance*?"

"Are you serious?"

My face was blank.

"Ok. We're watching *Deliverance* when we get off the trail."

A little snooping revealed that the small apartment had a half-eaten birthday cake in the fridge, clothes still in the drawers, and already-slept-on sheets on the beds. It was as if the tenants had just vacated the place that morning. Yet the door had no lock, there was no soap to be found, and the blinds wouldn't shut. We watched a news update on the dilapidated TV, sang along with the radio, and drank beer and wine coolers. In a moment of hiker hunger, we seriously considered eating the cake in the fridge. I even examined the container for an expiration date. Deciding I'd better not tempt food poisoning, I fell asleep hungry on the wrinkled sheets of the musky bed. My head was uncomfortably close to an unidentifiable stain. *Is that birthday cake?*

Sometime after the sun rose, I fell asleep and dozed fitfully until mid-morning. We got to the trail around ten and had an excellent day of hiking. The unplanned rest had significantly helped my body. I was feeling much less sore and much more motivated. I hiked at a good pace up and down rolling hills, enjoying the mild breeze on my face. I soaked in the colors of the trees, the scurrying of squirrels, and the rocks underfoot. As much as I had been hurting lately, I was still enjoying every minute on the trail. With Souleman, I laughed about Buck's and shook my head at how my mother would react to the tales of our evening. I tried to use the word "you'uns" in conversation, and we laughed so hard we had to sit on a fallen log to recover. Neither of us had actually heard that word spoken aloud before.

As my legs grew tired and we started looking for a place to pitch our tent, the sky became increasingly dark. It was as if the sun had decided to set hours too early. Looking up, I winged a prayer that we would get our tent set up before the rain started. Almost immediately, the gentle breeze disappeared and was replaced by gusting winds that carried heavy raindrops. I scrambled for my raingear and pack cover.

Setting up camp in the rain would not have been optimal, so we pushed on hoping to wait out the storm. Every so often I looked skyward. *Please let the rain stop!* No such luck. We trudged on, using the rain as motivation to hike further. About two miles up the trail, the rain lessened and eventually stopped altogether. The trail had become muddy and I was ready to stop hiking. But before I took my pack off, the sun came back out, and the chance to hike in sunshine and dry out our gear compelled us to continue moving forward another mile up the trail. One part of me protested the extra distance, while another part was grateful that those unexpected steps would be behind me in the morning.

We came down a small hill and found a camping spot where two branches of a stream came together at a fork. In the fork was a large, flat, sandy spot that was perfect for a tent. Overhanging trees surrounded the area, and a bridge with a white blaze led picturesquely across one branch of water, heading further up the Appalachian Trail. This would be an ideal place to spend the night. Thinking of my earlier prayer for a place to stop before the rain, I was reminded of the Garth Brooks song called "Unanswered Prayers."

We pitched the Blue Mansion near the stream intersection and immediately set about completing our chores. Souleman fixed dinner and purified water while I set up our sleeping gear, hung our wet rain clothes on a clothes line, and washed our muddy gaiters in the stream. Mud had completely caked the gaiters to the point where they were stiff and unwieldy. As I squatted over the water scrubbing them clean, I wondered what life had been like before the invention of the washing machine. Cleaning four gaiters wasn't too bad, but I couldn't imagine doing laundry for an entire family.

"Dinner's ready!" Souleman announced from beside the tent, pulling me from my musings.

I hung the gaiters on a tree branch, grabbed my spork, and plopped myself down so that we were sitting knee to knee. Sniffing the air, I asked, "Lipton noodles?"

"Yep."

I shoveled a giant, steaming bite into my mouth. "Thanks for cooking," I said around the mouthful. "I should get you an apron. You've been awfully domestic."

He shot a pointed look at me. "Then you better get one for yourself too. You get to do all the cooking after the trail."

I stared at him in mock horror. "That's a terrible deal."

He narrowed his eyes at me. "That's the deal."

"There will be way more after-trail nights in our life than trail nights," I complained.

"Do you want to cook tomorrow?" he asked, knowing the answer.

"No." I had a terrible relationship with our camp stove.

He grinned into the pot.

"I've cooked a few nights," I mumbled petulantly.

"Fair enough. I'll cook a few nights off-trail."

"A few nights a week?" I asked hopefully.

"Don't push it."

We ate in silence for a few minutes. When the pot was almost empty, I looked up at him with a huge smile. "Hey, how do you plan on my cooking for you after the trail? Am I to mail your dinners from Massachusetts to Vermont each night?"

Very seriously, he said, "I think they'd spoil."

"What will we do, then?" I feigned concern.

"I guess we might have to live together." He made a show of storing the pot and utensils. "Because of the food, I mean," he added, trying to hide his smile.

"Right. For the food."

In the tent that night, we studied Wingfoot's Handbook by headlamp. Recalculating our mileage, estimated days off, and possible finishing dates had become almost a nightly obsession. Although the data seldom changed much from day to day, we rarely went an evening without working the numbers. My Handbook had little math equations scribbled all over the margins and inside flaps, as though a mad scientist had used my book for scrap paper.

During the day, Souleman and I did our best to enjoy whatever was before us without stressing about mileage and destinations, but at night we rigorously studied and planned our course to Maine. We had read each page of the Handbook so many times that the edges were frayed and discolored, and we had much of the information committed to memory.

As we closed the book that night, I imagined our location in Tennessee on the map and asked, "Where do you think we should aim for tomorrow?"

"For tomorrow," Souleman said into the dark in a serious tone, "I say we shoot for Connecticut."

12

Sealed with a Kiss

The morning brought sunshine, which was a reason for much rejoicing and a boost in motivation. We saw many other hikers during the day, and most were headed for the same destination as us: Kincora Hiking Hostel. Due to a shortage of resupply locations, we knew we had to put our normal hostel aversion aside in order to purchase enough food until the next town. Our food bags were worrisomely light. Kincora had a fabulous reputation and was in an excellent location, just off the trail. Since we had spent an unexpected night at Buck's, we felt a little spoiled for staying off-trail again, but it was necessary for food resupply.

In typical fashion, we arrived at the hostel after many of our hiking companions were already there. I was happy to see Toolman and Vinnie in the mix. In fact, through the night's conversation, we learned that they were the other hikers who had slept at Buck's. They were as much in awe as we were. They had even eaten a piece of the questionable cake in the refrigerator. At Kincora, we also had the privilege of meeting the notorious Cycle Hiker, whom we had been hearing about for months. He was carrying a bicycle on his pack because he had biked to Georgia and was planning to bike home after hiking to Maine.

Due to our comparably late arrival at the hostel, we missed the pre-arranged shuttle to town. This hostel was located many miles from the closest stores. Our options were to wait until noon the next day or to find our own way to get there. Knowing we wanted to hike out before late afternoon, we opted to hitchhike. We left our gear in the hostel, shouldered our empty packs, and started walking in the direction of town, ready to stick out our thumbs at the first hint of engine noise.

The road into town was a winding and relatively isolated residential street. By some stroke of luck, the second vehicle that passed us stopped. It was a pick-up truck with four children and a dog in the bed, and the driver motioned for us to jump into the bed with them. We threw our packs over the edge and plopped ourselves down in the truck. One of the children, a three-year-old boy, was sitting on top of the toolbox and slid dangerously close to the edge as the truck careened down the mountain. *That kid is going to fall out of this truck.* I attempted to hold on tightly and avoid the dog while keeping an uneasy eye on the precariously perched toddler.

Miles later, at the end of the road, the truck lurched to a stop and the driver gestured for the children to get inside the cab. We accelerated haphazardly onto another road and then onto the highway. Souleman and I traded uneasy glances as we got further and further away from the hostel. *Surely there must be a grocery store closer than this.* As I clung to the truck, the wind whipping my hair into my eyes and making it difficult for me to see the road signs, I tried to pay attention to the route so that we could find our way back. *This is really unsafe.* As the driver stopped for a red light, we saw a grocery store across the highway. We motioned to him, threw our packs onto the median, and jumped into the road just before the light turned green. Holding hands, we climbed the divider, dashed across the highway, and scrambled over a fence into the parking lot. I gasped for breath, relieved we had made it alive.

We bought all the food on our list and shoved our purchases into our packs. Up and down the road we could see the colorful, glowing signs of fast-food establishments. We debated the merits of Burger King versus Wendy's, with me pulling for Wendy's and Souleman supporting Burger King. Our good-natured debate stopped abruptly when I saw a man on the sidewalk carrying a Taco Bell cup.

"I *have* to have Taco Bell."

Souleman nodded his approval. "We just have to figure out where it is."

"Sir, can you tell me where Taco Bell is?" I asked the man I'd seen with the cup.

He stared at me.

I gestured at his purple cup. "Taco Bell. Can you tell me where it is?"

He shook his head. "No English."

I tried again, breaking out my rusty Spanish. "Necesito Taco Bell. ¿Ayúdame, por favor?" I could've sworn he swallowed a smirk before answering me.

"No understand."

I *had* to have Taco Bell. I asked the next person we passed on the sidewalk. And the next. Finally, a gas station attendant was able to give us directions.

As we scurried down the sidewalk in the direction of taco holy land, a delivery truck pulled to the curb right beside us at a red light. The driver leaned out and asked, "You guys want a pizza?"

He held up a pizza box. *Do we look that desperate?* The traffic light turned green and the driver thrust the box through the open window. Souleman grabbed it and nodded a bewildered thanks. *We must look like we are starving.* We laughed so hard we had to stop walking. Unsure about eating a pizza from an unknown truck driver, we debated as we walked another block. *What are the odds he poisoned this? How old could it really be? Has anyone ever died from eating old pizza?* Ultimately we ditched it in the next trash can and kept walking.

The restaurant was much further than we had anticipated. Two hitches later, we ended up at Taco Bell. We ordered what seemed like half the menu and were debating whether to order dessert right then or later.

"Are you two hiking the Appalachian Trail?" the pony-tailed lady attending the cash register asked. Her nametag read Tonya. "I see your packs over there." She nodded in the direction of the booth we had set our packs in.

"Yes," I answered her.

"Oh, I'm so jealous. It's something I've thought about for a long time. I'm just too scared, I guess." She rearranged her visor and fiddled with her nametag.

"I won't lie, it takes a lot of planning, and every single day is hard."

"Would you do it again?" she asked.

"Absolutely," I responded without hesitation.

"I told myself I was going to start doing trail magic for hikers this year. I think I'll start with you two. Let me buy your meal."

"Oh, you don't have to do that," Souleman told her.

"He's right, it's really not necessary."

"What you're doing is amazing. I want to be part of your experience. I'm going to buy your dinner. Let's add two large drinks to that order. Anything else?"

We shook our heads no and smiled gratefully.

Tonya paid and handed the tray across the counter with a huge smile. After again encouraging our trail angel to pursue her dream of hiking and thanking her profusely, we gulped down our food smothered with copious amounts of hot sauce. Before we left, I handed Tonya a napkin with my www.trailjournals.com website and email address and encouraged her to use us as a resource as she planned her own hike.

Leaving Taco Bell, we heard music emanating from nearby and wandered down the next street. We ran straight into an old-fashioned car parade. Giddy from the delicious food, we wandered around the street looking at cars and getting odd looks from the townspeople. Souleman's arm was looped around my waist underneath my near-empty pack. We were far enough from the trail that a sweaty-smelling couple wearing dirty clothes and large backpacks drew attention.

Down the next street we spotted a movie theater. Going to a movie seemed like an unheard-of luxury. We checked the times and realized that we had arrived just in time for a showing of *The Amityville Horror*. The movie was decidedly awful, but that didn't lessen our enjoyment. Buttery popcorn, Sour Patch Kids, surround sound, and air conditioning—we were in heaven. The forced air was actually uncomfortably cold against the dried sweat caked on my skin.

It was dark outside when the movie ended, and we faced the task of getting across town and then back to the hostel. A pickup stopped and drove us back to the original grocery store. By this time it was starting to rain. We didn't have our pack covers or our rain coats since we hadn't planned on being gone for so long. Souleman and I scanned the area and, since we were becoming professionals, located the ideal hitchhiking location. We ducked our heads in the rain and stuck out our thumbs. Most cars sped by without slowing.

One car circled a few times, eyeing us suspiciously. We could see a nicely dressed middle-aged couple in the front seat. Finally, they rolled down the passenger window and the man leaned over his wife and asked, "Are you ok?"

"Yes sir. We're hiking the Appalachian Trail. We came into town for supplies and are trying to get back to our hostel."

After a whispered consultation with his wife he said, "We can take you partway."

Their teenage daughter was in the backseat, and I could tell that the mom was not thrilled about putting two dirty strangers into the car beside her. I sat in the middle and pressed myself up against Souleman, trying to keep our smell and filth as far away from her as possible. The teenager squished herself against the door and darted sideways glances at us in the darkness of the car. Following some unspoken code of etiquette, no one mentioned how terrible we smelled.

The woman fiddled with her pearls as she turned around to ask me, "Honey, what are you doing hitchhiking?"

"We have to get back to our hostel."

"I just don't think this is safe. Does your mother know you're doing this? I wouldn't want my daughter hitchhiking."

"My mom doesn't love that I'm doing it either. But she does support my hike. I call her from every town."

She nodded, but her brow remained creased. She turned to her husband. "Let's just take them all the way to their hostel. We aren't in a hurry."

Surprisingly, Souleman and I were able to remember the way back. I was increasingly impressed with my ability to navigate unfamiliar towns since my pitiful sense of navigation is often the butt of family jokes. Back at the hostel we climbed out of the car, offering apologies for the inconvenience. I had a feeling the teenager was about to get a lecture about the dangers of hitchhiking.

Our friends at the hostel were shocked at our good fortune—two long-distance hitches, a free pizza, free tacos, and a movie. Proud of our adventure, we hastily did our laundry and collapsed into bed together on a twin-sized bunk. Even after such a busy day, I could not sleep with the sounds of so many people echoing around one room. I tossed and turned on the wooden bunk in a state of exhausted delirium, wishing I had earplugs.

I scanned my tired mind trying to recall how many miles we faced in the morning. Hiking while tired was torturous for me. Rather than worry the minutes away, I forced my mind to change tracks and used the time to reflect on the trail. During the years I had prepared for my AT hike, I had thought extensively about nights in the woods, carrying the weight of a pack, building fires, cooking over my stove, hiking up mountains, braving difficult weather, and other such endeavors. Somehow, in all my preparations, it had never occurred to me that time in hotels, hostels, restaurants, post offices, grocery stores, and other town locations would be a fundamental part of my trip. My hike had come to include so much more than the camping and walking I had pictured.

Time spent in towns was a paradoxical complement to the serenity of hiking. In the woods I found myself lulled to sleep by babbling brooks, lost in thought to the background noise of wind in the trees, and completely at peace observing views off mountaintops. My interactions with other people were limited, and there was no distracting technology. Town time was hectic, busy, crowded, and often loud. While I replayed a slideshow in my mind of our trail experiences thus far, I grimly watched the hostel transform from dark to dawn to full-on daylight, still without having entered the world of sleep. The clatter and rustling of a dozen hikers organizing their gear started with the first rays of daylight.

Souleman and I were up and packed early and joined the train of hikers trickling out of Kincora hostel to head north. Our first scenic view was a gorgeous waterfall. The morning sun made the water glow and sparkle as it cascaded over the rocks into the pool below. We arrived at the same time as Jake Brake and Low Gear and stood staring at the view before taking pictures from every angle. I was so thankful to have a digital camera so that I could take a dozen photos of the same thing, knowing that later I could keep only the most spectacular shots. Ironically, I would never have the heart to delete a single photo I had taken on the Appalachian Trail.

The day presented a nice combination of rolling, flat expanses and challenging ascents. At one point I saw a yellow and black snake slither across the trail. Although he startled me at first, he ended up being completely harmless. One little tap of my pole on a nearby rock sent him slithering away.

Precisely in time for lunch, we arrived at a park that featured a huge, green lawn and a large lake. Hikers were sprawled out on the grass and picnic tables, their gear scattered about as if it were a yard sale. Tossing down our packs, we joined V3, Toolman, Jake Brake, Low Gear, Muleskinner, Rose, Bella, and Snowman. I pulled off my boots. My poor feet had been missing out on enjoying the outdoors since they were trapped in muddy boots all day. *Sorry feet. I'll try to include you more.* I shook out my socks and laid them on top of my pack to air dry. When I examined my feet, they were swollen, red, and sweaty. Gentle pressure on my soles reminded me just how sore they had been lately. I wiggled my toes in the grass and enjoyed the breeze as it dried my sweat.

While I examined my feet, Souleman took advantage of the chance to swim, ripping his shirt off and running into the lake. As he reached waist-deep water, he dove in until his whole body had been submerged. Moments later, he came out gasping for breath and shivering harshly. I had his dry shirt waiting to towel him off, but he shook his head and said he'd air dry in order to keep his shirt dry. He sat close by my side, shivering in the sun while we ate and laughed with our friends.

I think many people visualize the Appalachian Trail as a paved path that follows a straight line from Georgia to Maine. As evidenced by that day's trajectory, this belief couldn't be any further from the truth. The trail had spit us out at the middle of the southern side of the lake. While it had provided us with a perfect spot for lunch and swimming, it made for an annoying route over the next couple of miles. After lunch, we had to walk all the way around the perimeter of the lake in order to continue heading north on the other side. When attempting to hike north, there are few things more frustrating than having to head in a seemingly straight line in a different direction.

Although our route was circuitous, it afforded us an unusual sight: on one side of the lake, trees were growing straight up out of the water. It was as if someone had flooded a section of forest many years ago and the trees had just kept on growing. I was fascinated by this sight even though Souleman assured me that it was not an unusual phenomenon. I took pictures and stood on the bank, staring in wonder at those aquatic trees.

After a pleasant afternoon of hiking, we camped just past a shelter with a large group of friends. We woke at daybreak in our tent to the quiet noise of our trail friends stirring in their tents—zippers zipping, nylon rustling, and book pages turning. Quickly we were on our way north again. As sometimes happened on the trail, I was full of the deep thoughts I rarely had time for otherwise. I contemplated who I really was and worried that I hadn't figured out more on the hike so far.

I had always imagined that once I finished college, I would have my life figured out. Although I had missed my graduation ceremony, I had earned my bachelor's degree. But instead of starting a professional job, going to graduate school, or getting married like some of my peers, I was playing in the woods using a make-believe name. I did not feel like the adult I was supposed to be. I had so much unfinished philosophical business. I had expected to have unlimited time to think about the world and my place in it, but I found that I was spending most of my time thinking about day-to-day responsibilities and my overwhelming tiredness.

I wondered about my life plan after the trail. I thought about my stance on gay marriage and abortion. I considered my take on the war in Iraq and George W. Bush's performance as president. Mostly I wondered when I would be completely comfortable in my own shoes and really know who I was. *Do you just wake up one day and feel like an adult? Or does some life event cause that to happen?*

I reflected on the book *Catcher in the Rye*, which I had read, and greatly enjoyed, in middle school. I felt a kinship with Holden Caulfield and his endless questions about the world. The self-reflection fueling my brain must have also fueled my body that day because I turned into a speed hiker. I moved hastily over the day's 12.9 miles and was a little sad to see the shelter sign appear. I knew that setting up camp and focusing on chores would mean stilling the internal debates that were raging inside of me.

I woke up the next morning happy to be alive. The sun was out, the temperature was mild, and the air was fresh. As I readied my gear, I sang to myself the lyrics of the Travis Tritt song "It's a Great Day to Be Alive." The brilliant sunshine shimmered on the dew drops and complemented my perkiness. We hiked sixteen miles in six and a half hours. Souleman and I went to bed that night excited that we would arrive the next day in Damascus, Virginia, the unofficial quarter-way point of the Appalachian Trail.

"Can I read your journal sometime?" Souleman asked as we hiked toward Damascus.

"I don't think so."

"Why not?"

"I just don't want you to."

Souleman sulked along behind me. His footsteps sounded angry and his poles lashed out, striking at trees and rocks in frustration.

"What are you writing that's so bad you don't want me to see it?" He wouldn't let it go.

"Nothing."

"Then why can't I read it?"

I sighed in frustration. "A girl has to have some private thoughts, ok? Maybe I don't want you to read the *good* things."

"Riiiiight." His voice oozed with sarcasm.

My journal was my confidante. Not having a girlfriend with whom to dissect minute life details, I poured my heart onto the pages of my journal. I needed a private space to figure out my feelings and was hurt that Souleman didn't understand that. I wasn't hiding anything; I just needed some privacy.

Finally, after a miserable five miles, we sat together on a fallen tree and talked about the situation. I felt horrible for making him think I had anything negative to write about him and cried when I realized how I'd hurt him. After an hour of emotional conversation, we hugged, kissed, and continued on toward Damascus. My journal remained tucked away safely—and privately—in my pack.

We arrived at The Place, a house that had been turned into a hiker hostel by a Methodist church. Other guests taught us the ropes as they showed us around.

"Grab any bed you want. Pay in the box on the wall in the kitchen. And do some chores before you leave."

There was no one in charge. Hikers paid, cleaned, and otherwise managed things by using the honor system as they came and went. Trust like this was unparalleled outside the parameters of the trail. Perhaps we were bound by survival. Or maybe it was the shared experience of carrying everything of value on your back. It could have been the necessity of relying on other people. No matter what created this confidence, no hiker would dare break it.

Damascus was a small town with only one main road. The conveniences were few, but those that existed were extremely hiker-friendly. In fact, according to Wingfoot, Damascus boasts the title of "friendliest town on the Appalachian Trail." We visited Mount Rogers Outfitters first to tackle the task of finding me new boots.

I loved my Lowa boots, but they were no longer trail-worthy. The soles were peeling, the leather was cracked, and the tread on the bottoms had worn down completely. I could feel every stick and stone beneath my feet. Mount Rogers carried Lowas, and after a quick phone call to the company, they replaced my boots for free. Gear companies are incredibly generous with thru-hikers and will often replace even heavily used gear. In exchange, hikers recommend the companies to other hikers and perpetuate the cycle.

I was thrilled to have new boots with supportive soles but a little scared about breaking them in. I had been incredibly lucky with not getting blisters thus far and didn't want to risk facing that problem. Upon hearing about my sore feet, the outfitter also talked me into a pair of insoles. Sadly, the semi-expensive inserts didn't work for me at all. The insoles caused me excruciating pain, so I left them in a hiker box for someone else to try. Hiker boxes, which are sometimes found in towns and shelters along the trail, are a place to leave unwanted gear or food in hopes that another hiker might benefit from them.

That afternoon, I proudly wore my "town skirt" to the Dairy King restaurant for a peanut butter milkshake. The treat was so thick that my jaw ached as I worked to suck it through the straw. My tongue became frozen halfway through, and the stickiness of the peanut butter made me smack my lips together. Still, I didn't take my mouth off the straw until every drop was gone. Then, Souleman and I settled at the local bar for a few hours to relax and share hiking stories with trail friends, including Domino, Jake Brake, Low Gear, Tree Trunks, Slap Happy, Touk, Bassline, Hooky, Tiny Dancer, and Fireball.

While we were at the bar, we met four guys from Purdue University who were on a week-long hiking trip. They were fascinated by the stories of our hike and conversed with us for hours. When we left, they thanked us for providing entertainment and paid our bar tab. Once again, the unsolicited generosity of strangers had shocked me.

Dave's Place, a hostel in town, had a giant front porch with picnic tables that served as a hiker gathering spot. That night, Souleman and I played two games of Spades with Jake Brake and Low Gear and won both times. Afterward, as we sat chatting on the picnic tables, they told us about their lifestyle in retirement.

Jake Brake and Low Gear were nomads who traveled from place to place and adventure to adventure in their RV. After completing the Appalachian Trail, their plan was to learn to skydive in Utah during the winter and then visit Newfoundland, followed by Alaska. They had saved money throughout their marriage in order to prepare for this retirement lifestyle. Upon retiring, they had sold their house, packed a small amount of belongings into an RV, and started having adventures. Their mail was sent to a post office box in Florida designated for nomads. I had never heard of such a lifestyle before and was intrigued. I hoped I would have as much zest for life at their age.

As I stood in the hallway that night waiting for my turn to shower, Gypsy stopped to chat. "Brownie, your legs have gotten really skinny," she told me matter-of-factly.

I looked down skeptically. "Really? I hadn't noticed," I replied.

Curious about Gypsy's comment, I stripped off my clothes and stepped onto the scale in the bathroom. It announced that I had lost fifteen pounds. *Fifteen pounds? Wow.* I stood on my tiptoes and twisted and turned in front of the sink mirror, wondering from where the fifteen pounds had evaporated. I looked at my defined leg muscles, my thin arms, my shrinking waist. *Whose body is this?* The fact that I had been eating high-calorie foods, building stronger muscles, and still losing weight would have been a modern miracle were I not expending so much energy hiking up mountains every day while carrying a giant pack.

Before stepping away from the mirror, I turned my back to it and looked over my shoulder to stare at my tattoo. The five barefoot footprints walking across my lower back were my private rebellion. I had a lifelong reputation for being a "good girl." The discreet ink reassured me that I had a fun side too. I had designed that particular image to represent my desire to blaze my own path, to lead and not follow. Using footprints also symbolized my dream to walk the Appalachian Trail. The physical changes to my body were an indication that the trail was already transforming me.

Damascus is the location of Trail Days, a famous, week-long hiker celebration that takes place annually. Like most of our friends, we planned to attend, but our schedule had put us in town over a week before the festival would begin. Since we certainly were not going to spend two weeks away from the trail, we would have to continue hiking up the trail and then hitch a ride back. Luckily, hikers travel to the celebration from all over the trail, and securing a ride was rumored to be easy.

Planning the week following our departure from Damascus was tricky. We had to space our mileage so that we would end at a well-traveled road in order to ensure that we could hitch back to town for the festival. Souleman and I sat down at a picnic table and consulted our trusty Handbook, hunting for suitable roads. Once we found a road that seemed like a good fit, we had to work backward to decide where we would sleep each night. No matter how we split the distance, we kept coming up with an extra day in our itinerary. Unfortunately, there just wasn't another road further up the trail that would work. Deciding to stay an extra day in town to eliminate the extra day was not difficult.

We visited Dairy King numerous times for milkshakes and snacks, lazed by the river, napped, ate, ate some more, and talked with all the other hikers who were dawdling in Damascus while waiting for Trail Days. Two of the hikers had all of their gear stolen while staying at The Place. Fortunately, this was an isolated event, and the crime was not committed by a fellow hiker but by a local prankster. We were glad we had moved to Dave's Place, where our belongings were locked behind a private door. This was the first and only crime against hikers that we encountered during our trip.

After a full day of lazing around, we headed to the pay phones to call our families. We found V3 and Toolman sitting on the concrete steps by the phone. V3 had his elbows propped on his knees and his head in his hands. When we stopped in front of them, he met our gazes with tear-filled eyes.

"I think I'm done, guys."

"What do you mean?" I asked, hoping my interpretation was wrong.

He shifted on the step and stared off down the sidewalk, carefully avoiding eye contact. "I think I'm going home."

"Are you sure?" I asked, taking a seat beside him. "Maybe take a few days or a week and really think about it. This is a big decision."

"This could just be a rough point, man," Souleman pointed out.

He sniffled. "No, I really think I'm done."

"Even if you stop now, you've walked further than most people will ever walk at one time. Five hundred miles is *really* far," I reminded him.

V3 looked at us each in turn, with tears making lines down his cheeks. "I'm really glad I met you guys. You're awesome. Both of you."

We each gave him a hug and then sat with him and Toolman, offering words of praise and encouragement and trading stories about our trail time together. By the time we left them to finalize their plans, V3's tears had stopped, but his decision hadn't changed.

Souleman and I took turns phoning home. It was great to speak with my parents, but talking with V3 had made me somber. On the walk back to our hostel, I grasped Souleman's hand.

"I can't imagine hiking by myself. It must be so hard. On the days I'm going slowly or the trail feels too hard, you keep me going. How do people get through those days alone?" *I had planned to hike alone. I had no idea I'd meet Souleman. Would I still be out here if we hadn't become hiking partners? Do I actually have what it takes to do this trail alone?*

"I don't know," he replied, squeezing my hand and bringing my thoughts back to the present moment.

"Do you think Vinny's making the right decision?"

"It seems pretty sudden. I've never heard him even talk about stopping, and now all of a sudden he's just going home."

"Exactly. If one of us ever wants to quit for any reason other than injury, let's make a deal that we won't quit right away," I suggested.

"How about if we agree to keep going for at least one week?"

"Deal. Shake on it?"

We shook hands and sealed the promise with a kiss.

"I'm going to miss Vinnie. It's always so much fun to run into him. Do you think Toolman will quit, too?" I asked.

He shrugged in the dark. "Probably. I don't know."

"It's so weird that we might not see them again. One day they're out here with us, and the next they could just be gone."

"I guess you'll have that." He threw out one of his favorite Vermont phrases.

"Would you quit if I did?" I asked, trying to see his face in the shadows.

"I wouldn't let you quit."

Upon reaching the hostel, we found out that another hiker, Captain Chaos, had decided to stop hiking too. As other hikers told us the story, Souleman squeezed my hand silently. For the second time in one day, we found strength in being a team. That night we lay with our limbs intertwined, facing each other in the dark in our private room's double bed. We whispered about making it to New England and eventually Maine. Luckily for us, we both had family in New England, so we would know the area better and have more visitors. Most of our friends were leaving familiar territory and felt more nervous about hiking up north. We had a lot to look forward to.

"I just can't believe Vinny's done. Are you scared that that could be us?" I asked him.

"Sometimes. But I've got a lot to stay for." He pressed his forehead against mine.

"I love you," I told him, my hands moving up to touch his cheek and beard. It amazed me how quickly those words had become so natural.

"I love you too, Brownie."

Still tangled around Souleman, I fell asleep dreaming of Katahdin.

13

Want to Go on a Date?

The third morning in Damascus was as peaceful as the first two had been. Townspeople and hikers milled about in the streets in harmony. Not a single local resident looked strangely at the hikers wearing grungy clothes and Crocs. This was truly the epitome of a trail town. Knowing that we would return to this same town before long was strange. Other than our unplanned two-time visit to Erwin, we normally passed through towns enjoying the visit but knowing that it was a one-time stop on our journey.

We were ready to put some trail miles behind us. Too many days in town had made our legs antsy, and finding out that multiple people we knew were leaving the trail had made us edgy. The faster we moved north, the more confident we were that we would not become dropout statistics. Souleman and I hefted our packs and followed the sidewalk toward the edge of town.

Damascus was one of few towns that the trail actually went through directly. We followed the white blazes painted right on the sidewalk, intending to walk straight out of town. We got sidetracked by the smell of bacon wafting through the air from an outdoor diner. With our daily calorie expenditure so high, it was easy to justify any stop for food.

I stuffed a syrup-smothered bite of chocolate chip pancakes into my mouth before I had even swallowed the previous bite of sausage. "Do you think food will ever taste this good after the trail?"

"Probably not," he answered, still chewing, as he flagged down the waitress for more orange juice.

"Then I guess we better eat even more now." I finished my perfectly crunchy bacon while staring across the patio. The Appalachian Trail could be seen swirling up the mountain like smoke from a fire.

A few minutes later Souleman wiped his finger across his plate to wipe up the last of his syrup. He licked his finger and announced, "That was good."

"Mmmhmm." I had just polished off a blueberry muffin with cream cheese. "But now we have to hike up that." I pointed at the mountain.

Hikers live by the saying "down to town," which explains the near-guarantee that the trail will slope downhill on the way to each town. Unfortunately, that almost always guarantees that the opposite will also be true—that the trail will slope uphill on the way out of town. Since packs are heaviest when leaving town, this inevitable uphill climb seems like a cruel trick of nature. Upon leaving Damascus, the hike was predictably uphill, but it was also beautiful—the best climb out of town yet. After having spent so much time in town, I was thrilled to be back in the woods and away from all the people. For many miles we hiked in companionable, blissful silence.

We passed our intended destination of Saunders Shelter and pushed on to camp beside a pond. Although we hadn't begun our hike until after eleven o'clock in the morning, we ended up hiking almost twelve miles. It still dumbfounded me to think that when I had started the trail just three short months ago, I was struggling to complete eight miles in an entire day, and now I could tick off twelve miles in half a day with no trouble.

We erected the Blue Mansion and cooked a dinner of Lipton Noodles. I had recently learned to scavenge for ramps (wild onions), so I mixed some with the noodles, hoping to spice up the flavor. I was already pretty sure that I wouldn't be able to eat Lipton Noodles for a long time after finishing the trail. With full bellies, we settled inside the tent on our Therm-a-Rests to calculate our daily mileage. As we got quiet, we heard a loud, repeated slapping sound. The sound echoed all around us and filled the otherwise silent night. At first I was scared, and my eyes darted all around as I peered out of the tent's mesh opening. Then Souleman remembered having seen a beaver dam in the pond. He told me that what we heard was probably the sound of their tails popping the water.

In what I can only assume was an exhaustion-induced silly session, Souleman began to describe, with exaggerated seriousness, the plight of the beaver. According to him, beavers were the most powerful animal of all, but no one knew it.

"Beavers were around during the time of the dinosaurs and had wings," he explained. "They ate all the dinosaurs, which is, of course, why dinosaurs are now extinct. Then the beavers regressed and became small so that people wouldn't realize their power and kill them."

"But someday," Souleman continued in mock sincerity, "beavers will rise up and take over the world. Dinosaurs will return to help out the giant beavers. And the dinosaurs will eat people the way that cows eat grass."

Souleman laid back on his Therm-a-Rest with his hands behind his head. After a few moments of silence, he said, "I'll tell my children that story someday."

"Yeah?" I questioned, rising up on one elbow.

He pulled my head down onto his chest before continuing, "Yep, and I'll also tell them how their mom used to dig up vegetables for dinner on her hands and knees after walking up mountains all day."

I smiled into his sweaty, stinky shirt. After a few minutes of quiet, I assumed that he had fallen asleep. Being careful not to disturb him, I turned off his headlamp. As I was sliding it off his head, he surprised me by speaking.

"Brownie?"

"Mmmhmm?" I answered, settling back onto his chest.

"Want to go on a date with me tomorrow?"

I smiled. "What did you have in mind?"

"I thought maybe we could go for a hike."

"That sounds nice."

In the morning I awoke before Souleman. I brushed his hair off his forehead and ran my fingers through his hair. Keeping his eyes closed, he unhurriedly raised his arm and laced his fingers through mine. I leaned in and kissed him as he slid his other arm around my waist and pulled me on top of him.

A bit later we packed up our gear.

"So, how about that date?" Souleman asked with an easy smile. When I grinned, he clicked my poles with his and we started north.

That day I became a thru-hiker in my mind. Granted, I had already hiked almost five hundred miles, crossed Clingmans Dome and Roan Mountain, traversed four states, and passed through Damascus, the unofficial quarter-way point. But for some reason that day was a real challenge. We crossed Whitetop Mountain, and it took everything I had to finish the day and end on top of Mount Rogers. Each step seemed to take enormous effort. My legs felt like they were the size of an elephant's, and my pack seemed as big as a circus tent.

The day's scenery included two cow pastures with miles of little white flowers that covered the ground like freshly fallen snow. It felt as if we were walking in a winter wonderland, except that the weather was warm enough for shorts and a t-shirt. Tree Trunks passed us in one pasture as we were seated on rocks having a snack.

"Happy Mother's Day, Brownie," he called out.

"I'm not a mom, Tree Trunks."

"Someday you will be. It's appropriate to wish a Happy Mother's Day to future mothers too," he responded sincerely.

Despite the challenge of having to push my body to walk that day, I was in a good mood. The scenery was beautiful, and the memory of Souleman's recent sweetness curved my lips into a smile. My pace dragged the sixteen miles into an all-day affair, so it was almost completely dark when we arrived at the shelter on top of Mount Rogers. For the last two miles we could see our destination, but the trail that approached it seemed like an unending line stretching out before us. I alternated between staring ahead at the unattainable mirage of a shelter and glaring at my traitorously slow feet. I planted my poles before each step and pulled my aching body up to meet the poles. Each step was painful. Souleman trudged along behind me at my pace without complaining.

As dusk descended, we finally made it to the shelter. A family with three children was already settled in sleeping bags inside the shelter, their gear strewn everywhere. Although they offered to make space for us, intruding on their family time would have been awkward. We opted to tent just up the trail instead. After passing through a fence, we prepared to camp in a sprawling pasture on top of the mountain. Cows ambled around inside the enclosure. All I could see were walking cheeseburgers.

With practiced efficiency, we erected the tent and set it on the ground. Souleman dug in his pack for his sleeping pad as I searched for our stakes to secure the tent. Upon locating the stakes, I looked up just in time to see a robust wind pick up our tent and send it somersaulting across the pasture. Souleman took off after it, hollering, and I doubled over laughing. The tent bounced further and further away over bushes, plants, and—I'm sure—many cow pies. I knelt in the pasture and laughed until tears rolled down my cheeks. Souleman finally returned, out of breath, with the tent in tow. We threw our heavy packs inside to weight it down while we secured it with the stakes and guy lines.

The wind was too strong to keep the flame on our camp stove lit outside, so, against better judgment, we cranked up the stove inside the tent's vestibule. *Please don't let us set the tent on fire.* My rumbling stomach overruled my common sense. We chose mashed potatoes for dinner because they required the shortest cooking time and therefore the least amount of fire risk. Totally disregarding the adage that a watched pot never boils, I stared at the flame impatiently and awaited seeing bubbles in the water. At the first indication of a boil, I turned off the stove and dumped in the potato mix. Two titanium sporks dueled for massive bites of potatoes as we raced to eat our dinner before it became cold in the wind.

Fog rolled in while we ate, and soon we could no longer see the fence between us and the shelter. Together we braved the eerie whiteness to hang our food inside the shelter. I needed to relieve my screaming bladder but had no idea where I could find the privacy of a tree. I looked around at the thick, white fog that obscured everything beyond a five-foot radius. Deciding that the fog would create plenty of privacy, I walked about ten feet further and squatted right there. Momentarily, the idea of taking cover in the fog seemed brilliant. When I stood up and refastened my pants, though, I realized I had no idea where Souleman was.

"Souleman?" I whisper-yelled as I craned my neck, turning my head from side to side. I could see nothing. "Souleman?!" I raised my voice a little louder.

"Right here."

I flailed my arm around, grabbing for him in the dark. Our arms connected.

"How are we going to find the tent?"

"Umm . . . "

We squinted and peered around in all directions. Holding on to each other, we stumbled around in the dark until the light from my headlamp eventually bounced off of a reflective strip on the Blue Mansion's guy lines.

I expected to fall asleep right away after such a trying and challenging day. Instead we played a round of dots, a silly game from middle school, on a blank page of journal paper. We sat in our headlamp haze singing silly songs and reading our Handbook for the millionth time.

"We were made for each other," he told me before we finally closed our eyes.

I woke up the next morning and once again reveled in the simplicity of living and sleeping in the same outfit. I wove my hair into braided pigtails, tied on my bandana, and fastened my gaiters into place. I had become quite fond of my hiking uniform. I thought that the combination of gaiters and poles made me look very official.

I hurried down the trail, whistling to myself. According to our Handbook, we would soon pass through Grayson Highlands State Park, which was inhabited by wild ponies. Many repeat thru-hikers had told us about the amazing horses. I envisioned a dozen ponies with their manes blowing in the wind coming up to lick the salt off my arms.

Contrary to what I had imagined, I hiked all day and saw only one pony, and it was so far in the distance that I had to squint to know what it was. It could have been a My Little Pony toy for all I could tell. This section of the trail was beautiful, which slightly eased the let-down over the ponies. The path wound over mountaintops and little man-made, wooden bridges. We stopped and splashed in a stream during one of our breaks. That day's charm also included an interesting rock formation called "Fat Man's Squeeze," as well as a place where the white blazes lead hikers to wiggle through a cave-like hole in a giant rock face.

After six miles, I had completely run out of steam. For another mile I pushed my miserable body forward. *What is the matter with me?* I didn't know if my diet was lacking enough fuel in the form of calories or what else could be causing my consistent lack of energy. I tried to keep hiking but could only think about sitting down and eating. In my head I repeated the mantra from Lark's inspiration letter: *I am stronger than steel, faster than pain, and more intense than hunger. Trail, you are my bitch!*

I told myself to keep hiking until we found an appropriate spot to stop and eat. *You've only hiked six miles. You can't stop yet.* Although my mind urged my legs to walk a little further, my body was protesting. My ankles screamed, my knees throbbed, and my back spasmed. *I am stronger than steel, faster than pain, and more intense than hunger. Trail, you are my bitch.* I waged a battle with the part of myself that wanted to just stop and forced one foot in front of the other while leaning heavily on my poles. *I hate this trail. I hate it, hate it, hate it.* I sighed audibly. *The trail isn't the issue, my body is.* Finally giving up, I tossed my poles to the side and plopped down cross-legged in the middle of the trail with my pack still on.

"It's time for lunch," I stated.

For a few quiet seconds, Souleman stared at me with his mouth slightly agape. "Don't you want to at least move off the trail?"

I glared at him.

Without another word, he pressed his lips into a tight line and pulled the lunch food out of his pack. I ate ravenously without speaking. Crackers, cheese, cookies, dried fruit, peanut butter, and other goodies layered themselves on top of one another in my stomach as I attempted to infuse myself with energy. After having gorged on calorie-laden food, I was ready to tackle the trail again.

Ironically, on this day when I was feeling so guilty about moving slowly and not comfortably upping my mileage, a previous thru-hiker named CatDog ran into us. She reminded us to not focus on mileage and said that it was her biggest regret from her thru-hike. Souleman and I discussed how we could stay focused on enjoying the hiking and not just on counting mileage.

We sat alone on a tall rock that night and watched the sunset. The colors changed splendidly, and the sky reflected almost the full rainbow of colors before fading to black. This was the type of beauty we knew we should be enjoying.

My energy returned with the sun the next day, and we knocked off ten miles before one o'clock. As a reward, we hitched into town for more cheeseburgers. Back on the trail, the last four miles of the day were riddled with tollbooths, and we spent as much time kissing as we did hiking. By the time we set up camp, we were content to cuddle through the brewing thunderstorm.

14

A Damn Big Squirrel

On Friday, May 13, we hiked eleven miles and then hitched back to Damascus for Trail Days. Getting a ride was a little harder than we had expected, but we were successful after I made a sign and we changed our hitching location. The man who stopped was initially going to take us only partway, but he became interested in our stories and decided to go out of his way to take us into Damascus. For the millionth time on my trip, I reminded myself how much kindness I would owe the world after my hike was over.

During our absence, Damascus had been transformed. The streets and sidewalks were now packed with people and activity, and even the hostels and hotels in nearby towns were full of hikers. As soon as we walked into town, we saw familiar faces. A trail friend offered us a ride to Tent City in the back of his truck. Tent City was a fenced-in area of land over a one-mile square where the town allowed hikers to camp during Trail Days. Most of the hikers, including us, stayed there for the duration of the celebration.

I scanned the overwhelming sight as I hoisted my pack. Tents and tarps of all shapes, sizes, and colors were scattered around the entire enclosure. Many tents were grouped together, and some clusters sported flags or decorations to designate particular cliques. Port-a-potties lined the access roads, and vendors with hiking supplies had booths near the entrance.

Having no idea where our friends were camped, and rationalizing that we could visit anyone regardless of where we slept, we found a clear, flat space on the edge of the woods and prepared the Blue Mansion for a weekend of camping. This would be the first time our tent had stayed in the same spot for more than one night. As we were settling in, we heard a familiar voice.

"Souleman! Brownie! I heard that you two were here." Jax was striding toward us, grinning. He looked thinner than when we had last seen him, and his beard had grown.

"Hey, man!" Souleman gave Jax an enthusiastic hug. "Are you set up yet? Camp with us."

While the guys were catching up, I dressed in my finest attire—my wrap skirt, cleanest shirt, pink town socks, and Crocs—for our first venture back into town. The local fire department was sponsoring a free hot dog dinner, and Tent City was situated a mile and a half outside town. While this distance was nothing compared to what we normally hiked in a day, it seemed wasteful to expend so much energy on our days off when rides were readily available. Anyone driving between one place and the other made room for hikers.

We feasted on hot dogs, chips, and other treats while we met hikers, townspeople, and trail angels from all over. The pavilion was full of hikers, and we wandered from table to table catching up with friends who were ahead of and behind us on the trail. The reminiscing and sharing of stories continued late into the night once we returned to Tent City.

We awoke the next morning to the nearby sounds of dozens of tents being zipped and unzipped, fires crackling, and hikers yelling back and forth. It was time to head to town to embrace the spectacular celebration of Trail Days. First, we attended the Hiker Talent Show, where we cheered on Domino and his song "Mindless Switchbacks." There were entries of all varieties, and watching the happy hikers performing was good for a lot of laughs. We sat on the blacktop with Jax and many other friends, snacking and laughing until the last performer had finished.

Later in the day, we went to a screening of a new Appalachian Trail movie called *Walking with Freedom*, produced by a hiker we'd met by the name of Lion King. The movie was well made and full of passion, and the hikers who filled the auditorium were emotional as they watched scenes of the places they had been and those they had yet to experience. When the movie ended, the entire audience rose as one. We cheered and clapped—equally thrilled with the movie and the knowledge that we were living our own movie-worthy life event. I left the auditorium so motivated for the continuation of my hike that I almost wanted to pack up that night and push on toward Maine.

One of the much-anticipated rituals of Trail Days was the hiker parade, in which hikers from different years formed groups and paraded through town. Some groups made floats and banners, while others dressed in themed costumes. Everyone carried a water gun. As happened each year, a giant water fight broke out between the hikers and the townspeople. Our Dollar Store guns were pitiful, and we left the parade soaked but in good spirits.

Each night in Tent City, there was a huge campfire at the center of the "city," complete with a drum circle. The scene was primitive and haunting. I imagined that Burning Man and other such festivals had similar happenings. Women dressed like gypsies and shirtless men, all in various stages of inebriation, danced in a circle around the fire, chanting and banging on drums and other improvised instruments. The sound was simultaneously pleasing and eerie.

After several days of fun, laughter, and friendship, it was finally time to leave the festivities. We said our goodbyes to friends and laboriously packed our gear. Everything we owned was water-logged from the relentless rain that had fallen on the final night. With our food resupply, the wet tent, a wet sleeping bag, and wet clothes, Souleman's pack easily weighed fifty pounds. Mine didn't seem much lighter. We hated the thought of returning to the trail with heavy packs and wet gear.

"I'd take some of the weight from your pack if I could, but I'm not sure my pack can hold anything else without busting," Souleman told me as we prepared to leave.

"I'm tough," I said, trying not to wince as I shouldered my outlandish pack.

A friend of a friend named Taba offered us a free ride back to the trail. We asserted that we didn't want to impose and said that we would find another ride, but he insisted. We gathered our packs and headed to the meeting place for his shuttle.

Our ride was an unmarked, white, moving-type van that had been converted into a living space. The back area had two leather couches bolted to the floor, along with various other seats. All of Taba's worldly possessions were attached to the walls or ceiling by pulley systems, ropes, chains, and carabineers. A bike hung overhead, and rock-climbing equipment was attached to a pegboard on one wall.

Taba had dabbled at hiking the trail for a number of years without ever completing much mileage. Now, he spent a lot of time shuttling hikers to and from the trail. He ushered us into the van along with a number of other hikers and two dogs. *Yay, dogs.* After numerous delays, we heard the distinctive scrape of metal on metal as he latched the door shut from the outside. *So this is what it feels like to be kidnapped.* With no windows, no ventilation, and no exit door, I was immediately a little claustrophobic.

"There's only one rule in Taba's van," he told us over his shoulder from the driver's seat. "Have fun." He started the engine but turned around to say one more thing. "You can do anything you want, I don't care. Just share with the driver, ok? You can drink, smoke, smoke the good stuff, whatever. Just remember, share with the driver."

We're going to end up in jail.

Taba faced the front, and after steering onto the road, turned over his shoulder to face his captors again.

"Should we stop for beer?"

I stole a look at someone's watch—I had abandoned mine hundreds of miles ago—and saw that it was ten in the morning. To my relief, no one else seemed interested in drinking. Taba offered to stop for beer at least three more times. He swerved down the road and I nervously held on to Souleman. *Is this legal? We're riding down the highway in the back of a van, sitting on couches without seatbelts.* I was incredibly relieved that I didn't additionally have to worry about open alcohol containers and a drunk driver.

Taba drove for over an hour and then pulled over on the gravel shoulder. "Does anyone know where we are?" he asked. I exchanged an annoyed look with Souleman. *Seriously? Who just starts driving without knowing where they're going?* Another hiker climbed into the passenger seat and pulled out some maps. After at least three people had given input on which route would be best, Taba resumed driving. Thirty minutes later, he pulled to the side of the road again. *What now?*

"My socks are really bothering me. I have to change them," he explained as he climbed into the back of the van and started digging around for new socks.

I was incredulous. *This is insane. Socks? Will we ever get back to the trail?* Once he had changed socks, he offered, "Anyone want to get out and stretch?" No one moved.

After two more unnecessary stops, we finally made it to our destination. What should have been a forty-minute drive had taken over four hours. I was mildly carsick and not-so-mildly annoyed. I stumbled out of the van and stood blinking in the hotel parking lot. The long ride and late hour, combined with our heavy packs of wet gear, made us decide to spend a night drying out before we returned to the trail.

"Let's not *ever* ride with him again." I said to Souleman as the van sped across the parking lot, bouncing over a speed bump.

Returning to the trail was miraculous. I was so thrilled to be hiking again. At a distance of fourteen miles, our first day back was our longest day out of a town yet. My steps were strong and confident. With each stride I took, I could hear Katahdin calling me in the distance. On May 16, the beginning of our third month of hiking, we passed the official quarter-way point. I worried a little that we had three-quarters of the mileage remaining and only four more months to go. I was reassured, however, by the fact that almost everyone who had started on dates near ours remained in the same general vicinity.

Our second day in Virginia became our longest mileage day yet. Hiking nineteen miles seemed like a surreal accomplishment. The flowers were blooming and the sun shone brightly. By the end of the day, I had a long list of ailments: a pulled muscle in my back, poison ivy on my feet and ankles, a blister on one foot, blisters on each hand, a raw spot under my right arm, and aching feet. Somehow, the many days off had decreased my body's toughness.

As we passed the miles, Souleman told me of his passion for coaching children's football and his hope to do it again in the fall. Coaching Little League baseball was another dream of his. As he talked about the kids and the plays, I enjoyed the enthusiasm in his voice.

"When we have kids, I'm going to take them on cool adventures if you"—he paused abruptly, embarrassed—"uh, their mom, ever goes away for the weekend."

He wants to have kids with me!

I turned around and flashed a mischievous smile. "If you have kids with someone else, this relationship is doomed."

The happiness and easy companionship continued into the next day as we again put up big mileage. My legs were surprisingly cooperative with the increased distances. Only my feet were objecting. Over the course of that day's many miles, we encountered trail magic twice: first, apple juice left in a stream, then Oreos and strawberries.

We reached our target destination early and decided to eat a snack and hike on. During our snack break, we laid side by side in a patch of shade with our heads propped on our packs and our hands clasped between us. I thought back to the beginning of the trail when we had sought sun and warmth rather than shade and a breeze. We had come a long way already; in hiking from Georgia to Virginia, we'd gone from winter to spring.

Soon after we resumed hiking, we encountered a bridge. Waiting on the other side of the water for Souleman to cross, I leaned on my poles to ease the strain on my back. When the weight in my pack shifted, I lost my balance and fell backward into the stream.

Souleman looked up at the splash to see me seated in a foot of water. I saw the muscles in his face twitch as he valiantly suppressed the urge to laugh. *Chivalry lives.* When he heard me laughing, he gave in and laughed along with me. I remained seated in the stream until he crossed and pulled me to my feet. Nothing important had gotten wet, but I did have to hike with wet shorts and a dripping pack.

The trail seemed to be playing a trick on us that day because we could not find a flat spot for our tent when we were ready to stop. As we kept looking for somewhere to camp, our pace slowed—largely due to my aching feet—and it became difficult to gauge our mileage. To keep our morale high, Souleman pretended to be a reporter interviewing me after I had summited Katahdin.

"And tell me, Brownie," he began in a deep, animated voice, "what does it feel like to have hiked twenty-two hundred miles?"

Laughing, I played along. "It's wonderful. Surreal, really."

"And which of the fourteen states was your favorite?" he asked, holding out his hiking pole to me as a microphone.

"Honestly, it's impossible to say. Every state was unique."

He carried on, keeping us laughing and distracted until we found a flat enough spot to spend the night.

As usual, we found a new burst of energy when it was time to set up camp and eat. Sitting knee to knee with Souleman in the dirt, I leaned close to dip my spork into our shared pot. When he dropped a bit of food on his knee, I leaned down and licked it off.

"Now *that's* love!" he declared. "I've hiked eighteen miles today, nineteen yesterday, and I haven't showered."

Smiling, I shrugged and licked his knee again for emphasis.

Our streak of good weather ended abruptly the following day with a horrible thunderstorm. Rain whipped around us and wind howled through the trees. We were soggy and uncomfortable long before lunch. After very little debate, we added a mile to our day and accepted an invitation to split a hotel room with Hazy Sonic and Firefly in Atkins, Virginia. At the hotel, Hazy played songs on the guitar and we watched Animal Planet on TV.

During our overnight, we learned that these two were the couple we had been asked about on top of Clingmans Dome. I couldn't believe that Karis and Brian, who were strangers at the time of the conversation, turned out to be our treasured trail friends Firefly and Hazy Sonic. I would remain connected with these two long after our hike, and we would often mention the unexpected run-in with Firefly's parents.

Once we had settled in for the night, I opened my journal to a new page and saw Souleman's handwriting there instead. Somehow he had managed to borrow my journal while I had been filtering water the night before. I curled up next to him on the bed to read.

> *Together to Maine*
> *I came from the peach state,*
> *Many mountains ahead,*
> *Leaving all behind,*
> *Friends, family, and bed.*
> *In leaving my home,*
> *Many things have been gained,*
> *Knowledge, wisdom,*
> *And even some pain.*
> *In looking for nothing,*
> *And walking in the woods,*
> *I finally found something*
> *That can be understood.*
> *She has stolen my heart,*
> *And been by my side,*
> *Always there,*
> *With that look in her eye.*
> *A look so precious,*
> *So beautiful, so sweet,*
> *Making me wonder*
> *Why she chose me.*
> *No end in sight,*
> *But we might feel some pain,*
> *Together we can make it,*
> *Together to Maine.*

"You took my journal," I accused him after I had finished reading.

"Yes, but I didn't read it."

"Ok."

"Do you believe me?" he asked.

"Do you believe that I'm not hiding anything in my journal?"

"I think so."

"Then I *think* I believe you."

He wrapped his arms around me, and I leaned my head back against his shoulder.

"Your poem was really cute," I told him.

"You're really cute," he whispered into my hair.

The stay in town proved to be addictive, and the lure of rest and a bed to sleep in enticed us to stay one more night. It seemed that I just could not get enough sleep over the past several weeks. I fell asleep as soon as I closed my eyes at night. In towns I hit the snooze button on the alarm clocks repeatedly, and on the trail I begged Souleman for a few extra minutes of sleep before we packed our gear. For someone who had spent her entire life struggling to sleep, I had not expected to be sleeping so much. I chalked up the extra tiredness to the unusual amount of physical activity.

After sleeping in and eating, Souleman and I tackled chores. At the laundromat, I was sorting my mail drop and waiting for our clothes to wash when I heard my name from across the room.

"Brownie?"

I peered curiously around the laundromat.

"Hey. I'm Beantown. I think we're from the same hometown."

"You're from Wilbraham?"

This was quite a shock because Wilbraham is a tiny little town in Massachusetts. Most people have never even heard of it. We discussed mutual acquaintances and figured out that he was the cousin of a good friend of mine from high school. It was ironic how walking across the country was making me realize simultaneously how big and how small the world really was.

Our town chores took little time, and since Hazy and Firefly had returned to the trail that morning, we had the hotel room to ourselves. We spent the rest of the day enjoying TV, wine, and time alone together in a civilized bed. Souleman generously massaged my aching, tender feet, and I reciprocated by working the knots out of his shoulders.

Before we returned to the trail, we had to find a store. I was in desperate need of a new sports bra. Apparently bras aren't meant to be worn twenty-four hours a day for months at a time. Since the town lacked an outfitter, Wal-Mart was our only option. The walk to the store was long and slightly dangerous since the road was busy and had a narrow shoulder. After having successfully made our purchases, we lingered in the parking lot trying to figure out where to stand to hitch. An old woman drove past us twice and finally pulled over and handed us a fistful of change and one-dollar bills.

"Here. Go get something to eat," she told us.

I looked at the money in my hand in confusion. Then it dawned on me. *She thinks we're homeless.* Apparently, long-distance hikers and homeless people have the same ragged look. By the time I recovered enough to hand the money back, she had already driven away.

"What in the world are we going to do with this money?" Souleman asked, peering into my cupped hands.

"You heard the lady. Get something to eat."

"Let me guess, you want a cheeseburger."

I grinned and pointed at the McDonald's across the parking lot.

Souleman and I were still laughing about the money handout when we finally made it back to the trail. Dry, packed dirt lined the trail, and perfect white blazes made our route clear. The trail was wide enough that we could walk side by side and smooth enough that we could carry our poles in one hand rather than using them to walk. We held hands happily, swinging them back and forth as we walked down the trail. A side trail to a waterfall drew us in, and we watched daring locals test the frigid water. I was tempted to jump in, but since we were clean and the air was breezy, I held off.

The relative lack of progress in recent days had both of us itching to move more quickly, so we wasted no time heading up the trail. Virginia is a long state, and many hikers get the "Virginia Blues" and become discouraged by the long distance and repetitive scenery. So far I was enjoying Virginia as much as the rest of the trail, but I knew that we should increase our speed and decrease our town time in order to guarantee a timely summit date in Maine. The flat terrain kept me moving along, though I required numerous water breaks due to the unbelievable heat.

Just as we were discussing stopping for lunch the next day, we smelled cheeseburgers and were ecstatic to find more trail magic, including corn on the cob, cheeseburgers, salad, and soda. Boosted by the extra calories, we pushed up Pearis Mountain, where we planned to camp near Angel's Rest Overlook.

A couple of hours after lunch, I was hiking in front, lost in my own thoughts, when I saw motion out of the corner of my eye and came to an abrupt halt. Souleman bumped into me and also looked up. A large man was leaning against a tree just ahead. He had on jean overalls and big chunky boots, with a child's school backpack slung over one shoulder. A plaid blanket was tied to the bottom of the pack, and he was absentmindedly snapping a twig with one hand.

"He's scary," I whispered over my shoulder, switching both poles to the same hand and putting my other hand behind me to touch Souleman. I never took my eyes off the eccentric man.

"Just keep walking. Don't stop," Souleman responded quietly, nudging me forward.

Right as we passed the man, he shifted his pack on his shoulder and asked, "How ya doin'?"

We nodded and mumbled incoherent responses.

"I'm from this area. Go hikin' up here all the time."

"Great. Enjoy!" My voice sounded a little too high-pitched to my ears. I passed him hurriedly. Something about the man just gave me the creeps. *What is he doing this far up the mountain in town clothes? Why does he have a child's backpack?*

"Hey, how far to Angel's Rest?" he called after us.

Since that was our destination, we knew down to a tenth of a mile how far away it was. Not trusting him, and wanting to err on the side of caution, I said, "Oh, I'm not completely sure. It's up ahead." *He said he hikes up here all the time; shouldn't he know?*

"Where ya' headed?" he asked, falling into step behind us.

"We haven't decided," Souleman lied.

I took off at an astounding speed. My legs pumped furiously over the uneven ground. Even when I stumbled over tree roots, I kept my speed consistent. I could hear Souleman directly behind me. I glanced over my shoulder repeatedly and finally noticed that the man was out of sight. We sped right to the signpost for Angel's Rest and looked only briefly at the viewpoint. Sadly, we agreed that sleeping there was not an option with the strange man so close behind us. Not knowing what else to do, we kept hiking. It was already getting late. *I'm so tired. I don't know how much further I can walk.* My feet were throbbing and felt like Elmer Fudd's thumb looked in the cartoon after he had hit it with a hammer. I half expected to look down and see my shoes expanding and contracting.

In spite of my exhaustion, I hiked on. Souleman stayed right on my heels offering words of encouragement. He recognized that I was in pain and was sorry that we couldn't stop. We knew there was a town at the bottom of the hill and could soon see its lights. My swollen feet began to seem unwieldy, and I started tripping over rocks and roots. After stumbling a few times and catching myself with my hands, I had no choice but to take a break on a fallen log. I couldn't relax for fear of seeing the overall-clad man appear behind us.

"How are you holding up?" Souleman asked me.

"Terribly. My feet hurt so much," I replied, willing myself not to cry.

He squeezed my shoulder. "I'm sorry."

"It's not your fault. I'll be ok." I glanced back up the trail. "That man really creeped me out."

He nodded in agreement. "I got a bad vibe, too. I think it's a good thing we kept going."

"How will we know when we're far enough away?"

"I'm not sure."

Finally, anxiety overcame exhaustion and I resumed my awkward plodding down the trail. The downhill seemed endless, and I was nearing tears when the path suddenly spit us out on a road. The trail followed the street for a bit, and we seriously considered sleeping in an abandoned house we passed. We went as far as climbing the steps to the porch, peering in the windows, and even looking around inside. Fear of being arrested if we got caught was our only deterrent. Repeated glances behind us yielded no hint of the weird man.

By now it was dark and we had to pull out our headlamps in order to keep walking. A car pulled over and offered us a ride to town. While we did briefly discuss it, we knew we couldn't go back into town even in spite of the temptation of a free hostel. Thanking the driver, we hiked on. We decided to stay on the trail through town and camp in the woods on the other side once it seemed safe.

An awful smell soon hit us, and Souleman began spitting on the ground repeatedly, as if he could taste the noxious odor. After following the road through a questionable part of town, we were then thrown into darkness as the path headed away from town. The horrible smell continued. We passed a manufacturing plant with huge metal tanks. Its tall, metal barrier fences were covered with warning placards. A spotlight on one tank highlighted the words "WEAK ACID." We guessed this to be the source of the unbearable smell. Laughing nervously, we passed the plant and followed the blazes back into the woods.

True to form, the trail headed uphill as soon as we left town. Thick, sticky spider webs crisscrossed our path, and we took turns walking in front and breaking through them. Souleman was scared of spiders, and I was uncomfortable in the dark, so the going was sluggish. *So this is night hiking.* Our headlamps, which were great for reading and setting up camp, were useless for night hiking. Fortunately, we hadn't really needed to night hike until then. We occasionally stopped and peered into the darkness past the trail, hoping to see a flat spot. My feet had gone far beyond throbbing pain into an uncomfortable numbness.

We crossed two more roads and a stinky, sulfuric spring. We were losing hope for finding a flat spot, and our speed was getting slower and slower. The next shelter was still five miles away, and I certainly couldn't keep going that far. Just across one rarely traveled road, the trail widened into a patch of dirt. Right there, directly off a road in the middle of the trail, we pitched our tent. It was ten o'clock at night, and we had hiked 18.5 miles.

Inside the tent, I examined my throbbing feet in the light of my headlamp. The egg-shaped lump on my left foot was back and bigger than ever. After examining my injuries, I collapsed on my back beside Souleman.

"Do you want me to cook dinner?" I asked after a few minutes of silence.

"No. It's too late."

I agreed. For once food was not among our top concerns.

Just as I was drifting into the hazy realm of slumber, something large crashed into the bushes beside our tent. Souleman's entire body went rigid beside mine, and he reached for me in the dark.

"What was that?" I croaked out, my voice barely audible.

He sat frozen next to me, listening. "I don't know."

We heard rustling and crackling to our left.

"A squirrel?" I asked hopefully.

He paused a long time before whispering back, "That's a damn big squirrel." His fingers stayed tightly curled around mine.

"There's no way it could be that man, right?" I asked.

"Right." His voice lacked conviction.

My heart raced and my ears were on high alert, listening to every noise outside our nylon shelter. I know we both had visions of the overall-clad man standing over our tent. Just as I was drifting back to sleep, Souleman squeezed my hand urgently.

"Brownie? Did you hear that?"

It was going to be a long night for us both.

After dozing fitfully, we finally abandoned all pretense of sleep and emerged from the tent at daybreak. The bushes beside us were trampled, and we wondered what had made the ruckus during the night. Our breakfast granola bars did not even put a dent in my hunger. All morning we talked of nothing but food. Cheeseburgers, steaks, Buffalo wings, milkshakes, loaded nachos—no food was safe from our hunger-driven daydreams.

To really test our spirits, the trail went uphill all morning until we arrived at Rice Field Shelter. The shelter was gorgeous, and I immediately felt sad that we would not be spending the night. It was situated at the edge of the woods, inside a fenced enclosure. In front of the shelter, a rolling meadow opened up as far as the eye could see. The brilliant, blue sky filled with puffy, white clouds was welcoming and calming. Our fears from the previous night seemed very far away.

A stile was located directly in front of the shelter. These were an annoyance we had only recently begun to encounter. Stiles are little ladders shaped like the letter "A" that straddle fences and allow hikers to cross without letting animals out. The rungs are often rickety and the steps far apart, which makes them exceptionally hard to climb while wearing a pack. Mustering my last reserve of energy, I propelled myself up and over the stile and hopped up to sit on the shelter floor. With my pack still on, I fell over sideways and lay still with my face pressed to the sandy, wooden floor. For several minutes I neither spoke nor moved.

We needed some serious calories. Like kids emptying Christmas stockings, we dumped the contents of our food sacks on the floor between us. We sorted through our choices, hunting for the most filling option. Tortellini with marinara sauce won. Cooking in the middle of the day was a rare event for us, but I enjoyed the extra time to take in the unbelievable views. The clouds were so white and plump that they didn't look real. I considered the childhood question mentioned in my mom's encouragement letter: if I touched a cloud, would it be sticky?

Unable to wait ten minutes for the tortellini to be ready, I pulled out a bag of animal cookies. Souleman and I polished off half of the sugary elephants and zebras while our noodles finished boiling. Without even waiting for the food to cool, we forced ourselves to eat every single mouth-burning bite. It was very tempting to lie down in the field afterward and sleep the rest of the day away.

Instead, we hiked. With food in our stomachs, the rest of the afternoon was less torturous. The trail followed the ridgeline, and from the top of the mountains we could see for miles. Seeing the pathway unfurling up and over mountaintop fields reminded me of scenes from *The Sound of Music*. The trail remained picturesque and serene all afternoon. Our campsite that night was in a mountaintop meadow under a huge, sprawling oak tree. We marveled over the great view as we played Frisbee in the meadow with fellow hikers after dinner. Our game was interrupted by a pop-up rainstorm that produced a rainbow arching into the meadow.

That night, our mileage calculations revealed inspiring news. In order to reach Katahdin by our target date, we needed to average only twelve miles a day. This schedule would allow for five zero days a month.

"We can do that easily," I exclaimed.

"We could even get there early," Souleman agreed.

"Let's not go too fast."

"True. This isn't a race. The first person to Katahdin loses."

15

Caught with My Pants Down

Waking up the next day to rain did not deter us. As droplets of water rolled down our faces and soaked our clothes, we hiked on. We passed many shelters full of hikers who were seeking refuge from the relentless weather. They often offered us space to sit and encouraged us to stop and rest or dry out. Instead, we pressed forward, embracing the emptiness of the trail and the tough condition of our bodies.

"Hey, Brownie?" Souleman called over the rain, about ten miles into our day.

We had just stopped and inhaled granola bars under the overhang of a crowded shelter without even removing our packs. "Yeah?" I asked as I fiddled with my pack cover, trying aimlessly to keep the water runoff from splashing into my ear.

"I'm really proud of you."

"Thanks," I said, hiking a few more steps and then stopping and turning around to face him. "Why, though?"

"You're doing so great today. I know you hate to be wet. And you've been hurting lately. All these people we've passed are holed up in shelters and you're out here trucking through the rain without complaining at all."

I stood on tiptoe and kissed him. The salt and rain mixed together on our lips. "Thank you," I said into his mouth.

"For what?" he mumbled between our lips.

"For encouraging me."

We stomped in puddles, sang songs about rain, and yelled for no reason. By that evening, we had finished our first twenty-mile day. *Twenty miles? I hiked twenty miles in* one *day. This trail's my bitch.* I glowed all night in spite of my sore body. When we had settled into our tent and turned off our headlamps, I was too full of pride to be tired. Instead, I rolled over next to Souleman and pressed my lips against his. We poured our joy at our accomplishment into our affection for each other, taking full advantage of our secluded campsite and ecstatic moods.

After having stayed up far too late, I woke up achy and dizzy and at first attributed it to the increased mileage. I soon came to realize that I had started my period. Hiking as a woman could be hard. Having to squat to use the bathroom, especially when the ground cover included thorns and snow, was uncomfortable. My sports bra trapped sweat against my sensitive skin. Having to deal with menstrual cycles in the absence of modern conveniences like showers and trash cans was, to put it simply, gross. Thankfully, I had my Keeper, a reusable feminine hygiene device, so I didn't have to deal with packing out dirtied pads and tampons like some of my female hiking friends.

All that morning, cramps shot down my legs and caused me to bend over at the waist. *So much for those trail books that claimed many women stop having periods on the trail.* My head throbbed and I felt dizzy and nauseous. I was hiking to the mantra, *No pain, no gain, no Maine.* The cramps did at least take my focus off my sore feet. In an attempt to concentrate on something other than pain, I daydreamed about my future with Souleman. I imagined going on family vacations with our children to ski lodges, campgrounds, and Disney World. I envisioned baseball-themed nurseries and ice cream sandwiches after Little League games.

As usual, Souleman was patient with my afflicted body and provided encouragement. He offered to stop hiking six miles early when we came upon a perfect little campsite. I figured I might as well be in pain while making progress toward Maine instead of in pain sitting at a campsite, so we pushed on. The trail followed a fence that enclosed a pasture full of giant cows. Feeling snarky, I stopped in front of one particularly large cow.

"Hey, Big Mac!" I yelled tauntingly with my hands waiving wildly over my head. Turning to the next cow, I called out, "And *you* must be Whopper!" I laughed until tears came to my eyes.

Souleman just shook his head in amusement.

We passed what our Handbook indicated was a five-hundred-year-old oak tree and stopped for a photo. With our arms out wide, fingertips touching, we *might* have covered half of the circumference.

"This tree is big," Souleman affirmed, "but it doesn't hold a candle to the redwoods out west."

"You've seen the redwoods?"

"I drove through there on a road trip."

I stared up at the massive tree. "I can't imagine trees bigger than this."

"I'll take you someday. There are actually trees you can drive a car through."

After hiking more than eighteen miles, we stopped at Niday Shelter and decided to sleep there for the night. We had been tenting every night for a long time. Sadly, the break in shelter sleeping had not improved my ability to sleep surrounded by a group of people. Keenly aware of my discomfort, I lay awake for most of the night listening to the sounds of zippers, coughing, snoring, swishing sleeping bags, and the scurrying of mice.

As the next day wore on, the trail presented a number of challenges. Some of the rocks along the trail were so large that we had to use our hands to scramble up them. While stopping for a rest after a series of rocks, we ran into Hazy Sonic and

Firefly. They were going into Catawba for dinner at an AYCE diner reported by Wingfoot to be the best restaurant on the entire Appalachian Trail. Souleman suggested that a delicious meal might be exactly what we needed.

Motivated by the thought of biscuits, apple butter, and sweet tea, I picked up my pace. Dragon's Tooth, a large pointed rock, was one of the spectacular sights we encountered on the way to town. I ditched my pack and scrambled up the pointy rock. Standing atop the jagged peak, I yelled, "I'm queen of the world!"

Souleman hurried up the steep rock after me. "Does that make me king?" he asked.

"No," I told him, holding up my left hand to show my bare ring finger. "We aren't married."

On the way back down, he slipped and almost fell. This served as a comical reminder that he desperately needed new shoes with functional grips.

The Homeplace Restaurant served what was by far the best meal I had eaten on the trail. In fact, I think it was the best meal of my life. Seated with Hazy and Firefly, we were treated to an entire table of good Southern cooking, served family style. We had ham, roast beef, fried chicken, mashed potatoes, green beans, coleslaw, corn on the cob, biscuits, and corn bread, all washed down with pitchers of sweet tea. Whenever a bowl was emptied, a server arrived to ask if we wanted another helping. *If I could eat this meal every day, I would be happy. And fat. Happy and fat.* When the plates were cleared, I knew I could not fit another bite in my bulging stomach. That was when the server showed up with dessert—blackberry cobbler with ice cream. To my amazement, I ate every last bite. After having hiked more than sixteen miles that day, I was entitled to eat as much as I wanted.

We were so uncomfortably full after our gorge-fest that I didn't think I'd be able to buckle the waist belt of my pack. We wandered around in the gift shop, not wanting to leave the air-conditioned environment quite yet. I found a children's coloring book entitled *The Real Story of the Civil War: From the Southern Perspective. Really? Seriously?* Unable to contain myself, I called my fellow hikers over so that they, too, could see this atrocity. I do not remember a thing about the contents of the book, but the title alone struck me as absurd.

Outside, there was a large gazebo where a handful of hikers were lazing. We joined the group and stretched out with the buttons of our pants undone. The restaurant owner came out and told us we were welcome to camp in the grass behind the restaurant once it had closed for the night. Thrilled at the prospect of not having to move more than a few hundred feet, we happily relaxed and listened to Hazy play guitar while our food digested.

I woke early the next morning on a cushy bed of grass. The woman who gave us a ride back to the trail that day was a lifetime Girl Scout whose daughter was the first person in the United States to earn her Gold Award. As a lifetime Girl Scout and Gold Award recipient myself, I felt an immediate connection with this woman. We spoke enthusiastically during the short ride, and she was excited to learn that a Girl Scout camp had initiated my desire to hike the Appalachian Trail. She asked to be added to our email list to hear about the rest of our adventure.

That day turned out to be my favorite day so far on the trail. We didn't see another thru-hiker all day, so Souleman and I were alone in the wilderness. We passed Tinker Cliffs and McAfee Knob, the most photographed spot on the Appalachian Trail, and took the obligatory dozen photos. Since we didn't have someone else to snap photos of us together, we repeatedly set the camera timer, propped it on rocks, and ran to beat the clock. A picture of our boot-clad feet hanging off the cliff turned out to be one of my favorites of the whole trail.

After the long mileage of the previous few days, I wasn't moving quickly, but we still managed to tick off more than sixteen miles before dinner. Along the way we saw lizards, more walking cheeseburgers, a stunning blue butterfly, and countless deer. I was relieved to have finally seen some wildlife on the Appalachian Trail.

A fellow hiker's nine- and twelve-year-old children had joined him for a few days on the trail. We all camped in the same place that night, and Snowman's younger son "helped" us set up camp. When we settled down for the night, I could hear deer in the woods all around us. I woke up in the middle of the night needing to relieve my bladder and felt something warm pressed against the length of my back through the thin nylon of the tent. Quietly sitting up and turning on my headlamp, I saw a deer lying against the outside wall of the tent. *I'm snuggling with a deer.*

The trail ran "down to town" the next morning. After a speedy 9.4 miles, we hitched into Daleville. I was desperate for a shower and barely waited for the hotel door to close before I headed to the bathroom. The sweat, dirt, smoke, and grime had left a visible grunge on my skin. After three lathers with soap and shampoo, the water finally ran clear. Based on the length of his shower, Souleman faced a similar challenge. Once we had rid ourselves of the layers of scrubbable dirt, we collapsed in bed and remained there for most of the day. It was nice to be able to curl up together without worrying about our Therm-a-Rests sliding apart.

After more than ten hours of sleep, we completed our town chores and ran into Hazy and Firefly. We offered to share a room that night and showed them back to the hotel. Before retiring to the room with our friends, Souleman and I went to dinner with Domino and his girlfriend, Debra. Domino had been a constant presence in our trail lives, and we were excited to meet his girlfriend and spend some time with them. In the weeks that followed, we spent a lot of time teasing Domino about when he would propose to Debra. It turned out they did marry a couple of years later.

Without meaning to, we stayed awake talking to Hazy and Firefly until two o'clock in the morning, which made it tough to get out of bed and back on the trail the next day. Much to my dismay, my new boots hadn't made a difference yet. I had secretly hoped that new shoes would mean the end of my foot problems. Unfortunately, neither the shoes nor the time off in town had helped. Every few miles, I had to stop, remove my boots, and massage my tender soles. Somehow we still made it more than sixteen miles that day before setting up camp. We stowed our gear under our tent vestibule right before darkness abruptly descended and fat raindrops started to fall.

We slept late the next morning and didn't get started again until almost ten o'clock. The morning passed uneventfully as we both hiked while listening to the radios we had purchased in town. My body repeated a painful cadence of step-step-pole, step-step-pole as I tried to focus on the country songs crackling through my headphones. With few breaks, we hiked steadily until stopping for a late lunch. Knowing we had a tough climb ahead of us, we allowed ourselves time to splash in a river after eating. The icy water numbed my throbbing feet for a few blissful minutes. Pushing on, we finished the day with a five-mile, 2,400-foot climb. My feet whined with every excruciating step.

In the evening, we tuned our radios to the same station and obnoxiously belted out Delilah's love song selections. The sappy romantic lyrics and our goofy off-key enthusiasm fueled our march to the shelter. Twelve hours after starting, we had ended the month of May with a twenty-mile day. We had now hiked over 750 miles.

The first day of June brought clear skies and tolerable terrain. We passed numerous deer and got so close to one young fawn that we were able to snap some close-up photos. The tracks on the ground suggested that there must be more deer in this area. In the afternoon, I came to a stop when I heard a loud noise.

WOMP, WOMP, WOMP.

Souleman stopped behind me. The strange, deep thumping continued and seemed to resonate all around us.

WOMP, WOMP. WOMP, WOMP, WOMP.

I spun in circles, listening intently.

WOMP. WOMP, WOMP, WOMP.

"What is it?" I asked.

"I have no idea." He peered into the woods.

I pulled out my water bottle and took a few tentative sips as I continued to look around the woods, perplexed. *What the hell is that?*

WOMP, WOMP, WOMP.

My heartbeat sped up. *Is it a helicopter? A plane?* I looked up into the sky. *A weapon?* I peered into the woods around us.

A hiker rounded the corner and saw us looking around wide-eyed. "It's a turkey," he informed us. "That's his mating call."

My shoulders sagged visibly as the fear left my body.

After having solved the mystery, we continued almost eighteen miles before dinner. Our latest mileage calculations indicated that we could finish as early as September 1 if we hiked only 13.5 miles a day. Since we had already been hiking nearly twenty miles a day, averaging 13.5 miles seemed more than manageable. This would also put us well ahead of our desired end date of October 1.

In the morning we hiked a short distance to the town of Glasgow to resupply. In town we learned through registers and other hikers that Tex, Fireball, Tunes, and Bottoms Up had all left the trail. Not long after departing from Springer Mountain, the hordes of thru-hikers began to dwindle, and by the time we arrived in

Pennsylvania, it was obvious that they had thinned out considerably. Finding out that people we knew had left the trail made Souleman and me even more thankful to be going strong. It also gave us strength that night to avoid the pull of town and make it back out to the trail.

The next morning found me grumpy again. I was tired and my feet hurt before we even left the shelter. Souleman took the opportunity to ask me what I needed from him when I was in that frame of mind. His thoughtfulness surprised me, and we had a truly insightful conversation about each of our emotional needs in a relationship. He told me that he was in this partnership for the long haul and wanted to learn everything about me in order to help make it successful. The conversation distracted me from my relentless foot pain and lifted my spirits. By lunch, my sour attitude had long been abandoned in favor of laughter and smiles.

Flat, rolling terrain seemed to mirror my changed attitude that afternoon. The hiking should have been easy and fast, but my sore feet kept the pace painstakingly slow. It seemed that every single pebble, root, stick, and uneven surface had been placed directly in line with my footsteps. I couldn't take a single step without hurting. Though outwardly my disposition remained positive, inside I was absorbed in selfish thoughts.

At one point during the afternoon, I hobbled by a memorial and came to a stop. Our Handbook told us that the body of a four-and-a-half-year-old boy had been found in this spot in the 1800s. The boy, Ottie, had gone out to collect wood for his schoolhouse during a snow storm and had never returned. Ottie's body had been found five months later, more than seven miles from the schoolhouse. I wondered about poor Ottie as we finished out our 18.9 miles. *His poor parents. How long had he been out there alone and scared before he died? Did he suffer?* It was good to think about someone else instead of my own petty worries about my traitorous feet.

I was ready for bed that night as soon as we had completed our domestic duties. After journaling for a bit, I began the process of getting comfortable in my mummy bag. It seemed as though I had just gotten still when I woke up having to pee. Heaving a huge sigh, I disentangled myself from my sleeping bag, found my headlamp, stuffed my feet into my camp shoes, unzipped the tent, and hobbled away from our campsite. I squatted beside a tree. *How many minutes of sleep has my miniscule bladder cost me during this hike?* The part of my mind that was awake noticed a wet sensation on my foot. I was squatting on a slope and peeing on my own foot—again. *Awesome.*

A sign reading "Trail Magic in Hog Camp Gap" greeted us not long after we started hiking in the morning. After consulting our Handbook, we realized we weren't far away. The thought of food compelled us to hike slightly faster than usual. We sang along with our radios, laughed at our own jokes, and dreamed about a cold soda or cookies at the trail magic spot.

As we walked along, my insides began to growl and gurgle. It felt like someone had lit a fire in my intestines. *Oh, what I would give for a toilet right now.* This section of the woods had nothing but tall, mostly branchless trees. The undergrowth was virtually non-existent, and even boulders seemed conspicuously absent. *Why now?* I squeezed my butt cheeks together and hiked as quickly as possible in the hopes of finding some trees. The terrain was not changing. My bladder was unbearably full and the mountains of junk food I had been consuming had churned into an evil burning in my intestines. *Just let this pass. I'll eat healthfully from now on,* I mentally lied to the bathroom gods. My body was pleading for relief. *This is so embarrassing. Please let us find some trees.* For at least a half mile I scoured the trail around us, looking for any place that might provide a little privacy. As far as I could see, there was no hope for cover.

Finally, at a bend in the trail, I stopped hiking and announced, "I have to go to the bathroom. *Now.*" The urgency of the situation became clear when I dropped my pack and pulled out the toilet paper. When I only had to pee, I typically just grabbed a leaf. "Stand here, ok?" I said to Souleman, pointing to a spot by a bend in the trail. "And do *not* turn around."

I ducked behind a leafless tree about fifty feet off the trail. *Oh, I'm going to explode.* I hurriedly started to dig a hole with the heel of my shoe. The dirt didn't budge. *Why is this ground so hard? Are you kidding me?* I kicked at the dirt desperately and then grabbed a stick. My digging was barely evident, but my body did not care. My insides were rumbling furiously. The hole was maybe three inches deep. *This will have to do.* I lowered my pants to my knees and squatted just in time.

In spite of my embarrassment, I felt better almost immediately. Then, with my bare rear end pointing toward the trail and a wad of toilet paper in my hand, I saw movement out of the corner of my eye. I tried to make myself smaller behind the tree. Through my legs I saw a hiker coming down the trail toward me. A male hiker. *Where is Souleman!?* I shoved the toilet paper into the world's smallest privy hole and tried to wriggle my pants back up. Since I could see this hiker, he could clearly see me—including my naked, white bottom, which was facing his direction. I finally succeeded in wrestling my pants on after a near fall. Absurdly, I then tried to hide behind a tree that was about half the circumference of my waist. I held my breath and hid my face with my hands.

When I was positive the stranger had passed, I returned to the trail in search of my failed guard. Our packs lay abandoned on the trail, and Souleman's head was visible down a small hill. He was squatting by a stream, whistling and filling a water bottle. I stomped up behind him.

"Hey. What the heck?"

He stopped whistling and looked up in surprise.

I narrowed my eyes at him. "You were supposed to be my guard."

He looked up from the stream. "I thought I'd get us some water while we were already stopped."

"Well, some random guy just saw my butt."

He laughed out loud.

"It's not funny." I poked out my lower lip in a mock pout.

When our water bottles were filled, he followed me back up to the trail. Leaning close to wiggle my water bottle into my pack, he whispered, "At least it's a cute butt." Then he kissed my ear before he slung his pack onto his shoulders and took off whistling up the trail.

The trail went up in spirals until finally we summited one last mountain and jubilantly began the descent. As I was calculating exactly how far we had gone and in how much time, I started to feel a little cocky at the realization that we had hiked more quickly than usual. I was singing along loudly with a country song on the radio and giving myself an imaginary pat on the back when I suddenly rolled my ankle and landed face-first in the dirt. At the speed I was walking, it was a hard fall.

I looked up at the sky. "Got it." Clearly, I had needed to be humbled.

"What happened?" Souleman asked, kneeling beside me.

"God knocked me down."

"What?"

"I needed a lesson. God handled it."

He narrowed his eyes at me in confusion.

"Never mind, don't worry about it. I got the message." I gingerly tested my wrists and ankles to make sure I was ok and then dusted myself off. Upon determining that there was no damage to anything except my ego, I let Souleman pull me to my feet and continued hiking a little more slowly. *I'm doing great here. In the past twenty-four hours I have peed on my own foot, shown my bare butt to a stranger, and fallen on my head. Maine, here I come.*

We passed hikers headed in the opposite direction, and they briefly described the trail magic ahead that included corn on the cob, hot dogs, hamburgers, barbecued pork loin, macaroni and cheese, sandwiches, beer, soda, ice cream, and juice boxes. It sounded too good to be true. Knowing we still had ten miles to hike before the Dutch Haus Bed and Breakfast that night, the prospect of filling our stomachs was invigorating. We reached a trail crossing and stared in awe at the sight that greeted us across the street.

The field ahead was so full and colorful that it looked like a carnival. A massive orange tent was surrounded by numerous smaller tents in a scene reminiscent of Tent City at Trail Days. Nearby, multiple awnings were set up over tables, grills, and coolers. We approached and heard music emanating from a fire circle where hikers were playing various instruments.

We ditched our packs and were immediately offered a large assortment of foods. We ate with vigor and then wandered over to the fire to rest and visit. Initially, we maintained our original plan that we would hike on to the Dutch Haus B&B. But more food kept being presented to us, and eventually we decided to shorten our day. We agreed to hike just four more miles and camp so that we could enjoy the festivities a little longer. As more hikers trickled in and more food appeared, however, we lost our resolve and pitched our tent among the myriad of others.

That night we met the elusive Garland Five, a family that was thru-hiking together. The parents had their children, ages nine, twelve, and fourteen, with them. We had heard about this family for hundreds of miles but hadn't been fortunate enough to meet them. All three children performed camp chores so that each family member contributed to trail life. We relaxed and sang late into the night with this charming family and numerous other friends.

As is typical of hikers, eventually we all began trading trail stories. The hosts of the event were previous thru-hikers, so they had plenty of tales to add to our collection. After listening to so many others bare their souls, I decided to mention my embarrassing moment from earlier in the day when I had been caught with my pants down. I have always loved telling stories, and I grinned as my audience laughed. When my story wound down, the hiker behind me tapped me on the shoulder.

"Nice to meet you face-to-face."

Every hiker who had preceded or followed us that day got sucked into Hog Camp Gap for the night. We thought we were ahead of the game because we found the motivation to pack up and head out in the morning. Unfortunately, the enthusiasm we had been so proud of lasted only ten miles. We stopped at the Dutch Haus in Montebello to use the Internet and buy lunch. The Troll family we had met back in Georgia was there, and they had already arranged to stay the night. As we checked our email after lunch, they disappeared and then came back looking squeaky clean in plush, white robes.

"Where'd you get the robe?" Souleman asked Anchor.

"It comes with the stay. It's a great deal. For twenty-five dollars each, you get a home-cooked dinner, showers, a room, and . . . ," he spun in a circle, "a stylish robe."

I'm not sure if it was the food or the robes that sold us, but before I knew it we were dressed in our own white robes, sitting back on the porch. A soothing breeze blew through the screens while we sipped cold drinks and played Spades with Troll and Anchor. Oblivious ran around in the yard outside, laughing and yelling with joy.

The two comparatively short hiking days didn't negatively impact our progress. Even with a late arrival back on the trail in the morning, we ticked off 17.3 miles. We enjoyed getting to climb Spy Rock, which provided a fun rock scramble with Oblivious. His boundless exuberance for life never failed to energize my step.

After camping on top of Three Ridges that night, we got an early start the next day. At one point during the morning, I heard rustling in a tree off to the side of the trail. I stopped and turned to Souleman with my finger on my lips. We stood still and listened. Something moved in the trees to our left. Peering through the leaves, I saw my first bear of the Appalachian Trail—a baby cub climbing in the branches. Mama bear was certain to be nearby, so we scurried on. We crossed the Blue Ridge Parkway many times and ended our day in Waynesboro, Virginia.

The hotel where we stayed was unimpressive, but it had a bed and a shower, which was all we needed. Souleman felt sore and lacked all energy. The following morning he had trouble getting going, so we lazed in the room until check-out at eleven o'clock. We had planned only seven miles out of town, so a late start would be fine. Tackling chores took longer than we expected, though, and soon it was almost dinnertime. While waiting for laundry to finish, we showered at the YMCA.

Souleman came back outside with wet hair and a glum expression on his face. "I lost four more pounds," he told me.

"I thought love was supposed to make people fat," I teased, pinching his shrinking waist.

He smirked half-heartedly. "Maybe you should weigh yourself, too."

I returned a minute later and sat next to him on a stone wall. "I've lost four pounds, too."

He kicked at the wall with his Crocs. "We need to eat."

"We probably need to increase our calorie intake in the woods."

We decided to stay in town to fill our shrinking bellies and go back to the grocery store. In the YMCA field, some hikers arranged a cookout for that night. It was wonderful to see Cuppa Joe, Break-a-Leg, Scholar, Slap Happy, Tree Trunks, and all the others. Souleman was so tired that he barely moved from the picnic table all night. I was beginning to doubt I would ever be well-rested again.

After an early bedtime, we were up and checked out of the hotel by seven thirty in the morning. We played basketball at the YMCA, ate breakfast, checked our email on the library computer, and finally hitched out of town. That day we officially entered Shenandoah National Park. I was skeptical about hiking in another park after our dismal experience in the Smokies.

In the first seven miles of Shenandoah, we saw squirrels playing tag on tree branches, birds soaring overhead, and even a spotted fawn who was nursing a few feet off the trail. According to the rumor mill, this would be the hardest day of hiking in Shenandoah. Since these miles had been gentle, we looked forward to the days to come.

We arrived at our first shelter in Shenandoah, and right away I was confident that this section of trail would be different from the Smokies. The shelter did not resemble a prison, and there were ample legal tenting spots. Deciding to tent, we got our Blue Mansion set up just before it started raining. As we cooked under the shelter overhang, it began to thunder and the wind picked up.

Souleman was putting up our bear bag using a metal pole when a bolt of lightning crashed nearby. He slipped in the mud and fell on his tailbone, creating a bruise that would hurt for days. Eventually, we ditched the idea of the bear pole and threw our own bear bag line using rope and a tree branch. *I am a thru-hiker, I can do this. Getting soaked before bed doesn't really fit into my plan.* The next day was to be our first marathon distance day, and I didn't want to add a wet trail, heavy packs, and soggy clothing to the list of challenges.

A few miles into our planned marathon day, we met Princess and Nimblefoot. For miles, Nimblefoot talked about the blackberry milkshakes in Shenandoah. After thirteen miles' worth of details about the cold, thick, juicy milkshakes, I couldn't handle the temptation any more. We stuck out our thumbs at the next road crossing. I consider myself a pretty stringent milkshake critic, and the blackberry milkshakes rated a perfect ten out of ten.

While drinking our shakes in the visitor center, we spoke with a park ranger and were able to make reservations at a campsite for that night. Although we would not yet accomplish a marathon day, twenty miles of hiking seemed more than sufficient. I was disappointed that I couldn't cross off another hiking milestone, but in comparison to our elementary hiking feats back in March, it was miraculous to have walked twenty miles and stopped for a milkshake all before dark. In the miles leading up to our prearranged campsite, our Shenandoah animal count totaled eighteen deer, two rabbits, and one large, unidentified animal crashing through the woods.

In the tent that night, we had a talk about our mileage from Shenandoah to Katahdin. We had already established that by averaging 13.5 miles a day, we would make it to Katahdin by early September. There was no need to keep planning such long days back-to-back. We decided to relax a bit about mileage and let the trail guide our decisions, as long as we still averaged 13.5 miles a day. We also agreed that reducing our mileage on some days did not mean we should stop in towns all the time. It was important to both of us to surround ourselves with nature as much as possible during our journey to Maine.

The next couple of days, we easily hiked sixteen and thirteen miles. I was continuously pleased by the mild trail conditions in the park. Our deer count rose to twenty-six. With the miles ticking off so quickly, we had plenty of time for extravagant breaks, so we stopped for a lazy, two-hour lunch at a picnic pavilion.

The pavilion was deserted, so after lunch I lay with my head in Souleman's lap. He played with my hair and ran his fingers idly up and down my arms. The last few days had been so peaceful. The weather was warm, with a breeze and low humidity. After lunch we spent as much time kissing as we did hiking. We sat lip-locked on logs beside the trail, backed each other up against trees, and stood swaying mid-trail as we shared kiss after kiss. I was a girl giddily in love.

In the morning, we hiked seven more blissfully tranquil miles to a visitor center where we watched movies about the history of the Shenandoahs in an overly air-conditioned theater. We browsed the gift shop and wrote short postcards to send home to our families.

Grateful to have access to an actual toilet, I stopped in the ladies' bathroom. Sitting on the cold, plastic seat, I listened to the shuffling sounds of women in the stalls around me. I looked at the dainty, black sandals and flawlessly pedicured toes of the lady in the next stall and was amused by the stark contrast with my permanently dirty, baby-blue Crocs and dirt-crusted skin. I assessed the dirtiness level of the rest of my outfit. My zip-off pants were filthy. Handprints made of ash and dirt smudged my pants legs, a crust of unidentified food smeared across my right thigh, and salt lines from dried sweat were spread throughout.

Even the *inside* of my pants had traces of dirt and salt. Studying the thorough dirtiness of my pants in proud awe, I noticed something curious. The sandy-brown floor tiles were the same color as my pants. *Wait! Why can I see the floor tiles through my pants?* Deliberately I touched my hand to the opening, an L-shaped hole of approximately three inches.

Impatiently, I waited until the bathroom had emptied. I peeked under the stalls to make sure I was alone and then flushed and exited the stall. Standing on tiptoe, I turned my backside to the mirrors over the sink and looked over my shoulder. There was the hole, smack in the middle of my right butt cheek. My pale, commando butt was clearly visible through the conspicuous gap. *How long exactly have I been flashing people?*

The sound of the bathroom door opening interrupted my thoughts. I quickly turned my back to the sink as a tourist, complete with a fanny-pack, entered the bathroom. Offering a polite smile, I edged toward the exit with my backside facing the tile wall. In the hallway, I saw Souleman sitting on a bench waiting for me. I stood with my back against the wall and motioned at him. He raised his eyebrows.

"Come here!" I gestured urgently, leaning against the wall outside the bathroom door.

He sauntered over.

"I need help." I glanced around to make sure no one was watching.

"What's the matter?"

I turned around and showed him the situation.

He cupped his hand around my partially exposed rear end with a grin.

"This isn't funny!"

He half-heartedly choked back a smile. "Ok, what do you want me to do?"

He returned shortly with my duct tape, and I tried to tape over the hole. *My feminine pink tape is going on my filthy bottom—no irony here.* Even though the bright pink tape was extremely conspicuous, I preferred it to my naked bottom being visible to all the vacationing families.

Nine miles later, we sat on the roadside with Hazy and Nimblefoot waiting for our ride. Hazy, whose wife, Firefly, had been able to hike only part of the trail with him due to work constraints, was now hiking solo. Nimblefoot and Hazy had been hiking at about the same pace for a few days. The four of us had met a section hiker named Climber a couple of days before, and she had arranged to pick us up at the road and take us back to her condo for the night.

The condo was spacious, clean, and most importantly, air-conditioned. We shared a buffet of oven-baked pizzas and hours of conversation before taking turns in the gigantic Jacuzzi bathtub. During my turn in the bathroom, I discovered that the duct tape had fallen off my pants. The material was so saturated with salt and dirt that even duct tape wouldn't stick. I gave up the fight and resigned myself to baring a cheek.

In the morning Climber offered to have us all stay a second night, and we accepted with only slight hesitation. We had planned an 18.9-mile day. In order to arrange for transportation back to the condo, we had to get creative. Souleman and I would be dropped off at the southern end of the mileage (where we had left off) and hike north, since we were purists and would only hike in one direction. Hazy and Nimblefoot were not as strict and were happy to ride to the northern end of the mileage with Climber and hike south toward us. In the middle, they would pass off the keys so that Souleman and I could collect the car at the northern end and go pick up our friends to head back to the condo. While the plan may have sounded somewhat confusing, arrangements like this were not all that uncommon in the hiking world.

We had the option to slack-pack as we were returning to sleep in the same location, but we declined since part of our purist philosophy included always carrying our full packs. The weight of full packs may have slowed us a little, but knowing that hot food, a roof, and a shower were waiting that evening sure encouraged me to move quickly. During the day, we saw two bear cubs playing on the side of the road, a red fox, a giant frog, a spider being carried by an ant, and a blue-and-yellow butterfly.

Our trio of friends handed off the keys successfully when we passed each other around mid-day. When Souleman and I got back to the car, we drove back to the southern meeting point and found Hazy there waiting for us. Nimblefoot and Climber still hadn't arrived at dark. We were unsure whether they had headlamps, so Souleman and Hazy headed down the trail to "rescue" them. I sat on a rock and massaged my sore feet while guarding our packs. We were all reunited shortly. That night in the condo, I cooked casserole for everyone and we passed around bottles of red wine.

Climber insisted that we stay yet another night. We all weakly opposed her extreme generosity, but she insisted. She rationalized that she didn't need the whole condo to herself and that her husband had returned to work, leaving her to hike on her own. Gratefully, we hugged her and planned another long-mileage day with flip-flopped hiking and passing of keys. Souleman and I hiked another peaceful day in the Shenandoahs delighting in countless viewpoints along the fifteen miles and the same gentle, forgiving terrain. My enjoyment of the Shenandoahs renewed my faith in national parks following our disastrous experience in the Smokies. We returned once again to Climber's condo, this time by way of McDonald's.

Although we had been enjoying the luxury of hot showers and sleeping in a beautiful condo every night, we were still pushing out big miles each day. I felt well-rested from spending several nights in a bed, but my muscles were sore and my feet were still throbbing. Souleman and I took a zero day at the condo the following day in order to rest our bodies. Hazy and Nimblefoot had taken a day off more recently and decided to push on. We dropped them off at the trailhead along with Climber and returned to our temporary home via the grocery store. Alone in the condo, we watched movies, ate, and shared a magnificent, steaming bubble bath.

In the morning Souleman didn't feel well. He suggested that we go to an outfitter so that he could finally give in to his need for new shoes and I could buy replacement pants. This would simultaneously give him a few hours to perk up.

As the morning progressed, Souleman felt increasingly worse, and by the time we left the outfitter, he informed me that he needed to lie down. We found a hotel room and Souleman immediately curled up in the fetal position on the bed. I alternated between stroking his forehead and packing our things, anxiously wanting to be back on the trail. *This must be how he feels every time my failing body causes us to slow down or take a break.* I lay down beside him around dinnertime to discuss whether he felt up to eating. We both drifted off to sleep, and when I woke up it was almost midnight. Since dinner clearly wasn't happening, I covered us both with the comforter, spooned up against Souleman's back, and went back to sleep. With no alarm clock set, we woke up after eight in the morning. We had slept for over fourteen hours.

Souleman had made a complete recovery, and we were both ready to push out some mileage. As we walked down the street preparing to hitch back to the trail, a van pulled over in front of us. Taba's unmistakable puff of hair popped out of the driver's side window as he waved an enthusiastic hello. I sucked in a horrified breath. *Run. We should run.* Souleman's hand tightly squeezed mine and kept me from sprinting in the opposite direction. Taba got out and opened the back of the van. I peered into the dark. The Troll family, Silent Bob, and Padre were inside. *Why don't they bail while they can?* They remained seated on the couches and encouraged us to climb in. *No way. I'm not doing that again.* I looked down the road. It was mockingly empty of cars.

"Climb on in," Troll called.

I would rather give up food for the week.

Padre grabbed my pack. Against my better judgment, I handed it up and then allowed Silent Bob to help me into the truck. *How long will it take this time?*

Miraculously, we made it back to the trail this time without any unnecessary stops or wasted time. I was determined to put that town far behind us. My legs quickly covered the planned mileage. In my head I crunched numbers and dates as I worried that we were taking too many breaks and would not make it to Maine before Katahdin closed for the season. Right as I was contemplating the whereabouts of the hikers who had started at the same time we did, we rounded a bend in the trail and ran into a large group of hikers sitting on the side of the trail.

Gypsy, Touk, Sunshine, Cuppa Joe, Serenity, Feeling Free, and Turbo Joe were eating snacks while they took turns going down a steep incline to refill their water bottles in the stream. Gypsy, Touk, and Cuppa had all started within days of us. It seemed that no matter how many unplanned days off we took, we always stayed in the same vicinity as these hikers. Knowing that our pacing matched up with others' encouraged me.

Interrupting my thoughts, a voice inquired, "Hey, Brownie?" Oblivious was looking up at me expectantly.

How does this kid keep his Mohawk trimmed on the trail? "Yes?" I answered.

"Do you have a Snickers in your pack?"

"Yes. Why?"

"I'll go down that hill and refill your water bottles if you'll give me a Snickers."

"You've got a deal." I tossed him my empty water bottles and plopped down on my pack amidst our friends.

"Souleman, do you have a Snickers, too?" I heard Oblivious ask.

That afternoon we exited the Shenandoahs. Unlike with the Smokies, I felt a pang of sadness upon leaving this park. After covering more than sixteen miles, we stopped and erected the Blue Mansion. I was incredibly relieved to stretch out on my Therm-a-Rest and sleep in the woods again.

One of the most endearing aspects of trail life was that we could never predict what we would see. The next morning we hiked nine consecutive twenty-minute miles. During the last of these, we came upon an unusual sight. Off to the side of the trail was a rolling suitcase. We exchanged baffled looks and paused to theorize. About a mile further north, we ran into a man pulling a different rolling suitcase.

"Hey," he called out, scooting over to the side of the trail.

"Hey." I responded.

"Is that other suitcase back there yours?" Souleman asked, nodding back down the trail.

"Yeah. I can only pull one at a time. I pull one about a mile and then go back and get the second one."

"Oh." Souleman shot me a baffled look. "Well . . . good luck."

We managed to keep quiet until we were out of earshot and then launched into animated conversation about what in the world this man could be doing and why.

The rest of the twenty miles unrolled uneventfully. Even with my feet hurting, I found myself continuing up steep grades without stopping for breaks.

In the morning we hiked three miles into Bears Den Hostel. The hostel looked warm and comfortable, but we were nowhere near ready to stop for the day. Instead, we treated ourselves to pints of Ben and Jerry's while lounging around with hiker friends. During the conversation, someone else brought up the mysterious suitcase hiker.

Apparently, the suitcase hiker had stopped in at Bears Den the previous day and had requested directions to the nearest shelter. When asked which direction he was going, he had been unsure at first but had finally decided he was hiking south. The owner had given him directions down the trail, and he had left his suitcases unattended for a bit as he wandered outside. Cycle Hiker mistook the suitcases for hiker boxes, so he opened them and found them filled with canned goods. The group believed that this man had actually been homeless and was looking for the nearest homeless shelter.

After our break at Bears Den, we hiked Devils Racecourse and a part of the trail known as "the roller coaster." I was really enjoying testing my personal limits by pushing myself to power through long inclines without breaks, complete back-to-back high-mileage days, and increase my speed. To top off an excellent day, we crossed the West Virginia state line and put the 500-plus miles of Virginia behind us.

The first day of summer, June 21, was our first full day in West Virginia. To celebrate the arrival of summer, many hikers participate in Hike Naked Day. The idea of scratchy pack straps on delicate, bare skin, sunburn in places the sun shouldn't shine, and bug bites in sensitive areas was more than enough to convince me not to hike naked. To my dismay, however, we didn't encounter any other naked hikers, either.

With much whooping and hollering, we crossed the one thousand-mile mark and signed in at the Appalachian Trail Conservancy Headquarters in Harpers Ferry,

West Virginia. That night we walked through historic Harpers Ferry, reading all the historical markers before settling into our tent in the yard of a hostel. Two fathers with their kids were also camping at the hostel, and I was thrilled to see parents instilling a love of camping in their children.

The state of Maryland, which we would cross into the following day, was rumored to be almost entirely flat. I didn't believe the stories because the rumor mill had been historically inaccurate. Our walk from the hostel started on a completely flat gravel path. The flat, even terrain continued until our lunch at a campground. After lunch I prepared for the inevitable uphill, but the smooth trail lasted the entire 15.5-mile day. The even ground was less brutal on my sore feet, and it energized me. Not everyone enjoyed a pain-free day, though. We heard from other hikers that Anchor had fallen and split her head open, necessitating a trip to the hospital. She was going to be ok, but the incident still served as a reminder that injuries were a real possibility on the trail.

In the morning I was full of energy because we would be meeting my mom and sister that afternoon for a stay in town. We hiked only 13.7 miles of flat trail before our arranged meeting, and I was a bit disappointed by the short distance. Souleman reminded me that this distance was still above our target average for reaching Katahdin on time. My worry about the day's mileage was immediately forgotten when I was reunited with my mom and sister.

16

Hikers to Hospital

After three and a half months of unequivocal bliss—of living my dream of hiking the Appalachian Trail—I was forced to acknowledge a nagging fact that I had been consciously minimizing: my feet hurt. This was not the typical, thru-hiker "my-feet-have-been-trudging-up-and-down-mountains-with-extra-weight-on-them" type of ache. I had none of the "normal" thru-hiker complaints. Not a blister, nor a hot spot, nor a sprain. I had no bruises, no bumps, and no cuts. My feet *looked* fine. My foot egg had even gone away. But my feet hurt. A lot. I had been victimized by my own body.

I couldn't stand up in the mornings without help. For weeks, Souleman had been physically lifting me off the ground when it was time to get out of our tent. He would carefully lower my weight onto my feet until I could stand on my own. Each day after only a couple of miles of hiking, even on easy terrain, silent tears would escape without permission from my eyes. In towns, I crawled to the bathroom in the middle of the night because I couldn't bear the agony of walking on tiled floors barefoot. *If I don't talk about it, maybe the pain will go away. I'm going to have to get used to this. Surely my feet will adapt.*

The afternoon of our meeting, my mom and my sister, Allison, pulled up at the planned road crossing right on time. Hooky and Tiny Dancer were sitting beside the road with Souleman and me. I watched Allison's eyes bulge as she saw just how dirty and ragged we looked. To her credit, she did give me a hug, but I could almost see her holding her breath. Ever polite, my mom didn't allow her face to betray her reaction to our stench, but the towels covering the car seats indicated that she had expected us to be disgusting. I introduced everyone and then discreetly asked my mom if she minded squeezing in two more hikers for a ride to town. We piled in and she quickly rolled down all the windows so that she and Allison could still breathe over our noxious hiker perfume.

In the elevator at the hotel, Mom said, "How about all the hikers get showers—looong showers—and then I'll treat everyone to dinner?"

We all laughed and expressed our thanks.

"Does she have any idea how much we eat?" Tiny Dancer stage-whispered, patting his belly above his kilt.

"You can pay me back with trail stories," Mom whispered right back.

"You've got yourself a deal, Mama Brownie." He held his hand up and high-fived her.

As the door opened on our floor, Mom pointed at my pack. "That," she said to me, "will have to stay in the other hotel room."

I looked at my beloved pack that contained everything I needed to survive, and then at my mom.

"I'm sorry. I just can't stand the smell," she said honestly.

With a slight feeling of uneasiness at letting my gear out of my sight, I handed my pack off to Souleman and limped after my mom and sister.

When the hotel room door clicked shut behind the three of us, my sister said, "Sooo, I want to hear all about this 'Souleman' *after* you shower."

I nodded and treaded tenderly into the bathroom. When I slipped my Crocs off next to the bathtub, I could barely stand up. The pain of the unforgiving tile floor on my exposed feet was excruciating. I sat on the edge of the tub with my head in my hands. *Damn feet.* Finally I pulled off my filthy clothes and crawled into the tub. To avoid the intolerable pain of standing, I showered sitting down.

Mom had left face lotion, body lotion, Q-tips, and other town luxuries on the counter, and while sitting on the closed toilet lid I indulged in each one. Finally, I shrugged back into my hiking clothes and then my Crocs. Holding my breath, I pulled myself to a standing position and opened the bathroom door.

"You must feel better," Mom said when she heard the door open. She saw me round the corner and immediately said, "Oh, I didn't even think. Don't you want to wear some other clothes? Those are filthy."

"I don't have any." I glanced down at my comfortable but stained clothes, trying to see them through her eyes.

"You can wear some of mine. I brought plenty." She was already opening her flowered suitcase. Inside I saw neat stacks of folded clothes. I envisioned my mostly empty clothing stuff-sack and realized that my mom had more clothes for a long weekend than I had for six months.

"Mom, I can't wear your clothes." I'm small, but my mom is even smaller.

"I'll bet you can. You've lost weight. Here, wear these jeans." She tossed a pair in my direction and I could smell the sweet scent left behind by the dryer sheet.

"Good." Allison chimed in. "Those will hide her hairy legs."

"*These* legs?" I propped my leg up on the bed beside her, and tried to put her hand on my prickly shin. I tried not to grimace when all my weight was transferred to one shoeless foot.

"Gross!" she exclaimed, jerking away.

Surprisingly, the jeans did fit, and I wore them to dinner. It felt very peculiar to be in normal clothes while all of my friends were wearing their hiking clothes. It seemed like cheating. After doing laundry that night, I wore my hiking clothes for the rest of the visit even though I knew that the smell had not washed out.

I tried hard to hide the severity of my foot pain from my family. I shuffled from restaurant to restaurant and even managed to remain vertical for long enough to play mini-golf at a small family amusement park. Souleman and Allison egged each other on at the batting cages while my mom and I watched from nearby benches. I was greatly pleased that my mom and Allison seemed to like Souleman because I was very much hoping for a relationship post-trail.

I pampered my feet as much as possible that weekend. I soaked them in the tub, stayed off of them whenever possible, and tried some stretches recommended by a trail friend. I hoped that the special treatment would persuade them to behave on the trail. Mom and Souleman both knew I was in incredible pain, but they respected my pride enough to wait for me to bring it up.

Hooky had been debating leaving the trail because of a foot injury. She had already visited a couple of doctors and had tried cortisone shots unsuccessfully. She was still hurting and wasn't sure she could continue. After many tears, prayers, and conversations with Tiny Dancer, her intermittent hiking partner, Hooky called her dad and he picked her up from the hotel to take her home. *I support whatever decision makes her happy, but that will not be me.* Seeing another friend leave the trail thoroughly motivated Souleman and me to get back out there and put more miles behind us. We were eager to make it to the official halfway point.

When they dropped us back at the trail, Mom and Allison walked the first half-mile into the woods with us so they could see a trail shelter. We hugged them good-bye, thanked them profusely, and promised to call from the next town. I began limping almost from the first step back on the trail. The extended town stay should have rejuvenated us, and psychologically it had, but my feet refused to acknowledge the break. Bit by bit, Souleman and I crept northward. My feet insisted upon frequent breaks, though my ego griped. Miniscule pebbles felt like swords stabbing at my aching feet.

The day took us through a park, and the trail remained flat and wide. I suddenly understood why some hikers attempted to hike the entire forty-mile stretch of this state in one very long day. While I harbored no illusions that I was in any condition to hike forty miles in a single day, I was envious of those who could try. Our 13.2 miles flew by, and just as we were preparing to camp, we ran into Tiny Dancer and Hazy Sonic building a fire.

"Hey, join us," Hazy called.

"I'm making tacos and I have plenty to share," Tiny Dancer added.

"Tacos?" I raised my eyebrows. "I can't say no to tacos." I dropped my pack to the ground and sank down on top of it. My feet were so desperate for a break that I almost gasped in relief.

"Oh. There's one thing, though," Tiny Dancer stated very seriously, darting his eyes all around.

When I looked up at him, I realized he had lines drawn on his cheeks with ash. "This is a tribal dinner. You'll have to be the tribal lookout."

"Umm. Ok?"

Tiny Dancer had a vivid imagination, and I was never entirely sure when he was serious and when he was trying to be funny. Either way, he kept us laughing whenever we were in his presence.

After we had finished our tribal taco dinner, we tossed our bear line and walked toward our tent in the darkening night. From a distance, the outer surface of our nylon home was shimmering and appeared to be rippling in the reflection of my headlamp. Upon closer inspection, we discovered that there were so many spiders crawling around on the outside of the tent that it was actually moving. Souleman, who is terrified of spiders, stood back in horror as I shook the tent vigorously and sent them flying like popcorn popping. Souleman started doing what could have passed as some sort of tribal dance as he attempted to stomp every single spider to death.

"Die! Die!" he yelled as he continued his massacre.

Finally, I convinced him to get into the tent. He then proceeded to perform a spider inspection by looking under and inside of every single item in our tent. All night long he tossed and turned, frequently flipping on his headlamp in order to perform additional spider checks. To further complicate matters, I had an overpowering urge to pee almost every hour and was constantly climbing in and out of the tent. Each time I opened the zipper, Souleman frantically searched the tent for invading assassins.

After a long, restless night, we wearily climbed out of the tent. Souleman ran from the tent to the trail approximately thirty feet away. He refused to come any closer on the grounds that spiders were likely hiding in our gear, waiting to get him. Repressing the urge to tell him just how ridiculous he was being, I dutifully shook out each piece of gear to guarantee that no spiders had stowed away inside. *This is love.* I schlepped armloads of gear to the trail, where Souleman packed it away after checking each piece once more for spider trespassers. This painstaking process made packing take longer than normal, and it was already almost eleven o'clock by the time we started hiking.

The beautiful sunshine perked us up, and we started the day at a speedy pace. My frequent stops to relieve my aching bladder slowed our progress a little. As I shrugged out of my pack for about the twelfth time in five hours, I found myself feeling fervently jealous of men. *At least men don't have to take their packs off to pee. Wait. Did I just have penis envy?* I not only had to remove my pack, but also to lower my pants and assume a squatting position every single time I encountered the urge to go. Around mid-afternoon, I became shaky and atypically overheated. I carefully monitored my fluid intake to ensure that I was fully hydrated. My body still felt off-kilter.

During a water break, I pushed my forehead against Souleman's. "Does it feel like I have a fever?"

"How would I tell?" He moved his cheek to my forehead. "It's over one hundred degrees outside. Of course your head is hot."

"True." I dropped my head to his shoulder. "I think I have a fever anyway."

Even with my need for many breaks, we finished our 15.8 miles and arrived in Caledonia State Park by dinnertime. For fourteen dollars we got a campsite and settled in early. About two hours after we went to bed, I wriggled out of my sleeping bag, found my headlamp, eased the tent zipper open, slid into my Crocs, and stepped out of the tent onto my tender feet. I limped through the park to the restroom and squeezed a few drops out of my bladder.

A couple of hours later, I got up to go to the bathroom again. This time I abandoned campground etiquette and squatted behind a tree at the edge of our campsite. As I released a few drops of urine, a burning sensation forced me to clench my eyes shut and hold my breath. I waited, but those few drops were all that was going to come out. Breathing again, I noticed a foul odor to my urine. Something clicked in my head and I knew I needed to see a doctor. I had a urinary tract infection, and only medicine would provide relief.

I straightened to a standing position on my wobbly feet and limped back to the tent, where I eased open the tent zipper, took off my Crocs, wriggled into my sleeping bag, turned off my headlamp, and tried to find a comfortable position. Souleman scooted his body up against mine in his sleep. I concentrated on matching my breathing to his in hopes that I would fall back asleep. An hour later, I repeated the whole process, and again the hour after that. I continued this routine all night long.

Near sunrise, I once again had to pee. After expelling a few more burning drops, I eased back into the tent, trying hard to be quiet and not disturb my sleeping boyfriend.

"Brownie?" he called out sleepily, as his hand touched my lower back.

"Oh, I'm sorry," I half whispered. "I was trying to be quiet."

"I was awake. Didn't you get up just a few hours ago?"

"Yes." I sighed dejectedly. "And the hour before that, and the hour before that."

"Too much water at dinner?" He touched my face.

"No. I think I have a bladder infection."

"Uh-oh."

"Yeah. Uh-oh." I rested my forehead tiredly on his chest.

He kissed my forehead and stroked my filthy hair. "Try to sleep a little."

Relinquishing my pride and my hopeful, though childish belief that keeping silent would make reality cease to exist, I hitchhiked to the ER with Souleman in tow. A handmade sign made from a piece of cardboard that read "Hikers to Hospital" got us a speedy hitch.

After a mishap in which the hospital gave me an ID bracelet with the wrong name, the doctor wrote me a prescription for my UTI. Then, swallowing my pride completely, I asked him to look at my feet. I hadn't showered in a few days, and I was embarrassed to have the doctor touch my feet, which smelled of hiker funk and were covered in sock fuzz and dirt. The doctor didn't pass out or even visibly wrinkle his nose. After a thorough and painful examination of my feet, he announced his diagnosis: plantar fasciitis in both feet. *Ok. I know what that is. Mom has that.*

"Basically, plantar fasciitis is an inflammation of the thick band of tissue that connects the calcaneous—the heel bone—to the toes," the doctor said. "It most often affects active men in their forties to seventies (*not me . . .*). The risk factors for this usually include obesity (*no . . .*), sudden weight gain (*no . . .*), shoes with soft soles (*no . . .*), and long periods of weight-bearing (*finally, yes*)."

I glared at my traitorous pack sitting on the ground beside me. *Stupid, heavy piece of—*

"The pain is often worse first thing in the morning," the doctor continued, interrupting my silent pack-bashing.

I asked the obvious question: "How do I make it better?" I knew my mom had done stretches, worn orthotics, taken pain-killers and even tried cortisone shots. I was prepared to do anything to stop the pain and keep on hiking.

"Stop hiking." He clicked his pen cap shut as though emphasizing the finality of his statement.

No. I glanced down at my hairy, toned legs, then up at my hairy, hiker boyfriend, and finally at my dirty, disloyal, beloved pack before staring at the doctor in disbelief. *No.*

"This is an overuse injury. It will not heal if you keep hiking."

I held out hope. "Will continuing to hike make it worse?" *I've made it this far, right? I'm stronger than steel, faster than pain, more intense than hunger. I can make it eleven hundred more miles.*

"Possibly. It definitely won't get better unless you stay off your feet. It could become worse. If you don't already have heel spurs, those could develop."

I watched Souleman's gaze drop to the tile floor. *Ok. This can get worse. But I can get tougher.* Turning back to the doctor, I asked the question any thru-hiker would ask: "Is it *possible* to keep hiking?"

"Technically, you can hike, but it will hurt a lot. You'll be in pain every day, and it won't get better. Plantar fasciitis doesn't just go away. You'll need to do special stretches regularly, get custom-made orthotics, and will likely need a night cast. Icing regularly and staying off your feet are essential."

I swallowed hard. "Thank you for your help." *Jerk.*

Smugly, I rejoiced in the fact that I had not specifically agreed to stop hiking. I tied my boots to the outside of my pack and slid my aching feet back into my Crocs. *Damn feet.* For good measure, I gave my injurious, heavy pack a tiny kick. Souleman offered to carry it, but I stubbornly mumbled that I could do it myself before hefting it onto my shoulders.

I resisted the urge to glare at the doctor on my way down the hall. Souleman took my free hand as I picked up my prescription and began an awkward limp to the check-out desk. At that moment, it was a toss-up whether my feet or my bladder hurt more. Dejectedly, I leaned on the counter and waited to pay my bill.

"Are you," the lady behind the counter looked down at a sheet of paper and continued awkwardly, "Brownie?"

"Yes . . ." I toyed with the prescription paper, already dirtied by my hands.

"A man came in and left you this note." She held out a folded piece of paper.

I unfolded the note and read:

Brownie and Souleman, I'm glad I could help you get to the hospital.
I hope your doctor's visit went ok. Go across the street to the Italian
restaurant, where I've arranged for you to have a free lunch. Good luck on
the rest of your hike!

I was dumbstruck. Once again, I told myself that I would give back to others tenfold when I returned home from the trail. I couldn't believe that a complete stranger would buy our lunch. The owner told us to order anything we wanted. I sulked in silence while we ate delicious Philly cheesesteak sandwiches overflowing with cheese, onions, and peppers. Souleman drank about a bucket of Mountain Dew while I scowled at my water and wished it were sweet tea. Sadly, caffeine and bladder infections don't mix. We left a generous tip and then limped through town looking for a pharmacy, a grocery store, and finally, a hotel.

"Why are all these places so far apart?" I complained. I had resorted to using my poles on the flat sidewalk to ease the pressure on my feet.

"I guess because people drive everywhere these days," Souleman replied, stating the obvious. "When we get a room, you can take your meds and rest, and I'll deal with everything else, ok?"

I nodded and focused on dragging one foot behind the other.

He squeezed my hand. "So about what the doctor said . . . ," he trailed off, ". . . about your feet?"

"I don't want to talk about it." I kept my eyes on the sidewalk.

"Do you think we should take some time off? Let your feet rest? See another doctor?"

"I just need to deal with my UTI right now." I sounded petulant even to my own ears. *Why my feet? Couldn't I have a broken hand instead? I could hike with a broken hand.*

For the rest of the night, I remained broodingly quiet. I talked haltingly with Souleman about what to eat for dinner, what to watch on TV, who to call with updates, and where our next mail drop was scheduled.

The second night I was poring over Wingfoot, jotting notes in the margin, when Souleman sat up and muted the TV.

"What're you doing?" he asked me, though we both knew he already knew.

"Planning our mileage." I didn't look up from the tattered pages.

He frowned. "How are you feeling?"

"My bladder pain is gone. The fever, too." I knew this wasn't what he meant, but I kept on talking anyway. "I have four more days of antibiotics left, but I can take those on the trail. Anyway, it looks like we can make it to that park where everyone does the ice cream challenge for our next stop."

He was quiet for a few seconds. "I just wondered if you wanted to maybe take some time off. You know, rest your feet." He put his finger under my chin and tilted my head up so that I would look at him.

I kept my eyes focused to the side of his face. "I want to hike." I had hiked for over three months, more than two of them with foot pain. *Surely I can handle this for three and a half more months.*

"Ok, 'Chin.'" He placed a kiss on my forehead and then moved his lips toward my right eye, but I put my hands on his chest to stop him.

"Chin?"

"You poke your chin out when you're upset." He pinched it for emphasis.

"I do not." I lied.

"Uh-huh." He kissed my right eye, my left eye, my nose, and my jutted-out, pouty chin.

I pushed at my chin with my hand, trying to put it back in its natural place. "We're hiking tomorrow," I told Souleman.

Stubbornness dragged me about eighty miles further up the white-blazed trail. Painstakingly, I trudged through Maryland and part of Pennsylvania. These were easy miles compared to the relentless PUDS (pointless ups and downs) of the earlier portions of the trail. The elevation gains were minimal, and there were few rocks. My injured feet, however, took no notice of the milder terrain. They hurt as much as ever, and I was often reduced to an obvious limp just a couple of miles into the day. Knowing what was causing my discomfort did not make it any more tolerable.

I had to carefully choose each foot placement so as not to step on a pointy rock or errant stick. I was forced to take breaks often, removing my shoes to try and massage the tender ligaments in my arches and heels. One day, as I tried to hide my tears from him at lunch, Souleman took my throbbing feet in his hands and massaged them. His eyes carefully watched my face for indications that he was hurting me.

"Hey, Brownie?"

"Hmmm?" I answered, not looking at him and trying to stop my tears.

"Are you having fun?"

Of course I'm having fun. I swallowed hard and answered, "I've wanted to do this forever."

"I know. But are you having fun?" he countered. His hands slid up my legs and rested on my thighs.

I could feel him watching my face. I swallowed the lump in my throat. "I've always wanted to walk the AT . . ." I skirted the question again.

"Well, all I know is that you're out here to have fun. And if you aren't having fun, then you shouldn't be here anymore. It's not just about Maine. Maine will be there. It's about enjoying getting there. It's about having a good time. I want to see you smiling." His words were direct and serious, but not harsh. He wordlessly touched my rigid chin before pushing my mouth into a smile with his fingertips.

As soon as he let go, I sucked my lower lip into my mouth and bit it. Tears flowed down my cheeks.

"Just think about what I said, ok?"

Staring at the ground, I nodded almost imperceptibly.

After a few seconds of silence, I climbed into his lap and buried my teary face against his sweaty neck. He wrapped his arms around me tightly and rocked us slightly until my tears ran out. When I finally stopped crying, I didn't move from his lap.

"My feet hurt so much." I spoke into his neck.

"I know."

"I don't know what to do."

"No one would think less of you for stopping." He ran his hands up and down my back.

"I'm not worried about what people would think. I don't know if I *can* quit. I don't want to be a statistic. I want Katahdin. How can I stop? I hate my feet. I *hate* them."

"You have no control over this, Brownie. I don't want you to be hurting every day." He kissed the top of my head. "I love you even with your bum feet."

One side of my mouth lifted in a half smile, but immediately my face clouded back over. "I don't want to stop hiking."

Over the next couple of days, the terrain rolled gently up and down. Miles that should have ticked off quickly at this point in our hike were laborious and painful. I didn't complain much, but my silence and barely contained tears said enough. We arrived at Pine Grove Furnace State Park, a place we had been dreaming of since Springer Mountain. This otherwise unremarkable park is the location of the famous and much-anticipated Half-Gallon Challenge. Sitting in front of a tiny camp store at the unofficial halfway point of the trail, thru-hikers attempt to eat a half-gallon of ice cream in half an hour. We had been strategizing for months. *What flavor? Should we eat it frozen, or let it melt? Should we wash it down with drinks? Should we eat anything before the ice cream that day?* My stomach had been training for this for months. I was ready.

We had camped only two miles from the store and had risen early to make the short hike. Arriving at eight o'clock, we were the first hikers to reach the camp store that morning. Unbelievably, the store, which was known up and down the Appalachian Trail as the location of the Half-Gallon Challenge, was out of ice cream. The ice cream freezers stood mockingly empty.

I approached the counter to inquire about the missing ice cream. The attendant apologetically told me that the delivery truck would arrive sometime that day. There was no way we were hiking on without taking part in this trail tradition. We may have ignored Hike Naked Day and opted out of the forty-mile challenge in Maryland, but we were *not* going to miss the ice cream challenge!

Souleman and I planted ourselves on benches under the front awning to wait. We would sit on the porch all day if necessary. The morning dragged by. More hikers trickled in, and soon the front porch was littered with packs, poles, boots, and lounging hikers. Sometime in the afternoon, our hunger overwhelmed us and we gave in, begrudgingly eating cheeseburgers (and thus making less room for ice cream in our stomachs). There were at least a dozen hikers waiting by the time the ice cream truck finally arrived.

We peered over each other's grubby shoulders, watching as the delivery man wheeled boxes of food off the truck and into the store. When he started offloading the ice cream, a hiker stationed by the door read aloud the flavor listed on each carton as it passed by.

"Strawberry . . . fudge swirl . . . vanilla . . ."

Finally, the cartons were unloaded and stocked. Decision time had arrived. Souleman chose Fudge Swirl, and I ambitiously chose Chocolate Peanut Butter Swirl. Hikers gathered around tables, someone started a thirty-minute timer, and we attacked our ice cream without mercy. My titanium spork shoveled scoop after scoop of chocolate, peanut-buttery goodness into my rapidly freezing mouth. I don't even remember chewing, just an unending pattern of scoop, swallow, scoop, swallow. I was about two-thirds of the way through my half-gallon when Souleman held up his empty box in victory at the twenty-two-minute mark. I planted a sloppy chocolate kiss on his frozen lips and turned right back to my container of chocolate peanut butter soup.

With just eight minutes to go, I was doubtful my stomach could hold any more lactose-infused goodness. *You can do this! Ice cream is your favorite food. Just one bite at a time.* Already I was hearing unprecedented gurgling and rumbling sounds from within my body. I continued scooping the now-soupy brown mess into my mouth and forcing it down. *Swallow. Only a little bit more.* I swatted flies away from my face and scooped another big bite.

Touk, who was a tiny little thing and lactose-intolerant, raised her empty box across from me with a cheer. In response I shoveled a huge, careless bite into my mouth. *If she can do this, I can do this.* Souleman, holding his ice cream challenge "trophy," had his head on the table with his eyes closed and was turning various shades of green.

I spooned a huge glob of brown goo into my mouth and gagged as I started to swallow. Stalling, I began decorating my face with ice cream in hopes of diminishing the amount I had left to eat. I put a dollop on my nose, streaks on my cheeks, and a spot on my chin. I forced a few more painful, gag-inducing bites down my throat until finally, realizing that thirty minutes had passed, I stopped trying to distract myself from the inevitable.

I strode purposefully, though slowly, on my aching feet, to the trash can and threw away my half-gallon container. Only one-eighth of the chocolate peanut butter mess was still inside. *One-eighth.* Tears threatened against the backs of my eyelids. *So what? It doesn't mean anything. It's just ice cream.* But I couldn't stop the burning tears.

"Proportionally, you ate more than I did," said Souleman, trying to cheer me up.

I didn't care about proportions. I cared that my feet had been traitorous, my bladder had been merciless, and now even my stomach had turned against me. *Why is my body betraying me?* I walked my ice-cream-smeared self across the street, lay down in the grass, and cried all the tears I had held back for over a thousand miles. I cried for the times my feet had hurt all night, cried for the times I couldn't stand up straight first thing in the morning, and cried for the times I had crawled to the bathroom in town because I couldn't walk barefoot on the hard tile. I cried for how tired I was and for how no amount of sleep had been enough. I cried for the nights I had gone to bed hungry, for the bug bites, for the cold, the wet, and the heat. I cried for sunburns, poison ivy, hypothermia, and bladder infections.

My tears mixed with the ice cream on my face and ran down my neck and onto my shirt. I was a sticky, sweaty, tearful mess. Dirt and blades of grass stuck to my filthy face and arms, and ants crawled all over me, feasting on the salt and sugar painted on my skin. I was so caught up in my overwhelming misery that I didn't hear Souleman coming my way until he was sitting cross-legged next to me. He pulled strands of grass off my face and kissed my nose, which was coated with a generous portion of dried ice cream.

"I—can't—do—it," I lamented between the kind of sobs that break up words like inconveniently timed hiccups.

He scooted closer and pulled me into a sitting position between his legs, resting his chin on top of my head. "It's just ice cream. We can try again another day." But we both knew I was talking about more than ice cream.

"No. It isn't—just—ice—cream," I choked out. I took a haggard breath and squeezed my eyes shut. The next words that came from my mouth were unplanned. I heard them as though someone else had spoken them. "It's—a sign." Inside I screamed, *I don't even believe in signs!* Still, I took a shaky breath. "I'm—done."

Part Two

17

You Don't Have Hepatitis

And just like that, I knew I meant those unexpected words. I *could* make it to
Maine, but I wouldn't be having fun. This revelation slowed my sobs. Though
tears still ran down my cheeks, I could speak normally again. I twisted around to
face Souleman and grabbed his hands.

"I'll meet you along the way. We can hang out in towns and—"

"No."

"And I'll mail you packages," I continued as though he hadn't spoken. "Big
packages." I forced a smile. "And letters. Juicy letters."

Souleman was emphatically shaking his head side to side. "No," he repeated
quietly.

"And I'll—"

He put his finger to my lips to silence me. "This is *our* hike. *We* started this, and
someday *we* will finish. Together. Maine isn't going anywhere."

My tears picked up again. "You wanted to hike the AT long before you knew
me. I'm just some girl you met on the trail. You can't give up on a dream just
because of a girl."

He squeezed my hands tightly. "You're not *some* girl. You're the girl I'm going
to marry."

And somehow that fact, never explicitly spoken until then, decided it all. We
collected our packs and walked away from the trail, hand in hand, without saying
goodbye to anyone. Admitting defeat to all the other hikers who were pushing on
toward Katahdin would have hurt too much—or maybe it would have been too real.
We walked away from the trail shouldering the weight of disappointment and broken dreams. Our packs had never seemed heavier. Squeezing each other's hands, we
stood by the side of the road. Tears rolled down my ice-cream-painted cheeks as we
stuck out our thumbs. This time, we weren't headed to town to resupply. We were
hitching home.

All too quickly we were transported from the serenity of the woods to the hustle and bustle of society. The commonplace sounds of the modern world—car horns honking, gyrating music, cell phones ringing, and the ever-present drone of the TV—were inflicted ruthlessly upon our sensitive trail ears. Some of these impositions had been tolerable during our short interludes in town while hiking, but living full-time in a non-stop noisy environment was over-stimulating. I had many, many headaches.

Souleman and I spent the first awkward weeks back in society together. We moped around my parents' house as we mourned our separation from the trail. While my feet were relieved to have a break, my legs ached after switching from being in constant motion to being almost sedentary. I couldn't stop thinking about the trail. I missed the open spaces and fresh air. I thought back to our departure from the trail.

Normal, everyday activities that had come so naturally pre-trail were now overwhelming. Each morning, I stood for a ridiculous amount of time in front of my closet trying to choose an outfit. I had worn the same clothes for three and a half months, and it seemed pointless to put on new ones every day.

When I was cooking, it often didn't occur to me to use more than one pot. And one time I even found myself eating directly out of the pot in front of the stove. Showering every day seemed absolutely senseless, particularly when I hadn't hiked twenty miles up a mountain carrying almost a third of my weight on my back. Sometimes I forgot to turn on lights when it started getting dark in the house because I was so used to operating in the dark.

About a week after we left the trail, I was brushing my teeth when Souleman appeared behind me.

"It's time," he said.

I spat out the toothpaste. "For what?"

"To shave off my beard."

I set my toothbrush in its holder, then looked up at his reflection in the mirror. "Are you sure?"

He was stroking his beard nostalgically. "Yep. I have to go back to work. And even at the rec department, I can't get away with this."

I turned around and touched his mountain-man beard. "If you have to get rid of it, can I be the one to do it?"

"Sure."

We collected a razor, shaving cream, scissors, and a bucket of warm water and carried them to my parents' back deck.

First I used scissors to take off the bulk of the wild hair. Clumps of beard collected at our feet and were carried across the yard by a gentle breeze. Souleman's beard had grown in proportion to our completed mileage. Seeing it chopped off made our departure from the trail too real. I switched to a razor.

"Should I leave a trimmed beard? Or a goatee?" I asked him.

"No, I think it has to be a clean break."

Methodically, I swiped strips of shaving cream from his cheeks, chin, and neck. When I finished, his face was smooth and pale. I touched the naked skin with my palm in awe. I was looking at a stranger.

Saying goodbye to the beard seemed to snap us back into reality. We needed to earn money and figure out where to live. Souleman returned to Vermont, where his job was waiting for him. I spent time tending to my disloyal feet with trips to the podiatrist, night casts, painkillers, anti-inflammatories, and stretches. Though I dutifully followed my doctor's treatment regimen, the agony continued. Standing with any weight on my feet first thing in the morning was tear inducing. Even without my pack on my back, rocks underfoot, and mountains to scale, I found walking painful.

Healing my feet meant staying off of them as much as possible. I spent copious amounts of time napping or dozing on the couch. Since I seemed to be in a constant state of exhaustion, this served a dual purpose. Sleeping in, going to bed unusually early, and taking regular naps didn't seem to be making a dent in my recuperation, though. As someone who had never slept well, I wondered how in the world I could be sleeping so much. For the first couple of weeks I maintained the belief that my body was simply exhausted and needed time to recover from the trauma of the trail.

In addition to my feet, my ears had been bothering me for the last month on the trail. Changes in elevation, whether I was on foot or in a vehicle, were particularly miserable, although the pain came and went at other times as well. I thought perhaps that being outdoors in the wind and constantly changing altitudes while scaling mountains might have caused the pain. When the discomfort didn't disappear off-trail, though, I finally went to the doctor.

The initial diagnosis was an ear infection caused by fluid in my ears. Two rounds of antibiotics and two trips to the doctor later, my ears were still hurting. Limping slightly on my still-sore feet, I was sent to an ear, nose, and throat specialist for further treatment. The specialist looked in my ears, declared them problem-free, and was about to send me on my way when he glanced in my direction and noticed something about my posture. I was slumped in my chair, eyes heavy, face relaxed, and body largely limp. He paged a nurse and said he was going to run a blood test.

What will a blood test tell him about my ears? I normally hound doctors for specifics about my medical care, but I was just too tired to ask.

After leaving three vials of blood with a nurse, I staggered out to the car, practically holding my eyelids open with my fingers. My ears hurt, my feet hurt, and I was so unbelievably sleepy. I leaned on the steering wheel and cried. *What is wrong with me?* Giving in to my exhaustion, I locked the doors and napped in the parking lot.

My emotions were as out of whack as my body. I was devastated about leaving the trail and disappointed in my body for preventing me from reaching Katahdin. I had dreamed of completing the Appalachian Trail after graduation for ten years.

Now what? When I had finished college and embarked on my hike, I sure hadn't expected to be back home three months later with sore feet, aching ears, incurable tiredness, and no direction for my future.

When I had started the trail, I also hadn't expected to meet Souleman. I worried our relationship might change now that we were off the trail. *Will he resent me for his decision to stop hiking? Will he forget about me when he returns home? When will we see each other? Will we get along as well in the "real world" as we did on the trail?*

Outside of my uncertainties regarding Souleman, I worried about other things: *Will I ever make it back to finish the trail? When will my feet feel normal again? How long until I can move out of my parents' house? How will I find a job? Will I ever feel rested again?*

One day I stopped by the drugstore on my way home to buy some necessities. Completely overwhelmed, I stood in an aisle staring at the contact lens solution choices. *Why are there so many kinds?* I finally selected a bottle and moved on. While I debated types of chapstick—*Do I want "rapid relief" or "all day soft-ness"?*—I noticed a teenage girl staring at me. Self-consciously, I ran a hand through my hair and pulled at my skirt. She continued to stare. *Is there something in my teeth?* I followed her gaze and realized she was looking at my legs. *Is there toilet paper on my shoe? Is my skirt tucked in my underwear?*

Suddenly it dawned on me: it hadn't occurred to me to shave my legs. While my hairy legs had been a source of pride before, they made me stand out off-trail. A little bit sadly, I added a razor and shaving cream to my shopping cart. When I got home, I immediately headed for the shower with my razor. I had just turned off the water and was admiring my smooth legs when the phone rang. I hurried to step out of the shower and grab the phone from the counter.

"May I speak to Michelle?"

It was still strange to be called "Michelle" and not "Brownie." "This is she." I pulled a towel around myself and sank down on the closed toilet lid to relieve my aching feet.

"This is Stacy from ENT Associates. I have your blood test results."

"Oh, great."

"The good news is that you don't have hepatitis."

Hepatitis? They tested me for hepatitis? I digested this information while closing my heavy eyelids. Before I could ask any questions, she continued.

"The bad news is that you do have mono."

My eyes flew open again. "Mono?"

Stacy confirmed the diagnosis.

Per the doctor's recommendation, I made an appointment to discuss the results.

In the doctor's office the next day, I was told that according to the blood test, I had already had mono for quite some time. The doctor began explaining the precautions I would need to take, including drastically limiting my activity level.

"Didn't you hike recently?" he inquired, not looking up from his clipboard.

"About eleven hundred miles," I mumbled.

The doctor's eyes snapped up from his clipboard and widened considerably. "ELEVEN miles?" he repeated incorrectly. "You'll need—"

"No," I interrupted. "I hiked eleven HUNDRED miles."

The doctor stared at me, blinking deliberately. Finally, he told me that it was a miracle I hadn't ruptured my spleen. I was ordered into bed until the mono symptoms ended. The irony that I had managed to hike through mono, an illness that renders many people bedridden, but not through mere foot pain, did not escape me.

I spent many long days lying around the house. I was too tired to read and could only watch so many reruns on TV. Gradually, I regained the ability to walk without a noticeable limp. I had never been good at enjoying downtime, so recovering from multiple bodily malfunctions that required me to be inactive was almost unbearable.

Within a couple of weeks, I had lost all patience with recovery and decided I was finished with being sick. I dismissed myself from bed rest and earnestly began looking for jobs. I was anxious to figure out the next phase of my life. During my weeks of laziness, Souleman had returned to a life of productivity, resuming his job in Vermont. I was terribly envious of his employment.

I detested being idle and out of school, off the trail and without a job. I spent hours upon hours searching for *any* job for which I was qualified. Some places told me I was overqualified, while others suggested I needed more experience. It seemed unfair that my bachelor's degree rendered me too skilled for some places and not trained enough for others. *How do you get trained if no one will hire you? And what exactly does a philosophy degree qualify me to do, anyway?*

On top of the stresses of finding work, I was missing Souleman terribly. Going from non-stop companionship to weeks alone was unnerving. We had gone from worrying about an inch of space between our Therm-a-Rests to being two states apart. We visited each other as often as possible, sent countless emails, and spent too much time on the phone, all while brainstorming ways to get closer together.

"I miss you," I told him dejectedly during one of our long phone calls.

"Me too."

"I don't want to be in different places."

"Me neither," he agreed.

"I'm so sorry I made us have to stop hiking," I told him for at least the millionth time since leaving the AT.

"I do miss the trail, but I miss *you* much more." It was quiet for a minute. "Maybe you should look for jobs in Vermont."

"Really? You think?" *Is he serious?*

"Yeah. We could get a place together up here. Once your feet get better, we'd have lots of places to hike."

In late August I interviewed for a position at a preschool in Vermont. This was by no means my dream job, but it would allow me to fill my empty days, live near

Souleman, and have an income. I was offered the position and started making plans to move.

We lived in a small apartment over a farmhouse on a water buffalo farm, with a view of the mountains. Our time together was still much less than the constant companionship of the trail, but we were grateful to be able to see each other every day. Hearing one another called by our "real" names was awkward at first, but slowly we transitioned from "Brownie and Souleman" to "Michelle and Jeremy."

As the leaves began to change colors and flutter down off the trees, I laced up my boots for the first time since leaving the trail. Tentatively, Jeremy and I tried a couple of short hikes. My feet were still sore at times, but I was determined to convince them to hike once again. On weekend excursions we explored nearby areas in Vermont, including Moosalamoo National Recreation Area and Skylight Pond. *It isn't the AT, but it's hiking.* Even without the usual weight of a loaded pack, my feet were sore at the end of each practice hike, although I was excited to find that my legs remained sturdy and unaffected. I continued to wear my orthotics, use my night cast, and do my stretches religiously in efforts to heal my feet.

In late September, Jeremy and I were driving to visit my parents in Massachusetts when he suggested that we stop by the Appalachian Trail to "check out the foliage." This seemed a little odd since we were already running late and it was nearing dusk. Still, since I was *always* up for visiting the trail, I veered off the road. We walked hand in hand down the trail in the fading light, reminiscing about our hike and speculating what it would have been like to make it to this point. As we crossed a wooden footbridge over a brook, we stopped in the middle to watch the water rushing by below. He released my hand, pulled a box from his pocket, and dropped down on one knee.

"Our relationship began on this trail," he said. "I can't imagine being with anyone else but you. I want to be with you, on the trail and off the trail, for the rest of our lives. When I thought about proposing to you, no place seemed more perfect than the trail. I want the rest of our lives to begin on the same trail where our relationship began. Michelle—Brownie—will you marry me?"

I jumped into his arms. "Yes. Yes!"

We hugged and kissed, and finally I pulled away and asked, "Are you going to put the ring on my finger?"

I spent much of the remainder of the drive wiggling my sparkly ring finger in the fading light.

As we began to plan our wedding, we couldn't think of a single suitable location. We had visited a couple of completely awful venues (unless you consider moldy smells and Formica romantic) and were becoming discouraged. *We may never find a spot.* The more we talked, the more we realized we wanted an outdoor wedding.

"What if we got married on the trail?" he said one afternoon as we searched the Internet for venues.

"That would be awesome. But how?"

"If you're serious, I'll find a place."

"I'm serious."

Not expecting any results, Jeremy searched for wedding sites on the Appalachian Trail. Shockingly, he found a venue located right on the AT in Vermont. We set the date for June 10, 2006, and were soon immersed in planning a trail-themed wedding.

"So, we've figured out the wedding, but what are we doing to do for our honeymoon?" I asked one night as we were eating dinner.

"What do you want to do? We could go on a cruise? Go the beach?"

"We could." I twirled spaghetti with my fork.

"You don't sound enthusiastic. What did you have in mind?"

"Welllll . . . Planning our wedding has me thinking non-stop about the trail again. We met on the trail, we are getting married on the trail. Wouldn't the perfect finale be to finish the trail for our honeymoon?"

His eyes lit up. "Do you think we could?"

"Maybe."

After a lengthy look at our bank accounts, and many conversations about logistics, we made the decision. We were going to hike for our honeymoon.

From that point on, we alternated planning our wedding and our return to the trail. Our hike was to continue on June 15, 2006, five days after we said our vows. We planned to start in Pine Grove Furnace State Park in Pennsylvania, the exact same place we had walked away from after the ice cream challenge the previous July. This time, though, we would be married and more ready than ever to finish the trail together.

After we had made the decision to hike for our honeymoon, time flew by. It seemed like we had just gotten off the trail, but already it was almost time to re-embark on our adventure. Few people understood our desire to undertake a journey involving treading endless miles on foot and sleeping on the ground, much less our desire to do it more than once. When we added the fact that we planned to do this on our honeymoon, people were horrified.

"But you'll be dirty!" people protested. "You won't have any privacy!"

The year I had begun the Appalachian Trail, in an unrelenting attempt to make people understand *why* I wanted to hike from Georgia to Maine, I had concocted various explanations. The second year, I resigned myself to the certainty that non-hikers were incapable of comprehending this aspiration. Instead, I confidently assured those question-laden, worry-filled souls that we *did* know what we were doing and that we were *confident* we would have a *perfect* honeymoon.

Preparations for our hike the second time around were startlingly stress-free. The first year we had each been terrified of choosing the wrong, high-priced item and consequently ending up unprepared in some remote section of the woods. Like most hikers, instead of finding out we had brought too little, we discovered we had packed too much. By the time we left the trail, many of our carefully selected, "completely necessary" items had been mailed home or abandoned in hiker boxes.

This time we had the confidence of knowing that we had already made it eleven hundred miles and would be completely fine without any new equipment. Still, in an effort to lighten our packs and update our gear choices (we *were* closet gear-heads, after all), we made some new purchases. Instead of apprehension, there was only excitement. We eagerly awaited each delivery and immediately set aside time to test our selections.

I had entered a contest to win a free pack from Mountain Hardwear (MHW) and was one of approximately thirty applicants selected for their Exodus Tester Team. The company provided me with a bright blue MHW Exodus Backpack. It was a unique pack design with many exciting features, including a customized external frame, stretchable exterior pockets, and a removable water pouch. My personal favorite feature was the Velcro tabs that prevented excess strap material from dangling and making an annoying "slap-smack-slap-smack" sound.

Souleman also had a terrific new pack: an Osprey Aether 60. His was a compact pack best suited to loads under thirty pounds. Previously, he had carried the king of large packs, which he had purchased from a clearance rack without any knowledge about pack specifications. When it was fully extended, his old pack was almost large enough for me to stand inside. Having new packs that were better suited to our needs was going to be a whole new experience.

"We're going to have to get a new tent," Souleman told me shortly after his birthday. "The Blue Mansion is too heavy and bulky for these packs."

"You're right. I'm going to miss it, though."

After much debate (and one disaster in which we ordered, tested, and returned an insufferable, coffin-like tent), we settled on a Big Agnes Seedhouse SL2. The SL2 was significantly lighter than the previous year's Blue Mansion, weighing in at only three pounds, and was actually roomier. It had numerous storage pockets, which I loved, and was tall enough that we could both comfortably sit at the same time. It also had a large vestibule for gear storage.

"There's only one thing about this new tent that I'm not sure about," I told Jeremy as we practiced setting it up in the back yard for the second time.

He looked up from hammering the final stake into the ground. "What's that? I thought you liked this one."

"With all the extra space, will you still sleep as close to me?"

"If you're lucky."

To start our hike out on the right foot, I purchased new custom orthotics from an outfitter in Manchester, Vermont. They were hideous. Their splotches of red, yellow, green, and blue made it look as if someone had melted a handful of primary-colored crayons inside my shoes. Nevertheless, after the customary tender period of breaking them in, they were comfortable, and I was hopeful that their support would solve my foot problems.

We received our first wedding present from Jake Brake and Low Gear. Predictably, we promptly spent the REI gift card on hiking paraphernalia. Each day, we raced home from work and jockeyed to be the one to scoop any new packages off the steps and thus earn opening rights. Among our final purchases were a summer-weight sleeping bag for Souleman and replacement gaiters for me.

The anticipation of our hike alone was enough to keep me on edge and excited. I was so ready to be back out in the woods hiking determinedly toward Maine. When combined with the excitement and nervousness of our rapidly approaching wedding, the anticipation was nearly unbearable.

"You know, a month from now we'll be married," he told me one night as we boxed up our apartment.

"A month from now we'll be hiking the AT again," I responded with a huge smile.

Our wedding preparations moved along smoothly. Before we knew it, response cards were returned, flowers were picked up, the cake was prepared, and guests were arriving for our trail-themed wedding. We were fortunate to have many of our family and friends there to support us.

Our wedding rehearsal included silly games to teach our guests about our beloved Appalachian Trail. We had a crossword puzzle with trail trivia and a numbers guessing game with numerical facts about the trail. Following the games, we awarded trail-style prizes: a spa basket (hotel soap and a bandana), a gourmet dinner package (a box of macaroni and cheese), and drinks for two (two single-serve packets of Crystal Light and bottled water).

To end the evening, Jeremy and I invited our guests to join us for a presentation of our Appalachian Trail slideshow. We played a progression of our pictures from the first eleven hundred miles accompanied by music. The show started with "Georgia on My Mind" and continued to include songs we associated with our hike, such as "Take Me Home, Country Roads," "Ain't No Mountain High Enough," and "Rocky Top."

Jeremy and I sat holding hands in the middle of our family and friends while images of our hike flashed across the screen. The photos detailed our relationship from the Amicalola Falls State Park parking lot to eating ice cream at Pine Grove Furnace State Park. *Next week we will be back out there.*

In keeping with tradition, we slept separately the night before our wedding. Jeremy spent the night with his groomsmen, and I was with my bridesmaids. I woke early to the sound of rain tapping against the glass of the window. When I hurried to the window and moved the curtain aside, a dark, misty, wet day greeted me. *Oh, no.*

As I primped for the ceremony, the weather continued to intensify. I carefully pinned my hair into a bun and attached diamond accents. Glancing outside at the near-monsoon, I ensured that my mascara was waterproof before painting on makeup.

My mom appeared in the mirror behind me. "There's an old wives' tale that says rain on your wedding day is good luck."

Rain pounded against the window beside us.

"Is extra rain *extra* good luck?"

"One can only hope."

I slipped on my dress and spun to face myself in the floor-length mirror while my mom laced the corset. The bodice of the white sleeveless gown was studded with diamonds in floral patterns. At my waist the dress billowed gracefully where layers of petticoats gave volume. I spun, watching my dress twirl around me. *What a contrast to my hiking outfit.*

We moved the ceremony from a knoll overlooking AT blazes to a white tent. Although the rain continued, the ceremony itself was beautiful. The minister, my cousin's husband, had tailored his homily to our love of hiking, and our vows referenced walking together through the mountains and valleys of life. Even the decorations reflected our trail theme: our card-holder was a silk tent embroidered with "Brownie and Souleman," and our Ben and Jerry's ice cream cake looked like a mountain with a trail winding up it. Perched on top of the ice cream mountain was a miniature nylon tent with a tiny bride and groom peeking out.

My dad, always confident and in charge, carried me through the pouring rain and into the tent so I wouldn't soil my dress. My childhood piano teacher, Mark, began the traditional wedding march on the piano, and my dad gently pulled me toward the aisle. We passed family from across the country, friends from high school and college, Girl Scout friends, trail friends, and lifelong friends as we walked to the front of the tent. Dad pulled gently on my arm, slowing my entrance.

At the front row, Dad and I met my teary-eyed mom, who gave me a kiss on the cheek. Standing at the front of the tent, Allison, Lark, Meagan, and Ashley, Jeremy's youngest sister, looked radiant in their rose-colored bridesmaid dresses. Rachel and Anthony, the flower girl and ring bearer, were adorable. Jeremy's groomsmen, Jon, John, John, and Jed, all looked handsome, and atypically serious, in their tuxes.

As my dad and I took our final steps toward the front of the tent, my eyes fixed on Jeremy. He stood completely still beside John David, our minister, with his eyes fixed back on me. I studied his serious face and was relieved to see that he had kept his beard as promised. My mountain man would always seem most natural to me with some amount of facial hair.

"Who gives this woman to be married?" John David asked.

"Her mother and I." My father lifted my veil and placed a kiss on my lips before passing my hand to Jeremy. He took a seat beside my mom, and I glanced back to see him with one arm around her shoulders and his other hand on her knee.

The wedding was a beautiful blur. I remember saying the words "I do," my high school youth ministers, Kyle and Mike, performing a beautiful rendition of "Grow Old with Me," and Jeremy being told he could kiss the bride—me. *We're married!* Triumphantly we hurried back down the aisle as man and wife.

Our reception bonfire was rained out, but we danced under the tent and then spent a cozy evening inside with our friends and family. My dad started a rousing card game in the dining area, billiard balls clinked in the game room, and the bartenders were kept busy.

Finally Jeremy and I said goodnight and left the others to finish the party. We shared a bubble bath and champagne in the honeymoon suite, figuring we had better soak up some luxuries as newlyweds before we headed off to rough it in the woods.

After a lengthy breakfast with friends and family, we gathered our guests at the trailhead. Since our trailside ceremony had been rained out, and the morning water-fall hike with our guests had been canceled, we wanted to involve the actual trail in this final piece of our wedding. Holding hands in our matching "bride" and "groom" t-shirts and shouldering our new packs, we began walking down the AT to symboli-cally begin our honeymoon hike. In reality, we were walking just a tenth of a mile to our waiting car. We would drive to a bed and breakfast for a few nights of luxury before resuming our hike.

As we walked away, signs reading "Just Married" and "Newlyweds" were visi-ble on the back of our packs. Our friends and family blew bubbles and waved us off. I heard the strains of the song "Happy Trails" drifting down the trail from some of my camp friends as we started once more toward Maine.

Part Three

18

Rocks and Snakes and Thunderstorms, Oh My!

Maine was calling.

I took my husband's hand as I flashed back on the filthy, teary-eyed couple who had left Pine Grove Furnace State Park the previous summer. We parked in front of the camp store, and I looked out the car window at the momentous patch of grass. *We said we'd be back, and here we are.*

At the picnic tables in front of the camp store, we met our first few thru-hikers of the season. Remembering how hungry we had been at this point, we shared cookies and drinks with the other hikers. This was our first time on the magician's end of trail magic. Meeting new hikers was exciting, but it was also strange to realize that the faces we had grown so used to seeing the previous year were all gone, and we would need to make a whole new set of trail friends.

Sitting at those familiar picnic tables, we reminisced about our Half-Gallon Challenge attempt. I recalled my painfully full belly, the chocolate ice cream painted across my skin, the relentless throbbing of my feet, and my overwhelming tiredness. I remembered the tears and the heart-wrenching decision to leave the trail. Most importantly, I recognized that being here again meant that Souleman and I were back to finish the dream we had started. And this time around, my body was on board.

"Brownie?"

I smiled at Souleman's transition back to my trail name, and looked up. *Oh, I've missed that.*

"I told you Maine would wait."

I threw my arms around his neck and, with my nose pressed up against his pack strap, noticed that his new gear still smelled clean. *How long until we smell like thru-hikers? Wait. We aren't thru-hikers anymore.* It hadn't occurred to me until that moment that we were now section hikers. *Damn feet! You took away my thru-hiker label.* I pulled away and forced a smile. *The label won't matter when we make it to Maine. We'll still be two-thousand milers.*

"Ladies first," he said as he pointed up the trail.

Throwing a glance over my shoulder, I paused to click my poles together behind me. Then I took my first step north of Pine Grove Furnace State Park.

The first miles involved an incredibly easy walk, and I settled into a comfortable pace. We were at the shelter, completely rested, by two o'clock. I surprised both of us by suggesting that we push on. After another 2.5 miles, we camped alone in the woods. Although we were looking forward to meeting our fellow hikers, it seemed appropriate to spend the first night of our honeymoon hike alone.

We erected our new Big Agnes SL2 tent in the woods for the first time and immediately fell in love with our first home as a married couple. It was technically a single-wall tent, but the nylon could be rolled back over most of the top to reveal a mesh lining. I loved this construction because it kept out the bugs and made me feel protected from snakes and mice, yet permitted a cool breeze and stargazing from the comfort of my Therm-a-Rest.

That first night we slept with only the mesh separating us from the sky. We spent hours staring up at the stars and the trees swaying over our heads. Eventually, I fell asleep with my husband's arm holding me tightly against his side, the wind blowing across my face, and stars over my head. Life was perfect.

Apparently there were *some* aspects of trail life I had selectively forgotten. Memories of the many enjoyable parts of hiking, such as the touch of a breeze on my face, the joy of seeing shelter signs, and the incredible taste of gummy, slightly cold macaroni and cheese, had not faded. However, the incessant rotisserie-style sleeping, the cacophony of crickets, and the annoying routine of getting up to pee in the middle of the night were details I had somehow disremembered.

We had hiked with packs on for only one day, and already I had to flip from side to side every couple of hours during the night in an effort to lessen the discomfort in my throbbing legs. I could not even begin to imagine thru-hiking before the invention of sleeping pads. After a night of endless rotating, we were up and hiking early.

We hiked a few miles toward the next shelter. The highlight of this monotonous section was a circuitous boulder field in which we wound up, around, and between many giant rocks. After lunch, we came upon a couple of uphill jaunts that reminded us what the Appalachian Trail was all about. Just as I was cursing my ill-prepared, out-of-shape legs, the trail flattened and unceremoniously dumped us into a cornfield.

For more than two miles we wound through cornfields in the scorching sun. It was over ninety-five degrees in the shade, in which we were most decidedly *not* hiking. Sweat ran in rivers down my face, legs, arms, and back. I could visualize the sweat soaking into my brand-new pack.

Finally, we exited the sizzling field and found ourselves on the outskirts of Boiling Springs, Pennsylvania. We had intended to stay just outside town at the Backpacker's Campsite, but learned from nearby hikers that it was infested with ticks. Luckily, there was a man in town who allowed hikers to camp on his back lawn for a dollar each. We willingly turned over our two dollars and headed for a gas station to buy icy-cold beverages. It was so hot that our bodies were working like sieves. We couldn't put as much liquid into them as we were sweating out, even though we drank constantly.

In the morning we had an unprecedented early departure and were hiking again by seven o'clock. That meant I was awake and had eaten breakfast and packed my gear *before* seven o'clock. In fact, I'd also had a second breakfast of a ham and cheese sandwich from a gas station and had weighed my pack (twenty-six pounds). I was thrilled to be hiking without the exhaustion of mono or the pain of inflamed plantar fasciitis. Our fresh legs carried us more than ten miles by noon.

It was only June and already the temperatures were excruciatingly hot. Normally, heat doesn't faze me much, but this weather was nearly unbearable. Souleman and I were both sweating more than I ever remembered from the year before. As we picked our way through a blazing-hot field, we walked in relative silence because we were too hot to exert the energy required to converse.

I heard the tell-tale rattle before I saw a camouflaged rattlesnake sunning in the cornstalks. When my eyes finally landed on the snake, I reacted like a stereotypical girl: I screeched a horrible, high-pitched noise, flailed my arms, and went scurrying in the opposite direction. *Stupid snake.* Never mind the fact that the snake was not trying to strike at me and was not even directly on the trail where I would have had to step over it. This was the first snake we had seen despite the horror stories of their overwhelming presence in Pennsylvania.

"How about you lead for, oh, say, the rest of Pennsylvania," I said to Souleman.

"It was just a snake."

"Should I remind you about the night of the spiders?"

He took the lead. While Souleman scouted for snakes, I found blackberries along the path and dallied behind him snacking in the sun. I was really savoring the small opportunity for fruit, but I think Souleman was somewhat annoyed at my slow progress. Four steps, pick a berry, ten steps, pick three berries, six steps. . .

When we stopped for a break, I peeled off my shoes and socks and wiggled my toes in the sun. My feet felt remarkably good. I had no signs at all of the previous year's crippling pain. I did notice a couple of small blisters where the edges of my orthotics had rubbed my arches. Since the little bubbles didn't hurt, I left them unbandaged and made a mental note to re-evaluate them that night. My fears that being back on the trail and hiking every day would resurrect the unbearable foot pain of last year had been unfounded so far.

Throughout the fifteen miles we hiked, Souleman and I both felt energetic. I was really enjoying using my radio and new iPod and singing along as I trudged up hills or scurried down slopes. As we hiked in and out of range of different stations, I found silly talk shows and country music stations to entertain myself. Although I appreciated having the radio immensely, I made sure to spend more time listening to nature and my thoughts than the radio since part of the purpose of hiking the trail was to escape technology. The radio would still be there when I returned home.

With the help of our radios, we flew through our planned miles that day. I expected to need time to build back up to our old hiking stamina, but ten or more miles a day proved to be immediately doable. After having completed our planned mileage so early, we sat on a mountaintop overlooking the town of Duncannon and flipped through our Handbook. *Good old Handbook.* Since we weren't tired and there was plenty of daylight left, we decided to push four more miles into town.

During the evening, we hung out at the renowned Doyle Hotel. A legendary hiker named Warren Doyle had enjoyed staying at this hotel and had made it famous among Appalachian Trail hikers. Although everyone was extremely friendly, the food was fabulous, and the location was convenient, aesthetically it left something to be desired. The building was ancient and somewhat dilapidated, and the bar/restaurant was dark and smoky.

The bartender/waitress/cook rented out the rooms at the Doyle, and a rickety staircase led up to them. None of the rooms were air-conditioned, meaning that in order to avoid having a heat stroke, guests had to leave the windows open. None of the windows had screens. Some of the "deluxe" rooms featured ceiling fans or a single bare light bulb hanging from the ceiling. Souleman and I stayed in the "honeymoon suite," which actually had a fan *and* a light.

Bathrooms at the Doyle were dormitory style. With a ratio of about fifteen hikers to a bathroom, I could just imagine the scum buildup in the showers. A single, coin-operated washing machine was tucked into the shared bathroom. Shampoo and soap were not provided, and we weren't carrying any, so we bathed using a bottle of pump-style liquid hand soap we found under the bathroom sink. My hair did not appreciate the creativity.

I took my turn in the shower and tried desperately not to touch the slimy shower curtain, scummy walls, or stained floor with a single body part.

"I have a rash on my ankle," I called out to Souleman, who was sitting on the washing machine waiting for his turn to shower.

"Yeah?"

"Actually, it's on both ankles. A complete circle around the tops of my socks."

As I dried off, Souleman studied my ankles. "Poison ivy."

While we were starting to meet many of the 2006 thru-hikers, we still felt like outsiders. They had bonded over the last eleven hundred miles and shared stories, experiences, and trail friends that we could not relate to—they had encountered different weather, different hiking companions, different festivals, and different trail magic. We smiled through the awkwardness and did our best to establish our place in that year's hiker world.

The climb out of Duncannon was rumored to be steep and endless, but for us it was quick and steady. We crossed the Susquehanna River, which was the fourth-largest river on the trail. Souleman set a nice, constant pace, and I enjoyed the novelty of walking behind him. I was very proud of myself for keeping pace. Being the first day of summer, it was also our second Hike Naked Day. I seriously contemplated it, but I just knew I would be the hiker who came across an entire scout or church group. Fully clothed, we hiked our longest distance yet that year. While we had surpassed 17.1 miles countless times the previous year, it felt like a new accomplishment the second time around.

My poison ivy rash began to spread to my fingers, my lower back, my bottom, and my calves. It wasn't too itchy, but it was extremely uncomfortable. My skin burned when I sweated, which was almost all the time while hiking and wearing a pack. I was grateful that the temperatures had dropped a little because any more perspiration would have been unbearable. *These are the experiences that will make me tough.* Heald, a thru-hiker we had recently met, gave me some packs of Aveeno cream that helped. The patch of poison ivy on my back was right where my hip belt rested, so it had become rather irritated and raw from the constant sweating and rubbing. It was nearly impossible to find a comfortable position in which to sleep.

BOOM—CRASH—BOOM! We awoke at five o'clock the next morning to the sounds of thunder rumbling and lightning crashing in the distance.

"We'd better secure the fly," Souleman called over the thunder.

We had slept with the tent fly folded back in order to enjoy the breeze through the mesh. Hurriedly, we stuffed our feet into our Crocs and scrambled out of the tent.

"We have to get our packs. Oh, and the bear bag!" I yelled over claps of thunder.

Souleman ran for our bear bag line and hurriedly lowered it while I grabbed our packs and poles and threw them under the vestibule. It was inevitable that our tent would get drenched, but we were determined to keep as much of our gear dry as possible.

The moment Souleman pulled his second foot into the tent and grabbed the zipper, it started raining. The thunderstorm raged outside for hours.

"I'll bet our tent keeps out more rain than those windows in the honeymoon suite at the Doyle," Souleman offered after more than an hour of rain.

"Our tent has as many luxuries as that honeymoon suite," I stated. "We even have an overhead light." I hung my headlamp from the mesh loop at the top of the tent.

"And silky linens." He pointed at our sleeping bags.

"Maybe we should call this the Honeymoon Hotel."

Impatiently, we waited out the storm. Although it seemed like an eternity had passed, we were back on the trail with mostly dry gear by nine o'clock. The first few miles were uphill, and I faithfully followed Souleman up switchback after switchback. *What were the words to that song Domino wrote last year, "Mindless Switchbacks?"* We stopped only twice—once for a Snickers break after the uphill and once for lunch. The day went by fast and without further rain. I was proud of my ability to climb uphill without frequent stops. I felt great aside from the poison ivy.

We camped that night by a river, which happened to have a swimming hole nearby. After dinner, we bathed in the river. I marveled at the simple joy of rinsing salt and dirt from my skin and hair. As I rinsed I couldn't help but notice that my poison ivy kept showing up in new places—just out of reach of my fingernails, of course.

We stretched out in the tent in order to escape the mosquitoes. Having poison ivy while sleeping in such close proximity to Souleman worried me. Though I wanted to cuddle with my new husband, I did not want us both to be miserable.

As I wrote in my journal, I again heard thunder in the distance. Souleman lay beside me trying to get a Red Sox score on his radio. He sat up after a few minutes.

"Hey, it sounds like bad weather's coming," he said.

He stuck one of his ear buds in my ear and we lay side by side listening to continued warnings about the rapidly approaching extreme weather.

"Severe thunderstorm warning. Expect winds with sixty-mile-per-hour gusts and penny-sized hail. Seek shelter inside a building. Repeat, seek shelter inside," we heard the weatherman warn.

Does a nylon tent count as "inside?" Does a three-sided trail shelter?

"Hey, do you think we should try to get to that shelter?" I asked, propping up on one elbow and pulling out the ear bud. We had picked our tenting location because of the river and an idyllic, perfectly flat spot. We were exactly four tenths of a mile from the nearest trail shelter.

Pulling out his ear bud, he said, "I don't know. What if we got caught in the bad weather partway?"

"Yeah. I wonder how far away the storm is." I tilted my ear toward the sky. Thunder rumbled in the distance. I knelt at the end of my sleeping pad and stuck my head out of the tent to look at the clouds. "We'd better at least get our stuff secured."

We prepared for the storm as best we could, collecting all our loose belongings and stashing them inside the tent. We pulled the equipment that usually spent the night in the vestibule, including our packs, poles, and shoes, inside with us. We were not willing to risk having our valuable gear whisked out of the vestibule by a strong wind.

Thunder crashed closer and the ground underneath us shook. Souleman sat peering out the mesh of the door.

"Maybe we should go to the shelter," he wavered. "But what would we do about our gear?"

"We could take just our sleep stuff and come back for the rest tomorrow."

"Let's try for the shelter," he decided.

"Ok. Let's just loop our sleeping bags around our necks and take our sleeping pads and headlamps."

We sat up and unscrewed the air valves on our Therm-a-Rests. Before we could roll them, rain pelted the tent over our heads, and the nylon walls swayed furiously with the rush of wind.

"It's too late!" I yelled over the echoing thunder.

The rain came down as though a faucet in the sky had been cranked on at full blast. *How strong is that seam sealer we used?* Lightning crashed down all around our tent, casting eerie shadows through the nylon. The thunder was so deep and loud that the sound reverberated endlessly and shook the ground beneath us. *What are the statistics on deaths by lightning?* I saw a fiery bolt strike mere feet from our Honeymoon Hotel and heard the sizzle of leaves and grass being zapped with electricity.

"Do you think we could die?" I yelled as I curled up on my sleeping pad.

"If we do, at least we'll die together." He curled his body around mine, trying to make sure we weren't touching anything metal—our pack frames, our hiking poles, or the tent poles.

I made my body as small as possible and spooned against him. "Do you think anyone else has spent their honeymoon this way before?" I could feel his heart beating too fast against my back.

"Worried about dying in a tent in a lightning storm?" He chuckled tensely. "Probably not."

"You forgot to include the poison ivy." I squeezed my eyes shut and pulled his arm over my eyes as the next bolt of lightning struck.

"What does poison ivy have to do with a storm?"

"Nothing. But it can't be normal on a honeymoon."

Many anxious hours later, the storm subsided. I was both physically and mentally exhausted and succumbed to sleep with my body still firmly pressed against my husband's. Sleeping closely was not always comfortable for our sore bodies, but in this instance the security of being close triumphed over the desire to stretch out.

In the morning we trudged across a treacherous ridge made slippery by the rain from the night before. Rocks of all sizes were underfoot, and I imagined killer snakes hiding in each hole between them. The trail was so overgrown that branches, leaves, and prickly plants grabbed us from both sides and even occasionally from overhead. Many of the encroaching plants were poison ivy, poison sumac, and poison oak. I imagined the itchy patches already splotched across my body growing exponentially.

"The Pennsylvania slogan should officially be 'Rocks and snakes and thunderstorms, oh my!'" I told Souleman. "Actually, maybe the last words should be 'poison ivy.'" I scratched dramatically to emphasize my point.

"Maybe so."

"Why do hikers hate Virginia so much?" I asked. "Pennsylvania is way worse."

He nodded in miserable agreement.

We popped our headphones into our ears and walked without talking. The weather report on the radio indicated that even worse storms were headed our way. *I do not want to have to endure that for two nights in a row.*

At lunch, while Souleman read through the register in a shelter, I flipped through our Handbook. When he closed the register, I said, "You know, Pine Grove is only five miles past where we were going to camp tonight."

"Yeah?"

"Uh-huh." I darted a sideways glance at him. "And they have a McDonald's. And a hotel." I shoved another cracker with cheese into my mouth.

He raised his eyebrows and widened his eyes.

"And it's supposed to thunderstorm again tonight."

"I'm in."

Our town trip was quick. We ate at McDonald's, bought our food resupply, took hasty showers, and fell asleep. Early the next morning, we found ourselves back on the trail with five days' worth of food.

I couldn't believe we were getting so close to Delaware Water Gap. At midday, we approached an endless boulder field. The sun-warmed rocks were prime real estate for snakes, and I reminded myself to watch closely. The jagged terrain meant that I was forced to keep my eyes on every single foot placement, so it was difficult to scan the trail ahead. Each step was precariously placed on angled, uneven rocks. My ankles throbbed because of the increased pressure from landing and bearing weight at odd angles.

Eventually, we were given a brief reprieve from the boulders. *Maybe the worst of the rocks is over for today.* Almost immediately, though, another boulder field appeared ahead. Many awkward steps into the rock maze, Souleman suddenly cursed and flew backward into me. After hearing a loud rattle at the last minute, he had changed his direction just before stepping directly on a rattlesnake. In a comical, curse-studded scramble, he kept moving backward away from the coiled snake. Once his heart rate had returned to normal, he pulled out our camera and began inching back toward the snake.

"What are you doing?" I asked, bewildered.

"Documenting." He snapped some pictures from a safe distance.

For the rest of the day, the trail was relatively flat but still brutally rocky. My eyes spent so much time staring at my feet to determine the exact location of each step that I swore I could pick our trail runners out of any shoe lineup. Unfortunately, I couldn't tell you a single thing about the scenery around the trail in Pennsylvania.

To further complicate matters, someone out for a laugh had marked phony AT blazes in the woods. Since looking up while navigating the rocks was challenging, following the correct path could get confusing. Luckily, the pranksters had made the blazes the wrong size, and we were conscientious enough to recognize which blazes were official and not get off course.

As we sat eating lunch, I began watching one little ant trying to move a crumb. He was carrying something larger than his own body and seemed determined to make it to his destination. More ants appeared, and they all worked together to move the crumb toward their colony. I intentionally spilled some more crumbs, and the ants tirelessly transported each one. These industrious ants employed all sorts of moving techniques, including the Lift-It-Above, the Push-It-Ahead, and the Drag-It-Behind. Some ants even worked in pairs. Throughout lunch we jokingly compared the progress of multiple ants.

In addition to watching ants and navigating boulder fields, we hiked 10.7 miles out of town. For the first five miles, my heavy town pack had me dragging, but I had readjusted by the end of the day. While there had been many challenging days so far, I had taken them in stride and whined far less than I had on the trail the year before. The absence of foot pain and lack of oppressive tiredness from having mono made the trail a completely different experience. I was so thankful to be back and experiencing the trail in good health.

We arrived at the shelter late that day and had only a brief amount of daylight remaining. By dividing up our chores, we finished them speedily and were able to dive into our tent the very moment it started raining.

"This is unbelievable," Souleman lamented when we woke to find it still pouring outside.

"I know. I'm a little worried that God forgot about his promise not to send any more floods. Or maybe he didn't include Pennsylvania. Should we build an ark?"

"Maybe." He poked the wall of our tent with his finger. Water splattered down on us. "I don't think our tent can handle much more water."

"I think it must have rained almost every day so far this year."

"Yep, it's no good. I'm going to turn on my radio and see if I can catch a forecast." After a few minutes, he tossed the radio aside. "No signal."

"Have I mentioned that I hate this state?" I said, flopping dramatically on my sleeping bag.

We flipped through our Handbook, played a card game, and lay on our backs talking while trying to wait out the worst of the storm. Finally, the nylon walls began closing in on us and we simply had to get out of the tent.

When we peeked outside, our tent was completely surrounded by a giant puddle—a four-inch-deep, muddy puddle. Under the vestibule, our packs were sitting in several inches of brown, murky water. Sitting upright, Souleman poked the floor in dismay. Ripples waved out across the bottom of the tent. The word "wet" couldn't even begin to describe our surroundings.

I picked up my sleeping bag to stuff it into its sack. Then I set it right back down. "I do *not* want to do this."

Souleman lay back down on his sleeping pad and raised his eyebrows suggestively. "It won't be any wetter in fifteen minutes, right?"

"Fifteen minutes is all you've got?" I teased. "It may rain for hours."

Ultimately, we had no choice but to go out in the rain. We accepted the fact that we would be cold and wet and scurried out to break down camp. Just outside the door of the tent, I stood still with my eyes closed, adjusting to the cold and the rain.

"I'll understand if you're in a bad mood. This is miserable. You hate to be wet and cold!" Souleman yelled over the storm.

"You think *this* is wet?" I stomped my foot in a mud puddle so it splashed all over us both. "You think *these* hands are cold?" I stuck my icy hand on the back of his neck under his rain hood. I looked up at the sky and threw my hands up in the air. "Is that all you've got?" I yelled.

We stuffed our mouths with soggy Pop-Tarts, the red dye from the raspberry icing running down our hands. Finally, I hefted my wet, heavy pack onto my shoulders and stepped onto what was supposed to be the trail. A mucky river now wound through the woods following the white blazes. We walked through water, in water, over water, and around water.

We wrestled our poles from the greedy mouths of mud banks, as water-filled holes threatened to steal our boots and wet rocks became an extreme test of balance. Somehow we continued laughing, and the relentless rain kept us moving. We trudged more than thirteen miles without stopping or sitting down—we even ate our lunch standing under a dripping tree limb. Luckily, the terrain was moderate. The highlights of the day were seeing a large black snake slither across the trail in front of us and finding a turtle hiding from the rain underneath a fallen log. I had squatted down to touch the turtle and was just about to pick him up when Souleman spoke up.

"Don't you think that turtle's miserable enough?"

Poking my lip out, I settled for a photo instead.

With our rain hoods on, we couldn't hear anything over the staccato beat of raindrops on nylon. Our conversations were limited to "What? I can't hear you!" Eventually, we removed our hoods and dealt with wet hair so that we would be able to hear each other. As our skin became saturated with rain, we made up a million verses to the song "Froggy Went a-Courtin'." If nothing else, coming up with lyrics kept our minds off the rain. On the deserted trail, we sang at the top of our lungs and splashed straight through the mud puddles. Sharing our misery made it almost fun.

Saturated, dripping, and freezing cold, we made it into Port Clinton late in the afternoon. The townspeople allowed hikers to sleep in a pavilion in the center of town for free. A lot of hikers were already crammed in, waiting out the rain or recovering from it. By unspoken agreement, the picnic tables running along the back side of the pavilion were for cooking and socializing, one section of the pavilion was for sleeping, and the other side was for erecting tents to dry. Any available beam, rail, or nail was for hanging wet gear. I stepped over wet socks, muddy boots, and soggy packs, then ducked under bear bag rope strung out like clotheslines to add our stinky, sopping gear to the lineup. It looked like a hoarder obsessed with outdoor gear had lived in the pavilion for a decade.

There was so much moisture in the air, and so much rain coming down, that it seemed improbable that anything would dry. We erected our tent in a small space, and the last time I checked before going to bed, it still had standing water in it. Water seemed to be dictating so much of our hike.

The constant rain had started to affect my body. My fingers had turned a weird, grayish color, and my skin had become perpetually wrinkled. Under my arms, down my sides, and on my thighs I had a prickly, painful rash, and between my toes my skin had turned red and was coated with a clear, sticky goo. My clothes were soaked and felt gritty from salt and dirt, so the friction of the fabric against my skin added to my discomfort. With the rain still falling, no end was in sight.

In spite of my discomfort, we had chores to do. I planted myself at a picnic table to sort food and cook dinner. It continued to thunder and rain, but at least we were minimally protected under the pavilion. I felt very grateful that I wasn't cooking out in the woods at a campsite. We played cards by flashlight, socialized with our fellow water-logged hikers, and stared in amazement at the endless rain. Over the course of the evening, our pavilion turned into an island oasis surrounded by a twenty-foot-wide moat of rainwater.

Rain was still coming down just as hard the next morning. *Seriously?* Rumor had it that the trail had washed out in places and that some uprooted power lines were dangling in the water not too far north. Souleman and I easily decided to take a zero day rather than risk electrocution. A group of hikers decided to venture to Cabela's, a chain outdoor store, and we tagged along to get out of the rain for a while. *What is this place?* Colors assaulted me the moment I passed through the automatic door—fluorescent hunter's orange, green and grey camouflage, and red and black plaid seemed to be the colors of choice. A fake mountain reached almost to the ceiling in the middle of the store, and all around it taxidermied animals were posed on ledges and rocks. I could see boats in one corner, guns and bows in another, and car camping gear on a raised level above me. *At least it's dry.*

When we returned to the pavilion, the rain had stopped temporarily, though it was still overcast. Neither Souleman nor I could stand the idea of another night in the wet, crowded pavilion, so we decided to risk heading back to the woods. As a precaution, we secured our rain covers over our packs before stepping out of the pavilion. As soon as we left town, the trail became a river. The actual river in Port Clinton had overflowed and had purged all its excess water onto the Appalachian Trail. We walked through cold, rushing water that was full of debris and, at some points, well over my knees. I worried irrationally about snakes swirling around my legs in the water but trudged on anyway.

As usual, there was a steep uphill right out of town, and the terrain was slippery and wet. After we had hiked for only about thirty minutes, it started raining again. Luckily, the gear in our packs was secure under our pack covers this time and did not get any wetter. There was no hope for our shoes and socks, though, and our clothes were once again soaked.

When we saw the shelter sign that evening, I turned around to face Souleman. Rain splashed on my face as I looked up at him. "Our tent still isn't completely dry. I can't stand the idea of sleeping in a wet tent again tonight. Or packing it up wet tomorrow."

"So, you want to stay in the shelter?" He wiped at the beads of water collecting on his beard.

I looked over at the half-dozen people who were already spread out in the shelter and sighed. "Yeah. I guess so."

"Will you sleep?"

"Probably not." In some cases, though, practicality came before my sensitive ears. I was grateful to spread my Therm-a-Rest on the dry, wooden floor and see a solid roof over my head.

It poured all night. The sound of raindrops muted the noises of other people, and I slept better than I usually did in a crowded shelter. I appreciated being able to pack our gear without the burden of a wet tent. While getting dressed and slipping on my pack, I discovered that my poison ivy rash was mostly gone. I was smiling as I stepped out of the shelter into the temporarily rainless day.

It was a trick. The rain started again almost immediately, and there were four separate thunderstorms during the day with constant rain in between. The rain pelted from the sky with such force that, at times, the drops actually hurt on contact. Every fiber of my being was wet. My hair was wet, my skin was wet, and the insides of my ears were even wet.

"Can you think of a single dry spot on your entire body?" I asked Souleman as I wrung out one of my pigtails.

His eyes darted around, and I imagined him doing a head-to-toe inventory. Finally, he grimaced. "Nope, I sure can't."

"Me neither." *Eventually it will stop raining. Eventually I will be dry again.*

Even as wet as we already were, things just kept getting worse. The trail was still a river. At times it seemed almost comical to look up at the next trail blaze and then look down to see water flowing beneath our boots. We trudged for miles at a time through running water. Pushing through the resistance of the cold, rushing water significantly affected our progress.

My body hurt. I made a mental list of my rain-induced ailments. Gross things were happening to my skin. Strange, red rashes covered with sticky, clear film had appeared in a startling number of places on my body. The skin had been falling off my feet in long strips, and my hands had begun peeling where they had rubbed on my poles. My shoulders and waist had become raw where my pack straps had rubbed, and my fingernails had become abnormally pliable. *Think of something positive,* I commanded myself. Nothing came to mind.

19

It Works for the Frogs

"**B**rownie, do you smell a skunk?" asked Souleman as we were hiking the following morning.

"I don't think so." I stopped and sniffed in all directions.

"Stand over here," he suggested.

I walked over beside him and sniffed again.

"See?"

"It's faint, but it could be." I shrugged.

We carried on down the trail, stomping through puddles, wiping raindrops out of our eyes, and trying to carry on conversations over the noise of the rain. Not ten minutes later, Souleman stopped walking again.

"You smell it this time, right?" he asked, squinting at me through the raindrops.

I raised my eyebrows in question.

"It's a skunk, I swear."

I sniffed all around dutifully. Finally I had to tell him, "I think what you're smelling is *us*."

That night I could not get comfortable. The raw spots on my skin burned. My inner thighs were badly chafed from the constant rubbing of wet skin against damp, sweaty pants. I couldn't find a way to lie down that didn't put pressure on some sore spot. My discomfort kept me awake, and I wasn't sure I'd fallen asleep at all when the sun started to rise. I heard rustling and realized Souleman was awake too. We decided to pack up and start hiking since neither of us could sleep. It wasn't even six o'clock when we hit the trail. Starting so early made the miles fly by, and by lunch we had easily covered ten miles. It helped knowing that town was at the end of our mileage.

As we approached more of Pennsylvania's infamous rocks, I held my poles out wide and attempted ten steps with my eyes closed. *One, two . . . this isn't so bad . . . three* (wobble), *four* (place right foot on rock and roll ankle awkwardly), *five* (trip on unexpected boulder and catch self on poles), *six . . . seven* (trip over own pole and land on ground).

"Are you ok?" Souleman asked, offering me a hand.

I nodded. "I was trying to hike with my eyes closed."

He looked at me like I had lost my mind. "Why?"

"I read about a blind hiker named Bill Irwin who hiked the entire trail. I wanted to see what it was like." I brushed my hands off and shook my head. "I couldn't even make it ten steps."

We continued, perching precariously on top of wet, slanted stones. More than once, my poles saved me from long, potentially dangerous slides down steep inclines.

In between rock fields, we came upon a mountaintop covered in blueberries. We ate and ate until our dirty, wrinkled fingers were stained purple. We even put a bunch of berries into a water bottle to enjoy in town. The last miles ticked off pretty quickly, and soon we found ourselves standing on the side of a road.

Car after car whizzed by us. The speed limit on the road was fast, which made it hard for cars to stop in time, and our wet, dirty appearance certainly didn't help our cause. *I wouldn't stop for us either.* Since drivers stop for female hitchhikers more often, I stood closest to the road with my thumb stuck out. Souleman hung back holding the "Hiker to Town" bandana. Our water-logged packs sat at our feet with their "Newlyweds" and "Just Married" banners facing traffic.

Eventually, an older car with rust spots pulled off the road just ahead of us. The driver stuck a hand out the window and waved us over. When I approached the car, I could see mail envelopes, fast food wrappers, shopping bags, beaded necklaces, and all other sorts of clutter piled on the dashboard. An unnaturally thin, pale woman with a giant puff of hair asked where we were headed. After a brief conversation, Souleman and I piled in the car amongst its eclectic contents. As the woman careened around curves and skidded through stop signs on the way to town, she told us about getting evicted from her apartment, being abandoned by her family, and refusing to go to drug rehabilitation because she "just wasn't ready." I fumbled futilely searching for a non-existent seatbelt.

I thought back to riding in Taba's van as I anxiously watched for signs to Palmerton. A particularly fast curve sent me tumbling into the window. *I'm going to die!* When the car finally stopped, the woman insisted on leaving us with a souvenir from the ride "to remember her by." *This is a moment in my life I would like to immediately forget.* She dug through a box and handed me a green, plastic bangle bracelet and an open tube of hand lotion.

"Take care!" she yelled before she swerved up the road.

I stared in the direction of her car long after it had disappeared and then looked at my husband in wide-eyed astonishment. "I think I need a drink," I told him matter-of-factly.

First, we retrieved our much-anticipated mail drop package from the post office, and then we settled in at the Parkside Inn. The room was air conditioned and had a luxurious bed. Most importantly, it was dry.

We stripped off our wet, uncomfortable clothes as soon as we closed the door, draping them over every accessible surface in the room. By the time we were finished, our foul-smelling clothing dangled from the back of the desk chair, the light fixtures, the curtain rod, and the dresser. Then we thawed out with a hot shower, even as we laughed at the irony of purposely getting even more wet. The steaming water stung on my spots of raw skin, and a thorough exam in the bathroom mirror revealed my skin to be equal parts normal and angrily red. I carefully patted myself dry, trying to avoid rubbing the tender patches with the rough towel. Then I collapsed onto our dry bed.

We had scheduled a zero for the following day, and I planned on doing some serious relaxing. Town chores were a necessity, though, and we had a long list of them. *I love lists.* On the trail I had less need for lists than usual. Still, I made grocery lists, predicted mileage lists, and town chore lists. When I wasn't listing, I was recording statistics: number of miles each day, cumulative miles so far on the trip, and where we slept each night. For this town trip, I had a long list of tasks:

Zero Day To-Do List
  1. Sleep in
  2. Laundry
  3. Groceries
  4. Buy new shorts
  5. Eat pizza
  6. Buy replacement knife
  7. Shower
  8. Library (Internet)
  9. Relax
  10. Bed—early!

Palmerton was not set up for foot travel, so we walked many miles to complete our chores. In between tasks, we fit in a couple of showers. The soap and water were torturous on my raw skin, and no matter how hard I scrubbed, I could not get rid of the rotten, pungent smell. Even with stinging and stinky skin, though, it was still great to be dry.

The climb out of Palmerton was more or less a two-and-a-half-mile vertical rock scramble. I normally have no fear of heights, but the steep angles at which we were scrambling up cliffs, with heavy packs pulling us backward, raised my heart rate dramatically.

As we were hiking steadily upward at my ever-moderate pace, two guys we had seen before passed us. We exchanged pleasantries and continued on our way.

"I'll bet we never see them again," I commented to Souleman as they moved out of sight.

About an hour later, I was shaken from my hiking groove when I saw two hikers coming toward us—the same two guys. The shorter guy asked, "Are you southbounders?"

To which, of course, we answered, "No."

The men exchanged confused glances. The taller one asked, "Did you know you're walking south?"

It was our turn to look confused.

"We aren't. We're going north," I told them matter-of-factly.

We all pulled out our Handbooks in hopes of deciding which group was going the wrong way. I pointed at the sun, and at the neighboring mountains we had been paralleling, and explained that the same mountains had been on our left all day. They weren't sure about my logic but decided to turn around. Confident I was right, Souleman and I kept going in the same direction. It turned out that we had been going north the whole time, and they had somehow ended up making a circle.

As we continued scrambling over rocks, my ankles abhorred the uneven surfaces. Luckily, Pennsylvania would soon be behind us. Our planned tenting destination was a backpacker's campsite, but the sky became ominously dark about two miles before we reached it. A few raindrops fell, and we hastily unshouldered our packs and scrambled to attach our pack covers. Shaking my head at Souleman wordlessly, I resigned myself to the fact that I was going to get wet once again. This time, though, the rain held off and we actually had time to set up our tent before more raindrops appeared.

"Oh no," I lamented. "We forgot to dry the tent in town. It smells like a wet dog." I kicked the final stake in with my boot. "Next time, I'm adding 'Dry tent' to the to-do list for town."

Souleman finished hanging the bear-bag line and ducked inside the stinky tent with me just as the rain began in earnest. "Should we just cook in the vestibule again?" he asked.

"I guess. I don't want to get any wetter." I stared glumly at the water that was creating puddles outside our vestibule.

"Me either." He shuffled through the contents of the food stuff sack. "How about macaroni and cheese, Chin?"

I scowled. "Don't call me that."

"It's a cute chin . . . Chin." He touched my face as I scooted as far away as I could in the small tent.

"Stop picking on me."

By the time we had cooked and eaten our gourmet meal, the rain had stopped, and we were able to hang our smell-ables and get situated in the tent without bringing in any extra water.

We slept in on our final hiking day in Pennsylvania and didn't start back on the trail until almost ten o'clock. The sunny day with temperatures in the eighties was perfect. I enjoyed tilting my face up to the warmth of the sun. *I wonder what it would be like to hike naked and feel the sun on all of my raw skin.* The terrain seemed to consist of nothing but rocks, rocks, and more rocks. The strain from walking across uneven surfaces at odd angles was brutal on my ankles. Nonetheless, my legs felt strong, and I figured that once the terrain became less rocky, I would be able to complete our planned daily mileage easily.

The miles went by more quickly as I sang along with twangy country songs. When I wasn't listening to music, I spent a lot of time thinking about writing. I repeatedly wished I could write and walk at the same time. I had all kinds of ideas I wanted to get on paper—*I should invent a nose warmer and patent it. . . . A video game about hiking the Appalachian Trail would be really cool. How do you create a video game? . . . I think I'd be good at an organizing business. I bet that lady Dad knows might be able to get me started. . . . That conversation at breakfast would be great for my book*—but then I'd forget them by the time I pulled out my journal at night.

We made it six miles to Kirkridge Shelter for lunch and then continued into Delaware Water Gap. On the way, we tuned our radios to the same station and sang our way down the trail. We had plans to stay that night at a hostel run by a Presbyterian church.

When we arrived in Delaware Water Gap, hikers whom we had known for only a few hours or days greeted us warmly and showed us around the hostel. The easy friendships of the trail were something that constantly surprised and pleased me. It didn't matter whether hikers had known each other for hours or for a lifetime. These friendships bridged the gaps between ages, personalities, education levels, religions, and income brackets. Fellow hikers were automatically friends.

Grinds, Bravefriend, Squarl, Mr. Parkay, Chou Chou, and Heald were all in town. We also met Salt and her dog, Pepper, Energizer Bunny, and Low Gear. Low Gear—no relation to the previous year's hiker by the same name—had just been diagnosed with Lyme disease, which was a powerful reminder that we had to be extra vigilant about checking for ticks.

Before my shower that afternoon, I searched for ticks without result, but I did find two little hitchhiking spiders stuck to me underneath my shirt. In the shower I was relieved to see that my raw skin had begun healing. Once clean, we filled ourselves with cheesy, greasy, delicious pizza. That night, the church was hosting a bluegrass and jazz concert in the sanctuary. We lounged in the back pews with other hikers and relaxed to live music.

In the morning we said goodbye to the church volunteers and then, a short time later, waved a happy farewell to Pennsylvania as we crossed the bridge over the Delaware River. *Hello, New Jersey!* The first thing we encountered in our eighth state was trail magic from a woman whose trail name was Pokey. She gave us fruit, cookies, drinks, and even a bag of trail mix. A clear sky and a snack gave us a wonderful start to a new state.

We hiked with Mapman and Robin, whom we had met at the hostel the previous night. They were married and about the same age as our parents. Their upbeat attitudes and energy kept us moving. We all ate lunch by a glacial lake called Sunfish Pond, where we saw giant frogs that appeared to have been injected with steroids, and the largest tadpoles I had ever laid eyes on. We even spotted a snake swimming in the crystal-clear water.

For a change the terrain was very gentle, with a wide and gradual ascent. We hiked relatively quickly, but the humidity was bothering me. My breathing seemed labored, like I was trying to use a straw to suck air through a wet piece of fabric. *This must be what asthma feels like.* My noisy breathing was covered up only by the now-incessant, insufferable sound of my pack squeaking right near my ears. For the past couple of weeks, a part of my pack had been making an awful screeching noise. Everyone talked as we hiked, but I could hear only about every fifth word over the horrible squeak and my labored breathing.

When the four of us consulted our map during a break, we had to decide between stopping early or pushing on for another eight white-blazed miles, plus one blue-blazed mile, to the next guaranteed campsite. Since New Jersey had a lot of camping restrictions, it wasn't an option to just set up our tent when we were tired. We ended up stopping early at the Mohican Outdoor Center and staying in a site adjacent to Mapman and Robin. While I was disappointed at having to cut our mileage short, it was a relief to remove my noisy pack for the day. The awful squeaking echoed in my ears long after we stopped hiking.

Once we were settled, Souleman wanted to go swimming in the pond at the outdoor center. I thought back to the snake we had seen only hours ago and hesitated.

"Think of it as a free bath and clothes washing," he coerced, pulling me toward the shore.

I started inching into the water, trying to adjust to the cold temperature. Finally, I imitated my husband and dove headfirst into the frigid water. While it was great to be immersed in the chilly pond, I jumped every time something touched me under the water. *Is that a water snake? A leech?* Souleman splashed me playfully, and eventually I relaxed and enjoyed rinsing my skin and clothes. That night, however, my damp clothes chafed my skin as we sat around the campfire, and I regretted getting them wet in the pond. It would be my first and last swim on the Appalachian Trail.

In my still-damp clothes, I stretched out on my stomach on my Therm-a-Rest beside Souleman. Propped on our elbows, we completed our nightly math session with Wingfoot, which revealed that we were only one hundred and fifty miles from Connecticut. *We're almost to New England. We've almost hiked home.*

As I lay in the tent grinning into the dark at our accomplishment, the loud, unceasing sounds of mating frogs became unbearable. I visualized the numbers on an alarm clock rolling forward as the noise kept me awake further and further into the night. Eventually, I propped myself up on my elbows.

"CROOOOOOAK!" I whisper-yelled.

Souleman didn't move.

"CROOOOOOAK!" I got a little louder.

He opened one eye and raised his eyebrow questioningly but still didn't speak.

I scooted closer. "CROOOOOOAK!"

"What are you doing?"

"Trying to get you to kiss me." I flopped back on my makeshift pillow dramatically.

Both eyes popped open. "What?!"

"Hey, it works for the frogs."

I buried my head under Souleman's arm, trying to block out the deafening noise. The temperature dipped, and with my still-wet clothes, I got chilly and needed my long-sleeved shirt for the first time that year.

We left the Mohican Outdoor Center at six o'clock in the morning, figuring that the earlier we left, the earlier we could get to town. I was in the lead and kept stumbling all over the trail.

"Are you ok?" Souleman asked me. "You're walking like you're drunk."

I stopped and leaned my hand on a tree. "I'm really dizzy." A rock in front of me appeared to shimmer and swim. I closed my eyes and rested my head on the tree.

"Do you want to stop for a while?" he asked me.

"No. Let's just take it slow." Suspecting dehydration, I drank bottle after bottle of water during our monotonous trek up the trail. My dizziness seemed to subside as the day progressed.

In Branchville we landed in yet another slightly sketchy motel. The dry bed and hot shower satisfied our biggest needs, so I was willing to overlook the hair in the bathroom sink and the musty smell of the rattling air conditioner.

I woke up in the middle of the night completely soaked in sweat. My stomach and intestines were hurting fiercely. I stumbled into the bathroom, doubled over. My teeth were chattering, and one look at my glassy eyes in the mirror confirmed that I had a fever. After spending a miserable hour kneeling in front of the toilet, I crawled back into bed. Tucking the covers around me, I pressed my shivering body against my husband's to steal some of his body heat. I wrapped his arm around me as he slept, pressing the warmth of his hand against my churning stomach.

I slept fitfully for the next few hours. When Souleman woke up, I filled him in on my nighttime misery. He pressed the back of his hand to my forehead.

"You *are* hot. You need to rest. I'll take care of everything else." He dug two Tylenol out of our first aid kit and tucked me back in bed. "I'll be back with breakfast."

Later that day as Souleman holed himself up in the bathroom with our filthy hiking clothes and did our laundry in the sink, I watched TV. The news came on and I watched captions fly across the screen: Stock Market Dips for Third Consecutive Day, Unemployment Levels in New England Reach New High, E-Coli Outbreak Linked to Spinach. Everything seemed so far removed from my current reality. The information in my Handbook was so much more important. *What is the next shelter like? How far is the water source? Are there cheeseburgers in the next town? What about a Laundromat? Where can we get ice cream?*

Miraculously, I woke up feeling normal after a good night's sleep. The temperature was in the seventies without a rain cloud to be seen. We returned to the trail, and the terrain rolled along gently. We took many breaks. First, we stopped at a white-painted pavilion where we sprawled on the cool cement benches and ate Snickers bars. Later, we shed our packs on an observation deck and dozed in the sun. Three shelters along the way provided opportunities to read trail registers and find out about the hikers ahead of us. With mild terrain and a lot of time to rest, we maintained twenty-minute miles for the first twelve miles.

I spent most of the day lost in thought. My mind wandered aimlessly from one topic to another. *Where do snakes go in the winter? How do they not freeze to death? Oh, remember that time in high school that Meagan and I almost wrecked in the snow storm on the way to that concert? I wonder how you go about publishing a book. I'm hungry. I wonder how many calories we're eating a day now.* My mental aerobics kept my legs moving effortlessly.

After we had completed that day's miles, Souleman and I sat cross-legged in our tent planning town stops and mileage for the next stint. It seemed that trail towns, and the chores that went along with them, were becoming more complicated the further north we got. We were having trouble finding towns that could accommodate our needs. Laundry facilities and stores that carried cooking fuel were particularly scarce. For some reason, southern trail towns had seemed more suited to completing trail chores on foot.

We started back just after eight o'clock in the morning and walked three miles very quickly, then had a king-sized candy bar and went two more miles before stopping to refill our water bottles. Our MIOX, the water purifier which we had raved about for the whole trail, was giving us a hard time. Souleman patiently took it apart and tinkered with it but could only get it to work for long enough to purify three bottles of water.

"This thing was so great until recently," he complained as he fiddled with the pieces.

"I guess we've used it a lot. Maybe it's tired? Like when a computer needs to reboot?" I tried to earn a smile.

He shook his head. "Computers don't keep us from getting sick. We're going to have to get a replacement at the next outfitter."

"Any idea where that is?"

"Nope." He shoved the dysfunctional purifier into his pack. "Until then, we'll have to be selective with our water sources, I guess." He tossed me one of the three full bottles and stuck the other two in his pack.

Right before we made it to Pochuck Mountain Shelter, the mosquitoes came out in full force. Hiking became a series of step-SLAP, step-SLAP, step-SLAP sounds. Although the shelter was our targeted destination, we could not justify volunteering ourselves as an all-night banquet for mosquitoes. We pulled out Wingfoot to determine our options. The "no camping" rule in New Jersey meant pushing on to another shelter or into town. The road to Vernon, New Jersey, was 6.5 miles away. After an inventory of our bodies, we popped some "Vitamin I" (the hiking term for Ibuprofen) for our aching knees and headed toward town.

When we arrived at the road leading into Vernon, we shrugged out of our packs and stuck out our thumbs. The cars flew by us without a second glance. As the daylight began to fade, so did my hopes for a hitch into town. Eventually, we dejectedly re-shouldered our packs and began walking the road. My knees were screaming with each step on the hard asphalt. I counted steps to distract myself as I listened intently for the sound of approaching cars. *Fifty-eight, fifty-nine . . . .ninety-nine, one hundred . . . two hundred fifty-six . . .*

Lights came into view up the road and we were able to make out the sign for a garden center. As we got closer and could read the fine print on the sign, I saw two glorious words: ICE CREAM. *Please don't let that be a mirage.* To my relief, the words still glowed dimly in front of me when I set foot in the parking lot. Without discussion, we ditched our packs outside and jumped in line for ice cream. I had no idea where I was sleeping that night, no idea how I was getting there, no idea where I would eat dinner, and I was filthy and exhausted. Still, I sat outside in the dark on a bale of hay, holding my husband's hand and licking my mint chocolate chip ice cream cone. *Is there anywhere else in the world I'd be happier?*

Souleman's wedding ring pressed against my fingers, and I ran my thumb across it. The thick band still felt strange when we held hands. I nudged him with my shoulder, then shifted on the hay so I could look into his eyes.

"I love you."

"I love you, too." He wiped a smudge of ice cream off my lip before eating the last bite of his cone.

"I love you even more than ice cream."

He put his arm around my shoulder and squeezed me tight.

Just then a middle-aged lady came out the side door of the garden shop. She fished keys out of her denim purse before pulling her dark green apron over her head.

"You headed to the hostel?" she called in our direction.

We nodded.

"It's just up the road. I drive right by there on my way home. Want a lift?" She gestured at her Jeep.

We nodded and gathered our things.

"We really appreciate this," Souleman told her as he loaded our packs in the trunk.

"It's no problem. Hikers come through here during this season every year. Many of them provide our store business. The least I can do is provide a lift. I look at it as a little give and take." She offered a big smile.

Our home for the evening was a hostel at an Episcopal church. This hostel was perfect by hiker standards. Sleeping accommodations were on the floor, but we were used to sleeping on the ground. There was a hot, clean shower, laundry facilities, and a refrigerator full of drinks. They even provided stove fuel, which solved one of our major town dilemmas.

Everything at the hostel was on the honor system. A recycled coffee can with a slit in the lid sat on a table for donations and payments. No one checked to make sure you paid for your fuel or drinks, and no donations were required for use of the washer or shower. Dutifully we stuffed our share of dollar bills into the jar, grateful for all of the niceties.

During conversations while folding laundry, fellow hikers told us that hitchhiking was illegal in New York and New Jersey. *That explains our difficulty hitching today.* This rule would make our journey through the next couple of states a little more complicated, especially since towns up north had been much farther from the trail so far. Walking into town was not really an option.

There was a Burger King directly across the street from the hostel. We donned paper crowns and filled up on dollar-menu items before coming back to socialize with our hostel-mates, two ladies who had been childhood friends. They were now in their fifties and were section-hiking together. Their packs, which easily weighed fifty pounds each, were filled with unconventional items like scout-style multi-piece mess kits and bulky wool sweaters. The ladies sat in the hostel with their maps and guidebooks spread before them on a table and discussed which section they would tackle the following year. I watched from our sleeping pads on the floor.

"I hope I'm that adventurous when I'm their age," I whispered to Souleman. "But I hope I'm hiking with you."

"Second thru-hike in 2036?"

I laughed. "Maybe. We might want to go somewhere new, though. There are so many places I want to go. The Grand Canyon, Yellowstone, Alaska . . ." I trailed off.

"We aren't limited to one more trip together, are we?" He shook his head at me with a smile.

"I hope not." I pulled on his growing beard. "But I guess we should plan the rest of this trip before we worry too much about others." I pulled out our Handbook.

Stretched out side by side on our Therm-a-Rests, we did our daily math and determined that if we hiked 17.3 miles the next day, we would be a full day ahead of schedule. Even though that would mean three long days in a row, we decided to give it a try. Souleman claimed he could tell I was gaining endurance. *I hope I can hold up. In one hundred miles we'll be in Connecticut. And soon we'll be in the seven-hundred-mile range of Katahdin.* It still seemed amazing to me that having seven *hundred* miles left to walk was a dwindling number.

I fell asleep with my husband's hand rubbing big circles on my back and woke in the semi-dark of early morning to find his hand still on my hip. The lady-hikers were bustling around in the hazy light packing their gear, and Souleman was still asleep beside me. I lay quietly for a few minutes, listening and reflecting. *I'm so rarely awake to enjoy this time of day. Last year, having mono made mornings nearly impossible, and I had to be pried out of my sleeping bag every day. I never had this quiet time to reflect on the hike so far and look forward to the day ahead. I've missed so many of these delightful, cuddly, first-thing-in-the-morning moments.* I faced Souleman and tucked my head under his chin. *Five more minutes,* I thought to myself.

When we began packing gear fifteen minutes later, it was still dark enough to need a headlamp. I mentally prepared for another challenging, twenty-plus-mile day. However, as seemed to happen frequently, the day turned out very differently than we had planned.

A local trail angel came to the church to offer us a ride to the trail. He also mentioned a nearby store that carried hiking shoes. Since my Vasque trail runners no longer had any grips on the soles after clambering over the Pennsylvania rocks, I jumped at the opportunity. Unfortunately, the store literally had nothing in my size.

By that point, though, we were committed to the task, and we ended up an hour away at another store, Gander Mountain outfitter.

The shoe selection at the second store was large and overwhelming. Like a typical woman, I tried on nearly every available option. This time, though, I was not agonizing about which color I would wear more, which heel size was more appropriate, or which cut made my feet look smaller. *What if I pick the wrong shoe and make myself miserable? I could get blisters. My feet might start hurting again.* Finally, I settled on a pair of Merrells. They fit perfectly, and since Merrell caters to long-distance hikers, I considered them a good investment. Rather unceremoniously, I dumped my trail-beaten, mud-caked Vasques into the trash can outside the store.

Once Souleman and I finally made it to the trail, our hike began with a steep ascent and then leveled to a nice ridge walk. Breaking in a pair of shoes on the trail was risky, but initially I had no complaints. I stayed so focused on the mosquitoes that were feasting on me all day long that I barely thought about my new footwear. My arms were completely covered in huge, red, itchy welts.

We stopped for the day at Wawayanda Shelter and were surprised to find that its large metal bear box was not attached to the ground, but instead chained to a tree. Further inspection made it clear that the box had once been cemented into the ground. The dents and scratches in the bear box and the poor condition of the tree to which the box was chained indicated that a bear had tried to show the humans how ineffective their bear-stopping measures were. As we set up camp, the mosquitoes were still attacking viciously. They bit us with such frequency and intensity that I wondered if they had had a meal all summer.

"We haven't seen a bear yet, you know," I observed as we hurried to set up the Honeymoon Hotel. "Maybe tonight is our night."

Souleman scanned the campsite. "Alone in a remote campsite with obvious bear damage might not be the safest time for our first bear sighting."

When we got into the tent, it took a few minutes to kill all the mosquitoes that had snuck inside. Then I wrote in my journal while Souleman listened to his radio, trying to find a Red Sox game. Every so often, he peered out the mesh lining of the tent looking for a bear.

"Scared?" I asked with a wink.

"You won't think it's so funny if a bear actually shows up."

When I slapped my journal shut, I asked him, "You know what keeps the bears away?"

"What's that?" He glanced up.

"Noise," I told him. Scooting close, I pulled out his ear buds, pushed his radio aside, and clicked off my headlamp.

20

You Aren't Supposed to Get Mad at Me

The same amount of mileage could be manageable one day and unbearable the next. In this case, the following day's twelve miles seemed like twelve hundred. We encountered a bunch of rock scrambles completely unmentioned by Wingfoot, as well as a multitude of massive mosquitoes.

"What the hell is with these mosquitoes?" Souleman asked. He was kneeling by a stream with our MIOX, getting ready to purify the water bottle he had just filled with stream water.

"I think they're on steroids." I slapped at mosquitoes as I knelt beside him and filled the other water bottles. I set the full bottles in a line between us so that we could purify each one. "I swear I have no blood left for them to take. I'm going to become anemic."

"I know." He squished a mosquito on his forearm. "We look like we have chicken pox." For a few minutes, the only sound was the occasional slap as one of us killed yet another mosquito. Souleman sat down on the bank and held up the MIOX. "This thing is dead."

"Like, completely?"

"Like, completely." His tone betrayed no hope.

"Crap." *Maybe we should have carried a back-up purifier after all.*

"I hope it died a painful death. We're going to have to drink unpurified water now." He smacked another mosquito and looked at me glumly.

I collected our unpurified water bottles and offered him a choice of two. "Would you like giardia water or cryptosporidium water?" These were two of the common water-borne illnesses contracted by hikers.

He rolled his eyes.

"Come on. That's funny!"

The broken water purifier had not been the first challenge of the day. During the multiple rock scrambles, I had realized that my cushy new Merrells were pinching my toes. I had stopped, retied my shoes, and tried wiggling my toes again. There was no question that my toes were cramped and uncomfortable. I had followed standard long-distance hiking advice and purchased a size 9.5, which was an entire size larger than my normal 8.5 shoes. *How is it possible to wear an eight and a half in "real life" and need larger than a nine and a half on the trail?* Granted, my ugly orthotics took up extra space, the excessive amount of time on my feet caused swelling, and the weight of my pack flattened my feet. I was relieved to remember Merrell's satisfaction guarantee and knew I would have to exchange my shoes for a larger pair at the earliest opportunity. *Really, Feet? Really? A size ten? I'm only five-foot-two. I'm going to have clown feet. Forcing me to get off the trail for a year wasn't torture enough?*

My toes were pinched and squished with each step, but according to Wingfoot, a creamery with homemade ice cream awaited us at the ten-mile mark. I marched ahead all morning motivated by the promise of ice cream. When we at last reached the farm stand, we treated ourselves to large ice creams with sprinkles and a long break on a picnic table. While I licked my ice cream, I tried to count my mosquito bites. I lost count at thirty-seven, and I hadn't even finished with my left arm.

We could have filled our water bottles with an outdoor hose near the ice cream stand but chose not to because we would be coming to a stream in two more miles. Since we were about to go uphill, we didn't want the extra, unnecessary water weight. Of course, that same stream was where we had realized our MIOX was broken, so we mentally kicked ourselves for having been too lazy to carry the extra weight.

Finally, a long, stressful day ended with our first campfire of the year. When I had imagined thru-hiking before the trail, I had thought I would build fires all the time. Most of my camping memories from growing up included campfires, and I had been so proud of my ability to consistently start one-match fires. I had always loved the camaraderie of stories and songs around a fire. Surprisingly, though, I was usually so tired at the end of each hiking day on the Appalachian Trail that a fire was the last thing on my mind. That night, I enjoyed sharing the fire with fellow hikers and having a few minutes of happy distraction from my worries about our water purifier and my ill-fitting boots.

The next day, New York welcomed us with dirty, brown water. As we hiked, Souleman and I scoured our surroundings looking for water that at least appeared sanitary. While we were under no delusion that clear water meant *safe* water, we did hold as true the idea that murky water meant *un-safe* water. Late in the day, we had still had had no luck finding a clear source, and our water bottles were dangerously empty.

While worrying about water sources, Souleman and I tackled a section of trail which led us up, over, and around numerous mountains which were referred to as Agony Grind. We soon understood the name. We had to squeeze through gaps in boulders and even summit the same mountain twice from different angles. *Who the crap planned this part of the trail?* I wondered. One particularly interesting rock formation called the Lemon Squeezer required us to remove our packs and pass them through a small opening ahead of us.

We were working even harder than normal to complete our mileage, and we were both dehydrated. Just as I was beginning to seriously consider drinking yellow, smelly, unpurified water, we found a gallon jug of water and a milk crate full of drinks left by a trail angel. According to the register inside the milk crate, hikers often have trouble finding water on this notoriously dry section of trail, so trail angels sometimes place jugs of water near road crossings. We very gratefully filled our water bottles and thanked the anti-giardia gods who were watching over us. I drank a can of Nestea in one gloriously long gulp. *Ahhh!* Trail magic often consists of only sodas or beer, and since I drink neither, I was especially appreciative of the like-minded trail angel who had left a non-alcoholic, non-carbonated beverage.

The next section of trail was not well-marked, and twice we found ourselves turning in circles, searching for a white blaze. We had become so reliant on the comfort of those little white stripes of paint. When a blaze was not visible in any direction, a mild form of panic set in.

"Hey, Brownie? When was the last time you saw a blaze?" Souleman asked me at some point.

I thought about it and couldn't remember having seen a blaze for quite some time. "I'm not sure." *Are we lost?* After a deep breath, I looked down at the worn dirt beneath my squished feet. "We're definitely on a trail."

"It looks like it," Souleman agreed.

"But is it *the* trail? I don't see any blazes in either direction." I stopped and gazed hopefully at the trees in front of and behind me.

"We could backtrack," he suggested.

"Yeah, but what if we're on the right trail now? We'd be adding extra mileage." I was already tired and was not excited about hiking any extra distance.

"But what if we're on the wrong trail and keep going in the wrong direction?" he countered. "We'd end up having to re-hike even more."

There was no perfect solution. After consulting our Handbook and calculating our estimated hiking speed and the time of day, we determined that we should probably be hiking uphill. I looked at the flat trail in front of us. *This is not uphill.* We decided to turn around. *How far have we gone in the wrong direction?* Souleman led and I trailed behind. Each step seemed like a monumental effort since we might have been going the wrong way. I scrutinized each tree and rock for signs of a blaze. *Please let there be a blaze, please.* About a quarter-mile later, I bumped into Souleman, who was stopped in front of me. Sticking out my hands, I grabbed my husband's shirt to keep my balance and then leaned up against him.

"Brownie, look." He held up one hand, his pole pointing at a faded white blaze.

Thank goodness! I took the lead and powered up the trail. As we climbed the mountain steadily, we heard voices up ahead. In a sparse area we could see a group of what appeared to be college-aged hikers a few switchbacks ahead. *A freshman orientation group?* I pushed on. Sweat was dripping down my face, the foam pads on the handles of my hiking poles were wet with perspiration, and even more sweat was running down my legs inside my gaiters.

The exertion was exhilarating, though, and I continued to push myself up the endless switchbacks. Soon, I caught up to a hiker who was straggling behind the group ahead. With a wave, I passed her. Next, I caught up to the group, and finally, full of pride, I found myself passing the leaders of the young, energetic group. It was rare that my short legs passed anyone on the trail, much less on an uphill climb during a long, extremely humid day.

"I told you you're getting stronger," Souleman told me as he high-fived me at the top. He leaned in for a sweaty, salty kiss while I was still struggling to catch my breath.

My enthusiasm kept me happily moving, and at the turn for our planned stopping point, I suggested pushing on. When we finally stopped four miles later, Souleman and I were both giddy. There was much laughter as we worked together to pitch our tent, prepare dinner, and purify water using a borrowed water filter. Usually, we split up the chores, but this time we worked as a team, completing each task side by side. As we worked, we compared the Appalachian Trail to an amusement park. Finding the conversation humorous, I recounted it as best I could in my journal entry that night:

Please read the following in your best tour guide voice:

GOOD MORNING, and welcome to Appalachian Adventures Amusement Park. We're so glad you could join us. Today our first ride will be the Agony Grind. In order to enjoy this and all the other rides here at Appalachian Adventures Amusement Park, it's important for you to be properly outfitted. Please make sure that your shoes are tied tightly, a covering of some kind is secured to your head, and your poles are firmly grasped in your hands. You might want to turn now and introduce yourself to your neighbor. If you aren't comfortable sharing your real name, feel free to make something up—call yourself Cookie or Jumping Jack or Hop-Along.

Ok, now that we're all acquainted, prepare to board the Agony Grind. This is not your average park ride. There will be no glorious scenery or amplified sounds. This adventure will take you up rock overhangs, across cliffs, and over elephant-sized boulders. It will go up each and every mountain at least once and will always choose the steepest, most circuitous path. Whenever possible, this adventure will keep you away from water sources, except for those appearing toxically contaminated. As you're going up the fourth or fifth endless ascent, you may ask yourself, "Why am I doing this?" It is then that you must steadfastly remind yourself that although this experience is voluntary, it is a necessary part of successfully completing your goal of surviving every single ride at Appalachian Adventures Amusement Park. Now, sit back and enjoy the Agony Grind!

end tour guide voice

As soon as I put my pen down, I was ready for sleep. Ever since Georgia, we had heard warnings about Three Ridges in Virginia, the rocks in Pennsylvania, the Endless Mile in Maine, and numerous other challenging areas in between. But not once, until that day, had we heard a word of warning about Agony Grind and the surrounding area in New York. Since hikers seem to love building up hype about challenging sections, we found this omission puzzling. Our aching knees, swollen feet, sore legs, and otherwise decrepit bodies declared that this segment had been excruciating. We were in dire need of the zero we had planned in two days.

In the morning, Bear Mountain was the only real challenge that lay between us and town. Following the trail around that area was somewhat confusing because it crossed the road a number of times. We were both exhausted and covered in mosquito bites, and my feet hurt from my too-tight shoes. Our moods were not in the best shape either. In a particularly heated moment after some harshly exchanged words, I took off up the trail on my own, as fast as my legs would go. I figured he would come after me and catch up quickly with his long stride. A good ten minutes went by. *Why hasn't he caught up?*

I sat down on a log to wait. When ten more minutes had passed and there was still no sign of my husband, I became even more furious. *Why isn't he coming after me?* I stormed up the trail, my anger pushing me faster than I had ever hiked before. In my fury, I paid scant attention to the trail. When I reached a road and saw white paint splotches to my left, I turned and began following the road. *Did he think I was just going to wait on him? Ha. He'll have to catch me.* I followed the white paint splotches for quite some time, moving as rapidly as possible.

Finally, I stopped for a sip of water and noticed that the blaze in front of me didn't quite seem uniform. I looked around and realized that none of the "blazes" near me were quite right. *Oh crap. These aren't blazes. I'm not on the trail.* Dejectedly, I realized I had probably missed the actual AT blazes back when the trail hit the road. *How long ago was that?* I looked at my wrist before remembering I didn't have a watch. *At least twenty minutes—which means I've probably gone at least a mile on this road. Maybe more.* I sat down on the side of the road to assess the situation. *Dammit, Michelle. Really?* (In my head I had gone from "Brownie" back to "Michelle" in the span of twenty minutes. Clearly I could not refer to myself by a trail name if I couldn't even manage to follow a trail.) *The one time you hike alone on this stupid trail, you get lost?*

I took a big sip of water and then realized forlornly that this was the only water bottle I was carrying—Souleman had the rest. *Great. I'm lost and I have barely any water. Very responsible.* I shoved the bottle back into my pack in frustration. I wasn't scared of being alone. I wasn't even scared of being off the AT. What worried me was that Souleman and I were separated, and we had never made a plan for that scenario. *If he was trying to catch up to me, did he already reach the point where the trail crosses the road? If so, did he go the right way? And if so, how long will he continue to hike before he realizes I'm not in front of him?* I groaned out loud and then proceeded to have a conversation with myself.

Ok. Think this through. What do I know? asked rational Michelle.

I know I'm on Bear Mountain. I know the Handbook said there's a tourist area at the top of Bear Mountain. I know I'm on a road. So, this road has to go to the tourist area, right?

If this is the right road to begin with, rational Michelle pointed out. *Mountains can have more than one road.*

I decided I had three options. I could backtrack to find where I had gotten off-trail and continue on. *I missed it the first time, so I could miss it again.* I could hitch-hike to the tourist area. *Hitching alone is dangerous, and Souleman would kill me when he found out.* Or, I could keep walking up the road and hope it led me to the tourist area. *This is the safest option,* I told myself, even though I had no idea how long the road was, or if it would actually lead me to the right destination.

I followed the road, with its counterfeit white paint splotches, all the way to the summit of Bear Mountain. I was walking as fast as I could manage. The weather was miserably hot, and the asphalt felt so blistering under my feet that I actually checked more than once to make sure the soles of my too-small shoes weren't melting. The whole time I walked, I talked to myself. *Ok, when I get to the top and find the trail, how will I know whether Souleman is ahead of me or behind me? Surely he would stop at the top, right?* I sweated profusely as I mentally berated myself for acting in anger.

Finally, the road passed an empty ranger booth. *I have to be on the right road.* The fake blazes disappeared and I found myself in a parking lot. *Where am I?* I couldn't see buildings, trails, or another person. The road continued a little further up ahead. *This must be overflow parking.* As I continued walking, the sky became dark and I heard thunder. *At least it will cool off.* Sadly, it was just a cruel tease—the storm produced intense wind, lightning, and thunder, but very little rain. *Typical. It pours relentlessly for months, but the one time I want it to rain, nothing.*

Eventually I spotted cars and people off in the distance. I walked in their direction and saw buildings through the trees. I had found the tourist area. *Where is the trail? Where is Souleman?* I slowed my pace and scanned the sidewalks, parking lots, and grassy areas, hoping to see my hairy, sweaty (and probably angry) husband. The last hour, with my burst of anger and physical activity, had left me exhausted, and I wanted nothing more than to lie down. Even the hot asphalt looked appealing. I was increasingly worried that Souleman might have gotten ahead of me on the trail because of my blunder. *If he's ahead of me and keeps hiking faster to find me, how will we ever figure it out?*

I sat on a curb and pulled out my Handbook, scanning the lines near Bear Mountain. *If he hiked past here, where would he likely stop to wait?* I had no idea what to do, and my eyes teared up from exhaustion and worry. The sky grew increasingly dark as the wind swirled leaves and trash around the parking lot. Helplessly, I stared at the sky, rifled aimlessly through my Handbook, and darted my eyes around uneasily.

After about fifteen minutes, I saw movement out of the corner of my eye and looked up to see Souleman barreling toward me. I wasn't sure if I should be relieved to see him or scared of his obvious anger. I jumped up, wobbling under the weight of my pack and wincing as my knees and feet recoiled at the sudden pressure. He came to an abrupt stop about five feet in front of me and stood there leaning on his poles, breathing heavily. Sweat ran in lines down his red cheeks, and his shaggy hair was plastered to his head under his hat. After a long, tense silence, during which I intensely studied my already-dirty new shoes, he spoke.

"Where the HELL have you been?" he spit out.

"I—"

"What were you THINKING?" he continued as though I hadn't spoken.

"I was—"

"I had NO IDEA where you were," he interrupted angrily.

"Stop yelling at me," I pleaded, lowering my eyes.

"You just took off BY YOURSELF."

"Can you PLEASE stop yelling?" I asked, my own voice a little louder than I had intended. I looked around in embarrassment to see how many tourists were observing this immature marital battle.

"I had NO IDEA where you were. You just LEFT!" he raged, his voice as loud as before. He was waving his arms in the air. "You don't just TAKE OFF!"

I raised the volume of my voice to match his. "STOP," I slammed my hiking pole down on the asphalt for emphasis, "YELLING (slam) AT (slam) ME (slam)!"

He stared at my pole with a look of amazement, and then looked up at me with narrowed eyes. "Don't do that."

I narrowed my eyes right back, set my jaw, and stabbed my pole at the ground between his shoes after each of my next words. "Don't (stab). Tell (stab). Me (stab). What (stab). To (stab)—" I stopped short when my last stab of the pole missed the asphalt and landed squarely on his shoe.

He grabbed the pole from my hand and flung it on the ground.

I burst into tears, collected my pole, and awkwardly ran away holding the bottom of my pack with one hand to steady it against my back. *Is this really happening?* I was devastated to be fighting with my husband, embarrassed that people were witnessing my meltdown, and too tired to know how to fix the situation. I ducked around the back of a building and dropped my pack to the ground. Sinking down on top of it, I covered my face with my filthy hands and sobbed.

When Souleman's worn shoes appeared in front of me minutes later, I didn't look up. He started smacking his pole onto the cement block beside me. He smacked and smacked as he vented. "I'm MAD. I just do WHATEVER I WANT. I just TAKE OFF in the woods." He continued smacking his Leki pole against the cement and mimicking me until suddenly there was a loud snap. I jerked my head up to see him holding half of a pole in the air, mid-swing. He lowered his hand in slow motion and stared at the broken piece of metal with a look of disbelief. The other half of his pole lay beside the concrete block. He hurled the broken pole into the woods and lowered himself onto the concrete. We sat silently for many minutes, the anger between us still tangible.

"You didn't come after me," I mumbled.

"What?!" he asked incredulously, and turned to stare at me.

"Before. In the woods. When I started hiking. You didn't come after me." I said between sobs.

"Yes, I did."

I shook my head. "You're faster than me. I even stopped to wait and you didn't catch up. You didn't come after me."

"Yes. I did," he repeated, and then lifted my chin up to make me look at him. "I waited about ten minutes because I couldn't believe you just took off. I thought for sure you'd come back. Then I realized you must be thinking I would go after you. I took off at my fastest pace." He paused and took a deep breath. "I couldn't figure out how I didn't catch up to you. I knew I was going so fast." He looked straight in my tear-filled eyes to make sure I was listening. "I passed some other hikers going south and they hadn't seen you, so I didn't know what to do. I didn't know if you got on the wrong trail or got kidnapped or what. I hiked as fast as I could to the top of the mountain and looked all around, but you weren't there." All of the anger had left his voice. His concern was evident. "I didn't know if I should turn and go back south or continue north. I didn't think you'd go on past the summit without me, but I didn't know for sure. You have no idea how worried I was."

All of my own anger evaporated. "I'm sorry I took off." Tears poured down my cheeks, and I sucked my lower lip into my mouth.

"I know." He sighed. "I know you're sorry. So am I."

"I was so mad." I sniffled.

"Me too."

We sat in silence for a while, each of us staring at the ground. I leaned my head against his shoulder. Though the silence was the same as it had been a few minutes ago, the anger was gone.

"You aren't supposed to get mad at me," I told him, scrunching up my face as my lower lip quivered. "You're my husband."

The right side of his mouth twitched upward almost imperceptibly, and he shook his head from side to side slowly. "You aren't supposed to get mad at *me*; you're my wife." He took a deep breath and then asked, "Are you going to hug me now?"

I fell into his arms and cried against his smelly, sweaty, stale shirt while he rubbed my back. "I don't want to fight with you," I sniffled.

"Me either."

He picked me up and sat me in his lap. I tried to relearn how to breathe normally after so much crying.

Finally, we decided we had better hike on. We strapped his dilapidated pole to his pack for safekeeping and sheepishly walked back through the park, hand in hand, past the visitors who had witnessed our earlier blowup. I was still sniffling and wiping away errant tears. As we walked back toward the trail, I touched his wedding band repeatedly to reassure myself.

I paused to put my hand on the first white blaze we passed. *No more hiking decisions in anger,* I promised myself. For the first few minutes, I had to keep blinking my red-rimmed eyes to keep the trail in focus. My head was throbbing.

We settled into a normal pace as we descended the mountain.

"Oh no!" I cried out, stopping suddenly.

"What?"

"I'm not a purist anymore." Tears started rolling down my cheeks.

"Huh? What do you mean?" He stared at me, baffled.

"I didn't follow the blazes up Bear Mountain. I missed some white blazes. Now I'm not a purist anymore."

He cracked a grin. "Brownie, seriously?"

I nodded.

When he saw my solemn expression, he swallowed his smile. "You didn't miss any blazes intentionally. It was a mistake. The trail was poorly marked, and it could have happened to anyone."

I shook my head dejectedly. "Now I can't honestly say I did the whole trail."

"Brownie, it was maybe three-quarters of a mile. It doesn't count. Besides, who will know?"

"Me." I looked up at him with my eyes full of tears. "And you."

"It'll be our secret." He pulled me toward him and kissed my forehead.

Finally, we descended Bear Mountain and passed through the pedestrian tunnel underneath US 9W. The blazes led us to the Trailside Museum and Wildlife Center, a wildlife refuge and rehabilitation center for injured animals unable to survive in the wild.

The official Appalachian Trail goes through the wildlife center, so thru-hikers are able to enter without paying a fee. However, the center only allows a certain number of patrons inside at once, and it was over capacity when we arrived. As we stood waiting in line under the awning, it began to thunderstorm. I waited impatiently with my face tilted toward the ground to hide my red-rimmed, puffy eyes. Souleman rubbed my back soothingly in small circles beneath my pack.

For a few tenuous moments, the staff debated closing the park for the day due to bad weather. This would have forced us to follow the official alternative route, which was longer. The rain finally let up and we were able to pass through. Inside the wildlife center, in front of the bear exhibit, we passed the lowest elevation on the entire Appalachian Trail, at 124 feet above sea level. I stood in front of the enclosure and couldn't help but feel uneasy as I watched the small brown bear paw at the ground. So recently we had been trespassers in the woods that were the bear's natural habitat. We had seen bears just like this one in the wild. The one consolation was that the animals in this center were all rescued animals. This bear would not be alive without the medical treatments and habitat provided by humans. I shook my head at the irony. I had escaped society to experience the bear's world, and he had been forced to become captive in our world in order to remain alive.

We did not waste any extra time in the wildlife center because the day's events had drained us. Soon after we got into town, I found myself sprawled on a cushy bed in a frigidly air-conditioned room. After showers, Souleman and I watched a couple of *Seventh Heaven* reruns, and then he watched the All-Star baseball game while I journaled. We each drank two large bottles of Powerade and then refilled them with non-toxic tap water. We were so dehydrated that even after consuming 128 ounces of liquid, it was still many hours before either of us had to pee.

To erase any memory of our earlier argument, we spent the evening glued to each other's sides. We fell asleep intertwined on top of the covers, surrounded by empty Powerade bottles.

21

Food and Drinks
and Air conditioning

"**D**o you think it's acceptable to have a milkshake for breakfast two mornings in a row?" I asked Souleman.

He stretched. "Sure. I think you can have anything you want for breakfast if you plan to hike almost twenty miles after eating it."

"Good point. In that case I'll have a milkshake *and* a bagel." I scooted to the edge of the bed. "How about you pack and I'll go get us breakfast?"

He nodded and picked up his empty pack.

I returned fifteen minutes later with two thick, chocolate milkshakes and two "everything" bagels slathered with cream cheese. "Breakfast of champions," I declared. I handed him a bagel. "It has extra cream cheese, just like you like it."

We sat cross-legged on the bed and ate as we finished sorting our trail food.

"You're chipper this morning," Souleman observed.

"I don't think I would ever wake up on the wrong side of the bed again if I could have a milkshake for breakfast every day."

"Hmm," he answered around a mouthful of cream cheese.

After eating every last crumb of bagel and sucking down every last drop of milkshake, we finally headed back to the trail. We had zeroed the previous day and had spent the entire time running errands in the rain. The weather was overcast but not overly humid as we crossed the Hudson River on a footbridge heading out of town. In spite of the extra weight of our just-out-of-town, food-laden packs, we had a great day. The trail rolled smoothly up and down.

Not knowing what I would do for work after finishing the trail was weighing heavily on my mind. *I have a bachelor's degree in philosophy. But honestly, what am I going to do with that? There's not exactly a definitive career path. I'm going to leave this trail a married woman with bills and responsibilities and no idea what comes next.* My life path up until then had always seemed pretty defined: Graduate high school. *Check.* Get into college. *Check.* Graduate college. *Check.* Hike Appalachian Trail. *Almost check.* Get married. *Check.* Sure, there had been hiccups along the way. The first relationship I thought would lead to marriage hadn't worked out. The Appalachian Trail had become a two-part adventure instead of a thru-hike. Still, overall I had followed the plan. The problem was, the plan didn't extend any further. It was like staring over a cliff. *Now what?*

I knew what I desired a few years in the future. I wanted four kids—yes, four— and a white picket fence, so I'd need some money. I thought about all the careers that appealed to me and the resulting questions: *I could be a professional organizer (ooh, lists), but how do you get started in that field? I love to write, but could I write professionally? I'm passionate about the Girl Scouts, but how do I turn that into a career? People always tell me I'd be a great teacher, but really, am I patient enough?* I had the next seven hundred miles to figure it out.

With all the time to think, the comfortable terrain, and the pleasant weather, the day went quickly. I loved days like that, and I took frequent, short breaks to enjoy the scenery and re-energize. During one of these many breaks, I performed emergency surgery on my shorts. I stepped behind a tree, pulled my shorts off, and took out my knife. Standing half-naked in the woods, I used the tiny scissors on my knife to cut the mesh lining out of the shorts. I simply couldn't stand the wet mesh rubbing against my irritated skin any longer. With the clothing operation completed, I felt much more comfortable, but I was still looking forward to stopping at an outfitter where I could purchase actual hiking shorts. These makeshift shorts, which were actually boys' swimming trunks, had been my attire since a couple of towns back when my shorts had worn out and we couldn't find a store that sold hiking pants.

We got back into our groove, and Souleman and I each turned on our radios. I found a great country station that relayed random pieces of information between songs: Screwdrivers were originally used to help knights get into their armor. Changing clothes after work decreases stress levels (*Note to self: get job, then buy work clothes, then take work clothes off*), as does playing piano for fifteen minutes (*If job doesn't work out, buy piano instead*). Lemonade contains an ingredient that replenishes the brain chemical people burn when concentrating or thinking a lot (*Buy lemonade in next town*). The distraction of listening and singing propelled me happily, and quickly, north.

In a burst of energy, we continued four more miles and were hoping to camp at the edge of a wildlife preserve. When we got there, we saw a huge sign that read: "NO CAMPING next 5.1 miles."

"What do you want to do?" Souleman asked me. He squinted up at the disappearing sun.

"I *want* to stop. But we can't camp right by a 'no camping' sign. What if a ridge runner comes through?" I leaned heavily on my poles.

"Yeah. I guess we'll just push on." He tucked his sweaty hair behind his ears, and I noticed how long it was getting.

In frustrated silence, we continued 1.6 miles to another trail intersection. By then it was dark outside, and the air had become thick with bugs.

"I swear this 'preserve' is only preserving mosquitoes," Souleman observed, smacking the bugs on his arm as he spoke.

"I know. This is ridiculous. Should we just stealth?" I waved my poles in front of my body and simultaneously scratched a bite on my leg.

"I don't particularly want to hike another four miles. Especially in the dark."

"I don't particularly want any more mosquito bites. We're basically a big snack platter right now." For emphasis I slapped at a mosquito that was biting my arm.

We briefly debated the ethics of breaking a no-camping rule. While we paused to talk, our conversation was accented with smacks and slaps as we attacked the vicious insects. The mosquitoes sealed the deal, and we found a relatively flat spot off the trail to spend the night. In what I'm sure looked like some kind of voodoo dance, we set up our tent while constantly smacking at bugs.

"There seem to be a lot of hiking nuances in the north," I said as we snapped poles together. "No hitchhiking in some places. No camping outside of designated spots. No fires permitted in certain areas."

He slapped a mosquito. "Yeah, I know. And the stores and all seem further off the trail. Planning is getting harder."

"Right. And we aren't even near the White Mountains yet, where everyone says the hut system is so challenging to navigate." I threw our last piece of sleeping gear into the tent.

"So much for the idea that it would be easier to figure out details when we got closer to home."

We climbed into the tent just as another hiker named Dirt showed up. *At least now we're camping illegally with an accomplice.*

Fearing the wrath of a rule-enforcing ranger, or death by blood-sucking mosquitoes, we began our hike early the next morning. Even first thing in the day, it was painfully hot. I was sweating out water more quickly than I could gulp it down. Halfway through the morning, we needed more water and had to replenish at a stream. Since our water purifier was still broken, this was a risky endeavor. Thus far, we had been lucky enough to replenish only at springs or spigots, which were less likely to be contaminated. Knowing we had no choice but to drink often in this heat, we crossed our fingers and gulped our ice-cold "giardia water."

As I hiked, I imagined what it would be like to recommend Souleman's car for the MTV show *Pimp My Ride.* I decided that the pimped-out version of his car would be Red-Sox themed. I imagined a detailed paint job with the red socks on one side, the B emblem on the other, and Wally the Green Monster peering out from the trunk. Inside, the knobs would be miniature baseballs, and the floor mats would look like baseball diamonds.

Even with my ludicrous self-entertainment techniques, that day was officially one of the hardest days (if not *the* hardest day) on the trail. We were moving speedily and covered the first few miles rather effortlessly. We cheered exuberantly as we crossed the state line into Connecticut. *Our tenth state! Only four more state lines before Katahdin.* We were now counting how many states we had left instead of how many we had completed.

We ate an early lunch beside a beautiful river and were excited to have only eight miles remaining until our planned stop in Kent, Connecticut. Souleman had been hiking to a mantra that went, "Ice (step) cream (step), Mountain (step) Dew (step), ice (step) cream (step), Mountain (step) Dew (step)." Enthusiastically, we began the last leg of hiking before our zero days. We faced an uphill climb but were undaunted since every hiker knows the trail eventually goes "down to town." Apparently, the trail creators of Kent hadn't been aware of this well-known expectation. We walked up and up and up. Whenever we thought we had summited, we would round a corner to see even more uphill. *Does this mountain ever end?*

Even when we achieved the actual summit and expected to finally enjoy a descent, we were deceived. The trail would slope downward briefly and then shoot us straight back up to the top. This insanity went on for seven miles, after which we were completely exhausted and in a great deal of pain. Both of our bodies were revolting against the oppressive heat and the copious amounts of sweat. We were suffering from prickly heat rash, blisters, raw skin, and all sorts of other sweat-induced ailments. That was in addition to sore knees, bruised shoulders, and swollen mosquito bites. Our bodies desperately wanted to be still, clean, and dry. Not only was the trail steep and endlessly uphill, it was also rocky. We had to place each foot-step in exactly the right place in order to maintain balance. *This is like being back in Pennsylvania.* We practically crawled to the road.

We limped into town pathetically that afternoon, looking less like seasoned thru-hikers and more like refugees. We kicked our shoes off and sat on the cement on the shaded side of a gas station. While eating ice cream, we gulped two large bottles of Powerade each. Our faces were tomato red, our bodies were sore, and our clothes were soaked in sweat, but we had made it to Connecticut.

Summoning our last energy reserve, we stuffed our swollen feet into our Crocs, tied our hiking shoes to our packs, and stumbled across the street to the outfitter to see about our naughty, dysfunctional MIOX. Much to our relief, the outfitter was able to fix it, so we would no longer have to drink giardia water.

Before our sweaty clothes had completely dried, my dad arrived to pick us up. He was taking us to my parents' house in Massachusetts for two days of recovery. My mom must have warned him about how gross we would be because he had towels covering his car seats to protect them from our filth. I later overheard him tell my mom, "I played sports. I grew up in locker rooms. I thought I knew how bad sweat could get, but this was something else entirely." He accommodated our plea for air-conditioning but said the windows had to remain cracked to combat our stench.

"Sooooo, what do you guys want to do today?" Allison asked us the following morning. We were all sitting at the kitchen table in our pajamas eating a late breakfast.

"Eat." Souleman took a giant bite of cereal.

"Annnnnd?"

"Drink." I sipped coffee from the mug in my right hand and chased it with a swig from the glass of pineapple orange juice in my left hand.

"Ok. You want to eat and drink. Anything else?"

I looked at the thermometer outside the kitchen window. It already read 98.8 degrees. I leaned heavily on the table. "Air conditioning. I want to be in air conditioning."

Souleman nodded as he shoveled more cereal in his mouth.

"Food and drinks and air conditioning," Allison repeated. "Let's go to the movies."

We sat in the frigid theater and washed down popcorn and candy with swimming-pool-sized drinks Then we hurried home to enjoy a cookout with my family and Meagan. It was thrilling to eat a meal that wasn't one selection in one pot. We filled ourselves with grilled chicken, corn on the cob, salad, and fruit. *Vegetables, we meet again.* Then, after playing a new board game, we ate sherbet and brownies for dessert.

On our second zero day, we took care of some necessary town chores. In the afternoon, we spent many hours poring over our Handbook, planning out our next four weeks of hiking. We had never hiked with a fixed itinerary for more than a week in the past. Since we had so many friends and family members who wanted to visit with us in this area of the trail, we had to make a schedule in order to fit it all in. Our schedule had to be strict enough to give people predicted dates, but flexible enough to account for challenging terrain, weather, injury, and all the other unexpected factors that can delay progress.

For a lifestyle that was supposed to be so simple, long-distance hiking sure required a lot of planning and preparation. As we reviewed our itinerary one final time, my mom came in with her hands hidden behind her back.

"I have a surprise!" She flashed a smile, showing her dimples, and then set a white album on the table. "Your professional wedding photos are ready."

Souleman came to stand behind me. I ran my sunburned hand across the shiny cover and then flipped it open. We were greeted with an eight-by-eleven photo of me in my wedding dress. I barely recognized myself. My hair and makeup were fairly simple in the photo, but the contrast with my long, uncombed hair and naked face was evident. *Can these both be me?*

"I'll give you two some privacy," Mom said, ducking out of the room as fast as she had appeared.

We flipped through page after page showing our family and friends smiling and laughing. Our whole wedding weekend replayed before our eyes: Jeremy and our groomsmen. Me and the bridesmaids. The whole wedding party. His family. My family. The two of us during the ceremony. Us in our wedding attire with our packs on, walking down the trail. The last photo was a candid close-up of us after the ceremony. My hair was coiled into a neat bun with diamond pins, and my make-up was flawless. I turned toward Souleman and held the picture up beside my face.

"Which me do you like better?"

"I don't see a difference."

We bungled our planned departure time the next morning and didn't get to the trailhead until almost noon. Luckily, we had a relatively short day planned. The ascent out of Kent was short and easy, so the first 3.5 miles flew by. The woods near

Kent were very New England-esque and reminded us both of the woods where we grew up hiking. Pine trees, luscious, green ferns, and other familiar plants made this trail section seem comforting. We got to enjoy a few miles of riverside walking, which was refreshingly flat and breezy, and we even saw two beautiful blue herons. One of them took off suddenly, and we delighted in seeing the enormous wingspan and graceful flight of the beautiful bird.

The weather was pleasant, the terrain accommodating, and the company superb, but I nearly went insane listening to the squeaking of my pack. The noise had become so irritating over the past few weeks that I had contemplated switching to my old Gregory pack at my parents' house. But when I had packed it up and tried it on, it had seemed less comfortable and noticeably heavier. I loved the suspension system and fit of my Mountain Hardwear Exodus pack. Without the squeaking, I'd have been completely satisfied. In the next town, I placed a call to Mountain Hardwear and they agreed to send a replacement piece for my pack further up the trail. I tried to remain optimistic that it would stop the squeaking noise, though I worried I'd go crazy before then.

Shortly after lunch on the bank of the Housatonic River, we met our first southbounder of the year. Southbounders number fewer than northbounders, so it was a rare opportunity to be able to ask questions about the solo nature of hiking south and to glean information about what lay ahead on the trail.

In the morning, we climbed over Easter Mountain. We walked along the Housatonic River again and crossed it twice. It seemed counterproductive to keep crossing the same body of water. Looking down from the bridge, I wrinkled my nose at its icky brown color but enjoyed the breeze off the water nonetheless.

At a road crossing, we passed a hydroelectric plant with an outdoor shower. Since we were extremely hot and sweaty, a shower sounded enticing. The shower had no enclosure and was in the middle of a public place, so we showered in our clothes and delighted in the feeling of freezing water pelting our skin. Soaking wet, we sat on the steps nearby and cooked dinner while we let the sun dry our clothes. Cooking our hot meal earlier in the afternoon and then pushing out more miles before dark had become a habit of ours recently. This tactic worked perfectly because it split up the mileage and seemed to fuel us through the last section more quickly.

Setting up camp at night also seemed like much less work with cooking and cleanup already taken care of. That night, we set up camp at Limestone Spring Lean-to. (In the north, the shelters are called lean-tos even though they're constructed in the same fashion as shelters in the south.) Limestone Spring was a scenic area with a great spring as a water source, but it was located a half-mile off the trail. While this distance would have been inconsequential under normal circumstances, it seemed cruel and unnecessary tacked on to the end of a fifteen-mile day. Furthermore, it meant we would have to start out the following morning with an extra half-mile jaunt straight uphill before beginning our official 17.6-mile day.

The secluded shelter, with its steep entry path, did have the benefit of being deserted, so we spent a private night in our tent with nothing but each other and the sounds of creaking trees and scurrying animals. While meeting other hikers was always entertaining and enjoyable, I greatly enjoyed the occasional secluded evening. We may have chosen an unusual honeymoon, but we still welcomed nights alone. Lulled by the quietness of our surroundings, we nestled into our mated sleeping bags early and fell asleep curled up together.

Waking up well rested, we got an early start out of the shelter. Shooting sideways glances at one another, we gritted our teeth and powered ourselves rapidly up the steep, half-mile blue blaze trail without stopping. My thighs burned as I pushed up the rocky embankment. I considered a break, but my drive to reach the trail won, and I pushed on. When we rejoined the trail, I slapped the white Appalachian Trail blaze victoriously and, still out of breath from the uphill, nearly skipped down the path.

We met a hiker named Fred at the first road crossing about three miles into our day. Fred had scrawny legs and a graying beard. He was a northbound thru-hiker we hadn't run into yet, though we had many mutual acquaintances.

"I'm going into Salisbury, Connecticut, for breakfast," he told us. "You guys should come with me."

He looks like he could use an extra meal. It didn't take long for us to decide to join him. Souleman ordered strawberry pancakes, and I had a giant breakfast burrito smothered in hot sauce. With extremely full bellies, we returned to the trail. Though delicious, our unexpected breakfast had added *another* extra mile to our day. Our 17.6 miles had turned into 19.1 before we had really gotten started.

The last mountain in Connecticut was also called Bear Mountain, and it would be our first elevation over two thousand feet since Virginia. Our experience was much less traumatizing than it had been with Bear Mountain in New York. Next, we entered Massachusetts, and the state seemed to welcome us by saying, "Oh yeah, Connecticut? That's all you've got? Take *THIS!*" We proceeded to hike over two more mountains in the rain, each over two thousand feet high and both with extremely rocky terrain. Mount Everett (which sounds conveniently like Mount Everest) was a beast. We literally climbed straight up a rock face. The slabs of rock were huge, with very few good footholds and handholds, and of course the stones were wet and slippery from the rain.

"This sucks!" Souleman exclaimed as he once again slid backward down a slab of rock.

"Yeah. We take one step forward and slide back two."

"I just have no treads left on my shoes." He kicked at the rock.

"Well, if it's any consolation, I'm sliding even with my new shoes." I studied my already filthy Merrells.

Despite the frustrations of our progress, I almost preferred the mental challenge of treacherous, slippery slabs to the monotony of mindless switchbacks. Partway up the rock monstrosity, we heard a loud crashing off to our right, and I saw the rear end of a bear running away from us. We barely had a chance to register what we were seeing before he was gone. I couldn't believe we had hiked from Pennsylvania to Massachusetts before seeing our first bear.

This particular rainy day made it obvious that my new Merrell trail runners did not perform well in the rain. Even though the rain didn't last long, my feet were in horrible condition. I had raw, red spots on each heel and on the top of each toe. Also, the skin on both of my ankles was blistered, red, and painful. Since the shoes had been broken in already, these injuries should not be happening. With my feet hurting and Souleman sliding all over the place, the last 1.8 miles seemed to take *forever*.

We would walk a few dozen yards, then stop to lean on our poles and take a break. Rinse, lather, repeat. Fred was right behind us and the three of us kept stopping near one another.

"I do *not* know how it's possible that we haven't found the shelter yet," Fred lamented at one such meeting.

"I know. It seems like we should be miles past it," I responded while leaning on my poles.

"Do you think we could have accidentally passed the sign?" he questioned.

We all exchanged horrified looks and consulted our Handbook. No helpful information came to light.

"I guess we'll just have to keep hiking," Souleman said dejectedly.

Finally, at least half a dozen breathless stops later, we saw the shelter sign. I considered kissing it. The shelter was gorgeous and new, with a sleeping loft. Two weekend hikers were already there, but the rain cemented our decision to sleep in the shelter instead of tenting like usual.

Seconds after I had stopped walking, I peeled my shoes and socks off painfully. The raw, red spots were oozing clear goo, and my skin burned. Gently, I rinsed my feet with water, wrapped them with pre-wrap and tape, and slid them back into my cleanest socks. I gingerly donned my Crocs and stood awkwardly to tackle our evening chores. Each step caused friction and pain on the raw spots of skin. *I've about had enough of you, feet.*

The aching subsided once I had finished my chores and was able to take the weight off of my feet for a while. And, in a stroke of luck, we weren't eaten alive by mosquitoes even though we were without the protection of our tent's netting. Unfortunately, when I quit focusing on my feet, I realized I had other pains elsewhere. My aching bladder and a snorer in the shelter kept me awake all night. As I lay there, I worried I would need to see a doctor, which would mean changing our schedule. *See, we couldn't even stick to our schedule for one week. What will this mean for seeing all of our family and friends? Why can't my body just cooperate?*

22

CHAAAAARLIEEEE!

When the sun began peeking through the trees, I gently shook my husband awake. As soon as I saw his eyes open, I offered a half-smile and ran my fingers through his sticky beard before stating, "Good morning."

"Morning." He stretched his arms up over his head.

"Sooo, change of plans." I told him. "We have to go to town today. I have *another* bladder infection."

Souleman took it in stride and said we'd figure it out. A glance at Wingfoot revealed that Great Barrington, the next town, was eight miles up the trail. The camp I had worked at as a teenager (the same one that had inspired my yearning to hike the AT) was near Great Barrington, so I knew there was a hospital there. We had an uneventful hike into town and then hitchhiked to the emergency room.

As I had expected, I was given a prescription for a urinary tract infection. Dehydration and hot weather had caused the same problem for me the previous year. My body was not handling the heat well. It helped to know I was not alone. I had met another female hiker who told me she had suffered *three* bladder infections already that year. I would have to be more conscious about drinking plenty of water. The doctor's instructions were to stay off the trail for the night to hydrate and rest.

The receptionist at the ER tried to help us find a hotel room, but because Great Barrington stays so busy with tourists in the summer, the cheapest room would have cost over two hundred dollars. Since this price was way out of our budget, I flipped through our Handbook and realized there was a hostel for hikers near the north end of town. We decided to pick up my prescription at the drugstore and then figure out how to get to the hostel.

A man who had been in the waiting room for the ER with his three kids saw us walk out of the hospital with our packs. He generously gave us a ride to the drugstore and also wrote down his phone number in case we needed help while we were in town. As we waved goodbye, I again reminded myself how many favors I would owe strangers after the trail in order to balance out my karma. *Why can't my own body love me as much as these complete strangers have?*

As we walked up to the pharmacy counter, the pharmacist glanced up and asked, "Are you Brownie?"

"I am." I looked at Souleman bewilderedly. I didn't know a soul in town. Who could have been looking for me?

Souleman shrugged.

"You just had a phone call from a nurse at the ER. You're supposed to give her a call." She passed me a cordless phone and a sticky note scrawled with a phone number.

I called the nurse, who said she had a trail-angel friend who was going to meet us at the pharmacy in a couple of minutes. Mother Nature and her husband, Sourwood, soon approached. They happily drove us to load up on fluids and pick up dinner while they regaled us with stories about their own experiences on the AT. Then they dropped us off at the East Mountain Retreat Center hostel. Mother Nature and Sourwood even arranged to pick us up in the morning and get us back to the trail. *People never cease to amaze me.*

East Mountain Retreat Center was a silent retreat. This detail caused us to raise our eyebrows at first, but we decided it would be worth one night of silence to get a room for twenty-three dollars instead of two hundred. It turned out that we were the only residents that night, though, so we opted out of the rule and never discovered exactly what the silence mandate entailed. The hostel was a cozy haven from the rain and a great place to rest and rejuvenate before getting back on the trail. We even had an unexpected chance to do laundry and shower.

Souleman never once complained during our unanticipated trip into town. I still felt horribly guilty, though. I lay in bed that night and wondered, *Why must my body always ruin our plans? First there was my foot trouble last year, then mono, and now a UTI. What will my body cook up next?* I scooted closer to my husband and pulled the sheets around us. *I'm so lucky to have a partner on this adventure.*

In the morning we met Mother Nature and Sourwood at six-thirty for a ride back to the trail. We were so grateful that they had volunteered to shuttle us—and that they were early risers. Since we had shortened our mileage the day before, we now had to add mileage in order to remain on schedule. This meant that instead of our planned eleven miles, we would have to hike almost eighteen.

Immediately upon walking into the woods, we were accosted by massive swarms of mosquitoes. We found ourselves constantly swatting and swinging our hiking poles in an effort to escape the relentless biting.

After about a mile, Souleman stopped abruptly, threw his pack down, and declared, "It's time for war."

I stopped and turned around.

"Stick 'em up," he joked as he sprayed me liberally with 99 percent DEET, completely disregarding the printed warnings to keep the poison away from direct contact with skin. Once I was covered, he said, "Now me. Leave no spot unsprayed." After I had doused him, we doubled over in laughter as the mosquitoes veered away from us in an effort to escape the noxious poison.

After our victory against the mosquito army, the overcast sky and cool weather made for perfect hiking conditions. The temperature never rose above seventy-four degrees. In the afternoon, the fog cleared up enough to permit a few pretty views. About ten miles into our day, we passed a group of three hikers heading south who told us we would be extremely happy in about fifty yards. Smiles spread across our faces as Souleman raised his eyebrows. "Trail magic?" Sure enough, when we crossed the road, two men were sitting in the parking lot with a grill and a couple of coolers. One was Chubster, who had thru-hiked the previous year. Walkabout and Caboose, current thru-hikers whom we'd seen off and on since Duncannon, were already seated enjoying the treats.

The men asked, "Are you headed to Maine?"

We nodded.

"Are you hungry?"

"Of course!" Souleman exclaimed. His hunger had become insatiable. My hunger was growing, too. Two hot dogs, a cheeseburger, a Powerade, and about an hour and a half later, we stumbled north on the trail once again. Souleman and I had made plans for a Spades game that night with Walkabout and Caboose.

The rest of the day's miles ticked by smoothly as we hiked a steady, though unimpressive, two miles an hour. Apart from the incessant, unbearable squeak that continued in my pack, I was thoroughly content and happy. Smiling as we reflected on our day, we arrived at Shaker Campsite with a lot of daylight to spare. A group of men ranging in age from fourteen to at least seventy were camping there as part of a three-generation family backpacking weekend. One of the teenagers expressed an interest in hiking the entire trail, so we spent some time answering his questions.

"How did you research gear?" he asked first.

"Have you heard of www.trailplace.com? It's a website with forums and message boards all about hiking," Souleman told him.

"Wow. Ok. And how did you decide what month to start?"

"We started in the middle of March. Some people start in April, or even in February. The Trailplace forums can help you decide that, too."

"Oh, ok. This might be rude to ask, but how much money did you have to save up?"

"That's not rude. It's practical. The trail does cost money. People will tell you that after you've bought your gear, you can hike the trail for a dollar a mile. We haven't found that to be true, though. We've definitely spent more."

"Well, we do hike pretty luxuriously," I interjected. "We usually sleep in hotels in town instead of hostels or campsites. And we eat at restaurants instead of using our camp stove in town."

The boy nodded.

"We'll probably only get to do this once, so we're trying to live it up," Souleman agreed.

The boy asked us about food choices, resupply options, and daily mileage. As the fire died down, he said, "If you could only give me one piece of advice about hiking the trail, what would it be?"

Souleman and I traded glances. I knew we had the same answer.

"Don't stress about the miles," Souleman told him. "Maine will be there."

Convincing myself to get out of my sleeping bag early was always a challenge. Although I loved the peacefulness of the woods at sunrise, the ability to complete mileage without the heat, and the extra time to enjoy the day, I also relished being in a horizontal position inside my warm, snuggly sleeping bag. Once I got up, though, being awake for daybreak was always worth it. The hazy light filtering through the trees made the woods mystical—as if they had a secret to unveil. The sounds of the forest changed with daylight, and waking early gave me the chance to enjoy the entire symphony.

We were packed that morning by seven. As we took off down the trail in the early morning light, I remembered how long it had taken me to pack my gear each day back in Georgia. It was a brisk, pleasant morning. I hadn't been using my iPod very often because I'd been busy enjoying the sounds of nature. That morning, I pulled out my music and made good time up the trail as I sang along to familiar tunes. Time passed quickly, and before we knew it we were standing on Goose Pond Road, our target destination.

We plopped on the ground and leaned against our packs. Before long, a van pulled up beside us and five people tumbled out.

"Michelle!" The two smallest ones launched themselves at my waist.

I hugged them tightly and then stepped back to take them in. It seemed they had grown in the weeks since our wedding. I had babysat Rachel and Anthony since they were toddlers in diapers. Now here was Anthony in his Red Sox cap and Rachel staring up at me with big eyes that would soon break boys' hearts. Standing back a bit were two teenagers. The first was their older sister, Allee. She had been too old to need a babysitter when we first met, but we had bonded over late-night movies after I tucked her siblings in bed.

"Hey," she waved, almost shyly as I reached to give her a hug. Allee could be a model. She has natural beauty and poise beyond her years. She can look comfortable wearing absolutely any style of clothes. That day, she was in cargo shorts and a spaghetti-strap tank top, and a green bandana held back her blond, braided pigtails. "This is our cousin Amanda," she told me, gesturing to the teenager beside her with long, brown hair.

I greeted Amanda.

"Do you guys remember Soul—Jeremy?" I asked, stumbling over my husband's real name.

The kids nodded. As I turned to greet Donna, I could hear Anthony and Souleman already discussing the Red Sox. Behind the van, Donna was unloading bags. She ignored my filthy, sweaty state and wrapped me in a giant bear hug. Her eyes teared up immediately, and she fanned her hands in front of her face.

"I can't believe you're here. Are you ok? You look ok." She reached to hug Souleman too. "I want to hear everything, you hear me? *Everything*!" She motioned to the kids. "Come here. Put these on. Can you believe we are actually here with Michelle and Jeremy? Isn't this so awesome? Do you all have sunscreen on? Are you wearing bug spray?" I smiled as I listened to Donna talk. Technically, I had met Donna when she employed me as a babysitter, but she had quickly become a confidante and source of advice. As I grew from a teenager into a young adult, we had shared many cups of tea while working through life problems.

"Are you ready to hike?" I asked the kids.

Anthony ran toward the trail.

"Wait!" Donna yelled after him. "Now listen," she instructed the kids. "Michelle and Jeremy are in charge. You do what they tell you. Anthony, you have to stay where you can see an adult. Do you understand me?"

"Yes." He ducked his head and scuffed his sneaker in the dirt.

I bit back a smile. Anthony had developed a knack for hiding as a toddler. Once he disappeared while we were playing in the yard and I had found him standing on the kitchen counter, completely covered in pancake mix. Another time he escaped his mother's watchful eye and was found in the next neighborhood over.

Allee and Amanda led the way up the trail. Their long, lithe legs covered ground quickly, so we often rounded corners to find them sitting on rocks, waiting. Donna and I brought up the rear, chatting non-stop, and Anthony and Rachel plodded along in the middle with Souleman. He helped Rachel catch a frog and showed Anthony what moss feels like. Before I knew it, we had made it to Goose Pond Shelter. We had a picnic of sandwiches, chips, and fruit that Donna had packed.

After lunch the kids went swimming in the pond. I was tempted to join them, but memories of the painful chafing of wet hiking shorts kept me on the shore talking with Donna and Souleman.

As we continued hiking, Rachel and Anthony began getting tired.

"Have you ever played Twenty Questions?" I asked them. They hadn't. I explained the game and then said, "I'm thinking of a person."

"Is it a man?" Anthony asked?

"Yes."

"Is he alive?" Rachel wanted to know.

"Yes."

"Do we know him?" Anthony was warming to the challenge.

"No."

Donna and Souleman helped the kids come up with questions until they guessed that the person was David Ortiz, one of Anthony's favorite baseball players. The awful squeak in my pack made it hard to hear their tiny voices at times, but I played along, determined to help them enjoy the hike.

Just as Anthony and Rachel were almost overcome with exhaustion, we reached the I-90 bridge crossing.

"Hey, watch this," Souleman called. He demonstrated holding up his arm at a right angle and pulling down his fist. Below him, a trucker blew his horn. The kids' faces lit up. Before long the highway was echoing with the sound of horns. We ended the day's trek at US-20, Jacob's Ladder Highway, which made for a solid 5.3-mile hike for the family. We all piled into Donna's car, and all four kids fell asleep on the drive home.

In hushed voices, Donna, Souleman, and I continued talking until she pulled into my parents' driveway. We whispered thank you and goodbye and then went inside to enjoy a free night of restoration. My family was out of town, so we weren't able to spend time with them. Nonetheless, we enjoyed lounging around in a familiar space, and I was able to pamper my feet, which were still badly damaged from the recent rainy weather.

I sat on the edge of the bathtub doctoring my toes and thinking about how feet are a hiker's most essential body part. *The average person today is completely dependent upon a car, bus, or subway for transportation. A really ambitious or eco-minded person might ride a bike. If a person's car breaks down, what does he do? He drives a rental until his is repaired. If the bus breaks down, the company sends a different one. But hikers only have their feet. And mine are a mess.* My feet still had blisters, sore spots, and cracked, dry skin—the equivalent of rust holes, a broken radiator hose, and bad alignment in a car. I couldn't just buy new feet or take them to a mechanic, so instead I soaked, scraped, bandaged, and rubbed ointment on my damaged means of transportation. *They have to heal.*

Feet aside, I had been craving a zero day. We ate two large bowls of ice cream, went out to lunch, completed all of our errands, and rented movies.

The day off seemed to be exactly what my damaged feet needed. After the struggles of the previous year, I knew just how terrible hiking with aching feet could be. The blisters and cracks were nothing compared to my plantar fasciitis pain, but still I didn't want to take chances. Miraculously, all of the spots that had been so raw when we had left the trail seemed to have healed themselves.

My parents' neighbor, Mr. Phelps, was kind enough to drop us off at the trailhead the following day. It was almost ninety degrees outside, but the low humidity level made a huge difference when we were exerting ourselves and breathing so deeply. The elevation changes were minimal, but Souleman wasn't feeling well—he felt achy and his stomach was bothering him. We made sure he stayed hydrated and rested as often as possible.

During the day we met a family from Denmark who were hiking for a "fortnight." It turned out that the parents worked at a hotel in Vermont referred to by locals as "The Castle," which was a venue we had looked into for our wedding. This unexpected connection was another reminder that the world was not as big as we tended to think. After parting ways with the Danish family, Souleman and I talked about the "six degrees of separation" theory—the idea that any two people can be connected via acquaintances in six or fewer steps. The trail had emphasized to us the unlimited connections between people. It seemed that no matter where we went, we found people we were linked to in one way or another. In attempting to hike more than two thousand miles, we continued to realize how small, rather than how big, the world really was.

Our day ended with camping at the home of Marilyn, the "Cookie Lady." Just as our Handbook had suggested, Marilyn gave us homemade cookies, which she always had ready for hikers who were passing through. Then she and her husband let us pitch our tent on their grassy front lawn. We mowed around their blueberry bushes to compensate for our stay. Although mowing at the end of a hiking day was tiring, we enjoyed sampling a few blueberries as we worked. This was our first "work-for-stay" along the trail. The grass was soft underneath our tent, the water was cold and didn't need to be filtered, and we got cookies out of the deal. It wasn't a bad arrangement. Best of all, Roy, the Cookie Lady's husband, fixed my squeaky pack with some WD-40. I would have mowed his entire neighborhood in exchange for ending that unnerving, deplorable, stress-inducing squeak.

In the morning we hiked three gentle miles, took a break to inhale king-sized Snickers bars, and then hiked 3.5 more miles until the trail took us through Dalton, Massachusetts. We literally hiked right through the streets of Dalton, so we *had* to take advantage of the opportunity to support local businesses, especially since we were ahead of schedule. Our ever-changing plans on the trail made me smile because they so blatantly contradicted my obsessively schedule-driven existence off of it.

After an unimpressive meal at a pub, the white blazes led us right by a gas station. We were wilting in the heat, so I succumbed to the temptation to step inside, where I stood in front of the cooler soaking in the icy air while debating the merits of its myriad of rich, creamy contents. Ultimately, I chose Dove chocolate ice cream and consumed my first whole pint of the year while sitting on the curb outside the gas station. Wanting to arrive at our campsite in time to savor a little sunlight, I stood back up to follow my husband the last miles up the trail to camp.

At some point post-ice cream break, a sudden rain shower added a pleasant accent noise to our clomping footsteps. *Clomp clomp, splatter splatter, clomp clomp, splatter splatter.* The sky darkened, and the rain turned into a rumbling thunderstorm during our last mile. Fortunately, the heavy tree cover kept us dry, while the rain alleviated some of the humidity and made it a bit less difficult to breathe. The ice cream, which had seemed like such a wonderful idea in town, was revolting in my stomach in the intense heat. Growls of protest gurgled inside me as I placed one foot determinedly in front of the other. I tilted my face toward the refreshing raindrops and reminded myself that my hike was a gift. Rain, achy stomachs, and tired feet were all part of it.

After two blissfully mild days, we began a fifteen-mile day that would include Mount Greylock, the highest mountain in Massachusetts at 3,491 feet. Greylock was one of the trail highlights I had thought about since starting the AT in Georgia the previous year. Being from Massachusetts, I was certain that climbing the tallest mountain in the state would feel like a notable accomplishment. Surprisingly, conquering Mount Greylock turned out to be much less difficult than I had expected. The summit was foggy and rainy, but mountaintops without views had pretty much been the norm for us since Clingmans Dome in North Carolina, and I had expected nothing different.

In Greylock's summit lodge we consumed Gatorades and french fries. Warnings of a severe thunderstorm with lightning kept us hanging around on the porch of the lodge playing cards for a few hours. Seated at the table beside us were three older men who called themselves "The Weekend Warriors." They were funny and a little rowdy as they asked questions about our adventures and listened to our stories. Since I enjoy storytelling, Souleman let me do most of the talking. A couple of hours into trading stories, the gentlemen told me I should write a book and said they would read it (or in one man's case, watch the movie). The idea was already growing in my mind, and I began to feel more and more inspired to use my trail experiences as the material for the book I had always wanted to write.

All of the storytelling about our trip so far—and the planning for a book in the future—had me fired up and antsy to get back into the woods. We attempted to wait out the heavy rain, but it showed no sign of letting up. Finally, we decided to brave the rest of the storm in spite of suggestions that we stay the night. We packed our gear to the sound of splattering rain, but the raindrops let up just as we left the cover of the front awning. Although it remained foggy, we lucked out and made it to the shelter without getting into further rain or lightning.

Souleman and I were the only two people at the shelter that night. It was my turn for water duty, so I headed for the stream while he unrolled our bedding. Someone had left a bottle of champagne in the river as trail magic, and I brought it back with the refilled water bottles. We happily shared the bottle before spending a romantic evening in the secluded shelter. It seemed I had just drifted off to sleep to the sound of the bubbling stream when I awoke to my name.

"Brownie?"

I lifted my head.

Louder this time, Souleman whispered, "Brownie?"

"What?" I whispered back, squinting into the dark.

"Do you hear that?"

I blinked my eyes furiously and squinted again. Souleman was sitting straight up looking out into the woods. I tilted my ear toward the trees and waited a few seconds before asking, "Hear what?"

"I think there's a bear out there."

I listened again, turning my head in different directions. I heard the stream. I heard crickets. I heard the rustle of our sleeping bags. I strained so hard to hear any unexpected noise that I could practically feel the tiny hairs on my eardrums standing at attention. "I don't hear anything," I finally answered.

"It's been out there for a while," he whispered back, his head pivoting back and forth as he scanned the dark woods. The whites of his eyes were huge in the dark.

And? I wasn't particularly worried about a bear. Our food was properly stored and outside of that, a bear would have no interest in us. Dutifully, I held my head up a bit longer to appease my husband. My eyes scanned the darkness and my ears strained for any sound. I flashed back to the summer when I was a part of the Bear Squad at Camp Bonnie Brae. When a bear was sighted in the main area of camp, we would pile into the bed of an old, rusty pick-up truck, armed with air horns, a cow bell, and metal pots and spoons. We would scream, bang, honk the horns, and make a general ruckus as we chased the bear away from the main parts of camp.

"Do you hear it now?" I asked.

He shook his head in the dark.

"It's probably gone. Let's get some sleep." I laid my head back down on my makeshift pillow. Souleman was still sitting rigidly beside me when I dozed off.

"Brownie!"

It's going to be a long night. I pried one eye open and angled my head toward him. "Yeah?"

"You heard that, right?"

"No. I think I was asleep."

Souleman's headlamp snapped on. He scanned the woods in front of the shelter. Nothing.

I found his hand in the dark and intertwined our fingers, whispering reassurances before my head collapsed back onto my clothes-filled stuff sack.

Souleman stayed up most of the night worrying about noises in the woods, but I slept deeply. In the morning, we hiked three miles into North Adams. About two miles in, we met two day hikers coming south.

"Are you Brownie and Souleman?" they asked.

I was a little taken aback. *How do they know our names?*

They must have sensed my hesitation. "There's some trail magic waiting for you at the next road crossing."

Personalized trail magic?

When we got to the crossing, Draggin', a hiker we knew from the previous year, had left us a tray of brownies and a kind note. We gratefully sampled the brownies and tied the rest to the outside of my pack to share with friends.

As our appetites had become insatiable and it was nearly impossible to say no to any opportunity to eat, we pushed on to the Friendly's restaurant. Over bacon, eggs, pancakes, toast, and coffee, I expressed my concern that we would have to seriously alter our diets post-trail unless Souleman had a plan to become the next thousand-pound man.

As we were finishing our milkshakes (*It's ok to have dessert at breakfast, right?*), a man came in and introduced himself as Bird, owner of The Birdcage Hostel in Dalton, Massachusetts. He offered us a ride back to the trail, and we gratefully accepted. We hiked the next section fairly quickly even though the trail went almost entirely uphill and our bellies were gluttonously full.

In the afternoon, soon after crossing the Vermont state line, we passed by an impressive beaver pond called Sucker Pond. It was really an incredible creation. The trail ran about three feet below the dam, so we had to walk on wooden planks to avoid the mud and muck at trail level. We even saw a beaver, who smacked his tail on the water for us. I teasingly reminded Souleman of his story about beavers and dinosaurs from many months ago.

Just a little while later, we spotted the largest bear either of us had ever laid eyes on. He must have seen or heard us first because all we got was a glimpse of was his giant rear end running away through the trees.

The hikers at Congdon Shelter, our home for the night, were talkative and kind. Someone built a fire and everyone gathered around to share stories. The conversation continued non-stop all evening. It turned out that two of the hikers were from a town right near where we had lived pre-honeymoon. I marveled at the instant friendships that sprang up in groups of hikers. We would likely never see these people again, but for the night they were friends.

In the morning we rose early and hiked to the road to Bennington, Vermont, where we were expecting to meet a nine-thirty shuttle to town. The trail leading up to Bennington had some very steep inclines, and I fell twice, skinning my arms and legs. *Battle scars.*

A trail angel took us to town, where we borrowed bikes from the outfitter so we could get around more easily. Riding the bikes was unexpectedly rough on our knees. We did all of our town chores and ate ice cream twice. At the post office we loaded our packs with goodies from Aunt Barbie, Nanny, and Nicole. Then we escaped the grip of town.

Souleman and I settled into our tent for the night and pulled out our increasingly tattered Handbook.

"Guess what?" I asked.

"Hmm . . . ?" He pulled the headphones from his ears, taking a break from listening to the Red Sox game.

"We have only two state lines left in our hike."

"Wow, that's right." He took the Handbook from me and looked it over. "We have less than six hundred miles to go."

I laughed. "Isn't it funny that six hundred seems like a small number of miles now? I mean, compared to two thousand miles, it is, but compared to any normal distance . . ."

"I know. Can you believe we've already hiked more than twice the distance we have left?"

I leaned over and traced the trail map in the front of our Handbook with my pointer finger. With less than six hundred miles remaining until Katahdin, I felt confident. "It's hard to believe we've made it through Georgia, North Carolina, Tennessee—"

He cut me off and continued, "—Virginia, West Virginia, Maryland, Pennsylvania—"

"—New Jersey, New York, Connecticut—"

"—and Massachusetts." we finished together.

We've completed eleven states. Now we just have to finish Vermont and conquer New Hampshire and Maine. We may just make it.

In the morning, we said goodbye to the month of July in style. Considering our planned mileage, we got somewhat of a late start, but we made it more than seventeen miles with plenty of light for setting up camp and cooking. Camp chores were now a sprint compared to the drawn-out marathon we had gone through as brandnew hikers. We could set up our tent, lay out bedding, filter water, throw a bear bag line, and cook dinner in a matter of minutes, with little conversation.

For almost the entire day we had hiked with Charlie Foxtrot, a thru-hiker from England who had a charming British accent, and Dan, a businessman on a weeklong excursion. Charlie Foxtrot plodded along at the back of the group in his green plaid kilt and kept us laughing all day. Dan was an incredible hiker, and even though he lacked the many weeks of trail miles we had behind us, he enthusiastically kept up the whole time. I fell once during the day, and Souleman literally picked me up by my shoulder straps and placed me back upright.

Charlie Foxtrot said, "I've really got to look into getting me one of these husband things."

Right after lunch the following day, we came to an extremely tall lookout tower on top of Glastenbury Mountain. Once we had climbed the steps on our Jello-y legs, we could see Stratton Mountain, Mount Snow, Mount Greylock, Mount Equinox, and Okemo Mountain. The view was blissfully clear, especially considering our trail-long luck with horrendously foggy conditions at lookout points. Perhaps sharing the view with Dan and Charlie Foxtrot had improved our luck.

The next morning we would climb Stratton Mountain, a landmark that was significant to me for two reasons. First, Stratton was where Benton MacKaye had conceived of the idea of the Appalachian Trail. He had sat upon that mountaintop, looked at the mountain chains snaking in each direction, and imagined a continuous trail connecting all of them. His dream and the pursuance of that dream were the reasons we were lucky enough to have this journey decades later.

Stratton Mountain was also important to me because my parents had owned a cabin just off the mountain for years. I had many memories of skiing the slopes of Stratton with my dad, sister, and various friends. From that cabin I had taken many day hikes on the Appalachian Trail to prepare for my thru-hike. Hiking over Stratton would be like hiking home.

The view of Stratton and the jovial company made for a beautiful long-mileage day. I went to sleep anticipating the next day's attempt at a 21.6-mile day, ending at Route 11/30 in Manchester, where we hoped to hitchhike to my family's cabin. If we completed the long mileage, we would earn ourselves a double zero day. Otherwise, we would have one short-mileage day and one zero. It looked as though Stratton would be the only big uphill in the mileage, and thereafter the terrain would be relatively flat.

We said our goodbyes to Dan and Charlie Foxtrot before bed because they weren't sure about our plan to hike Stratton in the morning. Our trek to, over, and down Stratton went off without a hitch, even though the weather was extremely hot with record-breaking heat. According to a meteorologist on the radio, the heat was "not only uncomfortable, but a danger to your life." We consumed lots of water and looked forward to drinking some Powerade to restore our electrolytes once we made it to town. The climb up Stratton wasn't difficult, but we enjoyed very little view from the fire tower because of the haze created by the heat.

"Remember when we skied up here over Christmas?" Souleman asked.

"Yes." I turned in a circle looking off all sides of the tower. "Where are the trail signs?"

He pointed over my shoulder and I turned to look. A white blaze was barely visible through the trees. "No, not the AT, the ski trails. Where are the green and blue and black signs?"

"Oh. . . . I don't know. I guess they aren't near the AT. Remember how we took our picture by that big, wooden bear statue on top of the ski slope at Christmas?"

"Yes, but I don't see him."

"I'm sure there are a few summit spots. That must be on a different part of the peak. Near the ski lift."

"I see a ski lift over there." I pointed. "But I don't see the bear. It must be a different lift." We looked all around the top of the mountain. Before we descended the tower stairs, I mused, "The next time we're on top of Stratton, we'll probably be on skis looking for white blazes."

"Maybe this Christmas?" Souleman offered.

We hiked on to Stratton Pond, which was beautiful and looked like prime moose territory. Though we saw tracks in the deep mud, no actual moose were in sight. We made good time hiking, and even doing such long mileage, we were at the road to Manchester by quarter after seven. We had excellent luck with hitchhiking. In spite of the encroaching darkness, we were settled in my parents' cabin for the night by eight o'clock.

Just as I was peeling my filthy shirt off in anticipation of a long shower, I heard Souleman call out from the main room.

"Hey, Brownie? The answering machine is blinking. Want me to play the message?"

I peered over the loft holding my shirt. "Sure." I expected to hear my parents' slightly Southern accents relaying a welcome message. I was surprised to hear a booming British accent instead.

The message was from Charlie Foxtrot, and he was in Manchester at the Friendly's restaurant. We had told our friends in the shelter the night before about my parents' cabin and had given him them the phone number in case they needed anything in town. It appeared he had decided to hike Stratton in one day after all.

Souleman and I exchanged tired glances, and without a word I pulled my dirty shirt back on and he picked up the car keys. We had left one of our cars at my parents' cabin for the duration of our hike. As exhausted, hungry, and dirty as we were, we couldn't leave another hiker stranded—especially after such a long day and in such an expensive, non-hiker-friendly town.

We drove the twenty miles to Manchester in relative silence. After more than twenty miles of companionship already that day, we were content to remain silent. Our noxious odor was horribly obvious within the confines of the car. I cracked a window and tried to squelch my carsickness as Souleman navigated the dark, winding road to town.

Our stomachs grumbled furiously, and I mourned our missed dinner as we pulled in at Friendly's. It was after nine o'clock, and like most businesses in this small town, the restaurant was already closed. Charlie Foxtrot was nowhere to be seen. We checked in front of the outfitter and the pizza place. We tried McDonald's and asked at the front desk of hotels that seemed likely hiker choices. Nothing. After an hour of looking, we gave up and decided he must have returned to the trail or found another place to stay. Dejectedly, we drove home.

As soon as we walked into the cabin, the red, blinking light on the answering machine beckoned us. Closing my eyes and squeezing the bridge of my own nose, I pushed play. Charlie Foxtrot's British accent lilted through the machine.

"I'm guessing you guys couldn't find me in town. Guess I'll walk back up to the road and stealth camp somewhere in the woods off some side road by myself. Don't think I'll be able to get a hitch this late at night. Maybe I'll find you in town tomorrow."

Wordlessly, I took the keys from Souleman and walked back to the car. We repeated the winding drive to town in near silence.

"Where should we start looking?" I asked quietly as we neared the center of Manchester.

"I guess we'll start with the first wooded side street heading out of town."

I turned around in a parking lot and then pulled onto the first side road. The woods were thick with trees and underbrush. I couldn't imagine locating a flat spot for a tent. Glancing hesitantly at a nearby driveway, I rolled down the window.

"CHAAAAARLIEEEE!" I screamed out the window, interrupting the silent night. I inched the car forward almost halfway down the dark street, yelling my new friend's name every few yards.

"CHAAAAARLIEEEE!" Souleman alternated his yelling with mine and leaned over to honk the horn a few times. Nothing.

Dejected again, we turned around and headed back for the main road. I turned up the next side street and we repeated our endeavor. Adrenaline coursed through my veins as I screamed, "CHAAAAARLIEEEE!" into the dark night. We were exhausted after a good twenty minutes of yelling and flashing our headlights into the woods.

"This is insane!" I exclaimed, exasperated.

"I know. But what can we do?" He slouched in his seat, rubbing his dirty hand across his equally dirty face.

"I don't know."

Souleman sighed deeply and banged his hand on the window ledge. "I don't know either."

We exchanged bewildered glances.

"He's alone. In a strange town. At night." I looked out the open window at the inky blackness surrounding us. *I'd be scared out there alone.* It seemed much scarier to be alone at night on the edge of an unfamiliar town than alone in the woods.

"I know." Souleman nodded beside me.

I clicked my seat belt back on. "Let's try town again."

I steered back toward town and, on a whim, pulled back into the parking lot of Friendly's. There, seated on the curb, was our kilt-clad, British-speaking friend. We got out to give him hugs and threw his pack in the trunk.

"I know you're tired. I'll drive," Souleman offered.

"You sure? You hiked the same mileage I did."

"I know," he said, grinning sheepishly, "but this way you'll owe me a back rub."

The drive back to the cabin seemed short as we shared the stories of our respective evenings. Finally, the paved road changed to gravel as we turned onto the street to my beloved cabin. I took in the towering pointy roof, the glass front, and the framing made of rounded logs. We made our way across the tiered deck to the front door, which I unlocked for the third time that evening. The cabin was not air-conditioned, and the sweltering day had turned the closed-up house into a sauna. We opened all the windows, turned the fans on high, and retreated to the cool basement to watch old VHS movies on the cable-less TV.

Once I had finally stopped sweating, I ventured upstairs for a long, scalding shower. I lathered three times with the lavender-scented soap and scrubbed my hair an equal number of times. After drying off with a thick, soft towel, I stood in front of Mom's full-length mirror and tamed my wild eyebrows with tweezers. Then I slathered my tender skin in a thick layer of baby lotion. *Whose thigh muscles are those? Check out my tan lines.* Finally, I pulled on a pair of Mom's blue cotton pajamas. I fell asleep sprawled on top of my parents' comforter with the fan blowing at full blast.

We awoke to another sweltering day. Even in the comparably cool basement, we were sweating constantly. Just breathing was enough to make me break a sweat. We drove into Manchester to run errands and puttered around the stores, soaking in the air conditioning. While in town, we picked up fellow hikers named Kurly and Swansons to join us for the evening.

For dinner, we cooked enough spaghetti with garlic bread to feed a small army—or at least five hikers—and had a picnic on the floor of the basement to escape the heat as best we could. The night's activities consisted of many games, including pool, darts, board games, and cards. I looked around the cabin that night and again marveled at the ease of friendships on the trail. I had only known these people for a few days, and we were completely comfortable cooking, laughing, and playing games together. *How is it that friendships and trust are created so easily on the AT? Why can't the rest of the world be like this?*

In the morning, Kurly and Swansons hiked out and Charlie Foxtrot met his family. Souleman and I had planned another zero. While I had enjoyed hosting friends, I wasn't feeling very rested. The back-to-back long-mileage days had taken a toll on my body, and my hips and legs craved more rest. In addition to some treasured time alone, we were able to spend a few hours with my mom and sister, who came up to the cabin to meet us. They took us for a delicious dinner at Laney's, a barbecue place in Manchester.

As I repacked my gear that night, I turned to my sister and said, "You should come with us for a couple of days."

"Yeah, right." She rolled her eyes dramatically.

"Come on. It could be fun."

"Camping is your thing. I like my pillow. My bed. Showers."

"Wimp!"

"Whatever. I smell better than you. And my legs are shaved."

In the morning Souleman and I headed back out to tackle Bromley Mountain. Before long, we would find ourselves in the infamous White Mountains of New Hampshire. Neither of us had ever visited the Whites, so their notoriety had us eager with anticipation.

Bromley was exactly what I had thought Stratton would be. We walked up part of a ski trail, where we saw ski slope signs and jump ramps. Then, on the summit, we saw lifts and more trail signs. From the Bromley tower, we had unbelievable views of the mountains all around us. It felt like such an accomplishment to finally see what was on either side of the trail from Vermont Route 11/30, since we had driven that road so often when visiting family.

The rest of the day continued to be pleasant. Even after two zero days and a lot of high-calorie food, I was hiking much more slowly than usual, and we didn't get to the shelter until after eight o'clock. Our plan had been to continue half a mile further to a campsite, but we decided it was too dark.

We were hiking along the ridgeline the following morning when suddenly we came upon an area of forest with hundreds and hundreds of rock creations. Everywhere the eye could see, rocks were built into little towers, buildings, and designs: castles, crosses, piles, cones, and almost every other imaginable shape. It looked as though fairies had come in during the night and fashioned these unusual but beautiful stone creations. I expected to hear twinkling bells or see paths of glitter. We admired the strange artistic renderings, took some photos, and continued on. About half a mile further, we came upon another section of rock creations that was three times as large. Once again I stared in wonder. *Who in the world put these things here? And why?*

After leaving rock-fairy land, we also passed numerous swimming holes, a gorgeous lake, and a waterfall. We had to cross a narrow suspension bridge to get over the river. A large sign on the bridge read: "Weight limit: one person." This of course made me think, *Just what size person are we talking about? With a pack? Without a pack? Small? Large? Man? Woman?* I held my breath as we scurried across the swaying, bouncing bridge one at a time.

Unscathed, we began climbing Baker Peak, which was a scramble up a vertical slab of gripless rock. The climb was exhilarating, and the challenge took my mind off our mileage. Considering how slick the rock was, we appreciated our new shoes with good treads. Upon summiting Baker Peak, we could see for miles in every direction. Birds soared between mountaintops and the sun glinted off far-away rocks.

The many sights and obstacles made the day fun, and the weather was a perfect seventy degrees with a slight breeze and clear blue skies. Our attitudes and hiking speeds were probably also influenced by the knowledge that a steak dinner awaited us at the end of our sixteen-mile day.

During our visit the day before, my mom had asked if there was anywhere else they could meet us along the trail in Vermont. As Souleman and I huddled over our

Handbook, we realized that in two days we would actually be close enough to come back to the cabin with her. As we hadn't seen my dad since our wedding, we made a plan to meet them two days later, at five o'clock, at a road crossing.

We arrived at the road crossing an hour early and sprawled out in the shade to wait. Shortly thereafter, my mom arrived, and we spent a fun evening with my parents and sister eating steak and fresh vegetables and then telling stories around a fire pit on the deck. The temperature outside began to drop, and we all huddled around the fire passing around a bag of chocolate chip cookies. As I listened to my dad tell a story, I realized that this was the last time I would see my family before summiting Katahdin.

My parents and Allison retired for the night and left Souleman and me sitting beside the fire. I stood up and settled gingerly on my husband's lap, positioning myself so that I wouldn't hurt any of our sore muscles. He wrapped his arms around my shrinking waist and rested his chin on my shoulder.

"Can you believe we're back here?" he asked. "It seems like we were just here right after our wedding."

"I know. Why couldn't I have been this thin then?" I laughed.

He rolled his eyes.

"Remember how long the drive was from here to the trail in Pennsylvania?" After our post-wedding stay in a bed and breakfast, we had driven to Pennsylvania with his parents.

"And we walked the whole way to get back here."

"Hard to believe." I reached up and tangled my fingers in his growing beard. "You've grown all this since we got married."

We stared into the dying fire for a few quiet minutes.

"Are you glad we're hiking for our honeymoon?" I asked, spinning around to face him.

He squeezed me tight and kissed my nose. "I can't imagine doing anything else."

23

This Could Get Interesting

It had been a treat to spend another evening with family, but I was more than ready to push on toward New Hampshire. Six miles after being dropped off at the trail, we came upon Clarendon Gorge, which was by far one of the prettiest spots we had seen on the trail. Lots of people were there enjoying the beautiful weather, and I was grateful not to notice any litter or debris in or near the water. It was tempting to stop and swim in the sparkling water under the clear skies, but our late start dictated that we hike on. Luckily, the gorge was located right off Route 103 in Rutland, so we could visit another time.

We crossed a rickety bridge over the water to the parking lot on Route 103. After we crossed the road, a steep climb reminded us that we still had many challenges ahead. During the afternoon, we came upon trail magic twice. First, there were cold sodas left in the river at the five-hundred-mile mark. This trail magic was extremely professional as the donor had actually built a little cage into the river to hold the sodas and chill them. The trail angel also had a trail register and kept a running tally of how many sodas he delivered to hikers each year.

Souleman downed a soda in one gulp and placed the empty container in the provided recycle bin. I offered him my soda since I don't drink carbonated drinks, but he shook his head, saying there would be other hikers who needed it more. A little further up the trail, we came across a cooler and large Tupperware container with more soda and peanut butter crackers. We took one soda and two packs of crackers and collapsed by the cooler for a break.

We camped that night at a "secret shelter" located on private property near the Governor Clement Shelter. The Governor Clement Shelter was rumored to be in bad condition because there was road access to it and local youth tended to party there. This secret shelter was located on private land, and the location was shared only by word of mouth among long-distance hikers. When we arrived, everything was immaculate. I made yet another mental note to give back to hikers in the future. I would be in debt to society for the rest of my life.

We woke up invigorated and smiling because we would pass some very personal milestones on the Appalachian Trail that day. First, we walked up and over Killington Mountain, a place we had both been skiing and the peak just before the location of our wedding. The climb of over four thousand feet covered a distance of more than four miles. In the increasing fog, we saw little scenery. We stopped only twice for water breaks as we powered up the mountain.

"We made it to the spur trail," I observed as my eyes landed on a blue blaze. Originally, we had planned to take a spur trail that would add an additional 0.4 miles in each direction but would take us to the very top of the mountain. Stopping, I took out a water bottle. "Do you still want to go up?"

Souleman grimaced and studied the fog. "I don't see much point."

"Me neither. We'd be doing it just to say we did it. Skipping it saves us almost a mile round trip."

"I've summited enough mountains on this trail."

"Me too," I said, stuffing my water bottle back into its holster.

A mile before Mountain Meadows Lodge, we crossed a bridge on the trail and stopped to reminisce. This was the exact place where Souleman had asked me to marry him the previous September. It was as beautiful a spot as we remembered. It had seemed a much longer distance from the road the first time around with our jumping hearts and his sweaty palms. *If I hadn't hurt my feet, we wouldn't have been married when we reached this bridge. We might have gotten engaged somewhere else.* We took some photos and then hurried hand in hand up the trail to the spot where we had been married.

Although it seemed impossible, we had made it back to the exact location of our wedding ceremony. A couple of days after our June 10 wedding, we had driven down to Pennsylvania to start the second leg of our hike. Now, two months later, we were back at Mountain Meadows, only this time we had *walked* there. As we headed up the grassy hill toward the lodge, we scanned the familiar surroundings and reminisced about our ceremony.

A week prior to our wedding, the lodge had been sold to new owners, Bill and Anne. I had been a wreck after finding out that total strangers would be running my wedding. However, as soon as I had arrived at the lodge that weekend, my worries had been abated. They were an incredible couple with huge hearts and a desire to please. The wedding had gone off nearly flawlessly. It would be nice to see Bill and Anne again and find out how they were enjoying running the lodge.

Mountain Meadows Lodge was as rustic and inviting as ever. The converted barn had rough wood floors and wooden beam accents on the ceilings and walls. It was an ideal getaway spot for people like us who loved the outdoors and appreciated the tranquility of a remote location. We spent a relaxing evening playing ping pong, talking with Bill and Anne and the two other guests, and resting. Bill cooked us a gourmet dinner and even scrounged up some ice cream.

We awoke the following morning under a hand-stitched quilt and delayed getting out of bed so that we could savor being back at our wedding site. I propped myself up on one elbow and looked down at Souleman.

"You know, we're going to have to come back to the trail about a year after we summit Katahdin."

"I'm sure we will. But what do you mean?" he asked me sleepily, folding his arms behind his head.

"We met on the trail, dated on the trail, got engaged on the trail, got married on the trail, are spending our honeymoon on the trail. . . . We'll have to come back for the next big milestone, too."

He feigned innocence. "The next milestone?"

"A baby." I batted my eyes innocently.

"I don't know about a baby a year from now, but it won't hurt to practice."

Eventually, we stumbled down to breakfast. I was so hungry that I had actually dreamed about a continental breakfast. It was disheartening to find the countertops empty in the dining room, but Bill and Anne quickly brought an array of foods to our table. By the time we had finished our second round of food, we were both ready to face the day.

We hit the trail just before noon and made it six miles to the Stony Brook Shelter. It was a nice shelter next to a quaint stream. We decided to cook our hot meal at midday so that we wouldn't have to cook that night on the observation deck, where there would be no water source.

Sometime during the previous year, we had become unbearably tired of all the flavors of Lipton Noodles. No matter how good a meal was, we could only eat it so many times. We began a game of mixing different flavors together in an attempt to create new tastes. It was hard to believe there were any combinations left to sample after all the weeks we had spent on the trail, but in the last town we had come across a new flavor—jalapeño. We mixed the jalapeño and alfredo flavors together, and the result was surprisingly tasty. But then, at that point in our hike we probably would have eaten raw tree bark or marinated truck tires. Our taste buds were no longer very discriminatory.

After "lunch," which was really dinner, we loaded up with extra water at the stream to make sure we would have enough for our hike and to make it through the night at a waterless sleeping spot. Even though the extra water weight caused my pack to press uncomfortably on my shoulders and hips, I was hiking very quickly. We went up a large incline, and I pushed myself to maintain the same speed without breaks. *I am tough. I am tough!* I kept repeating to myself. *What was that mantra Lark wrote in her letter to me last year? All I can remember is, 'Trail, you are my bitch!'* When we finally stopped to consult Wingfoot, it seemed impossible that we were walking as slowly as the mileage indicated. Very discouraged, we scarfed down king-sized candy bars and pushed onward—up, up, and more up.

As my exhausted legs became increasingly wobbly, I was forced to rely heavily on my poles and arm strength to pull myself forward. My aching muscles burned, tingled, and quivered. Voluntarily hauling five pounds of water weight up a mountain so that I could sleep on top was starting to seem like a questionable plan. Finally, just as my internal motivation switch stuttered to the "off" position, we saw the sign for our destination: "0.1 miles to Observation Deck."

Suddenly, I had a burst of adrenaline. I glanced at the sky and the retreating sun and determined that we might just make it in time for a sunset finale. I huffed up the short trail as fast as I could. Soon, I saw the building towering over us. The platform was haphazardly secured to an extremely pointy roof in what appeared to be a rather unprofessional manner. Determined to catch the fading sun, we scrambled up the ladder without pausing to debate the safety of our endeavor.

From the vantage point of the platform, mountains of all sizes extended as far as we could see in every direction. The sun was still painting the westward sky dozens of shades of orange. Souleman snapped a million photos as I stared at the mountains in wonder. *Which of those have we hiked? Which ones* will *we be hiking?*

As the sun slid behind the mountains, I began to eye the platform and ladder skeptically. We were at least forty feet in the air with no way down except for that one rickety ladder. As I inspected the craftsmanship, I saw that the nails intended to attach the ladder to the platform were almost entirely pulled out and totally rusted. Also, the one handrail seemed barely attached. *Did I really just thoughtlessly ascend this ladder? How will we get back down?*

We discussed sleeping on the platform, but I was afraid I might need to get up to pee and did not want to have to climb down alone in total darkness. When the daylight was almost completely gone, we braved the ladder. Miraculously, we both descended unscathed and headed for the cabin's loft.

That night as I lay in my sleeping bag, I was grateful for my freshly brushed teeth. Being a long-distance hiker was helping me relish the simple pleasures in life. No other part of me was clean, but my teeth felt smooth as I ran my tongue around my minty mouth.

The next day was another one where the mileage according to the book and the mileage according to my legs did not agree in the slightest. We had hiked for eleven hours, from eight-thirty in the morning until seven-thirty at night, with only three breaks. We were shocked to realize we had made it only fifteen miles. *That means we're going even slower than thirty-minute miles. How embarrassing. We should be faster than that by now.* I tried to remind myself that our hike was not about mileage. It was hard not to dwell on distance, though, when completed miles were the only thing getting us closer to Katahdin.

During the day, we had to cross two roads that were listed in Wingfoot as being 1.5 miles and thirty feet in elevation apart. What wasn't mentioned was the enormous, straight-up-and-down mountain between the two roads. At the first road, we bought sandwiches, chips, and ice cream at a general store. Then, expecting a short and tranquil walk, we headed toward the second road. Much to our surprise, the trail kept climbing.

"I just don't understand. The Handbook sure didn't show this climb. How do you leave an entire mountain out of the book?" Souleman questioned, his voice rising in frustration.

Over an hour had passed since we had left the first road.

I stopped and leaned on my poles. "I don't know. It seems impossible that we haven't gone one and a half miles yet. This is crazy."

"I wonder if maps are more accurate for this section?" He wiped his sweaty forehead on his sleeve.

"Maybe. I guess it's a trade-off. We didn't have to spend money on maps since we don't carry them. But that also means we can't look at the elevation profiles to see what's coming up. Still, overall, I'd rather have unexpected climbs sometimes."

He nodded in agreement.

"Besides, I'm not so great at reading a map," I joked.

It seemed like an eternity later when we were finally spit out on the second road right near a farm stand. Despite the food we had consumed only two miles back, we stopped for more ice cream. Souleman's all-natural strawberry tasted good, but my organic mint left something to be desired. The chunky mint leaves in the ice cream got stuck in my teeth.

Finally, after the stressful and time-consuming first part of the day, the last two miles passed quickly. There were five other people at the shelter when we arrived. Two of them confessed upfront that they were snorers, so we pitched our tent. We collected some wood to contribute to a campfire that was already going and enjoyed sitting around the fire talking and relaxing with our fellow hikers. The pine branches gave off lots of smoke and helped keep the vicious insects away. I stood directly in the cloud of smoke in an attempt to cover up my hiker funk with trail perfume.

We celebrated two months of marriage by walking into New Hampshire, our second-to-last state. I was incredulous that we were about to enter the Whites and, before we knew it, Maine. I knew our trip would be over too soon, so I tried to embrace each moment. With only 442 miles left, I didn't want to miss a thing.

That afternoon, we heard on our radios that twenty-two Islamic fascists had been captured in England. According to the news report, they had been trying to bring liquid bombs onto planes flying into the United States, and if they had succeeded it would have been even worse than 9/11. It was surreal to hear such negative news while we were surrounded by the peacefulness of the woods. Sometimes we struggled to remember that although we were on a multi-month break from society, the rest of the world was continuing as usual. Hearing about this kind of potential disaster reinforced the reasons we were escaping reality, but it also reminded me how removed from current events we were. If the incident had taken place right over our heads, we probably wouldn't have known without our radios.

As soon as we walked into Hanover, New Hampshire, a van pulled up beside us and my mom's vibrant friend Kasia jumped out. Her oversized, colorful jewelry jingled as she ushered us into the car. With her hands animating every word, Kasia talked non-stop during the drive.

"Act like you're family," she told us when we pulled into the driveway. She bounced down the hall as she showed us to our room. "There's food in the fridge and towels in your bathroom. Oh, and make sure to enjoy the hot tub."

Souleman's dad picked us up before sunrise. We were settled at his parents' house in Middlebury, Vermont, before nine in the morning. We did the typical town chores and then begrudgingly prepared our packs for winter. We added hats, gloves, and extra layers to our clothing stuff-sacks, and swapped our summer sleeping bags for thicker winter ones.

At a family cookout with all of Souleman's relatives, we were peppered with questions about our hike.

"How far do you walk each day?"

"Where do you sleep?"

"How do you get food?"

"How do you get to towns?"

"How much weight have you lost?"

They marveled at the quantity of food Souleman ate and commented on his huge beard. While we answered questions, we ate all sorts of fabulous foods— meats, casseroles, salad, his mom's famous goulash, and even brownie sundaes for dessert.

The next morning, it was time to tackle New Hampshire and Maine. Our knees, feet, and backs objected to the added weight of our winter gear, but the heavier items were essential since the weather in the Whites was unpredictable.

We hiked only eleven miles that day, but there were two climbs of over a thousand feet that we traveled up without stopping. We were pleased to feel our bodies gaining strength and stamina, and I was hopeful about my ability to stay tough through the challenge of the Whites.

We got to the shelter before dark and set up for the night with daylight to spare. Our early arrival was especially nice because we had been in a routine of getting in late and performing most of our chores by headlamp. Every task became twice as hard when it had to be performed with your head held at just the right angle.

As we tackled our final camp tasks, a piece of our MIOX snapped off in Souleman's hand as he was cleaning it. *Uh-oh.* Having a broken purifier was incredibly bad news for two reasons: first, we still weren't carrying any backup water treatments, and second, New Hampshire towns were small, with unpredictable town amenities, so there was no telling when we might find a replacement water purifier. *How will we avoid getting sick?* While we were discussing options for the MIOX situation, I started getting out our supplies to cook dinner.

"Hey, Souleman? Come check this out."

He walked over to the picnic table and I handed him our suspiciously light fuel bottle.

"Oh, no." He raised his eyes to meet mine.

"Oh, yes. We forgot to get more fuel in town."

"So we're filter-less and nearly fuel-less." He hung his head in mock defeat. I bit my lip and raised my eyebrows. "This could get interesting."

In the morning, we accidentally slept in and didn't resume hiking until nine o'clock. We set a good pace and reached Lyme-Dorchester Road by lunchtime. Since we had no way to purify water, we hitched into town to get safe water at the town store. We lucked out and a woman and her son gave us a ride into town and then back out to the trail. At the store, we were able to buy Powerade and ice cream cones and fill up our water bottles.

After returning to the trail, we walked about a hundred feet and came across a sign reading "free water." I burst out laughing. Souleman leaned around me, saw the sign, and joined me in contagious, unstoppable laughter.

"Isn't it ironic?" I asked.

"A little bit too ironic." He smirked.

The arrow on the sign pointed to a house right off the trail. Even though our heavy packs reminded us that we now had plenty of drinkable water, we decided to check it out. A kind-hearted old man came out and spoke with us. He kept his own little statistics sheet about hikers. He recorded all our information and then offered us organic fudgesicles. Even though I'd barely swallowed my last bite of ice cream thirty minutes before, I accepted the chocolaty treat without hesitation.

We were just planning to head back to the trail when the man suggested we enjoy our lunch on the back deck. I glanced up at the sun and then back at the peaceful back yard with its large wooden deck, beautifully manicured gardens, and kind homeowner. It didn't take much convincing for me to unshoulder my pack and settle in on the picnic table. After all, the trail was about experiencing people, not just pushing out mileage.

The man brought out binoculars and bird books and regaled us with details of his sightings over the years. He even offered to let us use his bathroom before departing. We found out that he had gotten married at the same age we did and was still happily married fifty-two years later. I squeezed Souleman's hand under the table.

After lunch, we traveled uphill for six miles until we reached the shelter. It was a rigorous climb. About two miles before the end, we paused at a lookout point with a view of the fire tower where we would be camping. The tower was located straight up a huge mountain. After long gulps from our water bottles, we soldiered on toward the tower and its promised view. As tired as I was, I had been inspired by the vision of our destination. My thighs burned and my arms pumped vigorously as I dug my poles into the dirt to propel me up the trail.

When we finally made it to the fire tower, Souleman and I dropped our packs and stood staring out at the landscape. We silently took in the view as he wrapped his arms around my waist and rested his chin on my shoulder. Behind us, the trail we had already completed wound south as far as we could see, and in front of us, the White Mountains were beautiful and daunting.

I felt overwhelmed with gratitude for having the physical ability, financial security, and opportunity to be on the trail having such a life-shaping experience. I could have been stuck in an office, sitting at a traffic light, or standing in line at the bank. Instead, I was surrounded by trees and rocks, looking out over God's creation while standing beside the man I loved. Desperately, I searched my mind for something profound to say to capture the depth of the moment. As much as I loved words, I couldn't think of anything powerful enough. Finally giving up on sounding poetic, I wove the fingers of my left hand through his left fingers, which were resting on my hip. Our wedding rings clicked together, and I smiled and tilted my head back to look into my husband's eyes in the twilight.

"I can't imagine being anywhere else," I said.

He kissed my forehead. The silence stretched on for so long that I didn't think he was ever going to speak. I listened to the night coming alive around us and watched lights flicker on in the valley below as stars dotted the sky above. So quietly I could barely hear him, Souleman asked, "How many people do you think get to share something like this?"

I shook my head and turned around to embrace him. I was outside, surrounded by nature, completely in my element, and in love. I couldn't have imagined being happier. Standing on tiptoe, I slid my hands around his neck. My aching hiker calves rebelled against this un-hiker-like stance by sending darts of pain up my legs. Still, I withstood the discomfort long enough to share a lingering kiss with my husband. His lips were salty with sweat, but the taste was sweet on my lips. When my legs started shaking from the effort of stretching upwards, he grasped my sides firmly and held me up off the ground, prolonging our embrace. He kissed the tip of my nose as I dropped my heels back to the ground. I could feel him watching me as I shouldered my pack.

"Brownie?"

"Hmm?" I fiddled with a loose strap.

"Michelle?" I looked up, startled and surprised at the use of my real name.

"I love you."

I smiled. "I love you too." I squeezed his hand.

"No," he said. "I mean, I *really* love you."

I pecked his cheek and then stepped toward the shelter. As soon as my back was turned, I clicked my hiking poles together. His answering taps echoed behind me, and I could sense his smile without turning around.

24

Delaying Katahdin

"That one's a dragon." I pointed at a cloud above our heads. "See the fire he's breathing out up above?"

"Yep. And above him is a wagon."

We were sitting on a massive rock platform at the top of Cube Mountain. We had squished our sweaty bodies together on a "recliner" formed by the rocks so that we could look up at the clouds while we started to digest our huge lunch.

Not long after we started down the mountain, we stopped to study giant moose tracks on the trail. I noticed that Souleman's sweaty face had a different sheen than usual. Kneeling beside him, I put my hand to his forehead and found it hot to the touch.

"Are you ok?"

"I'm not feeling so well," he admitted.

"Do you want to take our packs off for a while? Take a rest?" I unclasped my chest strap.

"No. Let's just take it slow." He motioned me up the trail.

"We can stop. It's ok."

"I'd rather just make it to the shelter. I'm all achy. It's not normal hiking soreness, so if I stop I may not hike again today."

"You lead, then. Go at whatever pace is comfortable. I'll follow behind you."

We stopped often for short breaks. Sometimes Souleman would lean against a tree while he rested. During one such break, I stopped at a stream crossing and splashed my face with the frigid water. Washing the layers of dirt and sweat off my skin was incredibly refreshing, and I delighted in the simple pleasure of the ice-cold water on my hot, sticky skin. Splashing in the water brought our failed water purifier to mind, and with Souleman feeling ill, I began to worry about serious illnesses. *What are the symptoms of giardia, again?*

When we arrived at the shelter, I ran down the side trail to fill our water bottles while Souleman flipped through the register in the shelter. I looked for a spot where the water trickled directly out of the earth. Not finding one, I settled for a spot without much sediment. I shot a nervous glance upstream. *I hoped there isn't a dead animal in the water up above.* Thankfully, the other hikers at the shelter let us borrow their Aquamira filter, so we were spared one more potential exposure.

I dug through my pack for our remaining dinner options. "Do you want to choose what we eat since you're sick?"

"I can't even think about food," he said, burying his head in his arms.

"You have to eat. You're already weak."

"I know," he groaned. "What are my choices?"

"Instant potatoes, Mexican rice," I called out, digging a little deeper, "or macaroni and cheese."

"Do you really have to ask?"

Silently, I set about making the macaroni and cheese, our shared favorite trail dinner. Usually Souleman did all the cooking, but that night I was trying to make sure he rested. When dinner was ready, I handed him his spork and made sure he matched me bite for bite, even though he had no appetite.

We woke up early and Souleman said he felt back to normal. We walked just over seven miles to a hostel, where we were planning to refill our water bottles with safe water. The hostel owners told us that a huge group of northbounders had headed into the White Mountains that day. Sleeping space is limited in the White Mountains, so we did not want to be vying for a spot each night. We were easily persuaded to change our schedule a bit.

Our new plan left only a few miles to hike that afternoon, so we hung around the hostel and watched movies, checked our email and bank accounts, and rested. I was watching *Good Will Hunting*, and by the midpoint of the movie, my head had drifted toward the table and lay cradled in my arms. It was my turn for whatever bug Souleman had caught the day before.

Scooting beside me on the bench, Souleman touched my forehead and shook his head when he found it clammy and hot. He went to get us sandwiches and left me with instructions to drink an entire bottle of water while he was gone. I massaged my throbbing temples and hoped fiercely that I'd feel better after a night of sleep, just as Souleman had.

While I half-listened to the movie with my eyes closed, I reflected on how lucky I was to be hiking with a partner. *Who takes care of solo hikers when they're sick? Who motivates them and sets the pace on challenging days? Who watches out for hypothermia and heat exhaustion and low blood sugar?* The thought of managing all of those things alone seemed daunting, though I realized in astonishment that that was what I had originally set out to do. The Appalachian Trail had taken me time and time again to places I'd never have predicted and had showed me that no matter how meticulous a planner I was, God's plan was always better than mine.

As I tuned back in to *Good Will Hunting*, Robin Williams's character spoke about how important it was to experience life, and not just to know about it. He explained that reading a book about Michelangelo couldn't communicate what it was like to stand inside the Sistine Chapel, and reading *Oliver Twist* couldn't give a real understanding of what it was like to be an orphan. I thought back to the dozens of Appalachian Trail books I had read. Not one of them had truly conveyed to me what this experience would be like. I knew without a doubt that those people in my life who had not hiked the Appalachian Trail themselves would never understand my hike.

After eating our sandwiches, we finally made it back to the trail and camped at Jeffers Brook Shelter. I woke up feeling much better. We must have shared the shortest illness in existence, which was a blessing because the morning presented us with what was unquestionably our hardest day on the trail yet. Every hiker who had talked to us about the White Mountains had told us they would be tough, but their descriptions didn't do the mountains justice. Even the descent into the beginning of the Whites turned out to be astonishingly difficult.

We had climbed the four miles up Mount Moosilauke by eleven in the morning. From atop Moosilauke, every other mountain was dwarfed. It truly felt like being on top of the world.

"This is beautiful!" I tossed my pack to the ground and spun around with my arms spread wide. Souleman leaned on his hiking poles, taking in the view, and then plopped down on the ground and leafed through our Handbook. "We're at four thousand, eight hundred and one feet," he told me, staring into the distance.

I settled myself awkwardly in his lap. Our tight, sore muscles and the hard ground made it an uncomfortable sitting position, but I needed to be close while sharing the panoramic view. He must have felt similarly because he wrapped his arms around me and tucked his chin into my shoulder.

All around us were mountain ranges that had seemed high when we had climbed them, but next to Moosilauke, only the Whites were tall—tall and incredibly intimidating. *We're hiking up those?* I started shivering as the wind hit my damp shirt, and I had to pull out my windbreaker for the first time that year. Looking at the mountains surrounding me, I was reminded for yet another time on the trail that I was rather small and insignificant in this world.

"I don't think I've ever seen anything this beautiful," I said, sighing contentedly with my sweaty cheek pressed against his sticky beard.

"We haven't even started the Whites yet."

After a few minutes of silence, as we both lost ourselves studying the view, he stood and reached down to take my hands and pull me to my feet. With his pack already shouldered, he held mine up for me to slip into. Smirking, he said, "Hey Brownie? I'll race you to the Whites."

"What's the hurry? The first one to Katahdin loses, remember?" I tugged on his hand to pull him back toward myself.

"What?"

I stood on tiptoe and pulled him into a long kiss.

"What're you doing?" He murmured into my mouth as his arms slid around my waist.

"Delaying Katahdin a little longer."

The first two miles down Moosilauke weren't difficult. We enjoyed the continued vistas and walked around and over rocks to Beaver Brook Shelter. According to our Handbook, Beaver Brook boasted the best view from a shelter on the entire trail. We soaked in the scenery from the shelter's ledge while eating lunch. We knew we needed to consume a lot of calories in order to be able to put in another eleven miles, so we dumped our lunch bag out between us and ate heartily. It was two o'clock when we packed up to finish the descent.

I had always found downhill sections of the trail to be easier on my body, so when hikers discussed the horrible descent of Moosilauke, I didn't pay much attention. Surprisingly, the mere 1.5-mile hike down to Kinsman Notch dropped 1,800 feet and took us *three* hours to complete. I literally could not take more than one step without pausing to figure out my next move. We navigated around rocks of all sizes and shapes. I balanced on pointy nubs, jumped down drops equal to my height, and used tree roots and limbs as handholds to prevent myself from toppling headfirst down vertical rock slabs. It was excruciating.

Finally, we made it to Kinsman Notch. Taking many deep breaths and an equal number of swigs of water, we studied the sun. We still had eight miles to hike before bed, and they were all uphill. Though we were exhausted, there was no way we could take a break with so much mileage left and so little daylight.

We climbed back up steadily to 3,480 feet. The climb was painful and required the use of muscles we had not yet employed on the trail. Some of the steps were so high that I couldn't just push myself off the ground with one leg. I had to plant my poles, launch my whole body, and lean forward as I hurled myself up. This full-body maneuver was usually successful, but occasionally I didn't get enough power and slid back to the ground, only to have to continue trying until I made it up. Often I scraped my knees and shins in the process. When I did successfully scale a step, I then found myself teetering on the edge of a rock, trying not to let my pack weight pull me backward or throw me forward into the next obstacle.

Before many of these tall steps, I looked up to see Souleman offering me a hand from above. Initially, I shook my head stubbornly. *I can do it myself. I chose to do this hike. He shouldn't have to help me.* I was determined not to burden him any more than necessary and to be as physically independent as I could. Since I already relied on him to carry extra pack weight, set the pace on challenging days, and lift my spirits when my confidence faltered, I was acutely conscious of a need to tackle some aspects of the trail on my own.

When we weren't awkwardly scaling monstrous rocks, we were sloshing around in huge, deep mud puddles. I jumped carefully from roots to rocks to tiny dry patches of ground. Often the surfaces on which I found purchase were no larger than a child's tiny fist.

By six o'clock that day, I was thoroughly disheartened. Our microscopic progress and the sun's gradual progression across the sky were sure indicators that we would be night hiking. Before long, the trees around us were barely visible in the thick, black darkness. I reached up over my head to pull my headlamp from the top of my pack and strap it to my sweaty forehead. Tucking my chin into my chest and squaring my shoulders, I prepared to soldier on.

Souleman lifted my chin up with his fingertips. "Hey, it'll be ok. This could be fun."

"I hate night hiking." I kicked at a rock. "*We* hate night hiking."

"Think of it as a quest."

In the dark I rolled my eyes at his annoying optimism. "Remember our last night hike? We went so slowly. There were spider webs everywhere. We camped on the side of a smelly road with toxic water without eating any dinner."

"We're a lot tougher now. We've made it to New Hampshire. Plus, this time we don't have a scary man following us. We can just enjoy it."

I started off down the trail. *I'm tired. I'm hungry. This stupid trail is wet and slippery and full of rocks. It'll take even longer in the dark. We won't get enough sleep. My feet hurt. My shoulders hurt.*

"Hey!"

I stopped walking but continued to stare at the ground.

"You forgot something."

I turned around. "What?" My exasperation was evident.

Souleman planted his hands on his hips in mock anger. "Kiss me."

Exhaling forcefully, I went back and gave him a peck on the lips. "Ok? Let's get this over with."

"What was that? You call that a kiss? A couple of hours ago, you were all about kissing to delay Katahdin."

"A couple of hours ago, I wasn't exhausted and night hiking in the mud with many miles to go." My eyes teared up.

He pulled me against his chest. "Chin up, Brownie. You're tough, remember?"

I nodded with my lip quivering slightly and reminded him quietly, "I'm delicate, too."

He kissed my forehead and started to release me.

"And my nose," I requested.

He kissed the tip of my nose.

"And this eye." I tilted my right eye toward him.

He kissed my closed eyelid.

"Now I'm uneven." I tilted my left eye toward him.

He placed a kiss on my other eye.

I kept my eyes closed. "And my forehead."

He placed a long kiss in the middle of my forehead.

I opened my eyes to look at him. "And here." I pointed to my lips.

This time, he took my face in his hands and kissed me deeply. "You're covered in kisses. Let's move toward Maine."

"Not *completely* covered."

Our lights made eerie shadows on the trail, and the woods beyond were cloaked in thick darkness and seemed to pulse like some strange optical illusion. I was having trouble seeing where the trail wound through the woods and could feel myself getting frustrated and cranky. *I'm tough. I'm a hiker. I can do this. What was that mantra again?*

Twice, we lost the trail and followed animal paths for a short distance, but we realized our mistakes quickly and did not lose much time. "Let's play a game," I called ahead to Souleman. I was desperate to find a positive attitude. "Remember that singing game we used to play?

"Sure. You start."

I sang loudly through the darkness. "Been hiking all day . . . doo doo doo doo doo."

His response drifted from behind me. "Our feet will soon pay . . . doo doo doo doo doo. My belly's real hungry . . . doo doo doo doo doo."

"My feet're getting stumbly . . . doo doo doo doo doo. I sure want to sleep . . . doo doo doo doo doo."

"And a massage for my feet . . . doo doo doo doo doo . . ."

We traded verses for a long time, letting our voices cut through the darkness and distract our tired bodies. Eventually, my usually reliable, internal mile-o-meter told me we should be nearing the shelter. Every so often, I stopped and strained my ears for shelter sounds.

At least four times, my nose deceived me into thinking I smelled a campfire or food cooking. Water gurgling over rocks sounded like people talking, and the wind rattling trees sounded like laughter. Time after time, I just knew we had arrived at the shelter, only to round the corner and see more trail winding ahead of me instead of a shelter sign.

When once again I heard laughter and muted conversation in the distance, I doubted my own hearing and didn't even slow my gait. I was shocked to see a shelter sign appear around the corner. Once again, I had to resist the urge to kiss the sign's splintered wood.

Miraculously, everyone at Eliza Brook Shelter was still awake. I glanced at the watch stowed in my pack and saw that it was already ten-thirty. This was our latest hiking night yet. The others made room for us and chatted as we got ready for bed. It was a relief to learn that other hikers had thought this section of the trail was as hard as we did. No one could believe we had hiked 15.9 miles over such treacherous terrain. *What were we thinking? The White Mountains are no joke.*

"Do you want me to cook?" Souleman asked.

"Yes, but no. I'm hungry but too tired to eat."

We set up our beds and collapsed down with relief. As gravity relaxed my muscles and allowed them to stretch, the relief was immeasurable. My hips pulsed and my feet had a strange tingling sensation.

"I'm exhausted," I whispered to Souleman. "This might be my tiredest day yet."

"Mine too." He leaned his head against mine.

"And I still don't like night hiking."

25

We've Got to Be Crazy

Despite our humbling introduction to the Whites, we were up and hiking shortly after seven the next morning. We were determined not to face another late night. Our day started with a relentless and endless ascent, including at least four false summits. When we reached the actual peak of South Kinsman, we had good views and could see a second peak, North Kinsman, about a mile away.

"Does this mountain ever end?" Souleman collapsed on a rock.

"According to our Handbook, it's downhill all the way to the road after the second summit."

Of course, the trail did not go downhill all the way to town. But we did walk past Lonesome Lake Hut, our first hut in the White Mountains. The huts are rustic wood and stone lodges run by the Appalachian Mountain Club. Tourists make reservations months in advance and pay over eighty dollars a night for lodging and two meals. Thru-hikers and long-distance hikers generally either cannot afford this rate or plan their schedules far enough in advance to make a reservation. Since camping outside an official campsite is illegal in the White Mountains and the huts are expensive, sleeping on that stretch of trail can get tricky.

The huts are run by the "croo," which consists of groups of mostly college-aged kids. Sometimes an option called "work-for-stay" is available to a limited number of long-distance hikers. This arrangement involves performing chores for the croo in exchange for the opportunity to eat leftovers from the meals and sleep on the floor of the dining room. Based on what we had heard from other hikers, the amount of food is unpredictable and often insufficient to fill ravenous thru-hiker stomachs. By the time chores are finished, though, it's usually too late to consider cooking more food.

Once the hikers chosen for work-for-stay have completed their work and eaten, they have to wait until lights-out at nine-thirty before they can set up their sleeping gear. All the guests go to bed, and then the thru-hikers invade the main room like a stealthy, undercover army and set up in the dark, sleeping on picnic tables and scattered about on the floor. They arrange an astonishing assortment of sleeping paraphernalia in minutes. The hikers, who normally go to sleep by eight o'clock, are beyond exhaustion at that point. All night the guests shuffle through the common room on their way to the bathroom.

After a sleepless night, the hikers in the dining room are awakened by the croo cooking an early breakfast. They rapidly pack up their gear, and by the time most guests awaken, the evidence of their overnight presence is gone. Hikers then wait for breakfast leftovers and complete a few light chores before leaving.

While we had obviously heard a great deal about the huts, our stop at Lonesome Lake Hut was our first time seeing one, and we were ready for a lunch break. Each of us bought a bowl of potato dill soup and a chocolate bar. We sat at a table with two other couples: Mom and Windtalker and Carbomb and Lichen. Sharing trail time with other couples was a special treat, and so was a hot meal we didn't have to prepare ourselves. With full bellies, we hiked on toward town with Carbomb and Lichen.

Arriving in North Woodstock, New Hampshire, we settled in at the Carriage Motel. Our battered, bruised bodies were extremely grateful for time to recover and relax, and lying down on a mattress after showering was positively heavenly. I now understood that the difficulty of the White Mountains had not been exaggerated. Muscles I didn't even know I had ached in my legs and arms. I was both surprised to discover new limitations of my body this far into our hike and incredulous to realize that we still had the majority of the Whites ahead of us.

While enjoying our zero day to prepare for the next round of body-beating, we ran into Chubster and his friend Victor, who had left trail magic for us back in Massachusetts. They had come up to hike in the Whites for the weekend. We hung out with them that evening after we went to dinner. Then, in anticipation of our early morning climb back up to the ridgeline, we went to bed early.

We woke before sunrise to a phone call from Mom and Windtalker. They had just watched the weather forecast, and the meteorologist was predicting terrible thunderstorms all day. Going up above the tree line to ridge-walk all day in thunderstorms didn't sound like fun, and it also posed safety risks from exposure. Plus, the ridge was supposed to have a spectacular view, and we hated to miss yet another lookout point because of bad weather. But another zero day wouldn't move us closer to Maine. We waffled on which was the best decision.

After a hushed conversation with Mom and Windtalker on the sidewalk outside our motel rooms, we decided to wait out the storm in the safety of our dry room. It ended up raining all day and was cold and dreary outside, even down in the valley. Personally, I was grateful that the weather had given me an excuse to recover a little more from our brutal introduction to the Whites.

Fully rested after an extra night in town, we started our ascent back into the Whites. As we had come to expect, the terrain was unbelievably challenging. Once we got up above the tree line on Franconia Ridge, the weather was horrid. It was surprisingly chilly and damp in late August on top of high peaks in New Hampshire.

We hunkered down miserably in our raincoats, ducking behind rocks to avoid the wind that was pounding our faces. The thirty- to forty-mile-per-hour winds whipped the rain against our skin and soaked us as we stumbled across rocks we could barely see due to the fog.

The view from the ridgeline was supposed to be one of the best of the entire trail, but we could see nothing. At one point when I extended my arm out in front of me, I couldn't see my own hand. The wind was so strong that I could barely stay standing, and the temperature began to drop drastically. It seemed like we would never get back to the shelter of the trees on the other side of the ridge. Every time we passed a large rock or small tree, we squatted down behind it to take momentary refuge from the assaulting wind and rain.

Behind one rock, Souleman put his arm around my shoulders as we hunched together, shivering. He yelled over the wind and rain, "We've got to be crazy!"

"No," I yelled back. "Just hikers!"

Grabbing Souleman's hand, I ran back into the driving wind with a loud whoop. We didn't stop for lunch or other breaks because we were so miserable. The terrain was rough except for on the very top of the mountain, but it was so windy there that we could barely stay on our feet. I fell twice, but luckily I wasn't hurt and easily righted myself to keep going. After eight hours and forty-five minutes of hiking, we had traveled barely over ten miles.

The next morning the weather gave us a break, and we were treated to a pleasant day while still tackling challenging terrain. The clouds cleared enough to afford us one view. We could see the ridge we had walked the day before. It looked rather impressive from afar. Mount Lincoln, Mount Lafayette, and Mount Garfield were daunting peaks even in good weather. We decided that it was a backhanded blessing that we hadn't been able to see off the ridges the previous day in bad weather.

We made it to Zealand Falls Hut before dinner and were able to do a work-for-stay. Our chore was stacking wood. The pieces of wood were poorly cut, so stacking them evenly was difficult, especially with my throbbing muscles. Souleman took on the brunt of the labor even though he was probably equally as tired. In spite of the lower mileage, I was exhausted. Just lifting my arms seemed to require more effort than I could muster. When I added the weight of firewood, I could scarcely move. The evening passed in a blur as I waited impatiently to be able to stretch out my aching body and sleep.

We learned in the morning that departures from the huts were always later than ideal because of inevitable delays with chores. Finally back on the trail, we almost immediately came across four men stopped at a trail-crossing intersection. They were blocking the trail signs.

"Where are you headed?" one of them asked us.

"Maine," I answered proudly.

"On the Appalachian Trail?" another man questioned.

"Yes," I said, nodding my head. They pointed straight ahead.

"The AT goes north that way?" Souleman asked.

"Right," he verified helpfully. "Happy hiking."

We passed them and hiked onward. The trail was flat, so we made good time. Noticing no blazes after about three-tenths of a mile, we stopped to consult our Handbook. Two of the men from the intersection caught up and radioed to the other two men behind them to ask if they had seen blazes recently. They said yes, so we assumed that blazes behind us suggested the presence of blazes ahead. On we went, letting the two day hikers go ahead of us. Another two-tenths of a mile further, we came across the two men staring at a tree.

I looked up and saw a blue blaze.

"Is the AT always marked with white blazes?" one of them asked.

I groaned. "Yes."

We were on the wrong trail. Bummed, but grateful that it had at least been easy terrain, we retraced our steps and turned at the first trail intersection. Excited to be back on the AT, we hurried along. Souleman came to a halt about two-tenths of a mile down the trail, and I literally slammed straight into him. Wordlessly, he pointed at a yellow blaze with his pole. We were on the wrong trail—again.

Slightly less patiently, we retraced our steps once again. This time we went all the way back to the first trail intersection where the men had originally directed us "north." They had in fact pointed us down the wrong trail to start with. I heaved a huge sigh and touched the white blaze with my palm.

Souleman and I had heard that the trail could be hard to follow in the Whites, and this encounter taught us to be extra cautious at trail merges. Once we finally got back on the white-blazed trail, we hiked with haste. The weather was cool enough that we needed long sleeves when stopped, but warm enough that we could hike in shorts and a t-shirt. I really appreciated the sun after all the rain on Franconia Ridge, and I was much happier since we were conquering the terrain more easily.

When we made it to Crawford Notch, we hitched to a campground where we resupplied, reserved a campsite, and finally, as it became completely dark, headed toward the showers. I eyed the dark building skeptically. This was one of the only times we had stayed in a non-trailside campsite, and we were closer to a main road than I would have preferred. In front of me, the bathrooms were surrounded by deep shadows without a single outside light.

I went into the ladies' bathroom to find a cinderblock room with one dim bulb and spider webs everywhere. The corners were shadowy, and I saw that the shower stall had no door. I hesitated only a moment before walking right back outside.

"Souleman?" I stood outside the door to the men's room.

He appeared shirtless in the doorway.

"Is anyone else in there?"

"No. Why?"

"I'm coming in."

Souleman held the door open, and I ducked under his arm. He locked the door behind us. The water was cold and a breeze blew between the cinderblocks of the building, but I felt safe with the door locked and my husband inside.

Chilly but clean, we settled in at our campsite with Rising Sun. Four other thru-hikers were staying at the campground, and we all planned to hike to Lakes of the Clouds Hut the next day. Lakes of the Clouds was located one mile before the summit of Mount Washington, so we would be positioned the following day for an early-morning summit of the tallest mountain in the Northeast.

The climb out of Crawford Notch was the longest-mileage day we had planned in the Whites, so we got an early start. Rain pants and raincoats were essential gear as we walked along above the tree line. The hike was almost entirely uphill, but the unfurling views of mountains, trees, lakes, and seemingly untouched wilderness took away the agony of our endless trek up, up, up. I hiked in front and set a steady pace. Even with the steep climbs all day, we stopped only once.

Our arrival at Mizpah Hut was timed perfectly for a lunch break. We arrived at the same time as Burner, Feng Shui, and Rising Sun, so we all shared a picnic table inside. I drank about a gallon of "all-you-can-drink" hot chocolate. All day long, Mount Washington loomed in front of us. We hiked steadily toward it, watching the mountain gradually get bigger and bigger before us. Smoke from the cog train that goes up Washington billowed up in a black swirl as the train trudged up the mountain. The train whistle sounded loudly in the distance.

The highest wind speed ever recorded on Earth had occurred on this mountaintop. As we hiked along, it became easier to understand the unpredictable weather patterns up in the Whites. Even with the body heat generated from hiking, we needed rain pants and jackets in August. Many of the people we passed were bundled up with hats and gloves.

Since Souleman and I had both grown up in New England, we were familiar with the White Mountains and had visualized crossing them on our hike. We took what seemed like a million pictures in an attempt to capture the splendor of this part of the trail. As beautiful as the mountains were, our bodies ached from the physical challenge, and we both suspected this would be our last visit on foot to these imposing peaks. The rocks, steep climbs, and treacherous weather had left our muscles throbbing. Many times since the start of our hike in Georgia, we had stood together before beautiful vistas and promised or hoped we would be back to visit that particular spot. In the Whites, though, we stood together and expressed gratitude for the chance to see the sights, just that once, as we were pretty sure we would never return.

Finally, the mileage was behind us and we found ourselves inside the Lakes of the Clouds Hut (fondly called "Lakes of the Crowds" by thru-hikers due to its numerous guests). We had planned to stay in the "dungeon," a basement storage room that had been converted to a bunkroom. But one look into the gloomy dungeon was all I needed to decide that work-for-stay was a better option. We washed some dishes and silverware and wiped down tables for the croo. Our backs ached from standing at the sinks for so long, but at least we got to sleep inside and saved the money we would have spent on the dungeon.

When we had finished our chores, I was disappointed to learn it was only nine o'clock. I was exhausted and ready to sleep. Souleman and I sat in a corner of the hut flipping through our Handbook and talking in quiet voices about the rest of our hike. I rested my head on his shoulder and rubbed his back lazily as we waited for the clock to strike nine-thirty.

Many hikers raved about the huts, but it was frustrating for Souleman and me. We liked to be in control of when we ate, slept, and hiked. Given my consistently slow pace, I couldn't afford the extra time constraints of the huts. While I was thankful for the hut option, I was happy to be getting out of the Whites so that we could go back to sleeping at campsites and free shelters.

Breakfast leftovers were cold, clumpy bowls of oatmeal. Forcing myself to swallow the gelatinous calories, I had flashbacks to dreaded "oatmeal mornings" at Camp Bonnie Brae as a child. Sadly, unlike at camp, no one showed up to sing a silly song and make the oatmeal marginally more palatable. As soon as we had washed the breakfast dishes and completed our chores, we grabbed our already-packed packs and pushed out the door. From the entrance to Lakes of the Clouds Hut, Mount Washington wasn't even visible through the fog.

Climbing Mount Washington had seemed so important, yet in actuality, the only reason this summit was different from any other was because of its notoriety. The sky was so foggy as we ascended that we couldn't even see the giant lodge perched on top, much less a scenic view. The temperature, not accounting for wind chill, was twenty-nine degrees. We took the obligatory summit photo, though with the lack of visibility we could have been standing anywhere. It was so cold that we had to put on every single clothing item in our packs just to stand still for the photo.

I worked hard over the next 5.5 miles. The terrain was largely uphill, and I scaled rocks without complaint. I watched Mount Washington disappear behind me. The last three miles to the campsite were excruciating. My knees and ankles throbbed, and my thigh muscles quivered. Even the rocks of Pennsylvania had not been this brutal. Each step actually seemed dangerous because the rocks were precariously placed and unsteady. I was afraid to brace on my poles for fear I'd plummet to my death on a pointy rock below.

I stood balanced on a long, flat rock and paused to collect enough energy to keep going. I was grateful for the reliable grips on my shoes.

"Have you heard of the Barefoot Sisters?" I asked Souleman when he stopped beside me.

"I don't know."

"Supposedly, they hiked the trail barefoot. I think there's a book about it."

He studied the ground around us. "Wow."

"I'm struggling with boots on. How did they do it?"

"I have no idea."

Somehow, we made it over four mountains and more than fifteen miles to Gorham, New Hampshire, the following day. It was amazing how motivating the thoughts of town food and a bed could be. It helped that the final 1.5 miles were like a literal walk in the park. But the ridgeline that morning had been one of our harder climbs. It also rained much of the day, and we had to wear rain clothes and long-sleeved shirts to stay warm. Luckily, trudging through mud and water was not nearly as horrible when we knew we could dry off and warm up in town at the end of the day. The rain did, however, make the rocks more slippery and dangerous, and once again I pondered the rumor about the Barefoot Sisters.

When we arrived in Gorham, we checked in at a hostel and consumed enormous quantities of food at Burger King. Then, while Souleman stayed up talking with friends, I crawled into bed early. I was looking forward to a day to rest and repair my aching body. The Whites were truly magnificent, but their toughness had taken a toll on me. I hurt everywhere. My knees screamed, my feet pulsed, my back spasmed, and my hands throbbed from their constant death grip on my poles. I desperately needed a day to recover.

Though the Whites were supposedly the most difficult of the New England mountain ranges, we still had the similar Mahoosuc Range coming up in Maine. My body was worn out, but I knew we had less than three hundred miles to go, which meant less than two hundred miles before the Hundred-Mile Wilderness, the homestretch of the trail. Before I knew it, our adventure would be over. I stretched out my aching body and fell asleep prepared to embrace the rest of the journey.

Over a huge meal at the hostel, appropriately named the Thru-Hiker Breakfast, we planned our day.

"I'm tired of town chores." I told him.

"We don't have many towns left."

"True. Are you sad about that?"

"In some ways."

I sipped my coffee. "I think I'm just about ready to be done." The monotony of performing the same tasks in different towns was becoming exhausting. Truthfully, parts of the trail were wearing on me too. While the views were different every day, our routine was mostly unchanging: Get up. Eat. Hike. Eat. Do chores. Eat. Sleep. The constant movement, changes in location, packing and unpacking of gear, and lack of predictability were exhausting.

I was going to miss the views, the people, and being constantly surrounded by nature, but I was also beginning to look forward to the very different routine of non-trail life. Soon we would eat meals that consisted of more than one selection. We would wear a variety of clothes and shower daily. I would drink coffee every morning. *Mmm.* But we would also wake up to an alarm clock instead of nature. We would no longer have everything we needed attached to our backs. We would have to deal with the hassle of the Internet and cell phones. *Am I ready to go back to all that?*

"Let's just get through this town," said Souleman, interrupting my thoughts.

We accomplished all of our errands, including getting new tips for our hiking poles, which had taken a beating in the Whites. My tips had gotten bent, and Souleman's were completely worn off. Even with only three hundred miles left, we would need reliable poles to get us over the Mahoosucs. One section of that range was called the Endless Mile. It was rumored to consist of huge boulders that created such demanding obstacles that help from a partner was required. That one mile would supposedly take at least an hour to complete. I was looking forward to the challenge. It was hard to believe that in just one day we would be in Maine. *MAINE! The final state. We've almost done it!*

I felt the pull of Maine and was excited about crossing our last state line. On our way out of town we stopped at Pizza Hut. We got out our trusty old Wingfoot to create a schedule for the rest of the trail. This was the first time we had made a schedule that might accurately predict the end date of our journey. With only two town stops and three hundred miles remaining, Katahdin was now a reality. Rangeley and Monson were the only trail towns left where we planned to take zero days. Allowing for low mileage days and a zero in each of those towns, our predicted summit date was September 22—eight days before our target date.

However, my mom had graciously offered to meet us at Baxter State Park to drive us home, and the only two days she was unavailable were the 22 and 23. Since speeding up our schedule didn't seem practical, we would have to take a double zero somewhere in order to finish after September 23. Upon consulting Wingfoot again, we found that Gorham had the cheapest hotel rooms and the most food options.

We boxed up our leftover pizza and cinnamon sticks and headed to a hotel. This was our third night in Gorham and our third sleeping location. We had spent the first night in a hostel, which had left us craving privacy and quiet. We had spent the second night in a hotel that had all the amenities we needed. However, since we had already checked out when we realized we would be spending another night, we had to stay in a different hotel the third night. The third hotel was our best choice-it had everything we needed and was the most luxurious. By that point, we were pretty much experts on travel accommodations in Gorham, New Hampshire.

We stashed our packs and headed to the library to use the Internet. During our walk through town, we saw at least ten other hikers. Many were debating whether to leave or stay another night. Gorham seemed to be a trap for hikers. When we had arrived in town on Sunday night, a handful of hikers had already been in town since Thursday afternoon. I guess everyone needed some R&R after surviving the rough terrain in the Whites. And some hikers wanted to draw out their adventure as long as possible. Souleman and I planned to enjoy our bonus day and then push on toward Maine.

26

Where's the Toilet Paper?

On the last day of August, we entered our final state: Maine. *Oh my gosh, we made it. We're in the final state. Only two hundred and eighty one miles to go! We're going to make it to Katahdin.* My thoughts soared all day long. Sadly, my body did not follow suit. My pack seemed to weigh a hundred pounds, my back ached, and I just could not get a good pace going. It seemed that double zero days sometimes did me more harm than good. So much sedentary time had resulted in the inevitable "hiker hobble." As I determinedly pushed through the miles, my body readjusted to the familiar movement and I became more and more comfortable.

Despite my slow start, we hiked twelve miles and ended up at Full Goose Shelter, putting us five miles ahead of schedule. I watched Souleman stir instant potato mix into the boiling water.

"I'm not going to miss those," I told him.

"You didn't like them to begin with."

"True. But now I abhor them." I wrinkled my nose when he passed me my spork. "Which trail meal will you miss the least?"

"The chicken-flavored Lipton Noodles," he answered without hesitation. "I doubt I'll ever eat them again."

We ate in silence. Eating cold instant potatoes was almost unbearable. When Souleman had swallowed his last bite and licked his spork clean, he asked, "What part of real life are you most looking forward to?"

"A bed. With sheets and a real pillow. I'm so tired of sleeping confined in that mummy bag with my legs stuck together and my arms pinned at my sides." I smiled just picturing a real bed. "What about you?"

"Watching Red Sox games."

"Seriously? That's what you miss the most?"

"Yep."

I shook my head in amazement. *Not showers, food, or clean clothes. Not a bed or uncontaminated water. He misses baseball games. Men!*

259

I settled down in the tent and pulled my journal out of its worn Ziploc bag. Reflectively, I flipped back through the pages. We had experienced so much during our hike. I thought about all the differences between hikers: *Some go north; others go south. Some use internal frame packs; others use external ones. Some hike in a group; others hike alone. Some use poles; others do not. Some drink from Nalgene bottles; others prefer water bladders. Some are purists; others are blue-blazers.*

I smiled as I thought about the choices I had made over the course of my hike. I was proud I had always hiked heading north, carrying my full pack and following the white blazes. I was grateful to have found a hiking partner. My choices had been very different from those of other hikers, but I had successfully followed the advice to "hike my own hike."

As I tucked my journal back into its Ziploc, I had a thought. *As many differences as hikers have, I bet one thing that* all *hikers use is Ziploc bags.* These bags were so handy: they squeezed into any conceivable space in my pack, they contained and protected against moisture, and they were reusable and disposable. They came in all sizes—snack, sandwich, quart, gallon—and held any piece of gear imaginable. I wondered briefly how many Ziploc bags Souleman and I had used throughout our hike.

"What are you thinking about?" Souleman asked. I was sitting with my headlamp on, staring at the Handbook in its Ziploc.

"I'm wondering how many Ziploc bags we've used on our hike."

"A lot."

"I know. We should've bought stock in them. I'm seriously wondering how many, though. We keep almost everything in them." I held up the Handbook in its well-worn Ziploc as an example. We attempted to go through our bags and count: Ziplocs for food, for clothes, for our water purifier, for my journal, for dirty socks, and for our radios. We gave up counting at twenty-five.

At the end of the next day, we encountered Mahoosuc Notch, the area hikers refer to as the Endless Mile. It is widely recognized to be the most difficult mile of the entire Appalachian Trail. Hiking the Notch was a challenge right from the beginning. I began to scramble up a slick boulder and had made it about six feet when I fell. My pack weight propelled me backward, and I landed on my pack with my body completely surrounded by jagged rocks. I lay there stunned for a moment. When I swiveled my head, I saw that only inches from my skill was a large, pointy rock fragment. *Close call.* Despite all the rocks surrounding me, only my bottom had made contact with a sharp edge. *Shake it off. Keep going.*

A little further along, I slid on my stomach down a steep, slanted rock and just managed to catch my toe on another rock to avoid falling into a crevice below. *Steady.* I'm normally very independent while hiking, but in this section Souleman had to help me a few times, and I had to take my pack off twice and push or throw it ahead of me. Once, I found myself standing in front of a chasm that my stride could not straddle. Souleman saw me assessing the situation, picked me up (pack and all), and deposited me with a kiss between boulders on the other side.

The end of Mahoosuc Notch became especially treacherous because we had miscalculated how long it would take us to navigate the playground of rocks, and it had become dark. Another hiker named Lightweight had caught up with us, and the three of us worked together, using our headlamps to finish the last third of the Notch. We traversed some small, cave-like areas and crawled through spaces too small to fit through while wearing packs. *I wonder how many bugs, snakes, and rodents are hiding in here?* We climbed, stretched, wiggled, pushed, pulled, and sweated. It took over two hours, but somehow we survived. It was well after dark when we arrived at the campsite, and we went straight to bed without even considering preparing dinner.

September welcomed us with a steep climb up Mahoosuc Arm. The trail was even prettier than usual because the leaves were beginning to change color. Getting to enjoy the beautiful landscapes helped make the challenging terrain more tolerable. We took many food breaks since we had skipped dinner the night before.

Partway through the day, I was hiking along like usual, when suddenly I hit the ground. I scraped my wrists on the pebbles covering the trail before I rolled onto my side in the soft plants beside the trail.

"Brownie, are you ok?" Souleman's voice towered over me.

"Physically or emotionally?" I rotated my wrists gingerly. Finally I worked my way to a sitting position, and then struggled futilely to heft myself and my pack back up. "I'm stuck." My legs were sticking out straight in front of me.

"I've got you," Souleman said, grabbing my pack straps and lifting me to my feet.

I took inventory of my newest injuries: additional scrapes on both wrists, a swollen right wrist, and bloody knees. I brushed the pebbles off my hands. My falls were becoming more frequent, and my body displayed the evidence. Just in front of me was a sign that read "FRAGILE ALPINE VEGETATION: STAY ON THE PATH."

I waved my pole in the direction of the sign. "Great. Now I'm a klutz *and* a murderer."

Souleman smirked but wisely remained silent.

When I returned from getting water at the stream near Baldpate Lean-to that evening, Souleman immediately approached me at the picnic table.

"Where's the toilet paper?"

"In my pack." I lined up our full water bottles on the bench.

"Can I have it?" he asked, shifting from foot to foot in front of me.

"Just a second and I'll get it." I grabbed the MIOX.

"I, uh, need it now." He crossed his arms and rocked from side to side impatiently.

I climbed up into the shelter and got the toilet paper from my pack and tossed it at him.

A little while later, Souleman returned from the privy.

"One thousand, nine hundred and ten point two," I announced, looking up from the pot of Lipton Noodles I was stirring.

"What's that?"

"The number of miles we hiked before you used a privy."

He smiled and pumped his fist in the air. "Also the number of miles before I pooped in the woods."

"No way." I stopped stirring and stared.

"Way."

"You haven't pooped for thirteen states?" I stared at him with my spork frozen in midair.

"I always wait until town. That's why I always want to find a bathroom first thing." He grinned and nodded in self-satisfaction.

"Shut up! Sometimes we've been in the woods for as long as eight days."

"I know. Trust me, I know."

By seven o'clock the next morning, we were back on the trail. We quickly climbed both West and East Baldpate, scaling sheer rock faces with only haphazard cairns marking the way. The windy conditions and rocky terrain reminded me of video footage of astronauts walking on the moon. I even mimicked moon walking in an effort to elicit a few laughs. Despite the fog, the summits were spectacular, with views that seemed to last for miles. We could literally see clouds blowing by us.

After conquering the two balds, the terrain became much less grueling. We made good time to the road to Andover, Maine. Some section hikers we had met earlier had offered us a ride to town, which was a relief since hitchhiking was becoming more difficult as we traveled further north.

We made quick work of our town chores and were discussing plans to head out to the trail in the morning when we saw that the weather report forecasted heavy rain. Not surprisingly, we opted for a zero day. This change of plans meant I got to see Andre Agassi's last professional tennis match. As a tennis player and fan, this match was a monumental and emotional one to watch. Souleman and I spent the rest of the day relaxing: we ate breakfast at the diner, played Clue with Lichen and Car-bomb, and napped to the sound of rain pummeling our window. The endless torrent of water reassured us that we had made the right decision about rescheduling our time off.

When we left Andover, we saw thirteen other hikers headed toward Katahdin. *Where did these people come from?* For months the number of hikers had been thinning out. We had expected to arrive in Maine and be more or less alone. In fact, I think we were actually looking forward to the isolation before our return to society. Instead, we found ourselves in the middle of a throng of thru-hikers reminiscent of the original Georgia crowds.

About halfway through the afternoon, a group of slack-packing southbounders passed us. It seemed as if more and more hikers were slack-packing large sections of the trail—probably at least half of the hikers we saw each day were wearing floppy, nearly empty packs, or in some cases had no packs at all. Even though slack-packing would have unquestionably been faster and less taxing on my body, I would have felt like I was cheating. I had made it my goal to hike north, from Georgia to Maine, passing every single white blaze while wearing my pack on my back. *I've followed my self-inflicted rules this far. I'm not giving up now.*

Even though I was confident in my decisions, it was hard to watch other hikers pull ahead just because they could do more miles with lighter packs. I sometimes envied their faster pace and had to remind myself of my ultimate goal. *In a few weeks, I'll be able to stand on top of Katahdin and know that I stuck to my principles the entire way.* Many hikers would be summiting Katahdin that year, but I believed a very small number of those would do so as purists.

As I toted my full pack onward, we passed some spectacular views on Old Blue Mountain and the Bemis Range. The sky in Maine seemed to be a unique, crisp shade of blue. I loved gazing off mountaintops and seeing no evidence of humans— no houses, no billows of smog, and no power poles. Every vista seemed nostalgic as we realized how little time we had left to be surrounded by nature.

Along these ridges we were pleasantly surprised to see Mom and Windtalker again. We also heard that Lichen and Carbomb, who had gotten ahead of us, had slowed down because Lichen had hurt her knee. While we were concerned about her injury, we were excited at the prospect of seeing them again. Hiking with another couple had been a fun change of pace.

More and more signs indicated that our hike was nearing an end: only a few pages remained in our Handbook, and our gear seemed to be breaking down all at once. My food bag and the stuff sack for our tent each had a large hole in them—as did the mesh of the tent itself. My boots had multiple holes. My poles were all banged up, the hood to my pack had a few rips, and Souleman's pack was tearing along the seams. Not wanting to spend a bunch of money on gear with so few days left, we were patching equipment and making do. *What would we do without duct tape?*

Amazingly, we were still having new experiences so close to the end of our hike. That afternoon on Bemis Range, we heard a rustling in the trees to the left of the trail. I expected it to be another chipmunk or squirrel, but I stopped and put my finger to my lips just in case. Souleman came to a halt behind me. I tilted my head and listened intently as the rustling continued. I craned my neck looking all around, and Souleman stood beside me peering through the trees.

"It's a moose," he whispered as he put his finger to his lips.

"No way! Where?" I'd never seen a live moose before.

Souleman pointed between the trees off to our right.

"I can't see it! Where?" I was whispering too loud as I craned and leaned and stretched.

"I think you're looking too low. My car could drive through her legs. Look up."

"I can't see." I wiggled all around, standing on tiptoe, squatting, leaning. "I can't see!" I whispered fiercely. I was desperate not to miss my first real opportunity to see a moose. Finally, I caught sight of a brown figure through the leaves. "Oh! She *is* big. I can't see her head. Can you?"

"Yeah. Come here." He put his finger back up to his lips, awkwardly picked me up, pack and all, and lifted me high enough to see the moose's head.

"Oooooh!"

After a bit he set me back on the ground. "Did you see how big her ears were?" he asked me.

"No. Pick me up again?"

The moose's ears alone were easily three times the size of my hand. She was as large as an elephant but stretched her neck to get leaves like a giraffe. We stayed until she moved off into the woods, too far away for us to watch any longer.

"I saw a moose," I told Souleman.

He laughed. "I know. I saw it too."

"But it was my first moose." I planted a huge wet kiss on his lips and then skipped and twirled down the trail. "I saw a moose, I saw a moose, I saw a moose, hey, hey, hey, hey!"

The trail in Maine was horrendously muddy. If Pennsylvania was the "rock state," then Maine was the "mud state." Much of the ground was covered in thick, oozy mud. We had to hop from rock to branch to log in an effort to keep our shoes the slightest bit dry. In spite of the slippery terrain, I managed to remain upright all day without falling. A few of my scrapes and bruises were finally disappearing as we put more and more distance between us and the White Mountains.

For the first time since before the Whites, we were able to hike two miles per hour almost all day. My spirits were high, and Souleman and I laughed and talked as we ticked off the miles. About a mile after our encounter with the moose, I came to an abrupt stop where the trail passed between two trees. I turned to face Souleman.

"Another moose?" he asked, looking over my shoulder.

"Nope. A tollbooth."

"Really? Way out here?" He feigned shock.

I nodded, trying to keep a serious face. "Two dollars."

He leaned his poles against the tree, stuck his hands in his pockets, and pulled the linings out to show me they were empty. "I don't have any money."

I crossed my arms across my chest and scowled. "You can't pass without paying the toll. Rules are rules."

"Hmm . . . " He pretended to ponder this. "Would you take kisses instead?" He slid his hands through the gap between my lower back and my pack and pulled me against him. My arms slid around his neck, resting on his pack straps. His lips were salty.

I grinned the rest of the way to the shelter. *A moose and tollbooths—what a day.* I was shocked to find seven people already settled into the small space. This crowded shelter reminded me of the early tenting areas near shelters in Georgia, where sites had been filled to capacity and we had slept shoulder-to-shoulder with strangers. Despite our reservations about sleeping amongst a crowd, we were excited for the opportunity to put faces to many of the names we had been following in trail registers.

One of the hikers we met was Model-T, the author of *Walkin' on the Happy Side of Misery*, one of the first AT books I had purchased in preparation for my hike. I had spent many hours curled up on my dorm-room bed reading about his first thru-hike. Now he was on his fourth thru-hike. *A celebrity*. I followed him around for much of the evening, trying to be unobtrusive as I asked endless questions about writing and publishing a book. He answered every one of my inquiries patiently, and even gave me his email address in case I wanted to ask him more questions later.

The days were beginning to blur together. The routine of preparing our gear, hiking, eating, and walking had long since lost its novelty. I tried to focus on enjoying the views and the conversations because they were constantly new. Our ever-present fog curse continued to prevent us from seeing many of the sights. The following day, we summited Saddleback Mountain, which was supposed to have views of Mount Washington to the south and Mount Katahdin to the north. As expected, the view of both peaks was obscured by fog.

We reached the top of Saddleback Junior just as the daylight began to slip away. Evening had burned off some of the fog, and the colors were visible through the trees. Souleman climbed onto the tallest rock he could find and pulled me up next to him. Our sweaty clothes stuck to our skin and chilled us as the temperature dropped, so we huddled together on the exposed surface. He shifted and pushed me back onto the freezing rock. His body pressed against mine, creating at least the illusion of heat.

"We'll miss the end of the sunset," I mock-protested.

"There will be another one tomorrow," he said into my mouth. "And the next day." He kissed my neck. "And the next."

Above him, the colors in the sky faded from pastels, to earth tones, to black.

We hit the trail early the next day and pushed hard over South and North Crocker Mountains. The climbs were consistent and relatively challenging. I was struggling to keep up, and eventually I came to a stop and leaned on my poles.

"What time do you think it is?"

Souleman looked up at the sun. "Maybe nine o'clock."

On the trail, time mattered so little. We ate when we were hungry, took breaks when we were tired, slept when it was dark, and woke up when our bodies were ready—the actual time of day was irrelevant. Unfortunately, our stops in town were sometimes constrained by time. That day we had to be at the post office in Stratton, Maine, by eleven thirty. "Why don't you go on ahead? I don't think I can keep going this fast," I told him as I breathed heavily.

He studied me. "Are you sure?"

"Yeah. We have to get that mail drop before the post office closes today or we'll be stuck in town until Monday. I just don't think I can make it in time. You go on and I'll meet you in town."

"What about hitching?" He looked at me questioningly.

"I'll be ok."

He pulled on his beard. "Are you sure?"

"Yeah. I'm tough, remember?" *No. Not at all. I've never hitched alone and I'm scared.* I tried to smile convincingly.

"Ok. So I'll meet you in front of the post office?"

"Yep. I'll be right behind you." I nodded in fake confidence.

"Be careful."

"Always."

We kissed quickly and Souleman placed one more kiss on my forehead before heading off down the trail. He clicked his poles behind him and I tapped mine loudly in response: *I love you too.* He disappeared around a bend.

I tugged on my pack strap and started after him at my own pace. It had been a while since I had heard only my own footsteps on the trail. I settled into a rhythm and embraced the silence all around me. It had not been five minutes, though, before I heard the *step, click, step, click* of someone walking toward me using poles. When I looked up, I was surprised to see Souleman.

"I realized I had all the water and our purifier," he told me, slightly out of breath. "There's no way I was leaving you without any water."

"Oh, you're right. I totally forgot."

We typically tried to be conscious of the way we split the weight of our gear because of my previous foot pain and how much smaller I was. During the day, he often carried more of our water since it was so heavy. He traded me a full water bottle for an empty one, pecked me with a kiss on the forehead, and headed back up the trail.

I shifted my pack on my hips, re-balancing the weight of the water, and headed up the trail after him. I moved hurriedly because I was nervous about hitchhiking alone and didn't want to be too far behind. As I pumped my legs furiously up the next small incline, I looked up to see another figure coming toward me. Once again, it was Souleman.

I raised my eyebrows at him in confusion.

"I realized you had the Handbook, and I didn't know if I was supposed to hitch right or left at the road."

I shook my head with an amused smile. "We suck at this splitting-up thing." I leaned forward so that he could retrieve the Handbook from my pack's top compartment.

We leaned together over the worn pages and determined we needed to go left. With another kiss, he was off again. I settled once again into a comfortable but hurried pace.

It turned out that all of our worrying and strategizing had been in vain because Souleman was still trying to get a ride when I arrived at the road. A little fear had put a miraculous amount of speed into my step. I had maintained a pace of almost three miles an hour all morning.

I stationed myself at the road with my thumb out, while Souleman lurked near the woods. In no time, a truck pulled over and offered me a ride. Souleman came out of the woods, and the driver said he would do his best to get both of us to the post office on time. He was the owner of a bar/restaurant in town and invited us to check out his band that night.

When we pulled over on the curb in town, I left Souleman to gather our gear from the cab and ran into the post office. The clock over the counter read eleven twenty-six. *Just in time.*

The crowds in Stratton reminded me of our time in Damascus, Virginia. A large group of hikers crammed around tables in the one restaurant, gossiping and strategizing. We pulled up chairs and joined in. Later that night, when all of the sensible hikers had retired, Souleman and I walked across the street to the bar. The music was definitely not going to be topping billboard charts, but the people-watching provided first-rate entertainment. Overalls, camo pants, baseball caps, leather miniskirts, tattered jeans, and plaid flannel shirts characterized the eclectic crowd. It was perfectly Maine.

The next day was scheduled to be our last zero day of the trail. With a little coercion, Carbomb and Lichen and Burner and Feng Shui agreed to stay in town too. Ideally, this meant our schedules would be aligned to summit together.

The next day was September 11. Before I even got out of bed, I flipped on the TV. Patriotic songs filled the room as I settled on a station playing a memorial program for the 9/11 terrorist attacks. Watching the too familiar images of the World Trade Center towers collapsing and emergency responders swarming the city, chills prickled down my spine. Like most people, I knew exactly where I had been at this time five years ago: it had been my first day of classes at Furman University. I had returned from my first-ever college lecture to find my dorm in mass chaos. People were crying in the stairwell. A guy was dialing his phone over and over on the landing. *What is going on?* When I had reached my hall, all of the girls were in one room staring at a TV. That was when I had seen the first image. A plane had crashed into the twin towers. I remembered watching the building burn as I dug out my phone. *My dad is on a plane.* I had dialed Dad. No answer. I had dialed Mom. No answer. It had taken almost four hours before I was able to connect with my mom on instant messenger and learn that my dad was safe. His plane had been grounded in Kansas.

I turned my eyes from the TV and stared at my half-full pack on the floor. On 9/11 I had been eleven hundred miles from my family when disaster struck our country. For the first time I had wondered what I was doing so far from home. Now, five years later, I was again far away from my family. But instead of heading off to my first day of classes, I was about to hike the last stretch of trail before the Hundred-Mile Wilderness. *Let's do this.*

I felt terribly nostalgic as I realized I had precious few mornings left to stuff my life into a backpack. We ate breakfast with Carbomb and Lichen, and then the four of us hitched back to the woods. It was somewhat slow going with our town-heavy packs, but we had great views off Bigelow Range. Model-T arrived as we were posing for pictures and pointed out our first official view—albeit so far in the distance it was hard to know what we were seeing—of Katahdin. The end, literally, was in sight. *That's it. The end. We are truly, honestly, for-real, almost done.*

As the day progressed, we crossed the two thousand-mile mark not once, not twice, but *three* times. Each time, a sign at a road crossing claimed we had hiked two thousand miles. The third marker was an arrangement of sticks on a road that spelled out the numbers "2-0-0-0." We took a snapshot of the numbers surrounded by one of each of our trail-worn boots.

This is getting real. We had no more state lines to cross, only one more trail town to visit, and since we were defining our hike by Wingfoot's book, fewer than seven Handbook pages remaining. We were getting so close to the Hundred-Mile Wilderness—essentially the victory lap. I had dreamed about the Hundred-Mile Wilderness since I first decided I wanted to hike the Appalachian Trail. It was the most remote section of the trail, and I was excited to be so far from civilization. Hiking one hundred miles with nothing but the supplies on my back—and no opportunity to bail if the going got tough—would prove once and for all that I could survive in the woods.

As we hiked along, we laughed and talked and even made up silly song lyrics about trail life. Since the four of us had so much fun hiking together, we decided to try to coordinate our mileage for the rest of the trip. As the day wound down, we were hiking on an old fire service road when we found ourselves ready to stop for the night. There were no campsites nearby and none marked in our Handbook.

I stared glumly at the rocky, steep trail beyond the road.

"We could just camp right here," Carbomb suggested.

"On the road?" Souleman asked.

"Sure. I doubt there'll be any cars."

I kicked at a dried tire track. "Let's at least move away from this curve."

We pitched our tents within feet of each other in the middle of a long straightaway on the road. *At least a car would have a long time to see us and slow down.* I was standing on dried tracks when I hammered our tent stakes into the ground.

We survived the night without being run over, and the four of us headed out together in the morning. Partway into the day, as I was leading, we came to an abrupt stop. The others leaned around me to see what was going on. A two-by-four plank lay across a wide stream in front of us. We saw a white blaze on the other side of the water. I kicked at the board with my toe and found that it was not secured in any fashion.

"Do you think this is really how we're supposed to cross?" Lichen asked.

"It sure doesn't look safe." I nudged it again with my toe.

"Let's check for other options," Carbomb suggested.

We split up and looked for a distance up and down the stream. Neither direction revealed a crossable route. The four of us stood in front of the plank once again.

"Well, I guess we have no choice," I declared, and hopped up on the plank without further conversation. My heart hammered in my chest, and my legs wobbled underneath me as I walked very quickly across to the other side. With a little bow, I motioned Lichen over.

It was amazing to consider the dangerous climbs and crossings that we undertook without question simply because the blazes told us to do so. Those blazes had dictated a lot about our lives during our months on the trail, and I had grown to find comfort in each splotch of white paint. *I don't have to decide where to go—the blazes tell me.*

We made up silly songs and talked as we kept hiking. That afternoon we reached the Kennebec River, where we caught up with Burner and Feng Shui.

"We're next in line to cross," Burner told us, gesturing at a canoe that was slowly making its way back across the water.

We knew from Wingfoot that the trail crosses the Kennebec River just below a dam. A thru-hiker had drowned in 1985 during a crossing attempt when water levels had risen too quickly. The unpredictable nature of the river and dangerousness of the crossing had inspired the Appalachian Trail Conservancy to create a safer alternative to wading.

Just then, the "ferry," which was actually a canoe operated by a nearby resident named Steve Longley, pulled up on shore. Steve's white-blazed canoe had become the official AT route. During certain hours each day, Steve transported hikers and their gear across the river. We watched as Burner and Feng Shui donned bright orange life jackets and then climbed in. The water level rose visibly as we watched them cross.

Soon Steve returned, and Souleman and I prepared for our turn to cross. After we had secured our life vests, he helped me into the canoe. I sat at the bottom of the canoe, directly on top of the white blaze, and he loaded our packs on either side of me. Cold water soaked the seat of my pants, but I didn't complain. I would have gotten much wetter trying to cross the river on my own. Souleman picked up his paddle and used strong, confident strokes to help Steve paddle us across. We thanked him and waved goodbye as he turned to fetch Lichen and Carbomb. *I wonder how many times he does this every year?*

The trail had been flat and smooth before the river, but afterward it went steadily up and became rocky and root covered. Compared to many of the previous sections we had hiked, though, it was wonderful. Souleman and I stopped many times for tollbooths, and despite the uneven terrain, we still hiked the seven miles to Pleasant Pond Lean-to without needing to pull out our headlamps.

A steady drizzle began just as we saw the shelter sign and continued for most of the night. I greatly appreciated that everyone squeezed together to make room for us in the shelter. No one, even a hiker who has come two thousand miles, wants to be forced to tent in the rain. Surprisingly, the crowded shelter wasn't terribly uncomfortable, and I slept well. I did have to get up once in the night to go to the bathroom, however.

Trying not to wake anyone else, I snaked my hand out of my sleeping bag to reach for the headlamp that was stashed above my head. I slipped it around my neck but didn't turn it on yet, because I knew the beam would wake others. I held my breath, cringing at the noise as I undid the zipper of my sleeping bag halfway. Being careful not to bump Souleman or the hiker on my other side, I wiggled my hips and kicked my feet in an attempt to escape the confines of the bag. Finally free, I shivered in the cold Maine air while I felt for my Crocs. *Eww. What did I just touch?* I angled my head away from the other hikers and snapped my light on. *There they are.* I slid my feet into my Crocs and tried to stand up smoothly on my sore feet. I narrowly missed stepping on someone when I lost my balance.

Finally, I stepped gingerly off the sleeping platform and walked away into the trees to find a spot to relieve my bladder. Only seconds later, I reversed the process—walking back to the shelter, stepping up onto the creaky platform, navigating around sleeping hikers while trying to keep my headlamp beam out of their faces, sliding off my Crocs, scooting onto my sleeping pad and into my mummy bag, and snuggling up against Souleman. *Ten more days. Then I'll be able to get up and walk across the carpet to a real bathroom, where I can turn on a light and flush when I'm finished.*

Fall had begun in Maine. The leaves were turning from green to vibrant reds, yellows, and oranges. I stumbled across one leaf that was green with a splash of red in the middle. I imagined that if I remained standing there for a few minutes, I might actually be able to watch the color finish spreading over the whole leaf. The greys of winter had given way to the greens of summer, which were now changing to the reds of fall. The air was crisper, the leaves were ablaze with color, and the ground was even starting to have frost in the mornings.

Recently, it had been as cold as thirty-eight degrees when we packed up at daybreak. The rapid approach of winter weather solidified my relief that our hike was almost done. I did not want to experience winter on the trail.

I tried to savor each moment of the day's miles because I knew we had fewer and fewer trail days left. The following morning, we would walk into our last trail town: Monson, Maine. After that remained only the Hundred-Mile Wilderness and Katahdin. *How did it get to be so close to the end? Have I accomplished what I wanted on this hike? What will I do with myself now?* I felt pressure to make my next step something big.

I stopped to pull out a snack.

"You know one part of the trail I *am* going to miss?" I asked.

"What's that?"

"Snickers." I unwrapped the candy bar and took a huge bite. "We're going to have to give these up." It was my second one of the day.

Souleman came to a dead stop on the trail and widened his eyes in horror.

I crammed a third of the king-sized bar into my mouth. I winked as I said, "If I get a big belly after the trail, I don't want it to be from candy."

"Maybe we should get jobs before we work on growing your belly."

I sighed dramatically, but then my tone became serious. "We have so much to figure out. Where to work. Where to live. Are you worried?"

"Of course. But I'm not ready to think about it yet." He hooked his finger under my chin and turned my face toward him. "We have one hundred and twenty miles left. We can't figure everything out until we're off the trail. So, let's enjoy it for now. And when we've summited Katahdin—when we're two-thousand milers—we'll figure it all out. Just relax for now."

"I'll try." *Easier said than done.*

We barreled onto the road to Monson after 16.5 miles of hiking. My raw feet were screaming. While Souleman stuck out his thumb for a hitch, I sat on the edge of the road and pulled off my soaked trail shoes. A river ford a couple of miles back had been the final straw for my abused feet. I wrung out at least a cup of water from my socks and then squished out more from my shoes. The pre-wrap and duct tape covering my raw, red skin were caked in mud and sock fuzz. I put my wet socks back on and stuffed each wet, swollen foot into a Croc.

We made it to town just before four o'clock, right before the Monson post office closed. Souleman and I had four packages and two letters waiting for us. Balancing our collection of packages, our poles, and our packs, we walked through town to a hostel called Shaw's Lodging, where we shared a room with Lichen and Carbomb.

After we had each taken a steaming shower, we headed to a local restaurant for dinner. I ordered a cheeseburger, my town staple, and even tried a blueberry beer from a local brewery.

"Did you just order beer?" Souleman asked me incredulously.

"I did."

"But you don't like beer."

"I know. But I drank my first-ever whole beer in our first trail town, so I thought it was fitting to try to drink one in our last."

When my beer arrived, Souleman clicked his bottle against mine. "Cheers." He watched in amusement as I took a tentative sip. "Well?"

I cleared my throat. "It's official. Two thousand miles later, beer is still awful."

It wasn't only the beer that was off-putting to me, though; none of the food tasted right either. I merely picked at my meal while the others devoured everything in sight. I looked around nostalgically. *This is our last town. Our last restaurant meal as hikers. Our last hostel. Our last resupply.* The waitress stopped by to deliver more drinks, and the scent of her soap and perfume wafted in our direction. *Everything is about to change.*

"Brownie, what's wrong with your burger?" Souleman leaned over and asked me quietly.

"Nothing. I just don't really want it."

"Is it cooked ok?" He knew I was picky about my meat being well done.

"It's fine. I just can't seem to eat it."

He wrinkled his face in concern. "You need to eat."

"I know." I pulled a tiny piece of cheese off the edge and popped it into my mouth.

"If you aren't going to eat that, order something else. You have to eat. We have the Hundred-Mile Wilderness coming up, and we have to finish strong." He handed me a menu.

I never ate my burger or ordered more food. I figured I was too excited to eat. When we went to bed that night, I whispered to Souleman and tossed and turned. Finally, he dozed off and I could hear Lichen and Carbomb breathing rhythmically across the room. I lay awake worrying they would all be rested and I would be tired for the end of our hike.

I must have finally dozed off because I woke up at two o'clock in the morning to a searing stomach pain. Barely suppressing the urge to moan out loud, I curled into the fetal position. The pain tore through my body over and over, and I broke out in a cold sweat. I was completely miserable and was afraid I might be keeping everyone else in the room awake, too.

I climbed over Souleman as delicately as I could and tiptoed to the door. I flinched when the door hinges squeaked, but no one woke up. Stopping twice to double over in agony, I hurried down the hall to the bathroom. I must have made that trip to the bathroom more than ten times during the night. I had incredibly painful diarrhea and vomited until I could do nothing but dry heave. *Please don't let this be giardia.* My body was so exhausted that I finally lay down on the filthy floor in the community bathroom and fell asleep with my face pressed against the cold tile.

The following day was our final zero day, which would give me an opportunity to recover. Souleman, Lichen, and Carbomb had all slept soundly and were surprised to learn I had been sick. We had planned to go to a trail-angel-sponsored hiker feed—a feast to fill us up before finishing the trail—in Caratunk, Maine, but I was not feeling up to it. I tried halfheartedly to get Souleman to go along without me, but he refused. Selfishly, I was glad he had decided to stay—I had wanted him by my side because I was completely miserable.

We watched TV and relaxed for most of the day. I tried to eat some bland foods, but they didn't stay with me for very long. It was awful to be so sick away from home. Since the bathrooms were shared among many guests, I never knew if I would be able to get into one right away. The doors in the house were old and thin, so noises were not private. It was an awkward place to be ill, though everyone was as kind to me as possible. Every time I threw up or had diarrhea, I worried about the energy I was losing.

After a day of rest and a good night's sleep, I still woke up sick. I couldn't keep any food inside me. Even a banana went straight through. My body was tired and weak. Too Much, a nurse, and Enuff, an ER doctor, were also at the hostel and began checking on me regularly. Enuff's recommendation was that for three days I should just let my body try to eliminate whatever was bothering it. If I was still sick after that, I should see a doctor. I reasoned that I was on day two.

That morning, Lichen and Carbomb packed up their gear and headed back to the trail. Souleman and I had enjoyed hiking with them so much and had really hoped to summit Katahdin as a foursome. We hugged our friends goodbye and watched out the window as they walked away. Once again our plans had been sabotaged, and once again I was the one preventing our progress. Dejectedly, Souleman and I lay curled in opposite directions like mirrored bookends, with only our backs touching.

Over an hour later, someone knocked on our door. Souleman mumbled, "Come in."

I didn't even turn to look because I assumed it would be a housekeeper wanting to clean the room. The door creaked open.

"Oh!" Souleman exclaimed.

I turned around to see what was so surprising. Lichen and Carbomb were standing in the doorway.

"We got to the trailhead and both of us sat down," Carbomb said. "We just sat there without talking for like half an hour."

"Yeah, and then we finally talked and neither of us wanted to go on without you guys. We thought maybe Brownie would get better by tomorrow, so we just came back." Lichen plopped down on the bed opposite us with a hopeful smile. *They did this for me?*

Souleman pepped right up. I knew I had to be better in the morning or I would feel awful that Lichen and Carbomb had come back to wait for me. Plus, I was getting terrible cabin fever and was beginning to blame myself for once again holding Souleman back. I pictured the four of us standing on top of Katahdin and willed my white blood cells to do their job.

I woke up on the third morning in Monson and was devastated to realize that I still felt under the weather. Once again, we waved a sad goodbye to Lichen and Carbomb. The sadness was worse this time because I knew I'd never see them again, and they would summit Katahdin without us. I had been sick for long enough—I had to get treatment. With the help of a trail angel named Ilene, Souleman and I got to the hospital, where the doctor prescribed medicine and told me to stick to a bland diet.

With my prescription and a grocery bag of bland, stomach-friendly foods in hand, we checked back in to a private room at Shaw's. Souleman had just destroyed me at a game of checkers when suddenly I broke out in a sweat that went across my forehead and soaked the back of my shirt. My face was burning up and I couldn't stop shaking. I was so queasy that I finally ended up vomiting. As soon as I stopped heaving, I curled up and started crying.

"I'm sorry." Tears trickled down my face.

"Brownie, what's wrong?" Souleman sat down on the bed beside me.

"I'm so (sob) sorry."

"What? Why are you sorry?" His cool hand touched my hot forehead.

"I'm (sob) holding (sob) you back." It was like a repeat of our conversation when we had left the trail the previous year in Pennsylvania. I was crying so hard that I could barely get the words out. "I'm always (sob) holding you back. You have to hike slower because of (sob) me. You have to take more breaks because of (sob) me. You have to carry more weight because of (sob) me. And now (sob) you can't even finish the damn trail because of (sob) me. I'm ruining your (sob) hike. I'm too weak and too sick and my body doesn't want me to do this (sob) stupid trail."

He lay down behind me and curled his body around mine. "This is *our* hike. *We* have made it this far. *We* will finish." He stroked his hand across my damp forehead and held me until I quit shaking.

"I can't believe we're stuck in this stupid town with only eight hiking days until Katahdin. I'm going crazy. I just want to hike!" I shook my head in disgust. "Ugh, I hate this."

"Katahdin isn't going anywhere." He wiped the tears off my cheeks and pulled on my hand. "Come on. Let's go for a walk. I think it'll make you feel better."

We walked hand in hand through the one main street of town. We had spent so much time in Monson that we were practically locals. We had committed to memory the menus of the two restaurants and contents of the two stores' shelves. Some of the residents even knew us by name.

"Hey, Brownie," the man behind the counter at the drug store called out. "You feeling any better?"

I shook my head sadly.

"Brownie! Souleman!" the librarian greeted us.

We checked our email at the library and found out that John, Souleman's best friend and the best man from our wedding, was living ten minutes from Monson. John moves around frequently, and Souleman had had a difficult time keeping track of him during our travels. We couldn't believe he had been so close.

After a quick phone call, John picked us up and took us to his uncle's cabin. The house was a converted barn that his uncle had restored himself. It was very rustic but at least less crowded than the hostel. Souleman was thrilled to see John, which took the edge off my guilt at having slowed our progress. John and his girlfriend, Lauren, cooked and played cards with us that night.

The next day, we spent a lazy day watching movies and resting while Lauren and John were at work. By afternoon, my fever was gone, and my only remaining ailment was a sore throat. John built a fire outside that evening and cooked burgers, chicken, and corn. I ate heartily and waited nervously to see how my body would react. For the first time since arriving in town, I kept all of the food down and even managed to eat some sherbet.

I knew that one meal would not be enough to build my strength back. I had to be strong enough to tackle the Hundred-Mile Wilderness when we returned to the trail. For the entire hundred miles, we would have no bailout points if I relapsed.

The next day, I rested and ate more. Desperate to get back outside, I convinced Souleman to walk with me to check out the cows and pigs on the farm. The short walk exhausted me. *How will I make it a hundred miles carrying my pack if I can't make it across the back yard empty-handed?* Tearful and angry, I collapsed into bed.

27

One Hell of a Hike

I finally felt strong enough to hike the last 114.5 miles. John drove us to the trail-head and snapped our pictures by the Appalachian Trail sign. As I buckled my pack across my hips, I had to tighten the straps. I'd lost weight. My pack was extra-heavy since it contained enough food to last through the Hundred-Mile Wilderness. I toyed with my shoulder straps to distribute the weight.

"Are you sure I can't take some of your pack weight?"

Souleman had tried to get me to give him some weight when we were packing at the house.

"I've carried it this far. I have to finish it out."

"Man, you're stubborn." He rolled his eyes in exasperation.

"No, I'm tough."

"This would be an ok time to be delicate."

I shook my head. "I've got this. I've carried my full pack over two thousand miles. I can finish it out." *Even if I have to crawl.*

In spite of my heavy pack, it was wonderful to be back on the trail. In the five days we had been away, fall had officially arrived. The air was crisp, the colors were magnificent, and everything around us was beautiful. Bright, crunchy, fresh-fallen leaves covered the trail and made loud rustling and crunching noises as we walked. I kicked the leaves up with my hiking poles and stomped them with my shoes to embrace the crisp fall sounds.

"Are you sad we won't summit with anyone we know?" I asked Souleman that afternoon.

"Not really." He shook his head thoughtfully. "I'll summit with you. We took our first steps on the Appalachian Trail together, and we'll take our last steps on it together, too."

"True. And we will have gone from hardly knowing each other to being hus-band and wife."

"That's one hell of a hike." He tapped his poles together.

"Yeah. That *is* one hell of a hike." I tapped my poles back and saw him smile as I glanced over my shoulder.

We forded multiple streams over the course of the day, and I was grateful for sunny, mild weather because the water was frigid. I had expected to detest fording rivers since I hate being cold and wet, but it was actually sort of fun as long as I mentally prepped myself for the icy temperatures ahead of time. The adrenaline rush from balancing on slippery rocks also made the cold less noticeable.

One river we came to was wide with a swift current. We stopped again and pulled off our shoes. By that point, we had a system. We zipped off our pants legs and pulled off our socks and shoes before donning our Crocs. Then we stuffed our socks and pants legs into our boots, tied the laces together, and looped the smelly shoes around our necks.

Souleman crossed first. I rubbed my hands up and down my cold legs as I waited for him to get a few steps out. Gritting my teeth, I hurried into the cold water. The first few steps took my breath away. The far bank seemed to get farther away as I struggled across the slippery bottom, fighting the strong current that was trying to pull me downstream. I planted my poles as far out to my sides as possible and leaned forward to fight the pull of the water.

As I neared the middle of the river, water lapped at the edges of my shorts. Unconsciously, I rose up on tiptoe to avoid the frigid waters. The reduced surface area on the slippery river bottom sent me two giant steps to the side. As I fought to regain my balance, water soaked halfway up my shorts. I worried my pack might get splashed, but it stayed dry under its rain cover.

Finally, we both made it across and stopped on the far bank to dry off and put our shoes back on. As I rubbed circulation back into my goose-bump-covered legs, I noticed an unknown hiker appear across the water. He stopped, removed his boots, slid his sandals on, and began crossing the stream. His pack was huge, and he teetered back and forth in the swift current trying to keep his balance. When he was about halfway across, I noticed that his hiking boots were still sitting on a rock at the far shore.

I waved my arms and shouted, trying unsuccessfully to catch his attention. When the hiker stepped onto the bank on our side of the river, I walked over and introduced myself.

"Hey, I'm Brownie."

He introduced himself as Sleepy.

"I hate to be the bearer of bad news, especially when we just met, but you, um, left your boots over there." I pointed across the river.

He slammed his hand into his forehead and cussed. After shedding his pack, he painstakingly made his way back across to rescue his boots. My legs were still tingling from the coldness of the crossing, so I knew he had to be miserable going back across a second time.

On the far side, he stamped his feet and ran his hands up and down his wet legs. I could see his mouth moving but couldn't hear a word. Given the litany of curses he had unleashed on our side of the river, I could only assume it was more of the same. Looping his boots around his neck by their laces, he started back toward us.

I yelled encouragement as he sluggishly progressed across the freezing river. When he had gotten about two-thirds of the way back, I watched him wobble forward, then throw his arms out to the side and lean backward to right himself. He must have realized he had overcorrected because his hands started waving feverishly, and he yelled out as he pitched forward into the icy water in what seemed like slow motion.

The hiker was submerged up to mid-chest, and his look of shock was evident even from our distance. The boots that he had worked so valiantly to keep dry had plunged right into the water. I tried half-heartedly to suppress a snicker but ended up doubled over laughing, holding my stomach. Souleman followed suit.

When the hiker reached the shore, he was waving his arms and cussing exuberantly. He flung his soaked boots to the ground, kicked them with his bare feet, and then hopped around holding his toes. The pain must have really set him off because he started throwing anything he could get his hands on. He danced around barefoot for quite some time, cussing and throwing his poles, rocks, and sticks. As his fit subsided, we said a quiet goodbye.

Once we set up camp, I barely made it through chores before succumbing to sleep in our tent. I was glad for the protection from the wind and cold that our tent and my sleeping bag provided. While I would miss the fresh air, the open space, and the night calmness we had come to appreciate on the trail, I knew I would enjoy sleeping in a bed at home instead of a mummy sleeping bag. In bed, I could regain the movement of my arms and legs at night and not be trapped in a stifling cocoon.

The Appalachian Trail had been tough, and it had taken a lot out of me. I had experienced frustration, anger, defeat, and dejection, but more often excitement, joy, awe, and delight. As John David, the minister at our wedding, had predicted in his homily, we had been through the deepest valleys of despair and the tallest mountains of joy on the trail. Together, though, we had almost done it. In six days, we would complete our journey and achieve a dream. I had genuinely considered quitting in Monson when I had become so sick, but back out in the woods, I was grateful that Souleman had pushed me to finish.

"Wake up, sleepyhead."

I moaned and pulled my head further into my sleeping bag. "I don't want to."

"Come on," Souleman prodded me. "We need to hit the trail soon. We have a long day ahead of us."

"Is it cold?"

"Yes." He pressed his lips into a straight line and nodded. "And we have to ford a river first thing. But the sooner we start hiking, the faster it will be over. Come on. I'll break the tent down while you pack our bags."

Drowsily, I sat up and spun my pigtails into buns on the top of my head. Outside the protection of my sleeping bag, the cold air slapped me awake. I layered my warm clothes on and moved around our campsite stuffing various gear items into their assigned spots.

Barely past our campsite was the river. I unlaced the shoes I had just put on and slid back into my Crocs. Gritting my teeth, I planted my poles and stepped into the water. It was the coldest water I had ever had to put a part of my body into. All it lacked were ice cubes. The water was so frigid, it was actually painful. *How can my feet be numb and hurting at the same time?* Luckily, the water reached only mid-calf at the deepest point. I was too cold to even complain.

After the ford, we covered about three miles fairly quickly. Then it started drizzling. As we snacked at the first shelter, it started raining really hard. We secured our pack covers and kept trucking over four mountains. On top of White Cap, we were practically blown off the side of the mountain. I would pick up my foot to take a step, and before I could put it back down, it would be blown to the side of where I had planned to place it. Rain whipped mercilessly into our faces. White Cap was rumored to have a great view of Katahdin, but of course we saw nothing. It seemed to be a trail-long curse for us to miss nearly every single mountaintop view between Georgia and Maine.

At the next shelter, we decided to eat lunch standing up. I just knew that if we stopped for long enough to get warm and comfortable, I wouldn't want to continue. We were soaked, freezing, and wanted to hurry up and hike the final four miles. My fingers were so cold they looked almost translucent, and my nose and ears had turned bright red.

We ate giant Rice Krispies Treats and bit off hunks of cheese while standing in the part of the shelter most protected from the wind. I even left my pack on so that it would shield me from the wind. Resolutely, I tucked my chin into my chest as I chewed. As soon as we had taken the edge off our hunger, we quickly moved on. We completed the last four miles in ninety minutes in spite of the cold, rain, wind, and mud.

To distract ourselves from how uncomfortable we were, we tried to carry on a conversation over the sound of rain hitting the hoods of our windbreakers.

"Brownie, do you think you'll be happy or sad when we finish the trail?" Souleman asked me as we trudged along.

"Yes," I said confidently as I stepped directly in a giant puddle.

"It was a choice."

"I know. I choose both. Happy and sad. Happy we finished; sad it's over. Happy I got to spend so much time with you; sad I won't get to see you all day, every day anymore." I splashed through puddles noisily as I answered.

"Me too."

"I'll miss being able to have a plan and have no plan at the same time. And always working toward a goal."

Souleman slid a little in the mud. After he recovered, he said, "Well, we'll just have to make another goal."

"Like what?"

"The forty-eight four-thousands in New Hampshire? The Hundred Highest in New England?"

I jumped in, suggesting, "The tallest mountain in each state? Visiting every national park?" *Will I ever want any of those as badly as I wanted to hike the AT? Will I ever be able to plan enough time off work to accomplish another goal like this?*

According to Souleman's radio, the high temperature that day was fifty-six degrees. Together with the rain and wind, it was hypothermia weather. Luckily, the rain encouraged us to keep moving quickly, which allowed us to generate more body heat. When we arrived at the shelter, a hiker we had recently met by the name of Puffy Nipples was already building a fire.

I sat on the ledge of the shelter and shed my rain-soaked pack. I knew we had camp chores to complete, but I had to remove my hiking shoes immediately. The question was not *whether* I had blisters, but *how many* I had. I wrestled off my muddy shoes and peeled my socks from my feet. A layer of skin sloughed off with one sock. I held up the strip of skin in awe, then gingerly examined my feet. Red, raw, slimy spots covered each one. I cleaned the tender skin as best as I could and then wrapped them in athletic tape and duct tape before putting on my only dry pair of socks. I slid my dry socks into my wet Crocs and uncomfortably hobbled around the shelter.

After a dinner of macaroni and cheese, we stood shoulder-to-shoulder in front of the fire and rotated our bodies to dry our clothes. *How many more nights will we get to share in front of a fire?* Once I was mostly dry, I mated my sleeping bag with Souleman's and hoped that our combined body heat would finish drying our clothes and keep us warm through the night.

In the morning my feet were still raw, and my inner thighs had developed scabs where the wet material from my pants had chafed against my skin. Perhaps to make up for the pain I was in, the terrain that day was pleasant. I daydreamed about soft, dry cotton as I walked.

During the first few miles we had a real treat: we saw *three* moose. A mama and a baby moose were playing in the water while the daddy moose watched over them from the shore. I wanted to get a photo, but the mama must have heard me because she started making a warning noise and ushered the baby away. We quietly moved up the trail, and the mama and baby ended up walking right toward us. If we had been able to get our camera out quickly enough, we would have had an awesome photo. We tried to follow them, but it was as if they suddenly vanished.

How do such large animals move so quietly?

"I didn't know moose made noises," I told Souleman.

"I don't think I knew that either."

"You know, my mom thinks moose are mythical," I said, looking wistfully off in the direction they had disappeared.

"What do you mean?"

"Well, my parents have that cabin in Vermont, and she hears about other people seeing moose all the time, but she's never seen one herself. She jokes that they're made up to attract tourists."

He laughed. "And we didn't even get a picture to show her. Maybe your mom needs to hike the AT."

"Riiiiiiiight."

Because that section of the trail was full of muddy areas and fragile vegetation, we crossed many bog bridges—trees that had been cut in half lengthwise and laid flat-side-up to create walking platforms. Sometimes these bog bridges were single file, and other times they had been placed two-by-two to allow one platform for each foot. The idea was to keep hikers off of the vegetation. While I valued protecting wildlife, I was quickly learning to hate bog bridges and was convinced that the things were dangerous. They were inevitably wet and slippery, and no matter how carefully I stepped, it was easy to fall.

With only two days remaining before summit day, we finally and definitively saw Katahdin—twice. Not a wimpy, "that-might-be-it-over-there-behind-that-mountain-covered-with-a-cloud" kind of view like we had seen days before. First, while standing by a pond, Model-T confirmed that what we were seeing in the distance was definitely Katahdin and pointed out different peaks for us. *We will be standing on top of that peak, looking back over here in a few days.* It felt like seeing the finish line at the end of a marathon; I wanted to sprint the final leg.

Later that day, we summited a mountain and had another unmistakable view. Katahdin was incredible, even from a distance. According to Model-T, climbing Katahdin was equivalent to climbing a 14,000-foot mountain in the Rockies because it is so high and barren and has such unpredictable weather patterns. *What do you bet we miss another view?*

It had been a while since we had spent time around a group of hikers, but that afternoon two thru-hikers passed us. Souleman asked if anyone else was nearby, and they listed about ten people who were behind them on the way to the same shelter. At least that many hikers passed us over the next four miles. We later found out that a huge crowd had stayed at White House Landing, the stopping point near the midpoint of the Hundred-Mile Wilderness. Originally, there had been nowhere to stop during this hundred-mile stretch, but White House Landing had since opened as an option for hikers. Since the novelty of the Hundred-Mile Wilderness had become so widespread, many hikers chose to tackle the mileage without stopping. We were among that crowd and had leap-frogged past the hikers who had stopped.

Now we certainly wouldn't have to worry about summiting alone. Instead, we would have to worry about getting spots at The Birches campsite. Thru-hikers—defined by Baxter State Park as hikers who have come through the Hundred-Mile Wilderness—are permitted to sleep in only one area of the park before summiting Katahdin, unless they have a prior reservation. Since only twelve people can sleep there each night, a race for spots can ensue.

As the days and hours of our hike wound down, I tried to memorize every view, every feeling, and every smell in order to imprint the experience more firmly on my brain. We passed streams and lakes with beautiful vistas, and I basked in the gorgeousness of Maine. The terrain that day was fairly flat, though the trail was covered with rocks and roots. Thanks to sunny skies and cool temperatures, I barely broke a sweat all day even though we hiked fifteen miles.

That afternoon, we exited the Hundred-Mile Wilderness and were proud to realize that we had made it through in six days without stopping to resupply. While this had not been our greatest number of days without resupplying, it had been our longest mileage. Coming out of the Hundred-Mile Wilderness, we crossed the Penobscot River on a pedestrian footbridge.

In front of the Abol Bridge Campground, we used the pay phone outside the store—the last pay phone accessible from the trail—to confirm pick-up times with my mom.

"Hey, Mom."

"Well, hey there! How are the hikers?"

"We're good. We made it through the Hundred-Mile Wilderness in six days."

"Good. Are you feeling better?"

"I am. I'm still not back to my full strength, but I did fine."

"Good. Jeremy didn't get what you had, did he?"

I paused for a moment at the use of his real name. "Thankfully, no. I don't know if I've ever been that sick before. I really thought I wasn't going to be able to finish the trail at one point."

"Well, you're almost there now. Where are you guys?"

"We're right outside Baxter State Park. We have fourteen point four miles left to the summit of Katahdin. Then five more miles back down to the campground."

"You're almost officially two-thousand milers!"

We confirmed that Mom would meet us in two days, at the base of Katahdin in Baxter State Park, at three o'clock in the afternoon. *Forty-eight hours from now, I will have hiked the entire Appalachian Trail. I won't technically be a thru-hiker, but I'll be a two-thousand miler.*

Souleman and I spent a lovely night on the riverbank of the Penobscot. We had the site to ourselves, which was a treat since only two nights of our honeymoon remained. After cooking dinner, we sat together on Souleman's Therm-a-Rest holding hands and looking up at the stars. The woods were silent, and countless stars sparkled above our heads. We reminisced about our favorite and least favorite parts of the trail, our best and hardest hiking days, the most friendly trail towns, and hikers we would never forget. As the night wore on, we talked about our future and what it would be like to go back to life off the trail. Finally, we curled up together in our sleeping bags and took advantage of having one last shelter to ourselves before falling asleep nestled together under the stars.

Due to the influx of hikers we had seen the previous day, we knew that at least twelve of them were nearby. That meant that two people would not get a spot at The Birches campsite. Since the sign-up sheet was located 0.8 miles up the trail, we woke up early to make sure we got our names on the list. Souleman packed as quickly as he could and hurried the short distance to the sign-up board. I finished packing our gear in the semi-darkness and followed behind.

I joined Souleman at the sign-up board by six-thirty. He had waited for me so that we could sign the sheet together. We would be the first two names on the list. Squeezing my hand, he handed me the pen. I wrote "Brownie" on the top line and passed the pen back. He scrawled "Souleman" on the second line, and we stood staring at our names in silence for a moment. There weren't many more registers or places left to write our trail names. I took the pen back and added the symbol "&" between our names.

"Brownie and Souleman." I tapped the paper with the pen and looked up at Souleman with sad eyes. "We won't get to write these names for much longer."

"I guess not."

"It's going to be weird to hear you call me by my actual name. Michelle seems like a different person."

"A lot of things are going to be weird."

"True. Like sleeping in beds."

"And taking daily showers."

"And cooking in a kitchen." I stared off into the woods.

"Driving. Shaving." He scuffed his foot in the dirt.

"Who says I'm going to shave my legs? Maybe I've gotten attached to my leg hair." I propped one foot on the sign post and lifted up my pants leg.

"Hey, doesn't bother me. Does that mean I can keep my beard?"

"I hope you will. Maybe in a smaller form?" I reached up to touch it. I could barely imagine my husband without the shaggy hair framing his face. "That's a thousand miles' worth of facial hair. Think how long you've been growing that. Can you believe tomorrow's the last day?"

He shook his head.

"Did you see that view of Katahdin from the bridge?" I looked back down the trail.

"Not really. It was too dark when I crossed earlier."

"Let's go back then. It's only a tenth of a mile. We can get some great pictures."

We stood looking out over a foggy marsh and saw Katahdin looming just ahead. It was surreal to see the giant mountain appear out of the fog and know that we would be climbing it the following day. We took a snapshot that captured the autumn colors of the leaves, the glimmer of sun on the lake, the fog near the mountain, and the peak towering above. Katahdin, named by the Penobscot Indians, means "The Greatest Mountain." It was.

Shortly after leaving the bridge, we saw a baby bear playing on rocks in a stream. He was tiny and adorable, but we were afraid his mama would be nearby, so we started singing and whistling to warn her of our presence. We stopped often to enjoy the scenery and even took a couple of side trails to Big Niagara Falls and Little Niagara Falls. Since we had a guaranteed spot to sleep that night, we were in no hurry to rush this second-to-last day of hiking.

We normally avoided extra mileage whenever possible, but ten miles would make for a short day with such an early start. We were determined to soak up every second of our last full day in the woods. We must have said a hundred times that we couldn't believe we were really in Baxter State Park. Despite our best efforts, time moved quickly.

Right before the end of our hiking day, we had to cross a series of wooden planks over a marshy area. In some places we even crossed shallow ponds on these boards. Many of the planks were not nailed together and were only haphazardly piled on top of each other. I slipped on one wet, loose board and narrowly escaped diving into the water.

"Wow! Good save," Souleman commended me.

Seconds later, he lost his balance on the exact same log, and I heard a splash as he hit the water. He was standing thigh-deep in the pond and was trying valiantly to steady himself so that our camera, which was in his hip-belt, would not get wet. After a comical struggle against gravity and his pack weight, he straightened himself by balancing on his poles. The camera remained safe and dry.

When we made it to Katahdin Stream Campground, we immediately found the ranger station. Even with a reservation, we were nervous about the limited sleeping spots. The ranger was a dark-haired man in his early forties. He came out onto the porch of the cabin and took off his hat. "Are you guys thru-hiking?" Baxter State Park considers any hiker who has come through the Hundred Mile Wilderness to be a thru-hiker.

We nodded. "We made a reservation this morning for the Birches."

"Great." He confirmed our names and checked us off on his list. "All twelve spots will be full tonight, but you're the first two here."

The Birches was a three-sided structure just like most trail shelters had been. We claimed our spots in one corner and waited for the others to arrive. As it grew dark, someone built a fire and everyone gathered to tell stories. When the flames began to die down, Souleman and I huddled on a log studying Wingfoot by headlamp. In the morning we faced a 4,200-foot climb, most of which would occur over the span of three miles.

"Tomorrow is going to be hard," I observed.

"We'll have a lot of adrenaline to help us."

"I can't believe tomorrow's our last day. This is the last night we'll study Wingfoot," I observed sadly.

"The last night we'll sleep in a shelter," he responded.

As I laced our fingers together, his wedding ring pressed against my skin. We sat staring silently into the fire for a few emotional minutes. We were the first ones to retire, but I lay awake listening to the sounds of other hikers. The fire crackled, nervous giggles echoed, and twigs snapped. I didn't want this last night to end.

Tomorrow we tackle Katahdin. Tomorrow we become two-thousand milers. Tomorrow this adventure will be over. Tomorrow our honeymoon will be over. Souleman fidgeted beside me, so I knew he was awake with similar thoughts. I spooned behind him and wrapped my arms around him tightly.

"Even though I'm ready to finish, I'm not ready for it to be over," I said quietly into his neck.

On September 28, 2006, I woke up before the sun. My nose, peeking out of my mummy bag, could smell the cold. Still cocooned in my bag, I sat up and looked around. Even with my headlamp on, I couldn't see past the edge of the shelter. Souleman stirred beside me and I lay back down and pressed my forehead to his.

"Good morning, Souleman," I whispered, trying to sneak in as many uses of his trail name as possible before the day ended.

"Hey, Brownie," he played right along. "Are you ready to climb Katahdin?"

"Yes . . . no . . ."

"I know what you mean." He searched for his headlamp. "What's the weather look like?"

"Come on. You, me, a summit with a potential view . . ."

"Why did I even ask?"

We stuffed all our gear into our packs and pulled on our hats, fleeces, rain coats, rain pants, and gloves. Sticking our gloved hands into the straps of our poles, we tip-toed away from the shelter. No one else was moving yet.

We stopped at the Katahdin Stream ranger station to record our names and our route. Since the official Appalachian Trail terminus is on top of Katahdin, many hikers choose to take a different trail, called the Knife Edge, back down to the park. That was our original plan, but in light of the day's foggy weather forecast, the ranger had closed that route for the day.

The ranger encouraged us to store some of our gear on the porch of the ranger station so that we could summit with lighter packs, but of course we declined. We had hiked 2,169 miles with our full packs and were confident we could handle ten more. While technically we had already hiked over two thousand miles, we had not yet achieved two-thousand miler status by Appalachian Trail standards. Since the trail is rerouted each year to account for erosion and other factors, the exact mileage changes annually. To keep it simple, a hiker who completes the entire trail earns the two-thousand miler title. That day, we would join this elite group.

Hand in hand, we left the ranger station and stepped back onto the white-blazed trail. I paused to touch the first blaze we passed. *This is the last day we'll follow these blazes.* Souleman and I walked with our hands clasped until the trail became too narrow. It wasn't long before the trail also became steep, and I leaned heavily on my poles as I propelled myself upward. Though this was undoubtedly the most difficult ascent of our six-month hike, I didn't want to stop. We paused only for water breaks and photos during our march to the finish line.

The trail passed through some very difficult areas, and twice I had to take my pack off and have Souleman hoist me up a rock face and then hand me my pack. Other hikers with small day packs passed us. Even though we were moving more slowly, I was proud that all of our gear would accompany us to the summit. Our sleeping bags, tent, cooking gear, and other paraphernalia had helped us survive all this way. It seemed like the least we could do to bring it to the end point with us. After the trail, I would miss the security of knowing I always had everything I needed for survival on my back.

The wind blew briskly and a cold, misty rain drizzled down on us during the entire climb. I had on every layer in my possession and still shivered as I hiked. I was caught up in reflection and didn't want to talk, though the wind and rain would have prohibited conversation anyway. It was difficult to track our progress in the fog, so we had no idea where we were in relation to the summit.

After four hours, we stumbled quite unexpectedly on the summit sign. Usually, hikers can see the sign from afar, but in the thick fog we could almost touch the sign before we saw it. I had seen the red, wooden sign so many times in photos that it seemed familiar. Grabbing for Souleman's hand, I ran the last few steps to touch the sign. Katahdin. *We did it. We did it, we did it, we did it!*

We touched, hugged, and kissed that sign—the one we had dreamed about so much and for so long. We had completed the four-thousand-foot climb to the summit of Mount Katahdin, and at 5,267 feet above sea level, we were on top of the highest mountain in Maine. Even though we had hiked the mountain alone that day, we had not been the only people on the trail. Other hikers who were already on top of the mountain readily obliged as photographers for the clichéd Katahdin sign photos. I thought of other hikers taking naked pictures of themselves peeking out from behind the sign and shook my head. It was far too cold for such nonsense. We threw our arms above our heads and grinned below our winter hats.

Later, we would realize that the fog had made almost all of our pictures fuzzy. This seemed appropriate, though, because so many of our summits had been shrouded in fog, and the whole ascent of Katahdin was a little blurry in my mind.

Having obtained photographic evidence of our summit, we forgot the cameras, the other hikers, and even the nasty weather to focus for a minute on nothing but each other. We poured all two thousand miles of support, love, trust, and teamwork into a lingering kiss. When I opened my eyes, I could see nothing else in the fog besides the summit sign and my husband. Everything I needed at the moment was visible.

"I've never kissed a two-thousand miler before," he told me with a big smile. "How does it feel?"

"Hmmm, I'm not sure. Let me try it again."

We kissed again, smiling at the cheers around us.

"Yep, I like it. I think I'll keep you around."

I tapped his wedding ring. "I think you already made that decision."

Behind a big rock, a few thru-hikers sat passing around a bottle of wine. Over the wind, we yelled congratulations and slapped high fives. It was nice to be on top of Katahdin with other people who understood our accomplishment, but these were not hikers we knew well. I felt a pang of sadness for not being able to stand up there with some of our favorite friends. Every hiker leaves a little of himself on the trail, so I knew that every hiker we had met along our journey was on this mountaintop in spirit. I closed my eyes for a minute and saw the faces of so many trail friends whom I knew had celebrated in this exact spot.

After a few cold minutes taking in the summit, Souleman turned to me and asked, "Shall we?"

I shook my head no. I wasn't quite ready to leave. We had finished the Appalachian Trail after two seasons, six and a half months, and over two thousand miles of hiking. I looked out at the fog and visualized the trail winding beneath it through fourteen states, ending beside that plaque on Springer Mountain that I had touched so many months ago. I pictured myself sitting there as a slightly plump, recent college graduate with a lofty dream I wasn't quite sure I could reach. Katahdin, like so many dreams, had seemed so far away. Now here I stood at the opposite terminus: a strong, fit married woman and a two-thousand miler. *What a hike.* With one last glance at the cloud-shrouded terminus sign, I reached for Souleman's hand. For the first time ever, we headed south on the white-blazed trail.

Surprisingly, I was comforted by the fact that we had five miles left to go in order to get back to the park. I had five more miles to absorb the fact the fact that our Appalachian Trail journey was over. Five more miles to hike with my husband. Five more miles surrounded by nature. Five more miles to live my dream. *Five more miles.*

Just before the fog obscured the view of the Katahdin sign, I stopped and turned to face the summit one last time. Taking a deep breath, I yelled with all my might into the wind: "K-T-R!"

Beside me, Souleman smiled, and I could feel the smiles of every trail friend we had ever known.

Epilogue

Even though September 28, 2006, was the final day in a two-year journey, for me it was really just one more day in our Appalachian Trail adventure. While I was excited to reach Katahdin and the end point of the trail, the summit was not the sole climax of our trip. We spent only a few minutes celebrating on top of Katahdin because we knew that the real meaning of our adventure would be gleaned later as we reflected over all the things we had experienced over two years and two-thousand-plus miles.

The trail taught me about hard work, friendship, generosity, and kindness. I learned that I had strength far beyond what I had previously thought, both physically and mentally. But after reflection, by far the most important thing I had discovered on the Appalachian Trail was the innate goodness of mankind. Countless people contributed to my completion of the trail, and I was reminded again and again that human beings, overall, are generous, loving, and kindhearted.

After becoming two thousand-milers, Souleman and I transitioned back to living in the "real world." While our relationship had blossomed during our two seasons in the woods, it didn't fare as well off-trail. After fourteen months of marriage, we divorced in August of 2007.

Since then, I have had the opportunity to live in four states and meet memorable people around the country. Today I live in Greenville, South Carolina, with my cats, Georgia and Maine. I am happily enjoying a career as an emergency medical technician (EMT). I keep in touch with many of the trail friends mentioned in this book and make sure to hike as often as possible. In my free time, when I'm not outside hiking, skiing, or playing tennis, I travel, quilt, cook, and read.

"Springer Fever" has been burning in me more intensely each year since completing the Appalachian Trail. I'm excited to announce that I have planned my next long-distance hike. I will be doing the John Muir Trail in the summer of 2014. Finishing the Long Trail in Vermont and climbing Mount Kilimanjaro in Africa are currently the top contenders for future outdoor pursuits.